The Mojave Desert's Mysterious Secrets

by
Branton

With an Editorial by Timothy Green Beckley

and Assistance of
The Committee of Twelve to Save The Planet

The Mojave Desert's Mysterious Secrets by Branton

With an Editorial by Timothy Green Beckley

Revised Edition

Published in the United States of America By
Global Communications/Conspiracy Journal
Box 753 · New Brunswick, NJ 08903

CONTENTS

Artist's rendering of a UFO
striking a submarine

THE MYSTERIOUS MAN KNOWN AS BRANTON – ENEMY OF THE STATE

by Timothy Green Beckley

I first heard of the mysterious individual known as Branton when I received a huge carton of papers from him in the mail. In those days he was still using his given name.The box from Bruce A. Walton consisted of maybe a dozen folders on the topic of the Shaver and Inner Earth Mysteries. This was some time in the early 1980s, though the actual date is lost in the fog of time.

The material was of varied quality. Some of it was personal testimonials from those who claimed to have actually ventured down to a series of tunnels that had been carved into the earth hundreds of thousands of years ago by an ancient race who had to abandoned their cities on the surface of the planet because of some sort of radioactive catastrophe. The rest of the material consisted of photo copied pages from various newsletters, and out of print books on the same basic subject matter. At the time I was publishing a mimeographed zine printed on legal sized paper known as ***Searchlight.*** The vast majority of its contents was on the Shaver Mystery and the Hollow Earth theory which professes that there is a civilization at the core of the Earth. Several years later my buddy the late Gray Barker published ***A Guide To The Inner Earth,*** *which was more or less an index to existing material on these highly unsubstantiated but fascinating topics, which Branton summarized as follows:*

"To the Christian the Underworld is Hell. To the Greek pantheists it was a world of shadow accessed by the boat of Charon, and legion were the coins placed upon the eyes of the departed to pay that fearsome passage. To many an untutored savage, the world of caverns are the abodes of their ancestors, a truism common, perhaps to all of us, if we believe our for-bearers were cave men and women.

"To Richard S. Shaver the Hollow Earth was the abode of debauched Dero; to others it was the home of the Serpent Race or Agharta; still others saw it inhabited by a society with a Utopian model.

"To some, the Inner Earth may represent only caverns, a few hundred feet, or a few miles down. To other theorists it may represent a miniature cosmos of its own, complete with a Central Sun. But however we view it, the Inner Earth remains one of our strongest, if unproved, traditions."

We know something about the early life of Bruce A. Walton based upon what he revealed himself over the course of time in his various works: "I grew up in a Mormon household, and later left Mormonism when I came to realize you don't need to belong to a Masonic/Jesuit controlled religious group to know God and enter Heaven. I came to realize that knowing Jesus Christ as your Savior, you can hear from God through the Holy Spirit, and you will thus be assured a place in Heaven."

Branton often refers to the Holy Spirit as the Super intelligence, and has stated that its the Super intelligence (Holy Spirit) that is opposed to the Luciferian consciousness which influences and controls the secret societies that rule both the underground and above ground empires). Branton's spiritual/religious position seems to be based on the Protestant King James Bible.

IN BRANTON'S OWN WORDS

Below is a copy of Brantons personal testimony taken directly from his website:

"Branton" was born into a large family that lived near the western base of the Rocky Mountains, in the year 1960.

As he grew up, he realized that his neo-masonic "religious" background was somewhat restrictive, if not outright deceptive. Later on in life he came to realize that MOST mainline denominations of "church-ianity" had also been intentionally infiltrated by this Masonic virus.

However, before this realization came to pass, he was drawn into various secret neo-masonic (and so-called new age) cults which used mind-control in order to manipulate their "members'," as well as perverse 'molestation' rituals within their deeper levels.

Being '"nfected" with this psycho-spiritual poison caused him many mental and emotional problems later on in life.

Also, being trapped in a system of 'legalistic' religion merely drove him deeper into the pit of depravity and bondage to the evil one, just as the intolerant 'religious church-ianity of the Pharisees led to the execution and crucifixion of Jesus the Christ... the very author of LIFE !!!

He is not proud of the fact that he was 'used' by the evil one at one time in his life to harm others around him. However before his 'defection' from this parasitical kingdom of darkness, he did learn many of the 'deep' secrets and inner-workings of the kingdom of darkness, and now feels that it is his duty — regardless of the personal risk — to EXPOSE this darkness in the light of truth, so that others might escape the traps which almost ruined his life...

It eventually became apparent to him that his focus should NOT be placed on any particular pharasitical neo-Masonic "church", "denomination", or "religion", but rather on the savior, Jesus Christ, himself.

He became aware of how he was being used and manipulated by the lord of darkness and his 'hive' of vampirial and parasitical followers, as a result of childhood 'abductions' and other factors, such as 'alien implants' – which the top leaders of many of these cultic Neo-Masonic organizations were aware of ... and some of these secret society leaders were (and are) even reportedly in close contact with the darker 'reptilian' entities from beyond and within our world...

'Branton' was able to escape most of their hold upon his mind, with more than a little help from the Lord of LIGHT!

Jesus Christ, he realized, had many believers in many denominations. There is no one "true" denomination since in EVERY denomination in the world you have those who practice pharasitical "church-ianity" and then those who practice true apostolic "Christ-ianity."

In other words, if one were to believe that Christ died and rose again from the grave for THEM as the "Good Book" says, and APPLIES this belief into their lives, essentially allowing the Spirit of Christ to LIVE THROUGH THEM by faith in HIS Divine-Life-Blood-Transfusion, then THEY are forgiven... NOT by any faithless works or merit of their own (read the book of "Romans"). They/We can be COMPLETELY purged of all past wrongdoings, but ONLY because someone else chose to recieve the criminal punishment that they/we deserved (and of course, that 'someone' was/is Christ, the "Lamb" of God).

In short, those who are "saved" are those who allow the Spirit of God (which the Bible refers to as the pure WATER OF LIFE) to live in and through them. These are they who in essence ASKED FOR and RECIEVED this "divine life-blood transfusion" from Jesus Christ, the Living WORD or LOGOS of God, who is a being so powerful that He literally SPOKE the Metaverse or Omniverse (with its millions – or billions? – of galaxies, each containing millions or billions of stars and planets) into existence.

Jesus IS eternal life, and so the ONLY way for us to receive eternal life is to receive it from HIM, the SOURCE of all LIFE... the ONLY spiritual "OASIS" in the spiritual "desert."

Branton began to study "paranormal" phenomena at the age of 12, after reading Frank Edwards' book FLYING SAUCERS – SERIOUS BUSINESS, and he still lives surrounded by the beautiful Rocky Mountains, and he continues THE fight (within and without) to 'help' make this world, this country, and all people FREE from ignorance and oppression of all kinds... realizing that we are all individual 'cells' in the 'body' of humanity... so in essence the 'T-cells' (so to speak...) must work TOGETHER to rid this 'body' of the 'cancerous' draconian 'cells' that would devour all light and life — like a dead star or a black hole — if given the chance.

——End of Branton's personal testimony from his website——

A CONFUSED YOUNG MAN OR A SWORN ENEMY OF THE NEW WORLD ORDER?

When Bruce Walton stopped using his birth name and switched to merely using the singular Branton, I have no idea, though it was probably sometime in the 80s when he began to realize that something about him "was just not right." Something was going on in his head that obviously caused this transition. It all culminated when the now transformed Branton realized that he had been a "sleeper" for the CIA! According to the information that has come to us in drips and drabs, Branton stumbled upon some information that he was not supposed to know. He was, supposedly, given an alternative personality which was 'programmed' to serve his CIA Black Projects handlers and the Bavarian-Gray collective. In this alternate or "double life" he had access to several underground bases, and apparently over the course of time encountered several alien groups as well. It is even said that he had several alien implants placed at various locations on his body (NOT JUST ONE as in most cases!).

According to one source: "Branton also claims he has a number of hybrid children who are in the resistance movement. If I understand Branton correctly, he has mated with female reptilian shape shifters and has hybrid reptilian children of his own. However I could be incorrect about him having reptilian children, they could be another non human intelligent species, as I can only recall him stating that he has hybrid children. According to Branton there are many benevolent reptilian shape shifters (including some of his own children), who are resisting the Luciferian Jesuit NWO."

Chances are you are a "fan" of Branton or you would not have purchased this book. BRANTON IS NOT FOR EVERYONE! Truth is his material has limited appeal – but for those who can take all this in and digest what he has to say, Branton is considered somewhat of a savior to those who contend that there is a global plot to "take us all over."

I want to make it perfectly clear that I have not heard from Branton in years...but I do not know of anyone else who has either. When last spoken to, Branton had been in a roadside accident. He was riding his bike not far from his apartment when someone collided with him and took off down the highway. Those prone to conspiracy theories claim that the windows of the vehicle were tinted over, and the automobile was driven by representatives of the NWO in the form of their representatives known as the dreaded MIB, or Men In Black. Shortly after, he was in trouble with the "authorities," ending up in the clink. Nothing to report on him since, either as Branton or as Bruce A. Walton.

The Branton Files, as they have become known, are posted in various shapes and forms all over the internet. We were made the authorized publishers of *the printed version of* **The Dulce Wars**. *No suger coating the fact that Branton is* *not a terribly good writer when it comes to punctuation and spelling. We spent countless hours "cleaning up" the text of both this as well as his previous work. But we insist on not doing a great deal of editing as we do not wish to change the flavor of his work.*

*In closing, we welcome your essay and your thoughts on Branton's very strange revelations. Perhaps you can add to the mysterious **Branton Files**.*

Tim Beckley

www.ConspiracyJournal.com

HYPERLINK "mailto:mrufo8@hotmail.com"*mrufo8@hotmail.com*

Subscribe to our YouTube Channel

Mr UFOs Secret Files

The only known photo of Bruce Alan DeWalton (“Branton”)

Branton Interview by OneLight

Q:

We presently identify in this time space continuum we share as surface dwelling humans, not of another species, but genetically and culturally inclusive of ourselves. The species of the Serpent Race brings up thoughts of misadventure, serious difficulties, even emotional or spiritual dread to the psyche of human surface dwelling mortals.

Branton, over the many years you have become known something of an authority on the subject of subterranean caverns and their occupants. Of these underground occupants there are groups made up of what we presently call the "serpent people". From what we gather from ancient history is - these beings once dwelled among us and then through a break, perhaps a cosmic event, they are no longer in obvious contact with surface humans. Are there reasons for this break between serpent people and human surface dwellers, or stories you know of such a break?

Branton:

Well, I suppose that the original 'breaking' came near the very beginning, or in 'Edenic' times some might say. There IS the story in Genesis chapter 3 of a 'serpent race' which walked upright on two legs, and which rebelled against God and man, and being under the influence of fallen angelic entities the serpent race tried to overthrow humanity from their God-given dominion of the planet, just as the Luciferians who 'incarnated' the serpent race tried to overthrow the Godhead/Logos/Creator.

Like a 'spiritual black hole' (so to speak), Lucifer and the Luciferians (the fallen angelic beings that Lucifer deceived into following him/it) focused only on feeding their own insatiable lust for power... and since they broke away from the Creator – the ONLY source of life-essence or life-force – they became life-force vampires, ever sucking the life energy out of those around them – and even each other...

In the beginning, all life on earth, including the 'serpent' and its seed, dwelt in perfect harmony... that is until the Luciferians deceived the serpent race with the LIE that they could be 'gods' OVER other created beings.

In the book of Genesis (3:15), the Creator states that there would be WAR between the human and the serpent races, even until the end... and you read – or imply from — the book of Revelation (12:7) that the serpent race would be able to leave planet earth and conquer parts of the 2nd Heaven (the realm of the stars and planets - but never the 3rd Heaven from whence the fallen angels were cast following the original rebellion).

That verse talks about a "war in heaven" between Michael's armies and the armies of the "dragon". Most Christians do not realize that this REVELATION verse speaks of a LAST DAYS battle... since they believe that the Luciferians were cast out of heaven in the beginning and could not regain their lost ground... however they do not take into account the fact that the Luciferians "incarnated" into reptilian humanoid bodied.

These bi-ped reptilian-humanoids went underground or off-planet, and left only those non-biped reptilians on the surface. The reptilian-humanoids first went underground to escape the humans, who were getting pretty pissed-off by their vamperial atrocities against innocent humans on the surface. In order to escape extermination by the humans (which would have been well-justified) they went underground, and the fallen angelic entities which incarnated/possessed them, inspired them with the occult-technology necessary to build craft that could leave the planet earth altogether.

Then again, there is the Biblical account of the "tares among the wheat" (or serpents posing as humans – the so-called "reptilian shapeshifters") ... a verse that you can read as a quote at the top of this webpage:

http://www.angelfire.com/ut/branton/posers1.html

Some take the Edenic story as literal, whereas others take it as a very condensed or symbolic representation of actual events that were much more complicated... I tend to take the middle ground between the two...

Q:

From earlier time in history, from our modern day perception, there was born a myth structured in dark and light. Preferably we humans are seen as beings of light and the serpent folk are seen as beings of the dark. Or, the Serpent People are more disillusioned and we humans are closer to the spark of reality.

Have you found information, which would lead us to believe that the Serpent People were victimized by us? And in this, the blowback, seek revenge on us for some past injustice, perhaps favor of us by a particular god?

Branton:

As for the serpent race, we must realize that most of them are not of an 'individual' mentality as humans are. The great majority of the reptilians are under the total control of an electromagnetic 'borg-like' collective or HIVE mind... and this

Hive is ultimately controlled by the Luciferians themselves... those based in Alpha Draconis, Rigel Orion, Zeta Reticuli... etc. You can liken them somewhat to AIDS or CANCER cells, which are programmed ONLY to carry out the parasitical will of the central HIVE (or the 'psionic black hole' you might say). So the reptilians are in essence virulent life-forms.

HOWEVER, and this is a big HOWEVER... it must be understood that many of the so-called HYBRIDS/HUBRIDS possess a human-like SOUL MATRIX... whereas the reptiloids themselves do NOT possess such a soul matrix. So when attacking the Reptilians/Draconians (or rather the HIVE, which IS our TRUE enemy), we must be careful NOT to attack the Hybrids, many of whom possess a human soul-energy-matrix (and many of them are even trying to RESIST the HIVE, which is an enemy to their own soul-energy-matrix — which is the ONLY thing that gives us our INDIVIDUALITY and free will).

However we must not forget that we have the power to GIVE our free will away to other entities by violating the free will of our fellow humans. Let us say that each human has a psychic 'wall of protection' around them. This 'wall' represents their 'free will space'. So when someone goes BEYOND their God-given 'free will space' and invades the space of others, they must break down this protective 'wall' which protects OUR SPACE AND THEIR space as a result, and in doing so they/we allow OTHERS to invade THEIR/OUR space. So the BEST way to protect one's free space is to protect the free space of others! It's really pretty simple when you begin to grasp it.

By helping the HYBRIDS break free of the HIVE (through prayer, education, or whatever) we can then help them to help the reptiloids (those without a soul-matrix) break free also. The 'serpent' people were fairly beautiful in the beginning, before their fall, however eons of enslavement to the 'Luciferian Hive' has taken its toll. However, there is a chance that the HYBRIDS can help the reptiloids break free from the HIVE and be TAMED !!! The book of Genesis says that the serpent was created at the very TOP of all the animal kingdom. They were once the epitome of all the beasts... that is until they fell for the lies of the Luciferians and became (at least those on the surface) one of the least of all the beasts. So they were deceived into believing that they have to surrender themselves ENTIRELY to the Luciferians in order to regain their power, but in doing so they lost ALL of the little individuality that they had, as the fallen angelics began to incarnate them and use them as 'physical vessels' through which they – the fallen angelics – could control matter.

However, if the HYBRIDS are successful in breaking SOME of the Reptiloids free of the HIVE and TAMING them, then this would be the best possible route. Since the true non-hybrid reptiloids have no soul-matrix, nor individuality, they must be under the control of some force... be it the HIVE or the HYBRIDS.

I personally — being an implantee and an abductee, and having been severely (emotionally) abused growing up — all too often made the mistake of passing on that abuse to others... and it has caused myself and others around me much harm. However I am determined to break out of the 'programming' that I was fed during the abductions (through the implants, etc.), however my anger at the 'Hive' for what it has done to me, and also at the harm that I MYSELF have caused others by being under its influence, is growing.

Yes, there is the 'programming', however I know now that I STILL possessed free will, in spite of the fact that the HIVE tried to DECIEVE me into believing that I did not, and that I HAD to obey its instructions. But in the end it all comes back to free will. The reptilian aliens, in the end, have no power over you except the power that you GIVE them, and so long as you possess the power of free-choice, you can TAKE BACK what that power that is rightfully yours.

The fallen angels had individuality to SOME extent before the fall, however they gave that individuality ENTIRELY to Lucifer, and they can NEVER reclaim it...

Humans on the other hand CAN reclaim lost individuality (the only way to protect ones individuality is to respect the individuality and free-space of OTHER... it is a mutual defense mechanism)...

Q:

Is there evidence or speculation to: the Serpent People think of themselves as more exalted or closer to the supreme godhead than us, due to the fact that they have been able to hold onto their higher technology in the subterranean regions, while we surface humans seem to have to start from the cradle every 25,000 years or so?

Branton: Well you must understand that the reptilians have an entirely different mentality from man. You can learn a lot about them by watching the STAR TREK episodes about the BORG... except in this case the controlled entities have no soul and are not human (which in my opinion make them even more dangerous than the 'borg'). They are controlled by the HIVE, which is a completely parasitic Psionic control network which seeks only one thing... to DEVOUR everything around it... like I said, a 'Psionic Black Hole'...

Q:

Do you see our two species coming together in peace and combined efforts of growth and prosperity in the times ahead. Or, do you think the Serpent People need to get smite-d several times over to behave, and stop using us as a resource?

Branton: I believe that we should concentrate on helping the HYBRIDS to essentially 'tame' the reptiloids. Now the fallen angelics do NOT want to give up their 'material puppets' that easily, so I believe that there WILL be those reptiloids who (with more than a little help from the 'hybrids') will be 'tamed', and then those — the darkest and most parasitical ones — which will remain in the HIVE. I don't know exactly where the center of the HIVE thing is, possibly in Alpha Draconis... but I hear that it is a gigantic 'computer' type affair that links all the Dracos together in some sort of mind-net (again, kind of like the BORG of Star Trek). I don't know if we could obliterate this central computer like Luke Skywalker obliterated the 'Death Star'... ;o)

But I guess anything is possible...

—BRANTON
February 2008

CJ
Conspiracy Journal
PRODUCTIONS

THE MOJAVE DESERT'S GREATEST SECRETS

THE MOJAVE DESERT'S GREATEST SECRETS
(The Conspiracy Against Reality)
by Bruce Walton, aka "Branton"
Compiled by CONSPIRACY JOURNAL
Edited by Timothy Green Beckley

"AND I WILL SHOW WONDERS IN THE HEAVEN ABOVE...
"AND SIGNS IN THE EARTH BENEATH...
"BLOOD, AND FIRE, AND VAPOUR OF SMOKE..."
— Acts 2:19 —

The author of the following story is a Navaho Indian. He revealed this tribal secret which he learned from the Paiute Indians, who inhabit the Great Basin and Mojave deserts of Utah, Nevada, and California.

This native American, who went by the name Oga-Make, related the following account in appreciation for a story on the Navaho which appeared in the Spring of 1948 in a magazine which was carrying numerous articles on the mysterious "signs" or "fires" in the skies which were causing an enormous amount of confusion and debate during that same year, as well as the years following.

The article on the Navaho nation, which appeared in an earlier issue, told of the suffering that their tribe had gone through during past winter seasons, and encouraged the readership to send goods and supplies to help them through the upcoming winter of '48-'49, which many of them did.

In appreciation of this, Oga-Make related the following 'legend' which told of the secret history of the Americas which ran it's course, possibly thousands of years before white men set their foot en masse upon it's shores:

"...Most of you who read this are probably white men of a blood only a century or two out of Europe. You speak in your papers of the Flying Saucers or Mystery Ships as something new, and strangely typical of the twentieth century. How could you but think otherwise? Yet if you had red skin, and were of a blood which had been born and bred of the land for untold thousands of years, you would know this is not true. You would know that your ancestors living in these mountains and upon these prairies for numberless generations, had seen these ships before, and had passed down the story in the legends which are the unwritten history of your people. You do not believe? Well, after all, why should you? But knowing your scornful unbelief, the storytellers of my people have closed their lips in bitterness against the outward flow of this knowledge.

"Yet, I have said to the storytellers this: now that the ships are being seen again, is it wise that we, the elder race, keep our knowledge to ourselves? Thus for me, an American Indian, some of the sages among my people have talked, and if you care to, I shall permit you to sit down with us and listen.

"Let us say that it is dusk in that strange place which you, the white-man, calls 'Death Valley.' I have passed tobacco...to the aged chief of the Paiutes who sits across a tiny fire from me and sprinkles corn meal upon the flames...

"The old chief looked like a wrinkled mummy as he sat there puffing upon his pipe. Yet his eyes were not those of the unseeing, but eyes which seemed to look back on long trails of time. His people had held the Inyo, Panamint and Death Valleys for untold centuries before the coming of the white-man. Now we sat in the valley which white-man named for Death, but which the Paiute calls Tomesha—The Flaming Land. Here before me as I faced eastward, the Funerals (mountains forming Death Valley's eastern wall) were wrapped in purple-blue blankets about their feet while their faces were painted in scarlet. Behind me, the Panamints rose like a mile-high wall, dark against the sinking sun.

"The old Paiute smoked my tobacco for a long time before he reverently blew the smoke to the four directions. Finally he spoke.

"'You ask me if we heard of the great silver airships in the days before white-man brought his wagon trains into the land?'

"'Yes grandfather, I come seeking knowledge.' (Among all tribes of my people, grandfather is the term of greatest respect which one man can pay to another.)

"'We, the Paiute Nation, have known of these ships for untold generations. We also believe that we know something of the people who fly them. They are called The Hav-musuvs.'

"'Who are the Hav-musuvs?'

"'They are a people of the Panamints, and they are as ancient as Tomesha itself.'

"He smiled a little at my confusion.

"'You do not understand? Of course not. You are not a Paiute. Then listen closely and I will lead you back along the trail of the dim past.

"'When the world was young, and this valley which is now dry, parched desert, was a lush, hidden harbor of a blue water- sea which stretched from half way up those mountains to the Gulf of California, it is said that the Hav-musuvs came here in huge rowing-ships. They found great caverns in the Panamints, and in them they built one of their cities. At that time California was the island which the Indians of that state told the Spanish it was, and which they marked so on their maps.

"'Living in their hidden city, the Hav-musuvs ruled the sea with their fast rowing-ships, trading with far-away peoples and bringing strange goods to the great quays said still to exist in the caverns.

"'Then as untold centuries rolled past, the climate began to change. The water in the lake went down until there was no longer a way to the sea. First the way was broken only by the southern mountains, over the tops of which goods could be carried. But as time went by, the water continued to shrink, until the day came when only a dry crust was all that remained of the great blue lake. Then the desert came, and the Fire-God began to walk across Tomesha, The Flaming-Land.

"'When the Hav-musuvs could no longer use their great rowing-ships, they began to think of other means to reach the world beyond. I suppose that is how it happened. We know that they began to use flying canoes. At first they were not large, these silvery ships with wings. They moved with a slight whirring sound, and a dipping movement, like an eagle.

"'The passing centuries brought other changes. Tribe after tribe swept across the land, fighting to possess it for awhile and passing like the storm of sand. In their mountain city still in the caverns, the Hav-musuvs dwelt in peace, far removed from the conflict. Sometimes they were seen in the distance, in their flying ships or riding on the snowy-white animals which took them from ledge to ledge up the cliffs. We have never seen these strange animals at any other place. To these people the passing centuries brought only larger and larger ships, moving always more silently.'

"'Have you ever seen a Hav-musuv?'

"'No, but we have many stories of them. There are reasons why one does not become too curious.'

"'Reasons?'

"'Yes. These strange people have weapons. One is a small tube which stuns one with a prickly feeling like a rain of cactus needles. One cannot move for hours, and during this time the mysterious ones vanish up the cliffs. The other weapon is deadly. It is a long, silvery tube. When this is pointed at you, death follows immediately.'

"'But tell me about these people. What do they look like and how do they dress?'

"'They are a beautiful people. Their skin is a golden tint, and a head band holds back their long dark hair. They dress always in a white fine-spun garment which wraps around them and is draped upon one shoulder. Pale sandals are worn upon their feet...'

"His voice trailed away in a puff of smoke. The purple shadows rising up the walls of the Funerals splashed like the waves of the ghost lake. The old man seemed to have fallen into a sort of trance, but I had one more question.

"'Has any Paiute ever spoken to a Hav-musuv, or were the Paiutes here when the great rowing-ships first appeared?'

"For some moments I wondered if he had heard me. Yet as is our custom, I waited patiently for the answer. Again he went through the ritual of the smoke-breathing to the four directions, and then his soft voice continued:

"'Yes. Once in the not-so-distant-past, but yet many generations before the coming of the Spanish, a Paiute chief lost his bride by sudden death. In his great and overwhelming grief, he thought of the Hav-musuvs and their long tube-of-death. He wished to join her, so he bid farewell to his sorrowing people and set off to find the Hav-musuvs. None appeared until the chief began to climb the almost unscaleable Panamints. Then one of the men in white appeared suddenly before him with the long tube, and motioned him back. The chief made signs that he wished to die, and came on. The man in white made a long singing whistle and other Hav-musuvs appeared. They spoke together in a strange tongue and then regarded the chief thought- fully. Finally they made signs to him making him understand that they would take him with them.

"'Many weeks after his people had mourned him for dead, the Paiute chief came back to his camp. He had been in the giant underground valley of the Hav-musuvs, he said, where white lights which burn night and day and never go out, or need any fuel, lit an ancient city of marble beauty. There he learned the language and the history of the mysterious people, giving them in turn the language and legends of the Paiutes. He said that he would have liked to remain there forever in the peace and beauty of their life, but they bade him return and use his new knowledge for his people.'

"I could not help but ask the inevitable.

"'Do you believe this story of the chief?'

"His eyes studied the wisps of smoke for some minutes before he answered.

"'I do not know. When a man is lost in Tomesha, and the Fire-God is walking across the salt crust, strange dreams like clouds, fog through his mind. No man can breathe the hot breath of the Fire-God and long remain sane. Of course, the Paiutes have thought of this. No people knows the moods of Tomesha better than they.

"'You asked me to tell you the legend of the flying ships. I have told you what the young men of the tribe do not know, for they no longer listen to the stories of the past. Now you ask me if I believe. I answer this. Turn around. Look behind you at that wall of the Panamints. How many giant caverns could open there, being hidden by the lights and shadows of the rocks? How many could open outward or inward and never be seen behind the arrow-like pinnacles before them? How many ships could swoop down like an eagle from the beyond, on summer nights when the fires of the furnace-sands have closed away the valley from the eyes of the white-man? How many Hav-musuvs could live in their eternal peace away from the noise of white-man's guns in their unscaleable stronghold? This has always been a land of mystery. Nothing can change that. Not even white-man with his flying engines, for should they come too close to the wall of the Panamints a sharp wind like the flying arrow can sheer off a wing. Tomesha hides its secrets well even in winter, but no man can pry into them when the Fire-God draws the hot veil of his breath across the passes.

"'I must still answer your question with my mind in doubt, for we speak of a weird land. White-man does not yet know it as well as the Paiutes, and we have ever held it in awe. It is still the forbidden 'Tomesha—Land-Of-The-Flaming-Earth.'"

The preceding account, titled "TRIBAL MEMORIES OF THE FLYING SAUCERS", appeared in the Sept. 1949 issue of FATE magazine. Coincidentally or not, this same 'legend' was repeated in amazing similarity by an old prospector by the name of Bourke Lee in his book "DEATH VALLEY MEN" (Macmillan Co., New York, 1932). However, Lee stated that it was NOT a legend, but an actual account of the discovery of a (now abandoned) city WITHIN the Panamint Mountains as he heard it from three other people who claimed to have seen this ancient wonder beneath the earth.

Believe it or not, those who talked to Bourke Lee mentioned the ancient 'lake' within Death Valley, the ancient city within the Panamints themselves, and even the large tunnel-like 'quays' or ancient boat docks above the ancient shoreline on the eastern slope of the Panamints which led INTO the ancient city... ancient artifacts which they swore they saw with their own eyes.

The Editors of FATE magazine introduced the story which appears above with the following words:

"...FATE presents two new saucer stories in this issue. The first is a startling account of an aviation editor's encounter with two disks (two week's after he had photographed four and was frustrated in every attempt to get the photo into the big dailies and thus prove the flying saucers were real at the height of the 'scare'); and the second is a tribal secret of the Paihute Indians given to FATE magazine out of appreciation for FATE's Navaho story in the Spring, 1948 issue, which helped relieve their hardship in the ensuing winter. Your editor wonders about (these) stories, and presents them as a possible solution of the nature and origin of the famous disks. Both these stories arrived on our desk on the same day. They corroborate each other. We say that investigation will prove both to be true. We admit, however, that we believe it will be as impossible to prove the Hav-musuv story as it has been to produce a captive disk. Your editor, however, has been a friend of the American Indian for many years, and he has rarely known an Indian to lie. He is convinced of the sincerity of the story we present in this issue, and that it has not been distorted. What does it mean? What, really, are the Hav-musuvs?"

The story of the Hav-musuvs seems to be a major or key 'piece' of the overall puzzle of a wide range of aerial as well as subsurface phenomena which have mystified numerous researchers throughout this century.

Not the least of these unusual phenomena were the so-called 'contactees' of California who during the 1950's and '60's, in fact, described their own alleged encounters with 'benevolent' humanlike beings who were seen to emerge from aerial disks, not far at all from the mysterious Panamint mountains them- selves.

The Mojave Desert is also, believe it or not, the very place where William Shatner claimed to have had his UFO encounter with a 'silvery disk', which he alleges saved his life after he became lost in the Mojave's other-worldly expanse, and this long before he was Christened 'Captain' of the U.S.S. Enterprise!

The Mojave Desert of California is in this sense perhaps one of the most interesting areas in the world whereas encounters with strange aerial phenomena are concerned. In certain small California and Mojave Desert towns, like the small town of Anza for instance, one is more likely to be called crazy for NOT believing in UFO's than they are for believing in them. Sightings have been so numerous over the years that these aerial visitors are an accepted fact of life.

The interesting thing, however, is that the two most commonly reported types of 'occupants' which are described by thousands of witnesses with remarkable consistency the world over (in relation to these aerial phenomena) play a large part in the Mojave Desert scenario as well. These are the two groups which have often been referred to at the 'Saurian Grays' and the 'Nordic Blonds'.

Both types of 'entities' have appeared in many accounts describing encounters with not only so-called extraterrestrial beings, but also the lesser known — although nevertheless persistent — accounts of intra-terranean beings as well.

In this file we will document numerous accounts which seem to suggest that the 'Nordics' may be our ancient ancestors who, a few thousand years previous to the modern 'space race', may have attained the science and technology necessary to burrow deep into the earth in order to construct vast subterranean technological metropolises, and shortly thereafter like a slingshot from the lower depths of the earth they may have hurled them- selves in starships of their own devising through the interplanetary and perhaps even interstellar depths of space.

The strange allegation among 'UFOlogists', however, is one mentioned by many 'contactees' who allege that a neo-sauroid or reptilian race known as the GRAYS may have for hundreds if not thousands of years been in conflict, or even in even all-out warfare with the so-called 'Nordics' (as we will see further on, the "Nordic" appellation may be closer to the truth than one might think). The explanation given by some researchers as to the ACTUAL ORIGIN of this malevolent and predatory (other) race of 'grayish' aliens may shock you!

Since National Polls reveal that approximately 80 percent of all Americans believe in the phenomena known as UFO's to some degree, and that as many as 2 percent or 1 in 50 believe that they have been targets of 'abduction' by the same in the past, this file is written with the assumption that the reader is one of the 80% (and possibly even one of the 2 percent who have experiential knowledge of the UFO phenomena).

If the reader believes that they are part of the 20 percent who do not believe in UFO's and have no desire to do so, then the following may not be for you. If one does not like the idea of having the very 'fabric' of their concept of reality torn apart and woven back together again, then they might do well to pass on this information to someone with a more open mind. But if you desire to bear with us, we will reveal to you the hidden secrets of one place on earth which appears to be a 'doorway' to other worlds, to worlds and realities and adventures which may well make the reader's own perception of 'reality' seem absolutely mundane to the extreme...

But if you dare, then read on:

George H. Leonard, in his book "SOMEBODY ELSE IS ON THE MOON" (David McKay Co. Inc., New York., 1967), quotes Morris K. Jessup (the UFOlogist who died under mysterious circumstances after exposing the so-called 'PHILADELPHIA EXPERIMENT"), who asked the question: "Who has beaten us to the moon by hundreds or even thousands of years?"

Leonard, based on research gathered by himself and certain ex-NASA employees, confirms the suspicions of certain researchers to the effect that NASA is aware of the fact that an alien race (the Grays, etc.) AND a humanlike race has for centuries been fighting for possession of the moon, that mining equipment has been seen as well as many other evidences of lunar activity. Leonard says:

"More than one...race occupies the Moon - Culture traits and technology seen in different parts of the Moon vary considerably ... it appears from the body of reliable data that one or more of the (nonhuman) races regards us with disdain and values human life cheaply... Races capable of moving between star systems... and existing on the Moon must be capable of wiping us out at will. It is probably this (understandably) which PANICS the military."

Mr. Leonard, during one of his interviews with an ex-NASA employee whom he refers to as Dr. Sam Wittcomb (a pseudonym to protect his real identity), at which time he showed 'Whitcomb' the ms. for his book, learned the following disturbing facts:

"...And Sam Wittcomb read my manuscript in draft and then sat staring into the black night. When he spoke, it was in a hushed voice. I'd never heard him like that before. 'They brought scientists together from many countries in the Spring of 1975. The meeting was in England. They wanted to talk on the quiet about "extraterrestrials" and what they're up to. A lot of people at the top are scared.' A cold spot formed in the small of my back. Sam turned to me. 'They invited a physicist from Colorado, a man named Joachim Kuetner, who'd worked on the Moon program and know's what's up there. He could tell them about it first hand. About the frenetic building and digging going on, the spraying of craters and carving up of crater rims and ridges. I don't know exactly what they talked about. But you can bet they know it's not Earth-people's Moon anymore — if it ever was. It belongs to THEM.'"

As we've said, at least one of the races on the Moon is human, or identical to those of us on earth. If this is so, then we might ask ourselves "where on earth did these people come from, and how did they get to the moon before 'we' did?" It is certainly a reasonable question.

There exist several corroborative accounts taken from ancient Hindu scripts (again, as Ripley would say "believe it or not"), which we will quote shortly, stating that the ancient GREEKS had actually developed flying ships thousands of years ago. Is it possible that the Hav-musuvs (which as we've said, may have been a neo-Grecian race because of their dress and their marble- like cities) would have taken the next logical step after developing aerial travel: that is, attempt to land one or more of their kind on the Moon... eventually upon Mars... and possibly even later upon planets in a nearby star system?

The United States has made incredible advances in this area in a period of less than 100 years, thanks to the phenomena known as the technological curve (i.e. that a synchronous effort on the part of many contributing factors eventually leads to a multiplying explosion in technology). If America landed a man on the moon only 70 years after the Wright Brothers opened the skies to aerial travel, then can we expect anything less from the Hav-musuvs or others like them? For instance technology in our society is becoming thousands of times more sophisticated every year. Is it possible that the ancient Greeks or a similar ancient society had a 'technology explosion' thousands of years ago? If so, then it may have been possible for them to establish bases or colonies on the Moon, Mars, and perhaps beyond! We might add that there are some who even claim that the secret of "hyper- space" travel was inadvertently discovered only 40 years after the Wright Brothers successfully tested their aircraft at Kitty Hawk - during a super-secret Navy experiment called the Rainbow Project which was carried out at the Philadelphia Naval harbor in 1943.

If 'we' can go from the horse-and-buggy to landing men on the moon in LESS that 100 years (or from the horse-and-buggy to "hyperspace" travel in only 40 years!?) then how much exploration and colonization of other planetary bodies might have taken place by a race who three or four THOUSAND years ago possessed aerial craft and technologies equal to or greater than our own?

One 'contactee', incidentally, has stated that a large 'space port' does in fact exist in a network of caverns deep below present-day Death Valley.

In reference to this we will quote from a 'synopsis' of the experiences of Brazilian 'contactee' Jefferson Souza, as it appeared in a catalog put out by the UFO LIBRARY (11684 Ventura Blvd. #708., Studio City, CA 91604). Many of the individuals referred to in this catalog, which offers taped interviews or lectures describing their encounters, are either 'contactees' who have had friendly encounters with the so-called 'Nordic' or humanlike beings who pilot many of the 'alien' craft; or who have been 'abducted' by the more manipulating and predatory 'Gray' or 'saurian' entities. Quoting from their description of Mr. Souza's experiences:

"Reaction to the first sighting of a UFO is unpredictable. Jeff Souza had his first contact in 1979 when he was only 13. The memory of it was tucked away in the recesses of his mind. Twenty alien contacts during the next 10 years never fully restored the image. But those years were filled with excitement that would result in one of the most inspirational stories of alien contact ever recorded.

"The young Brazilian was possessed of intelligence and intuition. He studied and managed to complete one semester of medical school before giving up his formal education.

"In contact with two races of extraterrestrials, Jeff has met them in Brazil, Argentina and the United States. But where they occurred is unimportant when compared to the depth and cope of what he learned.

"The gentle VEGANS and the businesslike UMMITES taught Souza more than he could ever imagine about technology and life on all planets. He was transported aboard a spaceship by LIGHT (antigravity rays? - Branton) and taken to other planets and (other) parts of the world. On one such trip he suffered an unusual reaction - all his hair fell out. His watch broke at every contact.

"Jeff Souza has been questioned by experts in the field of alien contact. He has been clinically regressed through hypnotism to the time of his first contact but the answers came only in Portuguese. At that age, Jeff could not speak English.

THE MOJAVE DESERT'S GREATEST SECRETS

"The details he has learned are awe inspiring. Answers to questions about time, space, matter, energy, life and spirituality easily rolled from his tongue. All prompted by the alien contacts of his past and present.

"His interview and the recorded details of his many physical contacts PROVIDE HITHERTO UNKNOWN INFORMATION ABOUT SEVERAL ALIEN RACES INCLUDING THE MYSTERIOUS AND THREATENING GRAYS. FROM JEFF SOUZA WE LEARN ABOUT THE SEVEN RACES (possibly humanoid and/or saurian - Branton), THE ALIEN NAME FOR EARTH, A SUBTERRANEAN SPACE STATION IN DEATH VALLEY AND IF AIDS MIGHT BE CURED BY ALIENS.

"There is a final precaution from his contacts - we must all learn the lessons given to Jeff Souza because we are destroying our planet and if we don't change, not even the friendly aliens will be able to save us."

We see here then a definite connection between the subterranea of the Death Valley region, which is reportedly inhabited by the neo-Grecian (?) Hav-musuvs and the human societies in 'Vega' and 'Ummo', which as we shall see later on, according to other contactees, are "Federated" with other human colonies or civilizations in Tau Ceti, Epsilon Eridani, Alpha Centauri, the Pleiades and elsewhere.

Although Jefferson Souza claims to have encountered the Ummo People in landed craft, the Vegans are the ones who allowed him to travel on their craft most often. It was also the Vegans who showed him the MASSIVE basing complex below Death Valley, which contained chambers miles in diameter and numerous compartmentalized sectors which had been adapted to meet the gravitational, atmospheric and environmental needs of the various Federation world representatives who use the base as a way-station for their operations on earth. Apparently the Hav-musuvs have been VERY BUSY for the last few thousand ears, if we are to believe Souza's account.

In addition to the above, Souza learned of two other alien species that are in conflict to some extent with the humanoids with whom he maintained contact. One of these includes an "Insectoid" type race, while the other is reptilian. The latter consists of a tall, very reptilian-saurian appearing "master" race to which the shorter reptilian "Grays" are subservient. There are at least three types of "Grays", according to Souza: those that reproduce via egg-hatcheries, those that reproduce via cloning, and those that reproduce via polyembryony.

One might ask: if some of our ancient ancestors were so intelligent that they could develop aerial craft, then where is all the evidence? The evidence is there, but has been largely ignored by orthodox scientists who cannot fit the existence of advanced prehistoric civilizations into their own theoretical framework. For instance:

Ancient sophisticated artifacts discovered imbedded in SOLID ROCK (including ancient 'spark plugs', metal cubes, gold chains, metal vases, nails, screws, and even electric batteries such as those described in Rene Noorbergen's 'SECRETS OF THE LOST RACES' - Bobbs-Merril Co., N.Y.), as well as artifacts found on the ocean floor, give evidence to the fact that our ancient ancestors were FAR more intelligent in the scientific realm than we give them credit for. Yves Naud, in his book "UFO'S AND EXTRATERRESTRIALS IN HISTORY" (Ferni Publishers, Geneva, Switzerland, 1978) describes one such artifact:

"In 1900, sponge divers near Antikythera (Greece), found rusty fragments of a metallic apparatus on the sea floor. Scientists at first thought that they were remnants of an astrolabe dating from 65 B.C. In 1959, the English scientist, Solla Price, made a discovery which astounded the professional world when he published it in the NATURAL HISTORY review of March 1962:

"'It appears that this object is really a computer which can determine and describe the movements of the sun, of the moon, and probably of the planets.'

"This modern expert felt extremely humble and could only pay homage to the high science of our ancestors, although the homage was tinged with fear.

"'It is quite frightening,' he wrote in SCIENTIFIC AMERICAN (June, 1959), 'to learn that, shortly before their great civilization crumbled, THE ANCIENT GREEKS had come as close as this to our time, not only in terms of their thinking, but also in their scientific technology.'"

Back to the Mojave Desert mystery — it would seem that, based on the various reports (many of which we will record later on), that the Mojave Desert of Southern California and the deserts of western Nevada may in fact be a secret 'battleground' involving U.S. Government troops working in ALLIANCE with the alien races known as the 'Nordics'. Who are 'they' fighting? Their battle, according to SEVERAL sources is against the 'Grays' which have over the last century, possibly earlier, entrenched themselves below ground in underground 'bases' in the Mojave Desert region and elsewhere.

Just as the U.S. government is allegedly working with 'Nordics' based at Mt. Shasta near Weed, California and others in nearby star systems such as those mentioned above who have a base below the Panamint Mt.-Death Valley region; their neo-saurian adversaries are allegedly working with others of their kind within a huge subterranean network centered below the Mt. Archuleta region near the town of Dulce in Northwestern New Mexico (which seems to be the U.S. CENTER of activity in regards to MIBs or 'Men In Black', abductions, mutilations, disappearances, sightings of reptilian entities and so on).

These 'Grays' are allegedly working with other 'Draconians' who have established themselves in Alpha Draconis, Epsilon Bootes, Zeta Reticuli, Altair in Aquila, Rigel and Belletrax Orion, as well as possibly other NEARBY star systems. Why is this 'war' being carried on in secret? Partly because the U.S. Government does not believe that the American public can handle the truth. Just recall Orson

Wells' 'WAR OF THE WORLDS' radio program of so many years ago, and the panic it incited.

In reference to Zeta Reticuli, from where many of the Grays are said to 'originate', Jeffrey L. Kretch, in his article 'THE AGE OF NEARBY STARS' (which appeared in ASTRONOMY Magazine in response to Terence Eckerson's Dec. 1974 article 'THE ZETA RETICULI INCIDENT", describing the Hill abduction, an article which incidentally raised more interest among the readership than any other article the magazine had published), makes note of the METAL and CARBON deficiencies of this binary system. He suggests that carbon-based life could not have 'evolved' in such an environment, and he may be right, for the 'Grays' have 'told' some abductees that they are actually RETURNING to earth, their native planet. No doubt 'they' will try to use this argument, even if true, in an attempt to justify their planned takeover of the planet.

Recently one researcher, K.S., was approached by the family of a U.S. Intelligence worker (O.S.I.) by the name of 'Tucker', who had disappeared mysteriously. They were concerned and frightened as they had discovered, in a personal locker of his, SEVERAL papers describing INTIMATE details of activities surrounding the Dulce, New Mexico and Nevada (S-4, etc.) underground installations. Among this large stack of papers was hidden the following letter which was stamped 'SECRET'. The letter, copies of which were apparently also in the hands of a few other researchers as well, stated the following:

"Dear John...

"I am writing to you in the event that I do not return.

"There is a triangle surrounding the Nevada Test Site.

"There are in fact two of them. Each one frontiers on the other. One is the ELECTROMAGNETIC TRIANGLE, installed by MJ-12. This is a shield to protect the 'Benevolents' (very human looking) from the EBEs (so-called "extraterrestrial biological entities" or Grays - Branton) while they help us develop our counterattack/defenses. The other is the EBEs' 'trap' keeping the benevolents in the redoubt... At each corner of the EM Triangle you will find BLM stations and they are the transmitters of the shield.

"Facing each one of these is an EBE transmitter... There are MANY OF THESE STANDOFFS THROUGHOUT THE WORLD. It is important that you do not interfere by attempting to destroy one of their 'surrounds', they would be able to 'double-up' some- where else and overthrow that position. Once that link is over- thrown, our support team would fail. Their over extension is deliberate on our part. We are like the Chinese, we can't out technology them but we can out number them. Especially since they can't breed here and it is too far for them to go back home without our help. Many of our EM Triangles are ruses to keep them over extended. They can't get out of our solar system because our electromagnetic field (at this time - Branton) is the wrong frequency for their propulsion system to work efficiently. This explains why the EBEs can not commit more vehicles to our solar system."

The humans at the Nevada Test Site 'may' in fact, if we are to believe some researchers, be victims of subtle reptilian propaganda and intimidation. For instance, this source apparently believes that ALL the saurian-grays or EBE's come from extraterrestrial worlds. However as we've shown there is much evidence that saurian activity exists within deep sub- terranean levels and cavities throughout the earth, and has so for many centuries. This is a fact that the saurians have tried to hide from humankind, both terrestrial and extraterrestrial. Also, there are accounts suggesting that the sauroids, grays, etc., ARE IN FACT breeding profusely and reproducing them- selves via deep subterranean polyembryony tanks below Dulce and elsewhere, and are not as 'overextended' as they might have us to believe.

However, on the other hand, the fear the humans might have of prematurely attacking the 'enemy' positions might possibly be propaganda intended to keep humans from taking OFFENSIVE action, believing they are keeping the grays, etc., 'at bay' when in fact the Grays ARE ATTACKING OFFENSIVELY HUMAN SOCIETY on other hidden fronts via mass abductions, deception, implantations, psychic manipulation, recruitment of 'fifth column' humans and infiltration. We personally do not believe in 'standoffs'. In war there is no 'neutrality', one is either attacking (in various ways) or being attacked, in various ways — ways which those on the defensive might not even be aware of. The letter continued:

"The 'headquarters' of this particular 'surround' is Deep Springs, California. At this location one can find a 'school' for Communist homosexuals who have defected to the EBEs in exchange for a cure for AIDs and a promise to their own little world, including reproduction via cloning and artificial wombs. Their sperm fertilize eggs taken from abductees. You will not likely see the hybrids hidden inside the mountain, unless you have... starlite binoculars. Some homosapien APPEARING malevolents (mercenaries) are also there. Nine Soviets were there at the same time Soviets were at the NTS. They were there in the hopes of talking them into defecting back to our side. We are still hopeful.

"The collaborators use the cover organization Natural Resources Defense Council, with front offices in New York and 1350 New York Avenue, N.W., suite 300, Washington, D.C. 20005 [tel. (202) 783-7800]. It is headed by Tom Cochran, staffed by Kevin Priestly UNR, John Brune UNR, Holly Eisler UnSan Diego, Gary Reisling Univ. Ca. Pasadena, Holly Nelson NY, Mary Manning LV Sun, Ed Vogel LVR; and many others I can reveal later.

"One will also find that each corner of their triangle is at the base of a mountain. At each location you will find several entrances to underground systems. Do not attempt to enter, unless you wish to become liquid protein. You may however harass the EBEs' two other corners by placing a large magnet on the vaults... (placing a magnet on the other two entrances at each location will not affect anything). This temporarily interrupts their communications with Deep Springs until a collaborator team comes out to see what is going on. If you place a large magnet on this entrance (it has a large computer near the surface, you can hear it), it will affect an immediate interruption. So, you can take it off in a short time (1 hr) and take it with you. They will still have to come and reset the system. If you plant magnets (camouflaged like rocks) around these entrances, the EBEs won't come out & the sell outs won't be able to find them. The EBEs are also allergic to high concentrations of sugar. You will find that at two locations I have poured sugar around their exits. Always wear magnets near these locations, they interrupt the EBEs' sense of direction (due to an internal compass much like those found in migrating birds) similar to our loss of balance when our ear drum is affected.

"Please wait until I have returned, if you have an airplane, I would like to take aerial photos, we can photograph them together.

"Our alliance crest, symbolic of the EM Shield, and our sign/mark/graffiti is inclosed. Do not reveal them or else every- body will use them & you won't know the real from the pseudos.

"YOU DO NOT KNOW ME, I DO NOT KNOW YOU. THIS IS NOT FOR PUBLIC DISSEMINATION. ZEALOTS MAY DISRUPT THE BALANCE BEFORE V-EBE DAY."

Another researcher by the name (or pseudonym) of Jason Bishop has revealed that 'John', to whom the letter was addressed, is non other than John Lear (one of the most decorated test pilots in U.S. history, and whose father William Lear founded Lear Jet Corp., invented the 8-track tape recorder, and so on) who himself claims many connections with people 'in the know'. According to the letter, both the Nevada Test Site and Deep Springs are areas of conflict between U.S. Govt.-'Nordic' groups who are at war with the saurian grays or the 'reptilians' - since the internal makeup of the grays is reportedly reptilian- based rather than mammalian-based.

Jason Bishop also released some other information he received by way of John Lear, from this individual whose letter we just quoted. According to Lear, the author of the letter was actually a Security Officer at the Test Site who had called in to the Billy Goodman talk show (KVEG radio - Las Vegas, NV) on a few occasions. This person used the codename: 'Yellowfruit,' which he claimed was actually the codename of a top secret group that worked at the site, with which he was involved. YF also sent Lear a copy of the 'Benevolent' teachings. The 'Benevolents' are allegedly working at the Test Site with MJ-12 and are 'Blond-Nordic and/or Aryan-like' people. It is not certain whether these 'aliens' are tied in with the so-called exterran Nordic' Pleiadeans, the terran 'Aryan' Antarcticans, or the subterran 'Blond' Telosians - as all three groups allegedly exist according to different sources, and may have been confused with each other in the past. All three of these groups allegedly posses aerial disks, although in reality their societies may be somewhat distinct from each other.

The BENEVOLENT TEACHINGS (not limited to the below) were identified as follows:

"DISCOURAGED - NON PREPARATORY SPORTS (Activities That Can Not Be Used In Nonsporting Life) motocross, auto- racing, skateboarding, roller skating, football, baseball, hockey. Also Discouraged: Processed Sugar, Recreational Carbo- hydrates, Recreational Fluids, White Bread.

"ENCOURAGED - NONCEREMONIAL LESSONS OF THE MAJOR RELIGIONS & PREPARATORY SPORTS (Activities That Can Be Used In Nonsporting Life) swimming, running, hiking, martial arts, survival arts. Teach Your Children!

"FORBIDDEN - Alcohol, Illegal Drugs, Nicotine, Recreational Drugs, Unjustifiable Homicide.

"MUST - Avoid Weakness (evil grows in weakness). Execute Evil Prisoners In Order To Help Other Prisoners (Editors Note: One personal suggestion would be to place all 'unreformable' death-row prisoners together for life, without possibility of parol, in large though sealed single-entrance extreme-security closely-monitored DEEP underground 'prisons' with others of their own kind and gender. Provide minimum life provisions and possibly even religious-Christian consultation, or broadcasting, and hope at least that the 'Hell' that these people make for each other will motivate some of them to seek for a better existence in the afterlife - Branton).

"MUST - Quarantine Contagious Disease (AIDS) Victims Humanely. Show Strength. Stop Illegal Drugs. Stop Destruction of Environment. Stop Pollution. Use Nuclear Power.

"STUDY - Bill Of Rights, Biology, Computers, Economics, Geography, History, Latin, Mathematics, Philosophy, Survival Skills, United States Of America's Declaration Of Independence, United States Of America's Constitution, Vocational Skills."

Yellowfruit also provided coordinates for the Electromagnetic Triangles he referred to in his letter. These include: N 37 22 30 - E 117 58 0; N 38 21 0 - E 115 35 0; N 35 39 0 - E 114 51 0. Also: Yucca Lake: N 37 0 30 - E 116 7 0.

From what we can gather from the letter quoted earlier 'there are many' areas of conflict or 'standoff' between the humans and saurians around the world. Those who realize that the conflict exists, such as the inner government, have failed to warn the general population of the problem possibly out of fear. However, as we have seen, the documentation proving that such a hidden conflict between the human and serpent races has existed since ancient times is surfacing en masse.

We must realize however that due to the likelihood of the existence of recovered antediluvian technologies (as well as the apparent existence of hidden human and reptilian communities within the earth, which have utilized and added to such technologies since ancient times), the possibility exists that this 'war' began on the surface of the earth, spread to the caverns, and was later propelled out into interplanetary and interstellar space.

From the depths of the earth both 'races', as these technologies developed, apparently rushed to take control of as much territory as possible before the other side had a chance to, the humans - motivated more by their desire to expand their civilizations for the good of their overall societies; and the reptilians (and possibly humans "sellouts" who had collaborated with them) - motivated largely through Imperialistic tendencies, including the desire to establish godlike control over all creation without regard for universal law, a 'prime directive', etc. However, we must be reminded that man is partially to blame for opening the 'door' for these intelligent yet corrupted creatures to enter in and invade our societies, as well as possibly opening the way for their parasitical infestation of the heavens. Perhaps the 'war in heaven' between Michael and the 'Dragon' or the 'Old Serpent', referred to in REVELATION chapter 12, ties in with this scenario as well?!

Utilizing the ancient technologies and adding upon them through a multiplication process, it is uncertain just which 'race' was first able to land itself upon Luna and other planetary bodies, the humans or the reptilians? But there are indications that they both may have done so at least a few thousand years ago, give or take a millennia. According to John Lear's Intelligence sources, U.S. astronauts have even been warned of the dangers of space exploration by human 'UFO' occupants who have allegedly monitored and even accompanied many of the space shots - possibly something along the line of similarity to an older brother teaching a younger brother how to ride a bike, although in this case the stakes are much higher. Many of these 'dangers' would no doubt include malevolent alien entities.

UFO's have also allegedly followed U.S. space shots such as the Apollo and the Shuttle flights, the latter of which have actually 'filmed' what appear to be battles between alien craft and earth-based 'SDI' defense systems. The Apollo shots were allegedly followed FROM EARTH by UFO's, suggesting that an ancient Terran society which already went through the 'space race' phase, perhaps hundreds or thousands of years ago, was concerned with the feeble efforts of their 'little brothers' to move out into space. As we will see later on in this file, the possibility that an ancient Terran race developed space travel thousands of years ago is one which may be backed-up by actual evidence. When we realize that the United States itself became the major world power in less than two hundred years, and as we've said had essentially gone from the 'horse-and-buggy' to interplanetary travel in less than 75 years; then how much activity might have resulted in extraterrestrial realms over a period of two or three thousand years by human

AND saurian beings whose 'sciences' were increasing at a synchronous rate?

Also, do the 'benevolent' human-aliens allegedly working at the Nevada Test Site have any connection with the Hav-musuvs described earlier? Were the 'human' occupied bases on Luna as seen by NASA officials, according to George H. Leonard and others, actually installations placed there by the Hav-musuvs or another society affiliated with them? These are questions we intend to answer in this File.

As we've indicated, there are numerous accounts suggesting that an ancient race who utilize high-technology now resides in the bowels of Mt. Shasta in the Cascade Range of northern California. According to researcher William F. Hamilton, who claims to have met representatives of this society, the inhabitants of the subterranean 'city' under Mt. Shasta are usually tall, blue- eyed blonds who number in excess of over one-and-a-half million in their large 5-leveled, 20-mile long underground city.

Mt. Shasta has been a major site for UFO contacts for decades. Also Indian legends - as well as stories of strange people being seen on it's slopes - abound there. These accounts are so well-known that many of the travel guides to the Shasta area mention the legends of the ancient people who are said to dwell within this ancient volcanic peak.

Aside from the apparent 'Greek' connection with the under- ground city allegedly existing beneath Mt. Shasta (that is, the name 'Telos' itself, which is a GREEK word that literally means 'uttermost, purpose'), Mr. Hamilton also states that some of the 'Telosians' claim to be descended from ancient cultures such as the 'Quetzals' and the 'Naga-Mayas'. This seems to indicate a possible Meso-American connection or origin of some of the alleged inhabitants of Shasta. Is it possible that South American cultures AND Mediterranean cultures such as the ancient Greeks 'teamed up' in their obsession to explore the heavens?

James Churchward (who authored several books describing the history of an alleged sunken island-continent which he believed existed within the Indian Ocean and which went by the name of 'MU') has indicated that the 'Naga-Mayas' were a human tribe tied-in with ancient India. Whether the Telosians are descended from ancient Mayapan, India or Greece is not clear. It is possible as we've said that many ancient empires, such as was suggested in the Hav-musuv account, flowed-in to each other and traded and interacted with each other to a large degree.

Early archeologist Augustus Le Plongeon, one of the first researchers to do an in-depth study of the Mayan Language, came under criticism from orthodox scientists when he claimed to have broken the Mayan language code, and learned of the close connections the Mayas had with Egypt, India and an ancient island continent called 'MU'. Although Churchward placed MU in the Indian Ocean, Le

Plongeon placed it somewhere in the Caribbean, perhaps in the Bermuda Triangle region - possibly mistaking it with the antediluvian 'Atlantis' legends. Others however place MU or ELAM-MU off the west coast of North America or, in fact, identify modern-day California as none other than the ancient kingdom of MU which in ancient times was a peninsula or large island just of the California coast, as the Havmu-suv account seems to suggest. It is also possible that the 'MUrians' had several 'colonies' throughout the ancient world.

Zechariah Sitchin, author of many books, states that some Mayas may originally have came from Egypt. This might be the case when we realize the apparent similarities between the Egyptians and Mayas as they can be seen in the Mayan and Egyptian Pyramids, and so on. Another possibility is one suggested by Churchward, that the Mayas or Naga-Mayas came from India. However, even if they came from Egypt, a connection to India may still exist, for the ancient Greek writer Philostratus insists that the first Egyptians were originally navigators from INDIA! Whether or not the Mayas were originally descended from the Egyptians OR ancient East Indians, there is much evidence that the Mayas WERE never- theless a highly scientific society, who were well advanced in medicine, astronomy, architecture and mathematics. In fact, Charles Berlitz (author of many books on the Bermuda Triangle, the Philadelphia Experiment, and other mysteries) refers to the account of a Colorado art historian by the name of Jose Arguelles.

Arguelles claimed to have met an old Mayan 'sage' by the name of Humbarty Men who told him that his people, the Mayas, still exist as a civilization (underground? - Branton) and that they have in the last millennia succeeded in 'navigating' at least seven nearby planetary systems through advanced spacefaring technologies.

In relation to this, a man by the name of Morris Doreal, also of Colorado (a state which is or was believed to be the home of an advanced subterranean human culture), runs an organization called the 'Brotherhood of the White Temple'. Doreal claims to have visited a few of the ancient underground cities and alleges that several 'members' of his organization are Guatemalan Indians of Mayan descent who have told him of their own knowledge of subterranean cities inhabited by both good and evil (reptilian?) beings. It is true that there are many strange caverns in the regions of Yucatan and Guatemala. Eastern Guatemala has 'Silpino Cave' which has allegedly been explored for months in the direction of ancient volcanic cones without the daring Speleonauts' ever finding an end to the labyrinth; while the 'Loltun Caves' of Yucatan have an even more interesting history, being surrounded with accounts of ancient treasure troves, endless passages, encounters with people within it's depths who claimed to be centuries old, and even stories of lost tribes who vanished into the depths while fleeing their enemies, never to be seen again. Now back to the subject of the Hav-musuvs and the mysterious Mojave and Death Valley region.

THE MOJAVE DESERT'S GREATEST SECRETS

In addition to all of the above, there is much evidence that thousands of years ago the 'Nordic' Vikings landed on the west coast of the Americas. However, whether 'they' have anything at all to add to this scenario is uncertain. The best possible source however for the 'Hav-musuvs' and in fact the 'Telosians' themselves seems to be the ancient Greeks AND Mayas (Greco-Mayans?), although as we've indicated, possibly several ancient societies may have been working together. It is said by some that the Greeks borrowed much of their scientific thought from India during the time of Alexander the Great, and subsequently may have put this scientific thought into physical applications which were in turn shared with some of the leaders of India. As we will see later on, the ancient Greeks AND (Aryan?) East Indians may have been collaborating thousands of years ago in a 'space race' which propelled these cultures outwards to nearby star systems, possibly a millennia or more before the appearance of Christ.

In 1961, SEARCH Magazine published a letter in it's October issue, pp. 76-81, from a Gene A. Statler of (at the time) North Street, Jackson, Missouri. Excerpts from this letter are given here:

"Dear Mr. Palmer: A few days ago I wrote you a letter in which I brought to your attention an item which was placed by you in the Classified Advertisements section of the December, 1959, issue of SEARCH MAGAZINE. In this ad, you requested any information as to the whereabouts of L. Taylor Hansen, who had disappeared twelve years prior to that issue, and he was quoted as saying that he had discovered a black, polished shaft, leading down into the earth near Death Valley.

"You will remember that I mentioned that it was strange to have the poem, 'The Curse of Tippecanoe', listed as written by Hansen if the author had been missing for fourteen years. Well, my face is really red! While looking over some of the newest SEARCH and FLYING SAUCER magazines, I found that no less than five articles in the past three issues of your magazines have been written by Mr. Hansen. Therefore, I can safely assume that Mr. Hansen is not missing! Please accept my apologies for my rash statements. I'll try to be a little more comprehensive in my investigations the next time I try to make an earth-shaking announcement!

"However, my one suggestion still stands. Why not inform everyone, if you have not already done so, as to the real, whole story behind Hansen's disappearance and his discovery? What was his polished, black shaft?"

Ray Palmer's editorial reply to Statler's letter was as follows:

"...It is true that we searched for Mr. Hansen for all those years, and when we found him, he had this cryptic remark to make concerning his whereabouts: 'It would be best just to drop the subject.' However, we do have Mr. Hansen back doing articles for us, and not only that, but we have one book manuscript in production - one on Atlantis, and one on Lemuria. We feel sure that these will be quite sensational, and it may be they will answer a lot of unanswered questions concerning Mr. Hansen and his mysterious twelve-year silence."

As we have seen by the Hav-musuv and related accounts, hidden technological societies descended from ancient Grecia or other ancient societies, may very well have established aerospace travel several hundred, if not a few thousand, years ago.

Assuming this, once aerial travel was accomplished by ancient races such as those described by Oga-Make, William Hamilton and others, 'space' travel would be the next logical step. There are indications that the Hav-musuvs may have been only one of many ancient 'Terran' groups to discover 'free- energy' (electromagnetic) propulsion, and they certainly have not been the last. The problem is, when a segment of the human race, a scientific cabal for instance, stumbles upon the secret of electromagnetic propulsion (or even atomic, mercury, ion or tachyon energy drives - tachyons being an actual faster-than- light particle recognized by quantum physicists), they have a propensity to seclude themselves from mainstream humanity. This was usually done, according to various accounts, out of a fear that their technologies would be stolen and used for destructive purposes. It has only been in recent centuries that this 'techno-imperialism' on the part of the secret scientific fraternities has weakened, as the overall masses of humanity have demanded their 'share' of the technological 'pie', and with it they have also received the darker side of technology - machine guns, missiles, atomic weapons - the works.

Usually man has a suspicious outlook toward his fellow man, understandably, and this has apparently led many such sub- terranean cultures to develop their technologies in secret. Some hidden societies such as the MIB or 'Men In Black' have been especially defensive of intrusion and have used a type of 'psychological terrorism' in order to keep their secrets hidden from those on the surface, especially now that the technologies of the 'International' societies are becoming more refined. This defensiveness and paranoia on the part of the MIB might be explained by their own guiltiness which stems from their ancient associations with the serpent races, and the subsequent mental control which the reptilians have established throughout their own and other 'collaborative' societies. Many of the MIB' however are prisoners of environmental influence and cannot be condemned for being 'born' into such a society (we refer here to the 'humanoid' MIB, although androidal and even reptilian 'Men In Black' have also been encountered). There is no telling how many times such a scenario (of a society discovering the utilization of electromagnetic energy and subsequently disconnecting themselves from mainstream society) has run its course throughout the millennia.

As for the 'Men In Black', which according to researchers like John Keel are an 'Illuminati-like' secret society who may be collaborating with the malevolents (reptilians), their Black Automobiles have been seen entering and leaving underground areas, like for instance—according to one witness—a particular mountain near a road that runs between Hopland and Lakeport California, a road on which many automobiles including government vehicles have allegedly disappeared throughout the years.

The Haitians refer to these large black automobiles, which have sometimes been seen 'apparently' operating without a visible driver, as the 'Zobops'. The superstitious Haitians, many of whom are into Voodoo and serpent worship themselves, refer to the Zobops as a race of sorcerers, and add that if one sees one of these large black automobiles apparently operating without a driver that they had better leave it alone. As we have suggested, there are also many cases which suggest that many of the so- called 'Men In Black' are not human at all.

But whether good or evil, there are apparently numerous societies—many of them highly advanced technologically and many of them very ancient—who have hidden themselves away from mainstream surface societies, again for either benevolent or malevolent reasons. There is, in fact, evidence that such high-tech ancient cultures did exist in ancient times:

Yves Naud, in his book "UFO'S AND EXTRATERRESTRIALS IN HISTORY," records actual accounts of ancient metallurgy factories, as well as documented evidence that the ancients were very familiar with atomic sciences. He states that: "...The manufacture of metal objects (a very advanced form of metallurgy would be necessary in the construction of machines or aerospace craft - Branton) presupposes the existence of appropriate factories. In spite of the fact that the modern mind draws back from this conclusion, we are forced to accept the evidence. Dr. Korioun Meguertchian, brought to light a foundry where the Ancients worked copper, lead, zinc, manganese, steel, etc. Scientists who were doubtful of the existence of blast furnaces now have material proof: twenty-five of these constructions have been discovered, but it is calculated that there must have been at least two hundred..."

These ancient scientists as we've indicated also seem to have made persistent efforts to hide their knowledge from irresponsible persons, although some of this ancient knowledge apparently did fall into the wrong hands, if certain accounts of ancient nuclear explosions are to be believed. Yves Naud reveals: "We again encounter traces of the antique atomic sciences in India. The Brahman treatises VAISESIKE and NYAYA, the sacred book YOGA VASISCHTA, all speak of the structure of matter: 'There are vast worlds within the voids of each atom, as diversified as dust in the rays of sunlight.'

"Being wiser than we are, and aware of the danger that atomic force represented, the Ancients divulged none of the secrets of that science to the profane, in order that the atom would not be used for destructive ends. 'It would be the greatest of sins,' a Chinese wrote, a thousand years or more ago, 'to disclose the secret of our art to soldiers.'

"Antique people knew about the atom, but were they capable of producing an atomic explosion? Scientists spent a long time wondering about this question until the discovery of the DRONA PARVA, a Hindu text which recounts the explosion of an atomic bomb:

"'A flaring projectile with the brilliance of a flame without smoke, was launched. A great darkness suddenly obscured the skies. Clouds thundered in the uppermost air, releasing a downpour of blood. Burned by the heat of this arm, the world appeared shaken by fever.'

"...The physicist, Frederick Soddy, asks: 'In these old tales, can't we see some justification of the belief that prior representatives of a forgotten race of men not only achieved the level of knowledge that we have so recently attained, but even a power that we do not yet have?' Indeed, traces of ARTIFICIAL radioactivity have been detected in various parts of the world in the course of diggings into antique sites. In India a skeleton was exhumed which revealed a powerful intensity of radioactivity. This would tend to confirm the theory of atomic explosions in prehistory." Mr. Naud concludes.

Daniel Cohen, in his book "THE ANCIENT VISITORS" (Doubleday & Co. Inc., New York. 1976), also relates an account taken from an ancient text concerning what might have been aerial craft developed by an old race: "A number of ancient epics from India contain descriptions of fiery flying chariots. There are lines like this one, 'Bhima flew with his Vimana on an enormous ray which was brilliant as the sun and made a noise like the thunder of a storm.'"

Yves Naud related still other accounts suggesting that ancient Terrans did in fact attempt space travel...successfully:

"A CHINESE ON THE MOON 4,300 YEARS BEFORE THE RUSSIANS AND THE AMERICANS - The ancient people, making use of their astronomical knowledge, may have been able to launch out into the exploration of space.

"'The way was long, and as if enveloped in darkness,' explains Chu Yan, a Chinese poet of the third century B.C. Chinese tradition narrates the extraordinary adventure of Hou Yih, an engineer of the Emperor Yao, who decided, 4,300 years ago, to go to the moon with a 'celestial bird.' In the course of the flight, the bird indicated to the traveler the exact movements of the rising, the apogee, and the setting of the sun. Hou Yih thereafter explained that he 'sailed up the current of luminous air.' Could this current have been the exhaust of a rocket?

"'He no longer perceived the rotary movement of the sun,' the narrator points out. Effectively, contemporary astronauts have noted that, in space, it was not possible to discern the diurnal passage of the sun. And what did the Chinese engineer observe on the moon? He saw 'an horizon which appeared frozen.' To protect himself from the glacial air, he built the 'Palace of the Great Cold.' His wife, Chang Ngo, left to join him on the satellite, which she described as 'a luminous sphere, brilliant as glass, of an enormous size, and very cold.'"

If one such flight to the moon was successful, then we must assume that many others followed. Actually, Yves Naud quotes another ancient legend from China which suggests that at one point a great 'space race' to explore and colonize nearby planets was a reality, and that as a result of a perverted race of troglodytes the world was thrown into a dark ages which led to an almost complete loss of contact and communication between the other-planetary colonists and the ancient world. Quoting from the legend:

"...The Mao-tse were (a) perverted race which had taken refuge in the caverns. It is said that their descendants still live in the outlying areas of Canton. Then, under the influence of Tchu-Yeo, they stirred up trouble throughout the world, and it became ridden with highwaymen. The lord Chan-Ty (a king of the so-called 'divine' dynasty) saw that the people had lost every vestige of virtue. And so he ordered Tchang and Lhy to cut all communication between heaven and earth. From that time on there was no more going up nor coming down."

In connection to the above, it may not be any coincidence that John A. Keel states on pp. 93-94 of his book 'THE MOTHMAN PROPHECIES' (Signet Books, N.Y., 1975 paperback edition) the following concerning certain UFO witnesses: "...In some cases, ancient lettering like Greek or Chinese appears on the object. The effect is the same. Months, even years, later the same percipient may again see the same numbers or letters on an object..."

From the ancient text, the BRIHAT KAHTA, we read how the ancient inhabitants of INDIA were aware of the flying craft WHICH HAD BEEN DEVELOPED BY CERTAIN GREEKS who were very possessive of their scientific and mechanical knowledge. In the ancient account we read:

"Padmavit explains that Queen Vasavadotta wishes to fly in a chariot to visit the (other parts of) earth. Vasantoke, the Master of Entertainment, broke into a laugh and told her: 'The women servants of the king have exactly that same desire. I have told them to suspend a swing between two high poles and to use this to go to and fro in the air. And if the queen wishes these aerial voyages, then she must content herself in the same fashion!' Everybody started to laugh, but Rumanavit cut in, 'That is quite enough joking,' he said, 'now let us look at the facts.' 'We are talking in the void,' Yangandharayame interrupted. 'That is a problem for the artisans.'

"Rumanavit convoked the carpenters and gave them strict injunction to build a flying machine at once. The corps of artisans joined together and after a long period of shuffling about in an effort to avoid the whole problem, they finally sent their delegators, trembling in fear, to find Rumanavit. 'We know of four sorts of machines,' they told him, 'those made of water, those made of air, those made of dust, and those composed of a great many pieces. But as far as flying machines are concerned, we have never even seen one. The Yavanas (Greeks) are the ones who know about them.'

"Then a Brahmin spoke of a carpenter, Pukrasaka, whom the King had told (of) the existence of a certain Vicvita, who was mounted upon a mechanical cock. The foreign ambassadors whispered: 'We should never reveal the secret of the flying machines to anyone whomsoever, be he artisan or other. It is too difficult to understand for one who is NOT GREEK.'

"All of a sudden, a stranger (a Greek?) appeared. He called upon Rumanavit to supply him with necessary material, and he built a flying chariot in (the) form of Garuda (the eagle with a human body, the steed of 'Vishnu'). It was ornamented with flowers. The queen and her husband flew around the world and then returned to their city..."

This account, as we can see, indicates that the ANCIENT East Indians and Greeks were allies and were working together in the development of aerial craft. Could this explain the apparent involvement of neo-Grecian, and possibly 'Indian' and Mayan cultures in connection with the human civilizations living in the various cavern systems beneath California?

There are other indications besides those that we've just mentioned which suggest that the ancient Greeks were very steeped in the intellectual sciences and used this knowledge to explore the unknown regions. Is it possible that before the Grecian empire crumbled, certain members of that society continued to carry on their own version of their civilization in remote outposts beneath or beyond the earth? According to Judeo-Christian history and prophecy (book of Daniel), four world 'empires' would run their course before the Messiah Himself finally reigned as king of an incorruptible Kingdom. The first was the Babylonian empire, second was the Medo-Persian Empire, followed by the Grecian empire which would subdue "the face of the whole earth" (see: Daniel 8:5,21). The last empire would be the largest, cruelest and most oppressive, the Roman Empire. It would rise and rule the nations, and then 'fall' in a sense although still retain considerable control over the 'religious' world (Revelation ch. 17-18) and then revive into a '10-horned' empire ruled by a counterfeit messiah.

The idea that the Grecian empire went about "on the face of the whole earth" might be significant if we consider that the 'Hav-musuvs' for instance were connected with ancient Grecia. As for the highly intellectual nature of the Greeks, this was confirmed by the Apostle Paul, who alleged that during his visit to Athens, Greece, "...the Atheneans and strangers which were there spent their time in nothing else, but either to tell, or to hear some new thing." (Acts 17:21). Actually, when we consider the possibility that an ancient Grecian-like race developed aerospace travel thousands of years ago and compare this with modern accounts of human UFOnauts, there are indications that a connection between the two may be found. Many modern historians attribute our present sciences to the ancient Greek philosophers. However, when the Dark Ages of Roman Inquisition came these sciences were suppressed. But what if, as some suggest, certain of the early Greek philosophical-fraternal- scientific societies discovered for themselves hidden abodes far from the oppression of mainstream society and continued to develop their sciences with the freedom and creativity that only such hidden colonies could provide?

One very interesting account, which seems to indicate that hi-tech human societies on and within the earth did in fact colonize other planetary bodies thousands of years ago, appeared in SEARCH magazine. The article, titled "BRACE YOURSELVES", was written by an ex-NASA employee who identified himself only as 'The Doc'. His account appeared in the Winter, 1988-89 issue of that magazine. This ex-NASA employee related at the beginning of the article two very remarkable things that he'd heard while working at NASA. One of them included the discovery that the sun's surface may not be a region of continuous thermonuclear activity as has commonly been believed. Instead, scientists had found that it appeared to be in essence a tremendous electromagnetic dynamo or sphere which in turn generates the electromagnetic fields of the planets. In other words it seemed to be more of a gigantic electrical 'light' or 'sphere' than a gigantic thermonuclear reactor, although nuclear reactions might play a part, but not nearly to the extent that many believe.

Some have alleged that the 'heat' experienced from the solar orb on a planets' surfaces is not so much determined by their proximity to the sun, but more by the amount and type of atmosphere with which the solar radiations and rays interact to produce friction and heat. In simple terms, the sun is not 'hot' in the sense that most believe, but the solar flares and explosions taking place on the surface of the sun are more consistent with tremendous electrical 'arcs' than with nuclear explosions. The other 'revelation' he received from other NASA employees was that the U.S. Navy has for several year been making regular reconnaissance-observation trips to monitor alien 'bubble-cities' on the ocean floor.

Some years afterwards, while practicing homeopathic medicine in Phoenix, Arizona in 1984, 'The Doc' met a young man who had come into his office to pick up some 'UFO photos' he had loaned to a different doctor on a previous visit. The ex- NASA employee struck up a conversation with the young man. Following is an excerpt from the conversation which ensued between the young man and 'The Doc' during that visit. The young man said, after talking to 'The Doc' about the photos:

"So, do you know anything about UFO's?"

"Only what I've read since the 1950's and hear tell by others who have had encounters. How about yourself?"

"Well, there are such craft now in our atmosphere with bases underground and underwater. One group is very advanced and can take you anywhere in the universe."

"Should Einstein be upset to hear that?" I thought about it for awhile.

"There is a whole science concerning traveling above the speed of light. These people are so advanced that most of the world is not ready to understand or appreciate their values and their scientific attainment."

"Well, no matter how advanced their technology, spiritually they have the same plight as we. We are all spiritual brothers and sisters and must solve the mystery of returning to our Source."

He looked at me penetratingly and continued.

"When I was eight years old and playing with a friend out in a field, a craft came down, landed not far from us and a man and woman came out and walked up to us, smiling and calling us by name. They seemed to know all about me, what school I was going to, what subjects I liked best, and they told me that they would every so many years return and visit with me. They also said that they wanted me to do well in school."

"Did they return?" I asked, smiling, half in disbelief.

"Yes, surprisingly, they did. About five years later. I was about thirteen or fourteen. They told me that I was one of them and I was put on this planet to help them someday in the future."

"Incredible!" I played along with this.

"You haven't heard the best part. I was nineteen and was driving one night up through a wooded area in Connecticut, and suddenly this saucer swooped down over my car. I almost drove off the highway I was so shocked. It paced me, staying just above the car, and this voice came over my car radio speakers, but my radio wasn't even on! This voice knew my name and asked a number of times, 'Dave (pseudonym), when will you return home? You have been gone so long.'

"I was really shaken up by this, and then they somehow lifted my car off the highway and took me over a hill and brought me back down on the same highway, without my tires even squealing. They finally said that they would return again someday.

"I stopped at the first public phone and phoned my parents in Vermont. When my mother answered I was so shaken and anxious over the possibility of my parents having not told me the truth, I didn't bother to tell her what had happened on the highway. 'Mom, who am I?'

"'Why, Dave, you're my son.'

"'Mother, who am I really? How did I get into this world?'

"'Son, you got into this world just like other boys. I delivered you in a hospital.'

"'Mom, I don't believe it. Over and over I have been visited by people in starships who, somehow, know me. They say I am supposed to help them someday. Their ship just came down over my car, they called me by name and toyed with me about when I would come home to them someday. And then they picked up my car off the highway and gave me quite a shocker of a ride. I'm different, aren't I. I want to hear the truth.'

"There was a long silence at the other end of the phone."

"'All right. We were going to tell you someday as you have continued to mention these kind of things. Your father and I found you and your sister one evening as we were walking out behind the cabin like we did every evening after dinner. We found you and your sister wrapped in a blanket nestled between some boulders up on the hillside. We couldn't believe what we saw. You both were dressed in shiny one-piece suits. You were about a year old. We asked around and could not find anyone that might know your parents. We figured that you had been abandoned but we both had the strongest impulse to take care of you both until someone came into town and asked about you.'"

I was now shaking my head. "And have you continued to be visited by your friends?"

"Yes. More frequently, like a calendar."

"Where are they from?" He had me going now.

"Are you familiar with the Seven Sisters constellation?"

"I don't think so."

"It's also called the Pleiades constellation."

"Why are they, YOU here?"

"They won't interfere for the most part with the social problems and destiny of the Earth. It's a policy of theirs."

I was standing up now looking sad, "I'm sorry to hear that..."

"The Doc" then gave him a checkup, since the young man had originally come in for back problems. After he had informed the doctor that his back no longer bothered him, he told "The Doc" that he had to rush to catch a flight to Switzerland, and left the clinic.

"As I was turning into my office," the Doc continued, "one of the chiropractic physicians called as he was walking towards me down the hall carrying an X-ray.

"'Look at this X-ray. This guy is really different.'

"I looked at it. 'Two extra cervical vertebrae.'

"'Also abnormally low vital signs (blood pressure, pulse). Not sure about the placement of the organs either.'

"I looked at the helpless expression on my associate's face. 'Friend of yours?'

"'The guy that just left to catch a flight to Switzerland.'

"I found myself looking down an empty hallway, far off into the distance..."

In his book "LIGHT YEARS" (Morgan Entekin Books., Atlantic Monthly Press., N.Y. 1987), Gary Kinder reveals that the Swiss contactee Eduard 'Billy' Meier was told by the star travelers he allegedly encountered that 'they' were from the Pleiades, some 430 light-years from earth. The Pleiades are a relatively nearby 'open' star cluster consisting of hundreds of stars, and according to scientists the sun (or Sol) itself and some of its neighbors revolve around Alcyon, the central star of the Pleiades cluster. However, the Pleiades are a relatively young system of stars which are unlikely to have developed life of their own and, in fact, the Pleiadeans claim that they are not native to that part of the galaxy. The Pleiadeans claimed to have 'terra-formed' certain planets in that sector to support life and that their actual place of origin IS MUCH CLOSER TO EARTH, in the Lyra systems, some 30-or-so light years from our Sol-ar system. In other words, they migrated outwards from the general direction of the earth.

The Pleiadeans according to Meier look remarkably, almost exactly, like us although many of them are allegedly 'Nordic' appearing, some with blonde hair and others with darker shades. They number only a little more than 500 million on their Terra- formed planet of Erra, in the 'Taygeta' system of the Pleiades. This suggests that they have probably been living on that planet for a relatively short period of time as compared with the inhabitants of the earth, who number over 7 billion.

'They' also claim to have horses, cows, rabbits, fish, and other 'Terran' life-forms roaming about on their planet. This strongly suggests that the ancestrage of the Lyran-Pleiadeans and those on earth are intimately linked via ancient civilization, and in fact Meier was told that 'their' ancient lineage does in fact converge with that of earth's ancient inhabitants. When we consider that the Pleiadeans originally came from Lyra, which is much closer to planet earth, and consider the remarkable similarities between terran and Lyran-Pleiadean life, then one might wonder if Lyra itself might have been originally colonized by ancient explorers such as the Hav-musuvs, or by other civilizations such as the Mayas, Greeks, Chinese or Eastindians who according to many sources all possessed aerial and/or interplanetary exploratory craft a few thousand years ago. There is incidentally ANOTHER GROUP of 'extraterrestrials' who have made themselves known to various contactees and who claim to be tied-in with the Pleiadeans AND ancient earth, suggesting an even greater possibility that these as well as the Pleiadeans had their genesis originally on (ancient) earth thousands of years ago. Could planet earth be the original 'seed' from which all sentient life in the universe proceeded?

To be honest, there have been many claims — mostly through so-called "channeled" information — which would have us to believe that the Earth was originally colonized by beings from other worlds. We are of the opposite opinion, however, and suggest that much of the inhabited sectors of this galaxy were colonized by the many expeditions which, "unofficial" history tells us, were sent outward from earth by several hidden societies who had attained the ability to initiate interplanetary or interstellar travel throughout the past 3 or 4 thousand years, in post-diluvian times. The "other side" in this argument may present all the evidence they can gather to support their theory, however they must allow us the same privilege. We feel that if we are to suggest that planet earth was the original life-seed of the galaxy, then we have the duty to compile the evidence to support this theory, so most if not all of the information contained in these files is information which we have gathered in support of the above thesis and we make no apologies.

We present this possibility not because of any egotistical desire to place planet earth above any other 'world', but simply because it seems to be the one explanation which fits with all of the accounts given in this File. This 'other' spacefaring group who are allegedly tied-in with the Pleiadeans claim to come from the Tau Ceti and Epsilon Eridanus star systems, which are two of the nearest SOL-type star systems in this sector of the galaxy.

According to Meier, a great interplanetary battle and mass human exodus took place ages ago within the Lyran system, and as a result a large percent of the human inhabitants were forced to evacuate their planet within that system after many of their ancestors were apparently killed in the war. Meier was not told, to our knowledge, just who the 'attackers' were, but another 'contactee' claims that the attackers in the 'Lyran wars' were none other than the interstellar parasites known to us as the 'Grays'. Some who have been abducted against their will by the grays have even been shown holographic recordings of such an interplanetary war, as if the grays in their leviathan pride were parading their supposed invincibility to their frightened and confused abductees.

As a result of this war, according to Meier, a leader by the name of Pleiore allegedly led a mass exodus of surviving refugees from the Lyran system in an effort to reach and colonize the Pleiades, the Hyades and Vega. Even today as we've seen previously, some 'Contactees' have reportedly encountered the modern-day Vegans, as well as the Pleiadeans. Whether Tau Ceti was colonized as a result of this exodus, or whether it was an original 'link' in an apparent colonization by ancient Eartheans of the Lyran system, is uncertain. It is interesting however that, when viewed from earth, the three constellations of Taurus (Pleiades),

Cetus, and Eridanus are ADJACENT to each other and in the same sector of the sky. At this point in time, Meier was told, the Pleiadeans were part of a union of interstellar colonists and civilizations numbering over 127 billion humans. One interesting thing that Meier was told is that the 'Nordics' or 'Pleiadeans' were approximately 3000 YEARS advanced over us in technological development! (This extreme closeness in development when compared to the multi-billion year history of the galaxy may seem highly unusual, as well as the fact that nearly all human cultures in this sector of the universe who have contacted eartheans claim to be no more than a few thousand years advanced over us. The most likely explanation is that human life in this part of the galaxy appeared on one single world and quickly spread out to other systems, adapting themselves to their new environments, especially after "hyperspace" travel became a reality).

Are there any other accounts that might support the above scenario?

In the Spring, 1991 issue of "UFO JOURNAL OF FACTS" (Box 17206., Tucson, AZ 85710), researcher Forest Crawford gives a very remarkable description of a crash-recovery of a disk which was reported by a former deep-level government employee who Crawford refers to only as 'Oscar'. For reasons which should be obvious, 'Oscar's' last name was not given. His story, as quoted by Crawford, is as follows:

"'...The eggs had their typical lack of firmness and the sausage tasted more like greasy rope than pork links. The order to mobilize saved me from this breakfast experiment. We proceeded down six flights of stairs below the COMTRAPAC submarine base in San Diego to 'shoot-the-tubes.' After placing a few pieces of jewelry in a container I climbed into the cylinder to travel the tunnels to an unknown assignment. I wondered what was so important to upgrade our pay from E-3 to E-6 before we left and besides that, we could not even finish breakfast.

"'As I am told of our departure, a familiar uneasy feeling comes over me. When you push down on the accelerator in your car, one can feel the tug of inertia sinking you into the seat. When you travel the tubes there is no feeling of motion but you know when the door opens you will be in another place hundreds, even thousands of miles away. For some comfort I checked to see if the watch hidden in my pocket was still there. I quickly looked to see if it is still running. It seems to be working normally, so why no jewelry? Because of electrical charge buildup perhaps?

"The soft clang of the door opening made me tense again. I did not even feel us stop! Peeking at the watch I noted only 30 minutes had passed. We must be in California, Nevada or Arizona, I thought. As I stepped from the windowless capsule I heard a military policeman murmur 'Turners' Rangers.' Our reputation had preceded us. As I readorned my jewelry the first surprise of this assignment was about to come.

"'A high-ranking Naval O.S.S. Officer informs us that we will not be allowed above ground while in North Dakota. NORTH DAKOTA! Several of us were led to a large hanger-like room that had been quickly set up to function as a laboratory. Resting on heavy jack stands in the middle of the room was a large disk- shaped craft. The chief scientist present was introduced as Professor Bear. As his briefing and some discussion proceeded, I rapidly developed rapport with this talented, open minded and gentle man.

"'The craft had crashed near Phoenix, Arizona and was moved to this North Dakota base. Two dead alien bodies with fatal radiation exposure were found outside the craft. I reflected on my O.S.S. Training for crash retrieval and remembered thinking. 'Why bother, we will never get a chance to be involved in anything that exciting.' Well, not only was I involved, I was the security team leader. This meant that when the craft was opened I would be the first one inside! After all, one does not send in a high ranking officer or a chief scientist to possibly encounter an alien booby trap or extraterrestrial virus. Come to think of it, the prospects did not excite me either. As Professor Bear prepared his ultrasonic sound generators for opening the craft, my apprehension turned to intensity; after all, this was what my training was for.

"'As 'the Bear' tuned his equipment the smooth solid metal surface of the craft began to ripple like when you throw a stone in the water. When the ripples seemed to gain harmonic stability the now liquid metal parted in a circular iris-like fashion. As I stepped inside I noticed a fresh pine scent and a strange smoothness to everything. The interior was rounded off and continued with no seams or rivets. It was as if the walls, floor and ceiling were formed out of one piece of metal. Even a table in the center of the craft looked as though it had been pushed up out of the floor. What appeared to be control panels had no knobs, switches or dials. There were strange symbols highlighting these futuristic yet simple consoles.

"'The outside of the craft had no apparent damage yet the interior showed some distortion, possibly from the crash. Next to one of the panels I could see something that would challenge my training and change my perceptions of reality forever. The craft was just another piece of hardware, but seated next to the panel was a human! It's gender was obviously male. Aside from his unusual dress he could have walked past you at a grocery store and not command much attention. Upon noticing some injuries about his head I instinctively and quickly moved toward him to help. His skin was a bronze color, reminiscent of Mediterranean or South American cultures. His hair was similarly brown and very short in a Roman or crew style cut. The only real difference in appearance from earth humans were that his ears were slightly pointed. He reminded me of pictures of Quetzalcoatl, the deity of the ancient Toltecs (Note: This mythic being which was also known as the 'feathered serpent' may have been either human or serpentine, depending on the different 'depictions' given by the ancient Mayas, Toltecs, etc. - Branton).

"'He was conscious and in great pain. One leg was partially pinned by the shifting interior. I was examining cuts on his cheek and lip when I first touched him. An overwhelming feeling of compassion came over me as I heard his voice in my head. I could understand him clearly even though his mouth did not move. The communication was strictly telepathic..."

Note: In this case he mean 'empathic'. There is little evidence that actual mind-to-mind 'thought reading' is a reality, at least without the aid of sophisticated technology. Even if it were possible the 'words' formed in the mind of the human encountered by 'Oscar' would most likely be in a language completely unfamiliar to him. Most people who experience this phenomena claim that 'thought words' are not involved, but that so-called 'telepathy' instead involves the empathic 'feelings' or 'images' BEHIND these words. Emotions are the most common 'universal language' between the various different human races wherever they may be. Many experts claim that 'words' make up only about twenty percent of the actual 'communication' which passes between people. Sometimes body language, facial expressions, feelings, eye contact, and attitudes tell more about what a person is thinking than mere 'words' can. This is because humans have a duel physical and spiritual nature. Just as an astronomer can determine the chemical makeup of a star by looking at it's spectrograph, human beings are like 'lights' in themselves who can to a large extent be 'interpreted' by others who are sensitive to the feelings, expressions and words-attitudes which they are projecting. For instance emotions, sight, and even thoughts result from a combination of the physical and spiritual natures of human beings. So with this interjection, we now continue with 'Oscar's' account:

"'I perceived his fear of being harmed and told him that I would not let anyone hurt him. Suddenly, a voice from the doorway refocused my attention on the duties at hand.

"'I called back that we had a live one. The craft filled with gloved and masked medical personnel to help free the occupant. He was quickly carried outside and placed on a gurney. I remarked that he felt heavy for his size and a few others that had assisted agreed. As the alien was whisked off for medical attention, Professor Bear examined the inside of the craft. He found what he thought was a star map depicting the constellation Eridanus and wondered if that might be where the alien was from. After a brief discussion concerning the nature of the communications, Bear asked me to accompany him to the medical lab. As we talked along the way I referred to the alien being as 'Hank.' The professor asked if that was the name the alien had given me.

"I explained that it was not and that I had chosen that nickname based on it's native American reference to a 'troubled spirit.' The professor smiled and said,

'Hank it is,' and the name seemed to immediately stick. In the antiseptic, impersonal medical room Hank's discomfort was compounded by his complete undressing. While still in great pain he was examined from head to toe. No stone was left unturned, so to speak. They treated him as if he were a baby of some rare animal species being first born into captivity. It became evident that Hank could not communicate with everyone involved so I was asked to be translator. I had no trouble understanding that the normal anesthetics we were administering had little or no effect. Suddenly, with Hank's discomfort still a concern, everyone's attention became divided between the being and a new person arriving on the scene.

"'This new person was obviously important yet seemed to make everyone uneasy. Even Hank recoiled in fear when he came close. He barked a few stern orders and several people, myself included, marched into a nearby conference room. The man introduced himself as Frank Drake and told us he was the head of the operation. The reports would hence forth be titled 'Project OSMA' (with an 'S'). As the sound of his continued briefing faded into a day- dream, I thought about how my regimented life had just jumped track and was now speeding off in a totally new direction...'

Forest Crawford, commenting on the incident, states:

"This extraordinary story, according to the witness, is not fiction. Oscar is a simple country person from rural Missouri where he lives with his wife, three children, and a menagerie of stray animals. His life is seemingly uncomplicated and unhurried. However, his eyes reflect a clarity indicative of inner knowledge and understanding.

"We first came to meet this man as the result of a lead from nuclear physicist and renowned Ufologist, Stanton Friedman. At the 'Show-Me UFO Conference 1989' in St. Louis, Friedman asked Bruce Widaman, State Director of Missouri MUFON, if he would attempt to locate a witness that called responding to the 'Unsolved Mysteries' show on the Roswell crash. The person in question had possibly been involved in a crash retrieval while in the military. The tip had come from a former neighbor of Oscar's.

"Widaman of course agreed to follow up since Friedman felt that the witness did not have a phone. So with little else than a name, town, and rumor to go on, the search began. Widaman and Alex Horvat, Public Information Officer for Missouri MUFON, arrived in the small town near St. Louis after dark. After questioning a girl at a local convenience mart no further leads were found. Horvat suggested checking the local bar. This produced a description of a front yard that might be that of the elusive witness. After driving up and down the lane several times, one yard seemed more appropriate than the others so they hesitantly stopped. Stepping from the car into the country night proved harrowing enough as several large dogs snarled and barked from the surrounding darkness.

Widaman was further unnerved when a large black dog began licking his hand as he knocked on the door. Not knowing whether he was being greeted or tasted by the animal, Widaman was relieved to see someone answer. After a brief explanation of who or what our investigations were, an invitation to sit and talk came as a positive sign. The stranger said he did not know where 'Bill,' the name given Friedman, was, but that he was his brother. After Widaman and Horvat explained their purpose and some of their feelings and ideas he finally conceded that he was in fact the man they were looking for. He explained that his real name was Oscar and that the name 'Bill' had been given so he would know where any inquiries were coming from.

"As Oscar told the story that began this article it became obvious that, because of his military background, the name given was for his protection. The account unfolded further to reveal horrible injustices to Hank and to Oscar himself. At the direction of Drake the team conducted medical experiments such as spinal taps, marrow sampling, taking organ specimens and other exploratory surgery on Hank WITHOUT anesthesia. Oscar had spent many hours over three months communicating with and growing close to the alien. One day he stepped between Drake and Hank with his .45 cal. pistol drawn and demanded an end to the torture. Drake withdrew but the next morning Oscar had new orders to depart immediately for Saint Albans Hospital in Radford, Va., where he was incarcerated for debriefing. He remained isolated for several months until the efforts of Lt.(?) Charles Turner, Oscar's Commanding Officer, got him to move to a psychiatric ward. His family, who had now been out of touch with him for almost three months, was told that Oscar had suffered a head injury during a submarine accident. After spending time under psychiatric care, which would damage his military record, he was oddly enough given an honorable discharge.

"After having returned to civilian life he and his father embarked on a hiking trip to North Dakota. They purposely entered the restricted area surrounding the base where Oscar had been stationed. Perimeter patrol picked them up for removal from the area. While in their company Oscar asked how Hank was doing. One of the guards confided that the alien had died several months earlier.

"The next trip out to the country included myself and David Rapp, a physicist with 13 years experience in the aerospace industry and also Director of Investigations for Missouri MUFON. Because of our backgrounds in science the discussion focused on technical questions about Oscar's experiences..."

As for the alleged home of 'Hank's' people, Crawford states:

"The pattern from the panel inside the ship was confirmed by Rapp to match stars of the constellation Eridanus as seen FROM EARTH. It was later confirmed by Hank that the stars of origin of his people were Tau Ceti and Epsilon Eridani. In later sessions Oscar discussed some reasons for the presence of the aliens. He said THEY DO NOT LIKE THE SITUATION WITH SOME OF THE SMALL GREY ALIENS (emphasis ours - Branton). He corrected us when we used the term 'grey' and said that they are actually white. The Tau Cetians feel that the abductions being carried out by some of the Greys ARE A GREAT INJUSTICE TO HUMANITY. 'THEY ARE A PARASITIC RACE THAT HAS AND IS PREYING ON HUMAN CIVILIZATIONS THROUGHOUT THE UNIVERSE,' Oscar relayed. He added that our government's involvement with the grays IS VERY DANGEROUS AND OUT OF CONTROL... Oscar is ADAMANT that the bug people (i.e. Oscar's term for these creatures - Branton) are using HUMAN FLUIDS FOR SUSTENANCE. They feed by immersing their arms in vats and/or rubbing the fluids on their bodies. HE CLAIMS THAT THEY ARE ALSO KIDNAPPING CHILDREN..."

To our knowledge 'Oscar' had in no way at the time been in contact with John Lear nor any other researcher who has alleged this exact same thing. Oscar's claim that these creatures are more whitish or albino in color would seem consistent with accounts concerning SOME branches of the 'serpent race'.

As Oscar alleges, not all 'grays' have been described as having the same coloring. Some have been described as plain gray, others blue-gray, gray-green, or grayish white! One source suggests that the 'coloring' has a direct connection with the amount of 'protein formula' which they have access to. Also, Oscar's reference to the 'bug people' may be based on the fact that the reptilian branch known as the grays and others branches of the 'serpent race' are often said to resemble 'praying mantis' like creatures in that their eyes are sometimes bug-like and protruding, and their long arms which often reach down below their knees often appear mantis-like when in their folded or reposed position - elbows pointed downwards and clawed-hands positioned above. In fact, some of the early saurians such as the Tyrannosaurus Rex kept their arms in such a position, elbows pointed down, although many of the modern sauroids possess arms which are now much longer. But a more likely explanation is one that has been given by researcher Ray Keller. Keller's sources indicate that reptilian grays from Reticuli have created a sub-race by assimilating genetic materials from another intelligent (and malevolent) alien species of Insectoids. Therefore some of the "grays" being observed by abductees may actually be reptilian-insectoid genetic hybrids. John Lear stated in his infamous UFO document (which he posted on the Paranet Computer Bulletin Board) that some of the beings recovered from the earlier crashed disks were mantis-like and reptilian- skinned.

The possibility of little children being abducted and used for their 'secretions' and body organs is almost too horrible to contemplate. There MAY be other indications that such is the case, whether one chooses to believe it or not. For instance:

1) Bill English, son of an Arizona state legislator and a former Green Beret

commander allegedly viewed the top- secret "GRUDGE/BLUE BOOK REPORT NO. 13" years after he investigated a downed aircraft which radioed an encounter with a UFO, and whose occupants were later found mutilated. He stated that this secret document contained eyewitness descriptions of children who had been abducted by 'grey' type entities, one of them being abducted on a farm right in front of the parents, and never seen again.

2) The Aug. 1940 issue of NATIONAL GEOGRAPHIC detailed the disappearance of 30 children and their teachers in some catacombs below the island of Malta. Sources contemporary to the event stated that they had entered a 'burial' chamber in the third or lowest level of the 'Hypogeum of Hal Salflienti', an orifice which was rumored to lead to 'deeper' catacombs. The ancient catacombs were discovered below the small village of Casal Paula in 1902 when workmen literally fell into it while digging. They discovered over 30,000 bones and evidence of ancient human sacrifice conducted by an old Neolithic race. Witnesses to the disappearance said that a sudden 'cave-in' had blocked the opening after the last child had gone through, but the rope they used to tie themselves to the lower room was found to be clean cut, and many reported hearing the crying and wailing of children from below ground weeks after the disappearance. According to researcher Riley Crabb of the 'Borderland Sciences Research Foundation', a British Embassy employee by the name of Miss Louis Jessup entered the 'lower catacombs' a few days before the disappearance, catacombs which she described as being immense. She allegedly encountered a sudden and mysterious "wind" which blew out her candle, following which she felt something 'wet and slippery' brush past her. Needless to say she left the scene in a hurry. Nevertheless, this account indicates how children sometimes tend to 'disappear' in the presence of aerial or subsurface phenomena.

3) John Lear also claims — based upon accounts given to him by several contacts of his in the intelligence community — that there is evidence that a percentage of America's missing children have been taken by these creatures (the Grays), suggesting that the 'aliens' largely prey on the weak and defenseless among the human race. It is uncertain however what percentage of 'missing children' might be involved here. Lear, in his 'Press Release' of June 3, 1988, stated in reference to human abductees and victims of human mutilation: "The various parts of the body are taken to various underground laboratories, one of which is known to be near the small New Mexico town of Dulce. This jointly occupied (CIA-Alien) facility has been described as enormous, with huge tiled walls that 'go on forever'. Witnesses have reported huge vats filled with amber liquid with parts of human bodies being stirred inside... he secretions obtained are then mixed with hydrogen peroxide and applied on the skin (of the grays) by spreading or dipping parts of their bodies in the solution. The body absorbs the solution, then excretes the waste back through the skin." (like REPTILES excrete waste through

the shedding of their 'skins' - Branton) This would confirm 'Oscar's' claims to this effect.

(4) Researcher William Cooper, who was formerly a chief Petty Officer and Intelligence Worker in the Pacific Naval fleet, pointed out at the 1989 MUFON Conference in Las Vegas that over 3000 children disappear without a trace yearly in one part of Manhattan alone. We might relate this to other obscure though evident indications that Manhattan literally sits atop vast underground caverns which have been confirmed by different sources, including CON EDISON when they broke into a vast cavity at a depth of 200 feet while drilling in a Manhattan Park. Cooper also claimed to have seen top-secret reports stating that sections of human bodies were found stored on disks retrieved from crash-recovery sites, and that the government was extremely disturbed by this aspect of the alien activity.

5) There are hundreds, if not thousands, of accounts of women who had been a few months along in a pregnancy, most often an unexplained pregnancy, only to find after a UFO abduction experience that their babies suddenly 'disappeared'. These accounts are a reality. It is very unlikely that hundreds or thousands of women would collectively use the same 'bizarre' identical excuse if they themselves aborted a child and did not wish others to think that they did so, especially when many of these women were the ONLY one's who knew of the pregnancy.

6) Although many of the children who are allegedly abducted and never seen again are of the homeless or unwanted type, 'street' children of prostitutes, and so on — children who will not be 'missed' as much as others — it also appears that thousands of children who belong to middle-class families are also being abducted, IMPLANTED and returned. Since the disappearance of these would cause far more 'waves' than a child without a guardian, they are used instead for purposes of manipulation. It appears that these infernal creatures are EXTREMELY cautious and cunning, and have hidden their tracks and even their very existence well, at least up until the 1970's-1980's when 'abductions' started to make the news in a profound way.

Forest Crawford continues:

"...He (Oscar, based on what 'Hank' communicated to him) claims that they are also kidnapping children. The Tau Cetians have been preyed upon by these aliens before and they are working with other races and communities that were also victims. ONE SUCH RACE (emphasis ours - Branton) THAT OSCAR CLAIMS WAS RUN OFF THEIR HOME PLANET BY THE BUG PEOPLE WAS WHAT WE NOW CALL THE NORDICS OR PLEIADIANS. He claims, because of his ongoing contacts, he was made aware of the Billy Meier case in Switzerland and swears that is a real contact...

"I find all these comments interesting especially when you consider one investigative detail of this case. I have seen Oscar's house, his Mother's house, his work shop and truck, and at no time were any books, magazines, transcripts or movies about any subject, let alone recent UFO material, found... Could he be an avid reader of the latest and most controversial UFO documents and just be hiding them when we come over? This is highly unlikely since, without a phone, our visits were always unannounced.

"...(Oscar) wants people to know that if they are contacted by the Tau Cetians (humans such as he described) to not be afraid because they are here to help.

"This attitude is reflected in correlations with a totally independent case involving a woman near Springfield, Illinois. Jill Waldport (relates) an ongoing and very serious involvement with grey aliens. After Budd Hopkins (whose research inspired the May, 1992 CBS Network mini-series, INTRUDERS - Branton) spoke to her at length the case was recommended to John Carpenter, State Section Director of Missouri MUFON, and then to myself. The intensity and detail of the case is reminiscent of Debbie Tomies' (Cathy Davis) experiences.

"In my first interview with Jill she asked if anyone had ever been abducted/ contacted by more than one race or group of aliens. I told her that it was reported with some frequency and asked her which other one she had seen with the Greys. She said it was a totally separate contact and that they did NOT like the Grays.

"When asked about their appearance she reported that they were human, approximately about five and a half feet in height, 180-200 pounds but not fat, tanned looking skin with short hair cuts that laid flat against their heads. I asked her to describe their eyes, ears, nose and mouth. She said all features were essentially normal except the nose was broad and flat and their eyes were brown. Oscar reported the weight of Hank to be 190 pounds and five feet seven inches tall, he also noted the broad, flat nose (even this aspect is not unusually 'alien' to earth, being that many of the dark races posses broad facial features - Branton).

"Jill informed me that the aliens told her they didn't like what some of the aliens were doing to her without her consent. They had come to help her learn how to overcome the DECEPTIONS of the Grays and to protect herself. They explained that she needed to psychically build a shield around herself, like a brick wall, when they came for her. This would help keep her from being deceived by their MIND TRICKS. She tried it the next time the Grey's came for her and it 'seemed' to work."

According to many accounts, mere 'will power' does not always guarantee that one will escape the overlapping deceptions and psychic manipulations of the serpent race or the Grays. DIVINE INTERVENTION is, according to some, the only FAIL SAFE way to ensure oneself from being entangled by their deceptions, which are often deep, complex, and extremely subtle. There are actually accounts where people on the verge of being abducted began to pray, at which point the potential abductors left the scene. Also Clifford Stone, a high- level Military officer based at Roswell, New Mexico who has received much criticism from his higher-ups for his insistence on telling the public what he knows about the Grays, says that several 'skirmishes' between U.S. troops and alien Grays broke out in the jungles of southeast Asia during the Vietnam war, some of them ending in tragedy on our side. However one case involved a soldier who was a reborn Christian, who had a girlfriend in a particular village. During one visit he came upon a landed craft and some 'Grays' that were trying to entice some of the townsfolk to take a ride — possibly a permanent one — aboard their ship. The soldier came between the villagers and the Grays, and although his semiautomatic weapon had little effect against their bulletproof uniforms, the Bible he carried and the cross he wore DID have a definite adverse and weakening effect against the intruders, which immediately left the scene. Stone also confirmed that there have been many 'dogfights' between the 'Nordics' and the 'Grays' that the government is aware of (source: article by Robert W. Boyajian in UFO UNIVERSE, Spring 1988).

In reference to 'Jill', Forest Crawford continues:

"...At this point the correlation counter in my mind was working overtime, so I decided to go for gold and ask her if they told her where they were from. Believe it or not she replied, 'Tau Seat-eye, does that make any sense?' Later I mentioned to Oscar that I was investigating a case that involved intense interaction with Grays and Tau Cetians showing up to help. He asked where the case was from and I told him near Springfield, Illinois. He rattled off a very accurate description of Jill and said he was aware that she had been contacted.

"Horvat showed several pictures of people from the archives of ufology, one of which was Drake; Oscar immediately picked Drake's photo from the stack and one could see the anger come over his face at the sight of this man. Follow up research by Horvat produced an interesting set of circumstances. The crash in question happened in 1961. Some of you will remember that Drake headed the OZMA program, the predecessor to S.E.T.I. In 1961 Drake announced that OZMA, in it's search for intelligent extraterrestrial radio signals, would first look to the stars Tau Ceti and Epsilon Eridani..."

During one interview with Oscar, Crawford became concerned about the 'logistics' of a tunnel system stretching from California to North Dakota to Washington D.C., etc., attempting to correlate this with their background in science. According to what Oscar revealed to Crawford and his research companion:

"...it became evident that this was not feasible. With careful questioning it was discovered, according to Oscar, that the tunnels went only a short distance and did not actually connect to the North Dakota base. The capsule shuttle was accelerated and then a time/space window was opened. The 'exit door' of the time/space window simultaneously opened at the prescribed destination where the capsule would appear in a tunnel and decelerate."

One must wonder why an entire half hour was necessary for such an instantaneous transit, unless a tremendous speed was necessary to attain the subspace jump. There are accounts as given by researcher William Hamilton and others that some of the subterranean societies beneath America, the Telosians for instance, possess a tube-shuttle system. From his description it appears however that the Telosians utilized actual vacu-tube shuttle tunnels which stretch for hundreds if not thousands of miles. Perhaps the early shuttle systems constructed by ancient technically-advanced societies were of this variety, and were replaced or upgraded with time/space windows later? Is it possible that the government's eventual and alleged discovery of ancient tunnels, leading to this particular subsurface colony, has led to a JOINT Telosian-American use of the ancient sub-shuttle systems? Or are the tunnels referred to by Oscar entirely U.S. government constructions? Also, a similar network of vacu-tube 'shuttle' tunnels is also said to converge below Dulce, New Mexico, according to many sources. These are allegedly used mostly by the Grays, and possibly by certain mind-controlled 'CIA-MIB' type groups who may be working for them.

"The technology (for the teleport-tunnels described by Oscar - Branton) was supposedly a combination of our own knowledge, rooted in the Philadelphia Experiment, and acquired alien technology. Oscar also talked about the geological location of time/space/dimension doors. These places allow an easy entry of extraterrestrial craft into our atmosphere. Two such large natural doorways were reported to be just northeast of Seattle, Washington and south of the Apostle Islands in Lake Superior...

"An interesting possible correlation with the predicted natural time/space windows can be found in studying patterns on special energy maps. One such map is the Bouguer gravity anomaly map. Oddly enough A FAIRLY LOCAL low gravity area can be found at... the locations mentioned by Oscar (Not only near Seattle and the Apostle Islands, but also in Missouri where Oscar claimed to have had most of his subsequent contacts- meetings with the Tau Cetians - Branton)... My research is finding some interesting patterns emerging by comparing the location of gravity anomalies, Indian reservations, military bases and cavern entrances. These specialty maps can be purchased at great prices from GEO-SCIENCE RESOURCES., 2990 Anthony Rd., Burlington, NC 27215..."

One last note on the above account. William Cooper describes another incident involving a reptilian 'gray' which was allegedly recovered from a crash-retrieval in the southwest. Enormous efforts were taken to try to save the 'life' of this ugly little beast (which had a 'tendency' to LIE its way through subsequent interviews with Military Intelligence), yet when it came to an actual HUMAN alien like 'Hank', certain people could apparently have cared less for his/their personal welfare. Cooper also alleged that the 'secret government' for a large part refused to ally themselves with the 'Nordics' or human-aliens who warned them about the malevolence of the Grays, and chose instead to go ahead and form an alliance with the reptilian 'grays' since an Illuminati-Gray alliance would seemingly help the cause of the power elite (serpent cults?) who were making a 'killing' off of exploiting the masses, a practice which the Grays themselves encouraged and assisted in. One claim is that the serpent cultists working in the government already maintained an ages- old pact with these draconian powers, and one can reason that because of THIS they may have refused he advances of the 'Nordics'. Apparently these did not desire to accept the 'conditions' required by the 'Nordics', which included the discontinuation of nuclear weapons proliferation and the cessation of multi-billion dollar war efforts which, according to many sources, have also filled the pockets of the secret government (which covertly operates through secret societies in nearly every country).

Such wars-conflicts-revolutions-etc., many believe, have been directly influenced and orchestrated by the serpent-cult or secret-society groups. The pathetic individuals responsible for formulating the alliance-pact with the saurian grays (instead of with our 'Nordic' cousins who now make up an interstellar 'Federation' of worlds very similar to the one depicted in 'Star Trek') literally sold-out our nations to 'the Beast'. Let's pray that the situation is not irredeemable.

For one's information, a brief description of just what the 'Illuminati' is might be helpful at this point. Many researchers suggest that the Illuminati is a Jesuit invention or reinvention simply because Illuminati founder Adam Weishaupt who 'started' the order in Bavaria, GERMANY was a Jesuit. Also, the 'Scottish Rite' of Masonry which advocates the destruction of National Sovereignties in exchange for Illuminati government has allegedly been traced back to the Jesuit college at Clermont in Paris, as have been other Jesuit-initiated Masonic rites. The Jesuits themselves were founded by Ignatius Loyola, who had been previously arrested in Spain for subversive activities as a gnostic. The 'Order' was admittedly founded mainly for the purpose of crushing Martin Luther's Protestant movement (which 'protested' Rome's denunciation of the plan of eternal salvation by grace as it appears in the book of ROMANS). This is evidenced by the fact that the Jesuit oath (which advocated the killing of Protestant men, the cutting off of the breasts of Protestant women with shears, and the cutting open of the wombs of Protestant women so that their unborn children could be smashed against the rocks) - was fulfilled to the letter during the well-documented and bloody Roman Inquisitions. These took place during the Dark and Middle Ages of so-called 'holy' Roman Empire rule which 'began' when the last of the Emperors or 'Pontifex Maximus' of the Roman Empire, CONSTANTINE, declared himself to be the FIRST official Roman 'Pontiff' or 'Pope'. Constantine payed lipservice to 'Christianity' yet secretly held to the ancient Babylonean Mystery Religion of which he himself was High

Priest or Pontifex Maxiumus, one in a long line of many which can be traced back to Nimrod, the first King of Babylon, himself. (This statement may raise anger in some who religiously defend man-made 'traditions', however history is history and facts are facts).

If one doesn't believe that Constantine intended to carry on his Roman Empire and it's conquest of the world under the veneer of 'religion', then just remember what the Roman-Spanish Conquistadors did to the Mayas under Cortez (who slaughtered over 5 million of them - see: 'TRAVELS', PBS network - Feb. 15, 1993), the Incas under Pizzaro, and the Pueblos under Coronado. The Illuminati allegedly began in ancient Babylon and is said to be a mixture of Cabalism, the ancient Babylonian 'Mystery' religion, and ancient 'Baal' worship. Their vision was the same as that of Nimrod (aka Osiris, Baal or the 'Sun god' and consort of Semiramis, Isis, or Ashtaroth respectively). Nimrod was the original king of Babylon and the builder of the Tower of Babel. Some sources allege that the CIA and the NAZI movements were tied-in to the Illuminati, and that later these two organizations under the "Cult of the All Seeing Eye" joined forces in an effort to initiate plans for a world dictatorship. Part of this would of course involve working with the Grays and other saurian species in underground bases in a joint effort to establish absolute world despotism.

The Illuminati, or the 'Serpent Cult' is allegedly infiltrating political, economic, educational and religious institutions with the help of the Grays (which have ADMITTED to some that they have been the guiding power behind witchcraft and many of the ancient occult lodges over the centuries), which have 'promised' the Illuminati a part of 'the pie' once this world is under 'their' control. This infiltration is allegedly carried out through organizations like the 'International Working Man's League', which according to World Economists such as Dr. John Coleman 'molded' Karl Marx and his future as a Communist dictator. Another key figure in the Connection between the Illuminati, Masonry and the Jesuit Lodge was the Jesuit Priest Giuseppe Mazzini, the second in command to 'Universal Pontiff' of Freemasonry Albert Pike, and who according to some 'inside' sources even went so far as to organize a branch of the Mafia known as the 'Oblonica' within one of the 22 'Palladium' lodges which were initiated to oversee world Illuminati revolutionary activities, carefully hiding it's connection with the Grand Lodge in England.

The Illuminati headquarters in America may be hidden within the Masonic 'House of the Temple' in Washington D.C., (Scottish Rite Headquarters) which is curiously enough set atop the pentagram-like street layout of the city itself. Former 33rd degree Mason and Past Master of all Scottish Rite bodies, Evangelist Jim Shaw (P.O. Box 884., Silver Springs, FL 32668) tells of his own defection from the cult in his book 'THE DEADLY DECEPTION'. Shaw reveals the fact that the inside of the Scottish Rite headquarters is FILLED with carvings, murals and many other representations of serpents! The High Masons apparently revered the 'Serpent' symbol in what might be considered worshipful awe. Thus the name of their ancient cult, which William Cooper refers to as the 'Cult of the Snake' or 'Dragon', a Serpent Cult which was very active among the ancient Gnostic (serpent) cults of Pharaohic Egypt.

Even Gen. George Washington was a was a member of the Stone Masons Guild early on, however when he learned that it was being infiltrated by the Bavarian-German Illuminati he left the Lodge. This infiltration was also confirmed by the Presidents of Yale and Harvard Universities, who discovered that two fraternities, Yale's SKULL & BONES and Harvard's SCROLL & KEY had been infiltrated by this German occult lodge in an attempt to gain highly educated initiates who would be used to carry out their future plans for world control, plans which included the destruction of nation states to be replaced by a world dictatorship, which they called the 'New World Order'. There are even allegations that SKULL & BONES grads helped to finance the Communist and Nazi parties for the Illuminati's Machiavellian world scenario which included the orchestration of world conflicts (pitting various nations or factions against each other) for the purpose of eventually 'beating' the nations of the earth into a global dictatorship or NEW WORLD ORDER 'synthesis'.

If this report is beginning to sound like an over-budget Spy Movie or a Science Fiction Thriller, then... as they say, "you ain't seen nothing yet!"

The 'Knights of Malta' and the 'Club of Rome' are also, according to Conspiracy Researchers, players in the "End Game" in which the meek of the earth are the pawns. Both have advocated Genocide to curb the 'population problem' — since a true world socialist dictatorship can only survive if the population is kept to a 'controllable' minimum. The KOM and COR are essentially outward arms or branches of the Illuminati, according to many. There are even rumors that tunnels and Catacombs beneath Rome connect or at one time connected with others beneath the Island of Malta, and that a similar subterranean system utilized by the Western Illuminati exists beneath Washington D.C. as well.

In fact, Dr. John Coleman, in his report: 'FREEMASONRY AND THE ONE WORLD GOVERNMENT' (c/o World Intelligence Review., P.O. Box 507., Chalmette, LA 70044), wrote BEFORE the AIDS threat became widely known among the public, that a secret society equivalent to today's 'Illuminati' believed that it was their duty as the self-anointed 'gods' over humanity to keep the population of the world from getting out of control so that they could be more easily controlled. These ancient 'Alchemists', Coleman alleges, were responsible for the Black Plague and other scourges which killed millions. He was convinced that they were preparing to wipe away millions more through 'viral' warfare.

According to Coleman (who claims to be an ex-Intelligence worker for the

British Government who 'defected' when he learned the Horrible Truth), the 'Illuminati' consists of the duel lodges of Jesuitism and Freemasonry. He also documents all manner of infiltration of religious, political, and economic movements by the Illuminati of Jesuit-Freemasonry, as well as their seemingly endless manipulations of the nations by their behind-the-scenes orchestrating of economic turmoil, revolutions and wars.

In 1988, in apparent confirmation of this, a former high- ranking military officer by the name of F. P. Farrell, Lt. Col. Retired, U.S.A.F., released a disturbing report to several 'PATRIOT' organizations which alleged this very thing. Lt. Col. Farrell was a 1st Lieutenant, Captain and Jet Fighter Pilot in Korea; and a Lieutenant Colonel and Air Liaison Officer, 1st Infantry Division ('The Big Red One') in Viet Nam. In essence, Farrell accuses the UNITED NATIONS as being a trojan-horse cover for world socialist revolution, which intends to weaken and eventually destroy the INDEPENDENCE of the American Republic.

Farrell accuses the U.N. of being a Socialist-Communist controlled organization, and names at least 13 United Nations Secretary Generals who have been Communist Nationals. It was decided long ago, Farrell states, that no-one who was loyal to the U.S. constitution was to ever be UN Secretary General. He also provided documentation that the UNITED NATIONS 'police action' into which young Americans were drafted betrayed the American troops at every turn, by intentionally leaking U.S. battle plans IN BOTH THE KOREAN AND VIETNAM WARS to the Communists. This is why, he explains, both of these no-win 'wars' were lost to the Communists. In relation to Gen. MacArthur (who interesting enough publicly predicted that World War III would be fought against aliens in space!) Farrell states that:

"When General MacArthur WOKE UP TO THE TREASON OF PRESIDENT TRUMAN and the Soviets in the United Nations, he made one of the greatest military performances ever ventured in modern warfare. His dangerous but magnificent military engagement and sea landing at 'Inchon' on Sept. 15, 1950, enabled his military forces to slaughter the communist forces, destroy their massive supply dumps, and put the Red Chinese, North Koreans, and their Soviet advisors on the run.

"MacArthur never asked for permission from the United Nations Security Council (Soviet General Zinshehko) to perform this secret military operation. MacArthur hand picked close and loyal military officers in doing so, and they kept the lid on the entire operation. Originally, our forces were to never win any battles as planned by the Soviet Generals at the United Nations. But General MacArthur REALIZED THE TREASON AND TOOK POSITIVE ACTION NOT ONLY TO SAVE THE LIVES OF HIS FIGHTING FORCES AND DESTROYING THE ENEMY AND THEIR SUPPLY DUMPS, BUT ALSO CREATING THE 'TURNING POINT' OF THE

KOREAN WAR WITH HIS SUCCESS AT INCHON.

"For this 'positive action', General Douglas MacArthur was relieved of his command of the United Nations fighting forces in Korea by the traitor President Harry S. Truman, who met with MacArthur on the Island of Guam. MacArthur had figured out the whole picture OF TREASON and had to be relieved of his job.

"Truman feared MacArthur so much that just prior to General Douglas MacArthur returning to the United States from Korea, the traitor Truman, hid out at Camp David for over three weeks in fear of being arrested by General MacArthur who was a Five Star General and in command of all military forces in the United States... THE SAME MAN WHO HAD JUST SAVED THE LIVES OF THOUSANDS OF THEIR SONS WITH DARING MILITARY MOVES AGAINST THE WISHES OF THE UNITED NATIONS COMMAND, IN ROUTING THE RED CHINESE AND NORTH KOREANS AT INCHON, SOUTH KOREA. Now you know the real truth as to what really happened 'behind the scenes' during the Korean Conflict between the 'traitor' Truman and General Douglas MacArthur, THE REAL HERO!! Robert W. Lee, in his book entitled 'THE UNITED NATIONS TODAY' (CPA books., 33836 SE Kelso Rd, #6., P.O. Box 596., Boring, OR 97099), states on pages 20 and 21:

"'I (General MacArthur) was...worried by a series of directives from Washington (Truman) which were greatly decreasing the potential of my air force. First I was forbidden 'hot' pursuit of enemy planes that attacked our own. Manchuria and Siberia were sanctuaries of inviolate protection for all enemy forces and for all enemy purposes, no matter what depredations or assaults might come from there. Then I was denied the right (by Soviet General in United Nations) to bomb the hydroelectric plants along the Yalu River. The order was broadened to include every plant in North Korea which was capable of furnishing electric power to Manchuria and Siberia.'" Most incomprehensible of all according to MacArthur was the REFUSAL to let him bomb a supply target which was NOT in Manchuria or Siberia, "'but many miles from the border, (it) forwarded supplies from Vladivostok for the North Korean Army. I FELT THAT STEP- BY-STEP MY WEAPONS WERE BEING TAKEN AWAY FROM ME.'"

"This is exactly the same type of 'treason' that occurred against our military forces in Viet Nam. But Viet Nam was far more vile and dirty in the length or time that our soldiers were betrayed. MacArthur continues on page 21:

"That there was some LEAK IN INTELLIGENCE was evident to everyone. (Brigadier General Walton) Walker continually complained to me that HIS OPERATIONS WERE KNOWN TO THE ENEMY IN ADVANCE through sources in Washington... information must have been relayed to them, assuring that the Yalu River bridges would continue to enjoy sanctuary and that their bases would be left intact...

"General MacArthur then referred on page 21 to an official leaflet PUBLISHED

IN RED CHINA BY CHINESE GENERAL LIN PIAO:

"'...I would never have made the attack and risked men and military reputation if I HAD NOT BEEN ASSURED THAT WASHINGTON (Truman and U.S. Congress) WOULD RESTRAIN GENERAL MACARTHUR from taking adequate retaliatory measures against my lines of supply and communication.'

"J. Ruben Clark Jr., former Undersecretary of State and Ambassador to Mexico, who was widely recognized as one of the nation's foremost international lawyers, stated on page 27 of the book entitled: 'THE UNITED NATIONS TODAY':

"Not only does the Charter Organization NOT prevent future wars, but it makes it practically certain that we shall have future wars, and as such wars it takes from us (The United States) the power to declare them, to chose the side on which we shall fight, to determine what forces and military equipment we shall use in the war, and to control and command our sons who do the fighting.'

"In fact, A Soviet General in the United Nations still writes the plans for employment of United States troops all over the world, even in the Persian Gulf today. Former President John F. Kennedy also felt the wrath of the United Nations Charter (that Truman and the U.S. Congress signed) during the 'Bay of Pigs' invasion of Cuba against the Communist Castro. The Soviets in the United Nations would not allow Kennedy to directly use the United States military forces available in destroying Castro. The Soviets stated that in using United States military forces at the Bay of Pigs WITHOUT THE APPROVAL OF THE SOVIETS in the United Nations, would be a violation of the United Nations Charter THAT THE UNITED STATES HAD SIGNED AND HAD TO ABIDE WITH...

"By now you should have come to realize 'why' there were so many restrictions on our soldiers during combat in Korea and Viet Nam and 'why' WE WERE NOT ALLOWED TO WIN... not allowed TO BOMB CERTAIN TARGETS.

"...The Viet Nam war was also allowed to continue to weaken the resistance of the people in the United States against any type of war or fight against communism. To accept ANYTHING would be better in the minds of the masses... than (to accept) war and having their sons killed. Even if it meant the 'merging' of our entire government with that of the Soviet Union."

Other evidence which tends to confirm this Masonic-Jesuit connection, as exposed by Dr. John Coleman and others, comes from an essay titled: 'THE TWIN PINCERS: MASONRY AND CATHOLICISM', written (understandably) anonymously. The manuscript stated:

(1) Thirty-five years BEFORE the Jesuits were kicked out of France by a Roman Catholic king, Pope Clement XII issued his Bull against Masonry. The Bourbon French King, Louis XVI and his queen Marie Antoinette, were beheaded by an Illuminati inspired mob of masons and terrorists. Why was this Catholic family, the Bourbons, so opposed to the Jesuits? It is, by the way, very interesting that a

family like the Bourbons who had opposed the JESUITS, were brought down eventually by the French Revolution's ILLUMINATI-MASONIC reign of terror, pointing to the almost obvious fact that the Jesuits ordered the Masons to carry out the revolution.

(2) Why did... Frederick (the Great of Prussia) REFUSE to have the (so called) enemies of masonry, the Catholic Order of Jesuits, banned in Prussia in 1773? Could the insiders of the Jesuits ALSO BE Masons? (Note: Mackey's ENCYCLOPEDIA OF FREEMASONRY states that Frederick '...was initiated as a mason, at Brunswick, on the night of the 14th of August, 1738...')

(3) The Roman Catholic 'Stuarts' WERE masons from SCOTLAND... the Stuart, James II, tried to set up the Jesuits in positions of power when he became King of England in 1685...

(4) Between the STUARTS and the Jesuits at Lyons, France, and the Jesuit college of Clermont, in Paris... the RITE OF PERFECTION evolves; out of which, the masonic authorities have quoted, trace today's Ancient and Accepted SCOTTISH RITE OF FREEMASONRY.

(5) Rebold (a Masonic authority) and Mackey do not exactly agree on the part Chevalier de Bonneville played in THE RITE OF PERFECTION. Bonneville may not have been a Jesuit... but when we look at the part he played in the RITE OF STRICT OBSERVANCE... we see many indications that he was a Jesuit."

According to Burke McCarty's book 'THE SUPPRESSED TRUTH ABOUT THE ASSASSINATION OF ABRAHAM LINCOLN', several U.S. presidents who had come out in opposition against Jesuit-Masonry had been targeted by the Illuminati for assassination. McCarty states:

(1) President William Henry Harrison.

In 1841, General Wm. Henry Harrison of Ohio, was elected President by a large majority. The loyalty of the Union (toward) General Harrison was above question, and it was (the aim) of the power of Leopoldines, a great Jesuit Spy System, to defeat him.

"In his inaugural address... President Harrison... said: 'We admit of no government by divine right, believing that so far as power is concerned, the beneficent Creator has made no distinction among men; that all are upon an equality, and that the only legitimate right to govern, is upon the express grant of power from the governed.'

"With these unmistakable words, President Harrison made his position clear; he hurled defiance to the 'divine right' enemies of our Popular Government. Aye, he did more - for those words signed his death warrant. Just one month and five days from that day, President Harrison lay a corpse in the White House. He died from arsenic poisoning, administered by the tools of Rome. The Jesuit oath had been swiftly carried out."

Note: For a copy of the Jesuit Oath, refer to pp. 99-102 of William Cooper's book 'BEHOLD A PALE HORSE', c/o Light Technology Publishing., P.O. Box 1495., Sedona, AZ 86336. The oath appears in chapter 3 - 'Oath of Initiation of an Unidentified Secret Order'. Although Cooper 'suspects' the oath might have originated from the Jesuits or the Knights of Malta, he is uncertain. However, Dennis Passero and other researchers have published exact duplicates of the oath which appears in Cooper's book, and state that it IS the Jesuit oath, thus confirming Cooper's suspicions. It basically states that the Jesuit is through all means moral or immoral — the immoral acts can supposedly be 'forgiven' if they are done in the name of the Roman 'church' — to devote their life to bringing about the destruction of the Protestant movement, and to bringing all nations under the control of ROME for the glory of the 'Queen of Heaven', no doubt the same pagan goddess worshipped by the ancient Babylonians — none other than the ancient Queen Semaramis to whom we can credit the post-deluvian resurgence of witchcraft. There is much evidence that pagan Rome worshipped of the 'Queen of Heaven' previous to the rise of Christianity, and eventually gave her the name 'Mary' to win favor with the Christians. Mary was a virgin when she gave birth to Jesus, but scripture confirms that she gave birth naturally to other children following this. Jesus was born through the womb of Mary (The SON OF MAN) but was conceived by the Infinite Spirit of God (The SON OF GOD). Therefore Mary should not be mistaken as the "Mother of God" any more than Joseph should be accepted as the "Father of God", nor his parents as the "Grandmother" or "Grandfather" of God, etc.

Many allege that the Roman 'church' is nothing more than the continuation of the ancient Roman Empire which sought to dominate the world, and that they merely donned religious garb when they discovered that religious feeling was an ENORMOUSLY effective way to control the masses. The fact that Constantine was the last official Roman EMPEROR and the first official Roman POPE is cause for great suspicion.

McCarty continues:

"Allow me to quote for you from U.S. Senator Benton's 'THIRTY YEARS VIEW,' Volume II, page 21, regarding the death of President Harrison: 'There was no failure of health or strength to indicate such an event or excite apprehension, that he would not go through his term with the same vigor with which he commenced it. His attack was sudden and evidently fatal from he beginning.'

"And at the close of the chapter in Senator Benton's book, we read this significant bit of information which should be well pondered concerning Harrison's family: 'That the deceased President had been closely preceded and was rapidly followed by the deaths of almost ALL OF HIS numerous family, sons and daughters...'

"That is 'extirpation' with a vengeance, is it not? (Note: The Jesuit oath calls for members of the order to 'extirpate' the enemies of Rome - Branton)

(2) President Zachary Taylor

In his first message to Congress, he said: 'But attachment to the UNION of states should be fostered in every American heart. For more than half a century... this Union has remained unshaken...'

"The arch-plotters, fearing that suspicion might be aroused by the death of the President early in his administration, as in the case of President Harrison, permitted him to serve one year and four months, when on the Fourth of July, 1850, arsenic was administered to him during a celebration in Washington at which he was invited to deliver the address. He went in perfect health in the morning and was taken ill in the afternoon about five o'clock and died on the Monday following, having been sick the same number of days and with precisely the same symptoms as was his predecessor, President Harrison.

(3) Attempt on President James Buchanan

He was invited to deliver an address on Washington's Birthday, and made reservation at the National Hotel (which by the way was the headquarters of the Jesuit traitors), for himself and his friends.

"The gentleman had had his ear to the ground evidently and heard the rumble of the Abolitionists, and when the committee asked for a conference, he cooly informed them that he was PRESIDENT OF THE NORTH, AS WELL AS THE SOUTH.

"The following quotations from the NEW YORK HERALD and THE POST at the time chronicled what followed:

"'The appointments favoring the North by the Jeff Davis faction will doubtless be accepted, and treated as a declaration of war, and a war of extermination on one side or the other.' (Feb. 25, 1857)

"On Washington's Birthday, Buchanan's stand became known and the next day he was poisoned. The plot was deep and planned with skill. Mr. Buchanan, as was customary with men in his station, had a table and chairs reserved for himself and friends in the dining room at the National Hotel. The President was known to be an inveterate tea drinker; in fact Northern people rarely drink (i.e. drank) anything else in the evening. Southern men preferred coffee. Thus, to make sure of Buchanan and his Northern friends, arsenic was sprinkled in the bowls containing the tea and lump sugar and set on the table where he was to sit. The pulverized sugar in the bowls used for coffee on the other tables was kept free from poison. Not a single Southern man was affected or harmed. Fifty or sixty persons dined at the table that evening, and as best can be learned, ABOUT THIRTY-EIGHT DIED FROM THE EFFECTS OF THE POISON.

"President Buchanan was poisoned, and with great difficulty his life was saved. His physicians treated him understandingly from instructions given by himself as to the cause of his illness, for he understood what was the matter."

Researcher Dennis Passero also quoted the above in his 'CONSPIRACY TRACKER' newsletter (no longer being published). Being the avowed Catholic that he is, we cannot say that Passero had any particular bias against the Catholic church in his exposition of the Jesuits, but that he saw the corruption in the Roman Institution and exposed it. Passero has made some interesting comments in relation to Jesuit-Masonry and the assassination of one of the most popular Presidents in American history:

"...President Abraham Lincoln. The subject of Lincoln's murder is too vast to be covered here. McCarty believes that the Jesuits and their tools, the KNIGHTS OF THE GOLDEN CIRCLE were behind the crime. What is interesting is that President Harrison, Taylor, Buchanan, and of course Lincoln, were all strongly dedicated to the preservation of the Union — and all had made speeches indicating their stand. If the Jesuits wanted the Union split, they were not alone. In 1876, Otto Von Bismarck had this to say: 'The division of the United States into two federations of equal force was decided long before the Civil war by the High Financial Power of Europe. These bankers were afraid that the United States, if they remained in one block and as one nation, would attain economical and financial independence, which would upset their financial domination over the world. The voice of the Rothschilds predominated. They foresaw the tremendous booty if they could substitute two feeble democracies, indebted to the (European) financiers, to the vigorous Republic, confident and self-providing. Therefore, they started their emissaries in order to exploit the question of slavery and thus dig an abyss between the two parts of the Republic.'

"While McCarty links the Golden Circle with the Jesuits, Dr. Stuart Crane says that the Golden Circle was financed by the Rothschilds. (Note: Dr. John Coleman had stated in essence that the old-line 'Blue Blood' or BLACK NOBILITY families of Europe who claim DESCENDENCE from the ancient Roman Emperors make up the link between the Rothschilds, who control Masonry; and the Jesuits, who control much of the Catholic world behind the scenes - Branton)

"In order to create a rift using the slavery problem Golden Circle agents became known as Abolitionists in the North, and as Secessionists in the South. Even the fiery John Brown, who led the raid on Harper's Ferry, was financed by the International Bankers. Every member of the Southern cabinet belonged to the Golden Circle — as did every member of the Northern cabinet with the exception of Lincoln and Secretary Seward.

"When things began getting rough for the Confederacy, the Rothschilds even planned an invasion of the U.S. by British troops swooping down from Canada, and by French forces established in Mexico under the Emperor Maximillian, but this did not come off because the Russian Czar (who's government was later to be overthrown by the Bolshevik Revolution - Branton) said he would intervene on the side of the North if the European forces attacked. According to Mag-Gen. Count Cherep-Spiridovich, the Rothschilds had one of their agents in the Vatican, a Jewish- Jesuit named Father Fisher, convince the Pope that the Vatican should finance Maximillian who would in return reestablish Catholicism in Mexico, which had conveniently been abolished by Benito Juarez, a Freemason. Later, when the Civil War was over, the guerrilla army branch of the Knights of the Golden Circle, headed for Mexico to aid Maximillian who was running into trouble with the Juarez forces. This guerrilla force was under the command of Colonel William Quantrill, famous leader of Quantrill's Raiders, and of Col. Jesse James — later the famous outlaw. LIKE ALL MASONIC SECRET SOCIETIES, the guerrillas THOUGHT THEY WERE THE TOP OF THE LADDER, never realizing that there were higher-ups over them. For some reason, Jesse James earned the wrath of the Rothschilds — and the reward money later offered for his capture, came from coffers of the House of Rothschild (see: JESSE JAMES WAS ONE OF HIS NAMES, by Del Schroader).

"Abraham Lincoln was able to foil the conspirators at every turn. He was aware of the activities of the Jesuits (see: FIFTY YEARS IN THE CHURCH OF ROME, by Charles Chiniguy, c/o Chick Publications., P.O Box 662., Chino, CA 91710). He took the Union Army and turned it into the most powerful fighting force the world has ever known. He issued the famous 'greenbacks' — refusing to accept loans from the High Financial Power. For these reasons — and because he would not go along with the harsh measures of the Reconstruction — it was decided upon that He would die. John Wilkes Booth, a member of the Golden Circle and of the Carbonari (another Jesuit-connected lodge - Branton), was chosen as the tool to commit the crime. About a month before the assassination, Booth had traveled to Europe for a secret meeting with Napoleon III, also a member of the Carbonari.

(Note: A 1991 episode of UNSOLVED MYSTERIES alleged that Union sentries had been ordered to give Booth safe passage out of the city following the assassination - Branton). Napoleon III was surrounded by Jesuit advisors [see: THIS ONE MAD ACT, by Forrester, for a mention of the meeting].

"With Lincoln out of the picture, Golden Circle member Andrew Johnson became president. But, for some reason he pulled an about face, and also failed to go along with the harsh Reconstruction measures. Because of this he became the only President to be impeached, though acquitted by one vote... It appears that the Rothschilds intended the Reconstruction Period to be the Civil War equivalent to the French Revolution's Reign of Terror. Not content with the outcome of the war, it became necessary to keep the country divided via the injustices of the Carpetbag Governments. The High Financial Power realized that the South was really the heart and soul of the Republic. It was desired to destroy the economic base of the North, but to destroy the moral and spiritual base of the south. Individuality was the enemy of the collectivist conspirators, then as well as now!

"To keep a continual animosity going between the two parts of the country, it was decided that terrorism could be used against the Reconstruction Governments. This terrorism could be used as an excuse to further strengthen these bogus governments. Terrorism could be used to frighten foes of Abolition. Some of these terrorist acts included mutilation murders perpetrated by John Brown and his boys.

"According to Dr. Stuart Crane, the Terrorist organization born at this time was the KU KLUX KLAN, which emerged from the Knights of the Golden Circle.

"However, it appears that there were two Klans operating at this time. One was headed by Nathan Bedford Forrest. This Klan sought only to save the South and to avenge crimes and injustices. The other was the Golden Circle child. This second Klan was founded by Judah P. Benjamin - a Rothschild relative and Confederacy's Secretary of State -, Kuttner Baruch, Albert Pike - known as the Vice-Regent of Lucifer and as the Sovereign Pontiff of Universal Freemasonry -, AND BY AN UN-NAMED JESUIT PRIEST!"

Further evidence in support of the allegations that the Illuminati is composed of both Jesuits and Masons is given by Robold (the argument is that the Illuminati is a secret arm of Jesuitism reestablished by the Jesuit Priest Weishaupt, while subversive 33rd degree Masonry is a secret branch of the Illuminati. In other words Rome operates as the 'head' of the conspiratorial 'beast', the Illuminati is the neck, Masonry is it's body and the many neo-masonic political, religious, fraternal and economic cults are the 'tentacles'. Former 33rd degree Mason Jim Shaw has even exposed dozens of vatican officials who are also high-ranking masons). Rebold, in his 'GENERAL HISTORY OF FREEMASONRY IN EUROPE', reveals the following Jesuit-Masonic 'eggs' that were hatched during the 18th century:

"...RITE of the Old Daughter-in-law, by Lockhart, an emissary of the Jesuits... in 1749.

"RITE of the CLERKS OF STRICT OBSERVANCE or clerical Templar system, founded by the Jesuits, and united in 1776, with the SECULAR TEMPLARS, also a creation of the Jesuits...

"RITE of the Knights of the East, by Pirlet, a Jesuit Emissary... 1757.

"RITE of the Emperors of the East and West, Sovereign Prince Masons. This was the rite which Herodum extended to the RITE OF PERFECTION (from which the Scottish Rite of Masonry is evolved) of about 25 degrees, by the Jesuits, and propagated by Pirlet about 1758.

"RITE of the Flaming Star, founded by Baron Schudy, an emissary of the Jesuits in 1766.

"RITE of the Illuminati of Bavaria, by Professor Weishaupt (also a Jesuit)... in 1776."

Dr. William Campbell, M.D., a very knowledgeable virologist who to our knowledge had not even heard of Dr. John Coleman at the time when he first came out with his very disturbing revelations, seems to nevertheless confirm Coleman's suspicions of mass genocide through virological warfare. Campbell claims that in the course of researching the AIDS virus, he and his associates stumbled across a conspiracy almost too horrifying to believe. In an article titled "W.H.O. MURDERED AFRICA", which first appeared in the HEALTH FREEDOM NEWS (P.O Box 688., Monrovia, CA 91016), he presented a great deal of documentation that the AIDS virus was not only 'manufactured' artificially by 'splicing' the bovine leukemia and sheep visna retro- viruses in a laboratory in Ft. Detrick, Maryland, but that the WORLD HEALTH ORGANIZATION (which is an arm of the Illuminati-affiliated CLUB OF ROME according to Dr. John Coleman and others), as well as Socialist-Communist elements, and the UNITED NATIONS played a central role in it's creation and INTENTIONAL release into the world population...

Is it possible that Communism, like the Jesuit-infested Nazi Party itself, has acted as a secret weapon of the Jesuit- Illuminati in it's ongoing INQUISITION against Jews and Protestants (as well as governments such as the United States which through its CONSTITUTION, BILL OF RIGHTS, and DECLARATION OF INDEPENDENCE has challenged the world socialists to their face?) Dr. John Coleman has stated:

"...Karl Marx was one of the earliest members of the radical Mazzini movements starting in 1840... it is interesting to note that Marx, an avowed hater of religion, should so passionately espouse Jesuitism."

Also, cult expositor Dave Hunt, in his CIB BULLETIN (Dec. 1980) states: "During the summer of 1988 on PBS a number of representatives from the Kremlin were answering questions put to them by a live American audience. One of the Americans asked, 'What is the major cause of misunderstanding between the Soviet Union and the United States?' The LEADER of the KREMLIN DELEGATION unhesitatingly replied, 'The major problem is Evangelical CHRISTIANITY." (translated: Protestantism)

In his book, 'MASTER PLAN FOR YOUR DESTRUCTION', Arizona Pastor Lee Gerrard quotes from a Communist-Socialist instruction book on psychopolitics:

"...You must recruit every agency of the Nation marked for slaughter into foaming hatred of religious healing... that any religious practice which might devote itself to MENTAL HEALING is vicious, bad, insanity causing, publicly hated and intolerable. You must suborn and recruit any medical healing organization into collusion in this campaign."

Religious healing is largely a Protestant phenomena, the very group — revitalized by the German Martin Luther — whose destruction the Jesuit order in it's oath has sworn to carry out.

Now back to the subject of the 'Illuminati' conspiracy and it's alleged connection with aerial and subsurface phenomena.

There are some researchers who believe, aside from the revelations above, that there is a definite connection between the 'Illuminati' and the alien group known to many researchers as the 'Men In Black'.

Jim Brandon, in his book 'OCCULT AMERICA' tells of an alleged underground installation below Washington D.C. known as 'NOD' — suggesting that the antediluvian constructors of this 'Atlantean' substructure may have been descendants of Cain (see: Genesis 4:16). The present inhibitors of this subterranean installation are allegedly an underground race of 'power-trippers' tied into the highest levels of the NSA-CIA, who are in turn in contact with 'Sirius Star People' or a group that some UFOlogists believe is the extraterrestrial extension of the Illuminati, also known as the 'Men In Black' or the 'Nation of the Third Eye'. The 'NOD' and other similar facilities are reportedly NOT inhabited by ante-diluvians, but by people who later discovered these abandoned underground installations as well as the ancient technologies left there, which they learned to manipulate for good or evil. Brandon also mentions ancient tunnels discovered beneath Washington D.C. that have been investigated by government scientists, some of which, according to still other sources, contain walls with a glass-smooth but metal-hard glaze.

In connection with the German Illuminati, it is said that 'they' now possess aerial disks which may be capable of leaving the earth's atmosphere. These may explain SOME of the accounts of 'Aryan' saucer pilots, however Germans are not the only 'Aryan' civilization to exist (actually Hitler's 'theory' that the Germans were descended from Aryan stock may be just that - a theory), for instance there were the Aryans who ruled ancient India thousands of years ago.

Nevertheless the 'German' theory plays a definite role in UFOlogy, although if true it apparently makes up only a minor percentage of encounters with humanoid or humanlike entities. The popular theory is that sometime before WWII, German occultists — the same one's who gave rise to the Nazi Party, recovered a crashed 'disk' and began to study and eventually to utilize it's technology through various secret projects which allegedly utilized underground bases and factories that were used in attempts to duplicate the technology.

The top-secret Nazi 'aerial disk' research became more advanced throughout the Second World War, and reportedly utilized jet-turbine and later electromagnetic propulsions. As it became apparent that the Germans were losing the war, they allegedly transferred this technology to a base in Antarctica which had been established years earlier, complete with underground installations and all, and code-named the 'New Berlin'. Throughout the entire duration of the war the Nazis had allegedly shipped scientists, workers, technology and saucer components to this Antarctic base or bases.

U.S. Rear Admiral Richard E. Byrd some years later conducted and led an "exploration" of the Antarctic region. The strange thing about the "expedition" was that the massive operation involved nearly 4,000 well-trained military Naval troops, military vessels such as destroyers, subs, aircraft carrier and aircraft. Upon arriving at the polar continent they reportedly split into three separate groups and began a massive reconnaissance- like operation. One source even claimed that Byrd's Navy encountered 'resistance' there and that there was a photo-finish FIGHT between American and Nazi forces there, with losses on both sides.

When the Americans left two weeks later (also strange for a 'scientific expedition') Byrd, after arriving home, reportedly went into a rage and began demanding that the government turn Antarctica into a nuclear test range. Byrd was sworn to secrecy and his diaries are sealed to this day.

There are, in fact, some who claim to have encountered disks containing a swastika-like symbol, or occupants who spoke fluent German, yet these accounts are still relatively few in comparison with accounts of other types of human cosmonauts encountered in other incidents, suggesting that the majority of human-like alien encounters may come from the so-called 'Federation' which consists of the Ummo People or Ummites from the star Ummo or Wolf 424, the Vegans in Lyra, the 'Koldasions', Hyadeans, and the 'Solarians' with their alleged 'Tribunal' on the moons of Saturn, the Tau Cetians and Epsilon Eridanians, the Alpha Centurians, the 'Andromedans' from the Andromeda constellation, and of course the Pleiadeans—all of whom claim ties with ancient societies on earth. As for the 'German-Aryans', some sources indicate that they may have at one time been in league with the Grays, but that at least some of the second and third generations may no longer adhere as strongly to Hitler's mad obsession for global conquest, and 'some' of these may in fact now be in opposition to the Grays! Certain accounts suggest that two 'German' groups may possess antigravity technology - one based on the scientific developments of a group of German scientists who escaped Germany before the rise of Nazism, and the other group which consists of full-fledged Nazis!

Once again returning to 'Oscar's' references concerning time/ space windows... If Einstein's theories concerning the possibility of time/space anomalies are correct, then this might explain how a civilization could possibly travel from one star to another in a relatively short period of time. There is no evidence that time could ever be reversed without canceling itself out in a "paradox" (although some claim that reverse time travel is possible, but that it is not possible to "change" the past), yet there is a theoretical possibility that time/space might be SUSPENDED via some type of 'hyperspace'. There is allegedly much technical information contained in the elusive "GRUDGE/BLUE BOOK REPORT NO. 13" describing this aspect of physics. Some 'contactees' even state that the FORWARD flow of time is different in other parts of the galaxy, and that a day on earth could constitute a week on another planet. In other words a spacefaring race might have left earth only a few thousand years ago, yet the time differentiation might have allowed 10,000 years to pass in "their" time. Others believe that the forward flow of time (or rather a particular beings' passage through time) may also be altered through the manipulation of electromagnetic technology.

Also, in relation to the apparent 'tug-of-war' between the 'Grey's' and the 'Nordics'/Tau Cetians, etc., over individuals, as in the case of 'Jill' which we've related earlier, we have an apparently similar situation that was described in an 'Intelligence Report' released by 'Leading Edge Research' (Formerly Nevada Aerial Research). This report stated:

"One contactee that has been contacted by the blond/Nordic race was captured and examined (by the greys) after it was discovered by them that the blue beam used to paralyze people failed to have an effect on him. The implant device that the Nordics put in evidently neutralized the paralysis beam. It was said that the Greys came in a football-shaped craft."

This is one more confirmation, among others, that actual conflict if not warfare exists between various segments of the 'Nordic' Federation and 'Gray' Empire.

Now back to the 'center of the vortex' whereas both Gray and Nordic activity is concerned, that is, the Mojave Desert.

The Mojave mysteries are NOT known only to small groups of researchers who meet in secret to discuss their latest findings. The subject of aerial as well as subsurface phenomena is gaining more respect as more evidence and documentation comes to light. Major motion picture studios are becoming interested in the phenomena, for instance the Showtime and Speilberg productions of ROSWELL. Television companies are also beginning to take these reports of alien encounters seriously, and we have had numerous documentary productions such as SIGHTINGS, ENCOUNTERS, UNSOLVED MYSTERIES, X-FILES, and so on. TV News Magazines and TV Talk Shows have responded to the public interest. Even Radio Talk Show personalities who are heard by millions coast to coast see the potential importance of what is happening to untold thousands of people who are describing essentially the same things. Art Bell has his 'DREAMLAND' program, then there is Chuck Harder, Billy Goodman and others...

According to an item which appeared in THE LEADING EDGE Magazine, a well-known Los Angeles talk show host by the name of Ken Hudnell announced over the air on November 3rd, 1989, his intention to take a group to visit one of the ancient underground cities, which he says has an entrance 60 miles from Anaheim, California.

In 1962, a researcher by the name of Chuck Edwards released some of his own discoveries concerning what might be referred to as the 'Western Subsurface Drainage Network', which seems to cover parts of Utah, Nevada, and Southern California, where are located many drainage systems which do not ultimately flow into the Pacific ocean (via surface rivers, that is), but instead make their way underground into a vast subterranean drainage network. His letter appeared in issue A-8 of 'THE HIDDEN WORLD', one of the few specialized publications which grew out of the Palmer-Shaver controversy of 1940-45 which appeared in AMAZING STORIES science fiction/science fact magazine. The 'controversy' arose around Richard Shaver's claim's to have inside knowledge of two subterranean races which possessed aerial disks: the 'Deros' which have been variously described as a race of ancient out-of-control Atlantean robots, degenerate human troglodytes, or a race of reptilian non- humans (or all three) who were at war with another much more benevolent (and human) subterranean race known as the 'Teros'. The Deros were allegedly tormenting those on the surface of the earth through psychic attack and electronic mind control from their underworld lairs, in preparation for a possible future invasion of the outer world.

The answers to the aerial-subsurface mystery remained rather confused during the 'AMAZING STORIES-Shaver Mystery' period, possibly because of Shaver's perhaps well-intentioned but unwise attempt to inform the readers about the world beyond and the world below through science-fact-fiction stories (however, the readers were never clearly instructed as to where the fact ended and the fiction began), or because of editor Ray Palmer's attempts to 'occultize' many of Shaver's stories with his own mystic-occult philosophies, which Shaver accused him of doing.

So it was in the wake of this period that investigators like Mr. Edwards' were born. Some of the researchers of this period delved off into the metaphysical, seeking the answer to their questions from 'channeled' supernatural entities who tickled their egos, yet whose intentions and revelations could not be physically substantiated. The fact that many of these occultists ended up with severe emotional or psychotic problems — in essence seeing a 'Dero' under every bed and degenerating into schizophrenic paranoid behavior — would indicate that the greater majority of their 'sources' were no doubt astral or alien deceivers out to mislead these seekers after truth. Others however retained their intellectual and analytical sanity and, although not discounting the presence of evil influences, did not so easily open themselves up to their lies and misleading propaganda but set out to investigate the phenomena in a rational, sane, and intellectual manner. It is with this in mind that we quote from Chuck Edwards' letter (Note: These comments are addressed in a letter to Richard S. Shaver):

"This letter is in reply to your January 31 letter. Please forgive me for not answering sooner. Enclosed is some material I hope that you can glean something of value (from). Please be as candid as you have been in the past and if I am far off base don't hesitate to tell me...

THE MOJAVE DESERT'S GREATEST SECRETS

"Our foundation has located a vast system of underground passages in the Mother Lode country of California. They were first discovered in 1936, ignored by all even with our best efforts to reveal them. Recently a road crew blasted out an opening verifying our claims. ONE (of the chambers is) 200 feet long, 70 feet wide and 50 feet high. We have disclosed what we believe to be a vast subterranean drainage system (probably traversing the Great American Desert country for a distance of more than 600 miles). We believe this system extends out like five fingers of your hand to such landmarks as Zion Canyon in Utah, the Grand Canyon, another runs south from the Carson Sink in Nevada and yet another follows (below) the western slope of the same range, joining it's counterpart and ending somewhere in the Mojave Desert. We believe, contrary to orthodox geologists, that the existence of this underground system drains all surface waters running into Nevada (none, with the exception of the Armagosa runs out) and accounts for the fact that it is a Great American Desert. The hairy creatures that you have written about have been seen in several of these areas. Certainly there has been much 'saucer' activity in these parts. For two years I have collected material pertinent to these creatures and if you have any opinions along these lines I would appreciate hearing them.

"So much for now. I hope that I am still your friend. Much of my time has been devoted (to) helping a farmer near Portland who has made a fantastic discovery of incredible stone artifacts. He has several tons of them. They predate anything yet found (or accepted), let us say that for now. We are making slow but steady progress in getting through the wall of orthodoxy. - Chuck Edwards."

Several years ago, subsurface researcher Richard Toronto reprinted a news article in his SHAVERTRON newsletter describing a Municipal Water Director in Los Angeles. This official talked with a man who said that he was hired by the government to look for underground water sources for Camp Irwin in California.

At one point the man and a partner came across an abandoned mine and decided to follow it to the bottom. Near the bottom he was surprised to discover an ancient earth-fault which was wide enough for him and his companion to enter. They traversed this fault for a good distance until they finally emerged into a huge river-cavern. To his surprise he saw before him a crystal pure underground river over a quarter of a mile wide which flowed through the passage and out of sight.

Since learning of this incident the Municipal Water Director claims to have 'discovered' at least five similar underground rivers. Some of these have allegedly been die-traced and were found to emerge from the continental slope below the surface of the oceans, and at least one of them into the Gulf of California.

This might confirm the allegations made by one anonymous retired Navy officer that the Navy has knowledge of a VAST system or labyrinth of aqua-caverns which meander beneath the surface of California and even into other western states, and that these watery labyrinths exit out into the oceans via huge entrances in the lower walls of the Continental Slope. One of the more extravagant claims is that some of these aqua-caverns are so large that they can be navigated by submarine, and that one nuclear submarine on a secret mapping mission in fact became lost within the maze and was never heard from again. Two American nuclear submarines have disappeared without explanation in the past, the U.S.S. SCORPION and the U.S.S. THRESHER. It is true that one woman who claimed to have had a very strong emotional bond with her husband who worked on the Thresher, insisted at the time that she just 'knew' that her husband was still alive after the 'disaster'. She said that she and her husband had such a spiritual-emotional connection that they always knew when the other was in trouble (For information on the Navy's investigations of the aqua-labyrinths via nuclear subs, etc., see: 'CALIFORNIA FLOATS ON OCEAN?'; article in the March, 1980 issue of John J. Williams' "REBEL MAGAZINE", which at the time was available from: Consumertronics Co., c/o John J. Williams. Pres., 2011 Crescent Dr., P.O. Drawer 537., Alamogardo, NM 88310). The 'Thresher' incidentally 'disappeared' on April 10, 1963 with a crew of 129 men under the command of John W. Harvey, USN.)

Researchers Will Carson and Jeannie Joy interviewed the woman mentioned above shortly after the disappearance. She said:

"...My husband was on the submarine Thresher when it disappeared. I don't consider myself a widow. I don't believe my husband is dead. No, it's not a matter of just not being able to believe it, to accept reality; I just can't get over the conviction that he's still alive somewhere. I love my husband very much. I know he loved — loves me. We were very close. We could always tell when something was wrong with each other. Intuition, I guess. I should have felt something the instant there was trouble, if he was really in serious trouble and knew it — a matter of life and death — but I didn't."

"What do you believe really happened?" Carson and Joy asked the attractive young woman.

"Most people think I'm crazy when I say this, but I believe the Thresher was captured."

"By whom?"

"I can't say for sure, but there WAS a Russian submarine spotted near there that day (that is, near where it REPORTEDLY vanished 220 miles off Boston harbor) — only I can't imagine how even the Russians could CAPTURE a vessel like the Thresher without leaving the slightest evidence!"

John J. Williams' source, the retired Navy officer (whose credentials Williams verified), stated that "an eccentric billionaire" (Howard Hughes!?) financed the false Thresher "recovery operation" to satisfy the public and the media.

Still more revelations concerning the Mojave subnet can be found in Bourke

Lee's book 'DEATH VALLEY MEN' (MacMillan Co., N.Y. 1932).

In his chapter: 'Old Gold', Lee describes a conversation which he had several years ago with a small group of Death Valley explorers. The conversation had eventually turned to the subject of Paihute Indian legends. At one point two of the men, Jack and Bill, described their experience with an 'underground city' which they claimed to have discovered after one of them had fallen through the bottom of an old mine shaft near Wingate Pass. They found themselves in a natural underground cavern which they claimed they followed for about 20 miles north into the heart of the Panamint Mountains. To their amazement, they claimed, they found themselves in an huge, ancient, underground cavern city. This account will be quoted later on, however in addition to this, Lee recorded yet another story of a Paihute Indian (not the same one referred to by Oga Make) who may have stumbled into the 'deeper' underground kingdom of the ancient race who built the city within the Panamints, a civilization that was still alive and thriving after thousands of years.

During this lengthy conversation wherein they first revealed the secret of the underground city to Lee and others, the discussion turned to the topic of a Paihute Indian legend that they had heard which was remarkably similar to an ancient GRECIAN myth. The Paihute legend concerned a tribal chief whose wife had died, and who according to the tradition took a spiritual journey to the underworld to find her, and upon returning with her he 'looked back' and since this was forbidden he was not allowed to bring his wife back with him from the dead.

This legend would not be in the same vein as the more tangible story related earlier in the File, as told by the Navaho Oga-Make, concerning a Paihute chief who was allegedly PHYSICALLY taken into the underground cities of the Hav- musuvs deep below the Panamints. After this legend was referred to, the conversation turned to a discussion of an alleged subterranean race, who were believed to inhabit very deep caverns far below the Death Valley territory. Paihute legends of the 'Hav-musuvs' indicate that these ancient dwellers of the Panamints abandoned the ancient city within the mountain itself and migrated to still deeper and larger caverns below. Could the following story tie-in with the Paihute legends of the Hav-musuvs? We will enter the conversation with the following discourse from Bourke Lee:

"...The professor and Jack and Bill sat in the little canvas house in Emigrant Canyon and heard the legend all the way through. The professor said, 'That story, in its essentials, is the story of Orpheus and Eurydice.'

"'Yes,' I said. 'It's also a Paiute legend. Some Indians told that legend to John Wesley Powell in the sixties.'

"'That's very interesting,' said the professor. 'It's so close a parallel to Orpheus and Eurydice that the story might well have been lifted bodily from the Greeks.'

"Jack said, 'I wouldn't be surprised. I knew a Greek. I forgot his name, but he ran a restaurant in almost every mining town I ever was in. He was an extensive wanderer. The Greeks are great travelers.'

"Bill said, 'They don't mean restaurant Greeks. The Greeks they're talking about have been dead for thousands of years.'

"'What of it?' asked Jack, 'maybe the early Greeks was great travelers, too.'

"The professor said, 'It's very interesting.'

"'Now! About that tunnel,' said Bill, with his forehead wrapped in a frown. 'You said this Indian went through a tunnel into a strange country, didn't you?'

"'Yes,' I said. 'I think I called it a cave or a cavern, but I suppose a miner would call it a tunnel. Why?'

"'Here's a funny thing,' said Bill. 'This Indian trapper livin' right across the canyon has a story about a tunnel, an it's not a thousand years old either. Tom Wilson told me that his grandfather went through this tunnel and disappeared. He was gone three years, an when he came back he said he'd been in a strange country livin among strange people. That tunnel is supposed to be somewhere in the Panamints not awful far from where we're sittin'. Now! What do you make of that?'

"Jack said, 'I think Tom's grandfather was an awful liar.'

"I said, 'Tom's grandfather lived when the Paiutes were keeping their tribal lore alive. He probably knew the old legend. Powell heard it in Nevada only sixty-five years ago.'

"'It's very interesting,' said the professor.

"'I got an idea about it,' said Bill, thoughtfully. 'Tom's grandfather might have wandered into some tunnel all goofy from chewing Jimson weed and then come out an found some early whites an stayed with them. Tom told me that the people spoke a queer language and ate food that was new to his grandfather an wore leather clothes. They had horses and they had gold. It might have been a party in Panamint Valley, or even early explorers or early settlers in Owens Valley. How about that?'

"Jack said, 'Yeah. The Spaniards was in here, too. So it might have been Spaniards or the early Greeks. And, where is this tunnel? And why did Tom's grandfather have trouble speaking the language? This is an entirely different story than the one Buck told. We are arriving at no place at all with these Indians and Greeks... To return for a moment to our discussion of geology, professor; have you been in Nevada much?'"

From here the conversation took off in an entirely new direction...

Not only human 'UFOnauts' have been encountered in the Mojave Desert region, but the so-called GRAYS as well. Is it possible that the GRAYS had their genesis on planet earth thousands of years ago the 'Nordics' apparently did? This is the opinion of researcher Brad Steiger who is convinced that the GRAYS are actually descended from a mutation of the saurian race which mysteriously 'disappeared' from the earth, therefore giving rise to the theory that they became 'extinct' in spite of the fact that other saurians like the crocodiles, alligators and iguanas continued to survive.

In 1967, UFO researcher Brad Steiger coauthored (with Joan Whritenour - later Joan O'Connell) a book titled: FLYING SAUCERS ARE HOSTILE. Regarding the intentions of many of the occupants behind the phenomena, Steiger and Whritenour stated:

"...Certain saucer cultists, who have been expecting space brethren to bring along some pie in the sky, continue to deliver saucer-inspired sermons on the theme that the saucers come to bring starry salvation to a troubled world. The self-appointed ministers who preach this extraordinary brand of evangelism ignore the fact that not ALL 'saucers' can be considered friendly. Many give evidence of hostile actions. There is a wealth of well-documented evidence that UFO's have been responsible for murders, assaults, burning by direct-ray focus, radiation sickness, kidnappings, pursuits of automobiles, attacks on homes, disruption of power sources, paralysis, mysterious cremations, and destructions of aircraft. Dozens of reputable eye-witnesses claim to have seen alien personnel loading their space vehicles with specimens from earth, including animals, soil and rocks, water, and struggling human beings."

Steiger (who also authored the books: FLYING SAUCER INVASION - TARGET EARTH, and THE FLYING SAUCER MENACE, as well as several others) also believed that the entities most often encountered are not only hostile, as indicated by the above quote, but nonhuman and in fact REPTILIAN or SAURIAN in nature. In relation to this, there is the following statement which was recently made by Steiger in his popular video film "THE TRUTH ABOUT UFO'S". Steiger has, to some extent (in his video) "changed his tune" concerning the nature of these reptilian beings - supposing now that they aren't as evil as he made them out to be in earlier years. However, the facts just don't support this conclusion, and the only explanation which we can offer to this change of attitude would be the fact (as mentioned by a number of sources) that these creatures have the ability to manipulate from a distance the minds, emotions and spirits of humans through occult-technological or psycho- supernatural means, and that they would undoubtedly use this power to desensitize humanity to their actual nature. It may also be that Steiger succumbed to the pressure of the many New Age "Aquarians" with whom he interacts, who trust in "channeled" revelations which usually portray the Grays as benevolent "space- brothers" who are here to help establish a quantum evolutionary transformation and cosmic initiation into the fourth dimension of universal New Age god-consciousness, whatever that means.

THE MOJAVE DESERT'S GREATEST SECRETS

Certainly, if the true nature of the serpent races were widely known, their operations and even their very existence might be threatened. There are some who believe that the many movies, animated programs, etc., which depict reptilian-like 'alien' beings in a 'benevolent' fashion - are desensitizing America's young people away from their natural enmity toward these ancient, though elusive, enemies of mankind. Steiger, who is considered one of the foremost writers on UFO's and related subjects, said the following:

"In the late 1960's I presented my hypothesis that the reason why the most frequently reported UFOnauts resemble REPTILIAN or AMPHIBIAN humanoids may be because that is exactly what they are, highly evolved members of a serpentine or semiaquatic species. A provocative theory is that the dinosaurs didn't really vanish, they 'evolved' into a humanoid creature that eventually ran it's course, or was destroyed in an Atlantis-type catastrophe (i.e. such as the Great Deluge. Although Steiger and others may hold to an 'evolutionary' hypothesis, this may not necessarily be the case, especially when the 2nd Law of Thermodynamics and the laws of entropy are brought to bear. Instead of 'evolving' from a far less complex form, it is in fact far more likely that the serpent race MUTATED via natural selection, environmental adaptation, survival of the fittest and most intelligent, and so on, into it's various known and unknown branches, from a complex single species which originally inhabited the earth in ancient times. There is a BIG difference between the scientific fact of LATERAL MUTATION and the Darwinian theory of ASCENDING EVOLUTION - Branton).

"...I had developed this hypothesis considerably," Steiger continues, "...so I was delighted when I received word that Dale Russell and Ron Seguen of Canada's 'National Museum of Natural Sciences' of Ottawa, had fashioned a model of a humanoid dinosaur using Stenonychosaurus and Equallus as their inspiration. Stenonychosaurus, according to Russell, had a rather large brain and eyes with overlapping visual fields. The 90 pound dinosaur also walked on two legs, and it appears to have had a particularly OPPOSABLE THUMB on it's three-clawed hand. The result of such scientific speculation was an astonishingly humanlike creature that Russell terms a 'Dinosauroid'. The creature stands four-and-a-half feet tall, has a large, domed head, green skin, and yellow reptilian eyes. It should probably have had ears, Russell conceded, but the effect would have made it appear too human. As it is, the dinosaur on display at Canada's 'National Museum of Natural Sciences' almost EXACTLY fits the descriptions of UFOnauts provided by THOUSANDS of men and women throughout the planet who have reported close encounters..."

In his book 'THE UFO ABDUCTORS' (1988., Berkley Books., N.Y.), pp 5-6, Steiger adds: "In the greatest number of alien encounters, the UFOnauts were described as standing about five feet tall and dressed in one-piece, tight-fitting jumpsuits. Their skin was gray, or grayish-green, and hairless. Their faces were dominated by large eyes, VERY OFTEN WITH SNAKELIKE, SLIT PUPILS. They had no discernible lips, just straight lines for mouths. They seldom were described as having noses, just little snubs if at all; but usually the witnesses saw only nostrils nearly flush against the smooth face. Sometimes a percipient mentioned pointed ears but on many occasions commented on the absence of noticeable ears on the large, round head. And, REPEATEDLY, WITNESSES DESCRIBED AN INSIGNIA OF A FLYING SERPENT ON A SHOULDER PATCH, A BADGE, A MEDALLION, OR A HELMET."

The annual "NEVADA AERIAL RESEARCH JOURNAL" for Summer, 1989 confirmed Mr. Steiger's claims by reprinting a UPI news item which appeared in a Berkley, California newspaper. The article stated:

"Dale Russell, curator of fossil vertebrates at the National Museums of Canada in Ottawa, has developed a theory that intelligent life forms could have developed from the large reptiles that roamed the earth (in ancient times).

"Russell calls his imaginary creature a 'Dinosauroid' which would look like a hairless, green-skinned reptile with a bulging skull, luminous catlike eyes and three-fingered hands...

"The amphibians evolved into a humanoid species that eventually developed a culture that ran its course or was destroyed in an Atlantis-like catastrophe —just after they had begun exploring extraterrestrial frontiers. Certain UFOnauts, then, may be the descendants of the survivors of that amphibian culture RETURNING from their space colony to monitor the present dominant species on the HOME planet."

This is one possibility which was given in the article. According to certain sources the 'winged serpent' that is emblemed on the 'alien' uniforms represents another reptilian mutation which is near the very top of the alien or reptilian hierarchy, entities which have been referred as the pterodactoids, the mothmen, or the winged draco. These have allegedly been seen on rare occasions and have even been the subject of an entire book by UFO researcher John A. Keel.

Further confirmation comes from the 4-part documentary 'DINOSAUR', hosted by Walter Cronkite. This program also described the possibility that certain groups of ancient saurians may have developed or mutated into hominoid sauroids. David Norman, in a review of the series, stated:

"...The series finishes with an unusual flourish. In 1982 Dr. Dale Russell of the Royal Museum of Canada, Ottawa indulged in a half-serious thought experiment. He had described a small, HIGHLY PREDATORY, nimble troodont dinosaur from the Late Cretaceous, STENONYCHOSAURUS, which had AN UNUSUALLY LARGE BRAIN, large stereoscopic eyes, and grasping hands. He speculated about what might have happened to such dinosaurs if they had not become extinct. His answer was the 'dinosauroid' - a three-clawed, three-toed, large-brained, UP-

RIGHT, and TAILLESS dinosaur."

Norman also described the almost humanlike quality of the hand of one particular saurian branch, the Iquanodon: "...The flexible fifth finger moves a bit like a human thumb for grasping objects, while the middle three fingers are capable of little flexure. The large, stiletto-like thumb spike of Iguanodon would have been a devastating weapon. The sharp spike, coupled with the strength of the forelimb, could have punctured the toughest skin."

It is possible that if such a highly intelligent yet (according to many accounts) extremely insidious and predatory 'race' does in fact exist, then it might NOT have 'mutated' far from it's original form as it is 'pictured' — although in a rather obscure fashion — in the 3rd chapter of Genesis. If we are to believe the thousands of witnesses who have reported such creatures during UFO encounters (descriptions which would either be the result of a collective hoax, mass hallucination, or observation of actual encounters - the latter of which seems to be the most likely), then one could reasonably ask the question: "Where do they originate from?" If they had their origin on earth as Brad Steiger suggests, then where on earth are the infernal creatures? A better question might be "Where IN earth are the infernal creatures?" Although the 'serpent race' has largely succeeded in evading the scrutiny of most humans living on the surface of this planet over the centuries, there are many indications which nevertheless suggest a SUBTERRANEAN connection — not only to a large percentage of the UFO phenomena, but also to many of the creatures which lie behind the phenomena as well, especially the REPTILIAN creatures such as those described by Steiger.

Believe it or not, there ARE in fact many more very well documented accounts concerning alien, nonhuman 'entities' — aside from the one's mentioned earlier — which have been encountered in underground recesses throughout the world. Traditional Judeo-Christianity has more-or-less associated the depths of the earth with 'Hades' and 'demons'. We are certainly not denying this, but we are offering a much more elaborated exposition of this concept.

Before describing these, however, we will document some cases of reptilian hominoids which have been encountered on the SURFACE of the planet. The following accounts, which appear in 'CURIOUS ENCOUNTERS', by Loren Coleman (Faber & Faber., Boston, Mass. 1985) pp. 70-76, describe encounters with reptilian and/or amphibian bi-pedial creatures of a semi-aquatic nature:

"In 1973, during the summer, residents of New Jersey's Newton-Lafayette area described A GIANT, MAN-LIKE ALLIGATOR they had seen locally. Newspaper reporters wrote about an old Indian tale from the region that told of a giant, man- sized fish that could never be caught. In 1977, New York State Conservation Naturalist Alfred Hulstruck reported that the state's Southern Tier had 'a scaled, manlike creature (that) appears at dusk from the red, algae-ridden waters to forage among the fern and moss-covered uplands.'

"The New York-New Jersey record, however, cannot compare with the overwhelming series of narratives issuing from one place in the United States, the Ohio River Valley.

"Over twenty years ago, by digging into the back issues of the Louisville, Kentucky, COURIER-JOURNAL, I discovered one of those gems that has kept me pondering its meaning for two decades. The interesting little item was in the 24 October 1878 issue. A 'WIld Man of the Woods' was captured, supposedly, in Tennessee, and then placed on exhibit in Louisville. The creature was described as being six feet, five inches tall, and having eyes twice the normal size. His body was 'COVERED WITH SCALES.' This article now makes some sense.

"And then almost a hundred years later, again near Louisville, there are more stories of REPTILIAN ENTITIES. In October 1975, near Milton, Kentucky, Clarence Cable reported a 'giant lizard' was roaming the forests near his junkyard. Author Peter Guttilla described the creature Cable surprised as 'about fifteen feet long, had a foot-long forked tongue, and big eyes that bulged something like a frog's. It was dull-white with black-and-white stripes across its body with quarter-size speckles over it.'

"On-site field investigations by Mark A. Hall, however, indicated this 'giant lizard' RAN BIPEDALLY, according to OTHER Trimble County, Kentucky witnesses. The Ohio River is Louisville's, Milton's, and Trimble county's northern boundary...

"1972... In March of that year on two separate occasions, two Ohio policemen saw what has become known as the 'Loveland Frogman.' Investigated by Ron Schaffner and Richard Mackey, these researchers interviewed the officers involved but have not published their names, instead using the fictitious names 'Williams' and 'Johnson.'

"The first incident took place at 1:00 A.M. on 3 March 1972, on a clear, cold night. Officer Williams was on route to Loveland, via Riverside Road, when he thought he saw a dog beside the road. But when the 'thing' stood up, its eyes illuminated by the car lights looked at him for an instant, turned, and leapt over the guardrail. Williams saw it go down an embankment into the Little Miami River, a mere fifteen or so miles from the Ohio River. He described the thing as weighing about sixty pounds, about three to four feet tall, having a textured leathery skin, AND A FACE LIKE A FROG OR LIZARD. Williams went on to the police station and returned with Officer Johnson to look for evidence of the creature. They turned up scrape-marks leading down the side of the small hill near the river.

"On approximately 17 March 1972, Officer Johnson was driving outside of Loveland when he had a similar experience. Seeing an animal lying in the middle of the road, he stopped to remove what he thought was a dead critter. Instead, when the officer opened his squeaky car door, the animal got up into a crouched position like a football player. The creature hobbled to the guardrail and lifted its leg over, while constantly looking at Johnson. Perhaps it was the funny smirk on its face, but Johnson decided to shoot at it. He missed, he figured, since the thing didn't slow down. Johnson later told how he felt it was more upright than the way Williams described it. One area farmer told investigators he saw a large, FROG-LIKE OR LIZARD-LIKE CREATURE during the same month of the officers' sightings..."

Charles Berlitz, in his 'WORLD OF THE INCREDIBLE BUT TRUE' (Fawcett Crest Books., N.Y.), related the following incident concerning another hominoid predator or 'Lizard Man':

"There have been numerous Bigfoot sightings in the United States and around the world. The humanlike creatures are usually said to be large and hairy with glowing eyes. During the summer of 1988, however, residents of Bishopville, South Carolina, reported accounts of a rare breed of Bigfoot: A SEVEN- FOOT-TALL LIZARD MAN WITH GREEN SCALY SKIN. According to witnesses, unlike other Bigfoot creatures Lizard Man has only three toes on each foot, as well as long ape-like arms that end in three fingers tipped with FOUR-INCH CLAWS. Only the second Bigfoot to have only three fingers on each hand, and the first (known to Berlitz - Branton) to also have three toes on each foot. Lizard Man is the most unusual Bigfoot ever reported.

"Seventeen-year-old Chris Davis first encountered Lizard Man around 2:00 A.M. on June 29. On his way home, the teen stopped near the brackish waters of Scape Ore Swamp outside Bishopville to change a flat tire. While replacing the jack in the car's trunk, he glimpsed something running across the field toward him. Jumping into his 1976 Toyota Celica, he was quickly engaged in a tug-of-war with the reptilian creature as he tried to pull the door closed. Then Lizard Man jumped onto the car's roof, where he left scratches in the paint as evidence of his attack.

"Hysterical, Davis returned home and told only his parents and a few close friends about the experience. Law enforcement officers, however, interrogated him after neighbors said the boy might know something about the strange bite marks and scratches found on another car.

"Davis wasn't alone in his report. Soon other reports were flooding the sheriff's office. Teenagers Rodney Nolfe and Shane Stokes, for example, were driving near the swamp with their girlfriends when Lizard Man darted across the road in front of their car. Construction worker George Holloman also claimed Lizard Man jumped at him as he was collecting water from an artesian well.

"Investigating the area around the swamp, state trooper Mike Hodge and Lee County deputy sheriff Wayne Atkinson found three crumbled, forty-gallon cardboard drums. The tops of saplings were ripped off eight feet above the ground.

And there were, according to Hodge, 'humongous footprints,' fourteen-by- seven-inch impressions in hard red clay. Following the tracks for four hundred yards, the officers backtracked and found new prints impressed in their car's tire tracks. According to state wildlife biologists, the footprints matched no known animal species." (This 'Lizard Man' incident was covered in one of the episodes of Tim White's 'SIGHTINGS' documentary, - 'MONSTERS' segment, on the Fox Network - Branton).

Some sources have indicated that these Reptons or 'Lizard Like' beings, similar to those described above, have been seen in deep underground tunnel networks below the general southwestern areas of Albuquerque (especially Dulce and San Crystobel), New Mexico; Las Vegas (especially Groom Lake), Nevada; Salt Lake City, Utah; and within caves in the Black Mountains between Las Vegas, Nevada and Kingman, Arizona — among other areas. These creatures have also been encountered, sources allege, in deep underground installations below the Mojave Desert region of California... and even on the fringe of the desert itself near Lancaster and elsewhere. In many cases they have been seen working closely with the 'Grays', which regard these Reptons or 'Lizard Men' as being their superiors.

Researcher Michael Lindemann of the '20/20 GROUP' related the following in a public lecture in Lancaster, California, concerning a woman who had experienced an 'abduction' by the alien group known as the Greys, on the outskirts of the Mojave Desert:

"...Lot's of ordinary citizens in the Lancaster area...are having close-up alien encounters... the first one is a woman with a number of children who in 1972 was living with her then husband in Ridgecrest, California... This woman had never read any books about UFO's or aliens, and didn't have any interest in it. Indeed today she has not read any books. The first thing she tried to do recently when she realized that she had had alien encounters, was she went out and rented Whitley Strieber's movie 'COMMUNION', the video tape, and she stuck it in the machine and barely a minute into the movie she got very anxious and nauseous and ran out of the house. That was her only attempt to inform herself on, let's say, literature or information about aliens, and yet this woman has had astonishing experiences."

Following an entirely waking experience where she saw a seemingly half-physical or apparitional 'Grey', near her home which faced the open desert (the nearest neighbor being about two blocks away), she began having more intense experiences which she knew took place - but could not entirely understand or recall. She described the creature in the traditional 'gray' configuration described by so many other 'abductees' — short gray with a large head and large black slanted eyes — which in light of her ignorance of the overall UFO phenomena, according to Lindemann, only tends to substantiate her story. As a result of this initial experience, Lindemann explains, she contacted a hypnotherapist, a woman who incidentally had never read a UFO book herself. This psychologist concluded — through various tests and observations — that the woman from Ridgecrest was entirely sane and sincere. Michael Lindemann continues:

"...This woman has had lots and lots of experiences since then. Her next experience was also a waking experience which TURNED INTO an experience that she could not remember except through regression. But the 'waking' part of it was the 'clue' that she needed to start exploring her hidden memories.

"Her husband went off on a training program, he worked for a telephone company, (and) went off on a training program for a number of weeks some time later, toward the end of 1972.

"She was staying at home with her children. Of course because they were in an isolated spot, she slept in her bed with a loaded shotgun, and she was a very light sleeper, kind of nervous.

"One night she woke up because there was 'rustling' in her room. She looked and she saw what she thought was a sort of hooded, black figure over by her dresser. It looked as if somebody were sort of 'playing' with her jewelry box. And she of course felt as if someone had probably broken into the house.

"But as she was kind of thinking to herself, 'What can I do, what can I do,' kind of gripping her shot gun, she made a little involuntary gasp, and whoever it was turned around and walked over to her.

"She described this being as about...4 1/2 feet tall, very, very dark, with very... she said it looked like a lizard! Very rough skin, big yellow eyes...not the huge black almond shaped eyes...large, yellow with a slit iris, a muzzle, teeth. She said it looked like an iguana. And she said that IMMEDIATELY she could tell that this being was very menacing and didn't like her at all. This being was dangerous and nasty, and not to be trusted.

"She didn't remember what happened next, all she knew was she was terrified, because this being was literally leaning right into her face as she lay there in bed.

"And in regression she found out the rest of that particular story. She was floated downstairs and she found that some GREYS were PHYSICALLY CARRYING her three children outside to a waiting craft. She was levitated outside to the same craft.

"She recognized immediately that this black lizard-like guy, which she later learned actually had a tail... was actually WORKING WITH THE GREYS, but, she said, they did not (always) get along. It was the 'Greys' craft... she was literally 'listening' to their 'telepathy'. They were conversing about her as she was lying on a table in the craft waiting for their decision on what to do. She became convinced that the black one wanted to KILL her, and the Greys were 'saying'... 'No...

not on OUR ship.' She said she saw something horrifying at that point. She said the black one just 'swept' its hand across the chest of one of the greys and literally tore the greys chest open. It fell to the ground and she thinks it died. She says, 'I know they have GREEN blood, I saw it bleed.'"

Before one feels too 'sorry' for the 'greys', they should understand that many accounts indicate that the greys have participated in unknown numbers of animal and human mutilations in order to use the animal AND HUMAN secretions as a 'liquid protein' food source. And if we are to believe some of the more fantastic accounts of crash-retrievals, such mutilated animal and human organs have been discovered within or among the debris of crashed GREY craft. The 'reptilian' hierarchy seems to operate in an exactly opposite manner as the Judeo-Christian ethic, and instead of operating on faith, love and service the reptilian or sauroid hierarchy is said to operate on fear, hatred and competition. Since both the Greys and lizard-like 'aliens' operate on 'collective consciousness' and are neo-saurian in nature according to many sources, and since they have a similar agenda which seems to be imperial-conquest motivated, they inevitably work together in what Michael Lindemann calls a 'wedding of convenience'.

From one perspective, one should NOT see the 'iguanas' as being much worse than the greys. For what the green-blooded 'greys' lack in the way of demoniacal 'hatred' or contempt for humankind, they seem to make up in their profound 'indifference' to the human race. Over and over again abductees describe the greys as emotionless and methodical, and seemingly show no sympathy or pity whatsoever toward human suffering or death, but merely look upon it with scientific 'curiosity'. Although 'hatred' would seem to be the opposite of 'compassion', others would argue that 'indifference' is the antithesis of compassion, caring or love. From this perspective, 'indifference' to human life may be no less evil than raging 'contempt' for human life. BOTH may be the motivating factors behind all kinds of atrocities.

In reference to the case referred to above, Lindemann continues:

"...Her hypnotherapist said to us at this point, 'You know, you really ought to understand that this woman is a very, very good hypnotic subject and she actually relives her experiences in real time in the first person. She goes through all of the emotions and she has incredible recall of detail.' ...she says...as a therapist of long standing she has no reason to doubt that the detail that this woman brings forward is essentially accurate. It matches of course in many, many particulars the kind of information that other abductees have also told.

"...One of the other disturbing things that this woman has mentioned...is that in other sessions where she was abducted, she found herself in an underground facility which she feels quite certain was at George Air Force Base where she grew up. And in that facility underground she saw the greys were working side by side with human military personnel. And we do have other reports, not only 'we' but many people who study the abduction phenomena, collective reports indicating that the abduction phenomenon is occurring right under the noses of our own officials, that there is apparently some agreement operating here..."

The above account would seem to confirm that the SAURIAN GREYS (which are basically neo-saurian or reptilian in configuration according to alleged government autopsies) are being used by their larger reptilian superiors as the 'technical brains' behind some hidden agenda, and as a type of cosmic 'double agent' race. Numerous accounts indicate that the Greys are willfully subservient to the larger 'Draconian' entities and, because of the OUTWARDLY less-intimidating through nevertheless frightening appearance, the greys are used to 'interface' with U.S. military personnel. Also, many individuals within 'deep' military organizations have since come forward and implied that the 'Greys' used these interactions to establish foot- in-the-door treaties with the Military which were never meant to be honored, but were used only as 'platforms' to get control, via implantation and so on, of sensitive government-military personnel. The Greys are said to have used deception profusely to get their way. Part of the reason why the 'agreements' continue even after the 'Grand Deception' was discovered, some suggest, is simply because the greys have 'taken over' the minds of certain officials in high government positions. This continued 'pact' with the serpent race may also, in part, be explained by the malevolent influence of the 'Jesuit-Illuminati' or the 'Serpent Cult' in certain policy making groups such as 'MJ-12', the Jason Society, etc.

The following article describes what might be a similar group of beings as the 'Lizard Men' described earlier, although these creatures seem to have been somewhat more human-size in their configuration and apparently intent on passing themselves off as humanlike entities. The account appeared in the Omaha, Nebraska 'METRO UPDATE' for Oct. 29 - Nov. 4, 1990. Written by reporter Patricia C. Ress, the article was titled: 'LINCOLN MAN RECOUNTS ABDUCTIONS BY ALIENS':

"People have been talking about flying saucers for about 45 years now — longer if you count the reports of the so-called 'foo fighters' seen by pilots on both sides during World War II. But within the past 20 years we've been hearing more about a more frightening side to these visitations - abduction by aliens.

"The most famous case was that of Barney and Betty Hill, two New Englanders returning home from vacation and unable to account for a large block of missing time. Under hypnosis, a very frightening and detailed account of alien abduction emerged. Later there was Betty Andreason, who told of aliens who took her through walls and closed doors.

"Then came Budd Hopkins, who made a study of such abductions and chronicled one case in 'INTRUDERS-THE INCREDIBLE VISITATIONS AT COPELY

WOODS.' Next came the 'Gulf Breeze Sightings' in Florida, and most recently author Whitley Strieber's accounts of his own abductions in his books 'COMMUNION' and 'TRANSFORMATION.'

"While most of these abductions took place in the East, some say that visiting aliens have been just as busy in the Midwest — even Nebraska. A Lincoln man recently recounted his experiences during a talk at the Oakcrest Institute in Elkhorn.

"John Foster has been an engineer in Lincoln for a number of years. Lincoln, in fact, is his home town and the place where his abduction experiences began back in 1950. A soft-spoken down-home type of man, Foster reminds people of a young Joel McCrea.

"'Alien abduction is a terrifying and traumatic experience,' Foster told the audience. 'Psychiatric counselors don't know how to deal with this — even if you can get them to believe you.'

"Foster has gotten help and understanding from people like Dr. Leo Sprinkle of the University of Wyoming, who has dealt with numerous alien abduction cases. He also has been the subject of ridicule and rejection by both family and friends.

"'Often in a UFO abduction experience, things happen that are absolutely unbelievable. I have been told that IT IS NOT UNCOMMON FOR FAMILIES TO BREAK UP AFTER SUCH AN EXPERIENCE. I finally reached the point where I no longer care what people think of me.' Foster said.

"He said he wasn't fully aware of what had happened to him over the years until the 1980s. In 1981 he was sitting outside his home in Lincoln with a friend and on a lark, they both said a prayer (or incantation? - Branton) that they would see a flying saucer and soon after, one appeared, he said.

"On another occasion in March, 1966, he saw a light out behind the trees as he sat on his patio, he said, and the sight triggered a distant memory of something that had happened to him when he was in grade school in Lincoln in 1950.

"He said 40 or 50 people were outside watching a movie when swirling lights suddenly appeared, ALONG WITH A CRAFT THAT INITIALLY LOOKED LIKE A HELICOPTER.

"Foster recalled being INCAPACITATED AND FEELING STRANGE. He said he saw a craft appear WITH THREE LITTLE MEN who appeared to be fixing it. He felt an overwhelming desire to get inside the craft, but once he did, he discovered it was in a different form. 'We got a lesson about history, mankind and something about Indians and buffalo,' he said.

"When he looked around him, Foster said, he noticed that everyone else seemed to be FROZEN IN TIME. 'They all looked like statues,' he said, he saw a woman who told him she had FIXED HERSELF UP SO THAT HE WOULDN'T BE TRAUMATIZED.

"He said he was taken to an examining room BY CREATURES THAT LOOKED 'LIKE FROGS OR LIZARDS.' The 'woman' told him they were the educators and would supervise his learning experience, he said. Among other strange things, Foster recalled THAT THE LIZARD MEN ENCOURAGED HIM TO JOIN THE MASONIC LODGE.

"After he was examined, Foster said, he was sent back out of the craft to the crowd below. The woman (i.e. the being that had 'fixed' itself up to appear as a 'woman' - Branton) spoke to him in almost a scolding tone, saying that from then on he would be a good boy and mind his parents, he said. The woman seemed to know a lot about him, including the fact that he and some friends had stolen some pop and candy from a store across the street, he said.

"In October 1986 Foster went camping with his wife and children at Niobrara Park and he had a short visitation which awakened more memories of previous abductions, he said.

"By mid-December he recalled 50 abduction experiences, he said, and by January that number had grown to 2,000 and by January 1987, he had recalled 3,000 abductions.

"Foster has recorded memories of 50 of the abductions in detail, another 450 in short notations and many others by locations only, he said.

"'There are roughly two areas of the so-called close encounters,' Foster said. 'These may mesh together, but there are the abductees who seem to be taken aboard a craft to be examined and the contactees who appear to be contacted throughout life and seem to have an assignment.'

"In June of 1987 Foster and his daughter met with several other contactees and he had the feeling that he had known them all his life, he said.

"They helped him recall experiences from coast to coast and from Canada to Mexico, he said.

"'I believe the UFO experiences are directed at you personally,' Foster said, 'but there are times when they can seem to address the population in general.

"'THIS IS WHAT SEEMS TO BE THE CASE WITH THE MYSTERIOUS 'CORN CIRCLES' THAT FIRST APPEARED IN ENGLAND AND CAN NOW BE SEEN IN CANADA AND THE U.S. AND OTHER PLACES.' (Note: Many of these symbols are very intricate and are meaningless to most. Could they be some type of 'signal' to those who have been abducted-programmed, signals which are intended to 'trigger' some subconscious reaction in certain abductees? Admittedly, this is only one of many possibilities - Branton)

"Foster said profound things happened to him during his abductions and the world should know about them. HE WAS SHOWN HOW THE 'VISITORS' CAN MANIPULATE ATOMIC STRUCTURE AND CHANGE THINGS DIRECTLY AT WILL, he said, and was told things about scientific matters over the years, only to see them discovered afterward.

"WHILE THE ENTITIES HE INITIALLY ENCOUNTERED LOOKED REPTILIAN, HE SAID, THE SPIRITUAL 'GUIDES' WERE MORE HUMAN IN APPEARANCE AND WERE ABLE TO 'PHASE IN AND OUT AT THE DEEPER LEVELS.'

"On the initial level of the abduction experience there is a kind of excitement, Foster said, while on the deeper level, life plans emerge and there is interaction with people who have had similar experiences. Foster said there are four witnesses who can recall parts of at least three of his encounters.

"Foster said that to document his experiences, he has made several drawings and paintings. He believes he has encountered at least 13 different kinds of crafts.

"Foster said he remembers abductions that involved his friends when they were teenagers. A large 'floating phone booth' would descend from a dark fog, he said, and a voice seemingly from a loud speaker would urge them to 'gather around for eternal wisdom and knowledge — and something else about Indians and buffalo,' he said."

(Note: was the promise of 'eternal wisdom' the bait used to entrap them into the Reptilian agenda? We realize this sounds rather simplistic but ancient accounts do reveal that this exact same strategy was used by the original 'Serpent' race of Hebrew tradition, in their unholy alliance with INVISIBLE fallen angelic beings, to destroy man's connection with the Almighty — and subsequently, his divinely-given authority over creation, including his dominion over the BEASTS! In relation to this, the third chapter of GENESIS states that the serpent race was the most "subtle" of all the members of the animal kingdom — those "beasts" that had no eternal "soul" essence as does humankind. The Hebrew word for "subtle" is ARUWM, literally meaning "CUNNING [usually in a bad sense] or CRAFTY". Those who have seen Steven Spielberg's depiction of the 7 ft. tall RAPTORS in the movie "JURASSIC PARK" can gain a sense of just how "cunning" and cruel these creatures were and, according to various witnesses, still are today - Branton).

Foster, in reference to the floating "phone booth", stated that:

"The voice over the loudspeaker would call them by name AND COULD AT TIMES SOUND SARCASTIC (as a manipulator might sound? - Branton). On one occasion, his friends SHOT AT THE BOOTH WITH RIFLES AND THREW BEER CANS AT IT.

"When he was at Mahoney Lake in 1987, Foster said, he again saw both the booth and the saucer. He asked the entities to quit bothering him because he was disturbed when he COULDN'T RECALL his abductions, he said, AND THEY TOLD HIM IF HE REMEMBERED THE EXPERIENCES, IT WOULD NEGATE THEIR PURPOSE.

"They also told him that if he didn't want to have any more abduction experiences, he would meet some people who would 'HELP HIM BECOME MORE META-PHYSICAL,' he said, and he later met such people.

"He said he recalls being pulled up into a kind of floating bus and being taken into the future. He declined to say what he saw.

"Foster said he was given experiments to do as an engineer. 'They worked, but they shouldn't have, according to what we know,' he said.

"He said the 'guides' told him they were preparing people for a time when the chosen would be taken away.

"...'I was told to awaken people to other dimensions and to participate in these realms,' he said..." (i.e. opening themselves up to or surrendering to the occult and supernatural powers and realms which these Reptilians control, in order to be more easily controlled and manipulated by them? Just a thought - Branton)

In reference to the Saurian Grays and the Secret Societies they allegedly manipulate, researcher Bill Hamilton, who claims to have had contact with one 'Nordic' or 'Telosian' family, offers a synopsis of his own findings. Mr. Hamilton provides some informative research that may help us to understand this mystery in a fuller perspective. In an article which appeared in Patrick O'Connell's "TRENDS AND PREDICTIONS ANALYST" Newsletter, Vol. 6, No. 2 (July, 1990) issue, William Hamilton stated:

"...The cover-up was initiated soon after the Roswell, N.M. crash. We wanted to know - 1) Who they were, 2) Why they were here, 3) How their technology worked. The cover-up became a matter of NATIONAL SECURITY (a blanket word covering secrecy and deception). The cover-up involves secret organizations within our government such as MJ-12, PI-40, MAJI, Delta, the Jason Scholars, & known intelligence organizations such as Naval Intelligence, Air Force Office of Special Investigation, the Defence Investigative Service, the CIA, NSA, and more! It involves THINK TANKS such as RAND, the Ford Foundation, the Aspen Institute, & Brookings Institute. It involves corporations such as Bechtel, GE, ITT, Amoco, Northrup, Lockheed, & many others. It involves SECRET SOCIETIES who may be the hidden bosses of the orchestrated events (i.e. economic collapse, wars, assassinations, conspiracies to manipulate & control humans & thereby to exercise enormous power over the destiny of the human race) - the Illuminati, Masons, Knights of Malta, etc. The individual players are too numerous to list. The whole of this conspiracy forms an INTERLOCKING NEXUS. The goal is said to be a ONE WORLD GOVERNMENT (or Dictatorship)!

"'The Underground Nation' - The RAND symposium held on Deep Underground Construction indicated that plans were hatched during the 50's to build underground bases, laboratories, & city- complexes linked by a stupendous network of tunnels to preserve & protect the ongoing secret interests of the secret societies. These secret societies made a pact with alien entities in order to further motives of domination."

Actually, as it turns out, THEY (the secret societies) are now being 'dominated' by the 'aliens'. One can only assume that if certain humans would 'sell out' their own kind to an alien race and use such an infernal alliance to gain dominion over their fellow man, then they should consider the fact that they, according to universal law, must in the same way open THEMSELVES up to being manipulated and controlled by their supposed benefactors. As it is written, "the servant is not greater than his lord." There are indications, as we've said earlier, that an antediluvian race or races may have attempted this very same thing, the construction of vast subterranean systems like the ones now being built by the more modern secret societies.

There are also indications, as we have also said, that later societies and their underground networks intersect these ancient antediluvian excavations and outposts. This is evidenced by the many accounts which suggest that Masonic-related secret societies are utilizing both the ancient and modern subsystems. Many indications also point to the fact that entire human colonies, both peaceful and 'alien controlled', may exist within these deeper levels. These colonies are allegedly inhabited in part by ancient native American or meso-American tribes or explorers who crossed the seas from ancient Mediterranean and elsewhere in the eastern hemisphere thousands of years ago. These may also include more recent (past few centuries) American inhabitants or explorers of Anglo-saxon descent as well. Indications are that such explorers happened to discover some of these ancient antediluvian excavations, which led to deep tunnel networks and ancient hydrothermal and geothermal cavities containing conditions sufficient to sustain physical life.

Mr. Hamilton continues:

"...The underground complexes are not confined to the U.S. alone! A large underground complex operated by the U.S. exists at Pine Gap, near Alice Springs, Australia (Note: According to various sources, conditions in this complex are somewhat similar to those at Dulce, that is, this underground base contains replicated flying 'disks' based on 'alien' technology, and many workers there have allegedly been implanted and operate under a type of mental control of the Secret Government and Gray aliens which also reportedly utilize the base as part of the Illuminati-Gray "joint interaction" - Branton).

"...It appears that the secret societies among us have become aware of the coming planetary ecocatastrophe & the possibility of an earth polar shift in the near future. Surveying the earth from space, satellites & shuttles reveal EXTENSIVE DAMAGE TO OUR ECOSPHERE! Our planet is wobbling on its axis & its magnetic field is decaying! Ozone depletion & the greenhouse effect are rapidly endangering life on our planet. Alternatives, which include - 1) direct handling of the atmospheric problems, 2) taking shelter in underground domains, & 3) escape to other planetary bodies in the solar system, have been devised in secret. However there is a possible Alternative 4 which mostly depends on a completely different idea on how to save the earth (in essence, by escaping to another "dimension" - Branton)..."

Based upon the relatively elusive yet extensive accounts and relative data which has been gathered by a loosely-connected group of researchers, we can conclude that the subterranean network — whatever it consists of presently — is basically inhabited by both human and nonhuman reptilian beings. In those areas where the humans are not being controlled by the non-humans or saurians, there is obviously conflict between the two races as foretold in Genesis chapter 3. Many of the American subterranean networks, before the turn of the century (1900), were apparently inhabited mostly by human societies, yet it seems as if a reptilian 'invasion' of the substrata of North America occurred en masse in the early part of the 1900's, with a major 'push' into the U.S. subnet from already-occupied underground systems in Central and South America taking place around 1933. This, according to many accounts, involved reptilian beings which had been in possession of underlying cavern networks beneath Asia and the Far East, and according to their imperialistic-predatory nature these creatures began expanding their influence into the Western Hemisphere — first into Central and South America, and finally North America itself. Some unconfirmed reports tell of whole groups of humans (both surface exploration parties or even troglodytical tribes) who have literally been wiped-out in sudden attacks by the serpent race in a type of "battle beneath the earth".

Aside from the human and reptilian entities, there are some who speak of a third type of being, a (so-called) 'hybrid' between the humans and reptilians. The indications are that such a 'hybrid' would be impossible, theologically and scientifically speaking. The serpent races simply possess no soul-matrix (or 'conscience') as do humans, and even if it were possible to genetically or artificially produce an 'apparent' crossbreed, the creature produced could never be an actual 'hybrid', but would inevitably fall to one side or the other - a corrupted form of human being possessing a soul, or a mutated version of the 'reptilian' or 'serpent' race. Bill Hamilton explains another reason why such a natural (thank God) cross between the two could never be produced:

"...It is unlikely that the reptilian greys are crossbreeding with humans. Reptilians carry their sex organs internally and reproduce by eggs hatched by solar heat. Reptoids have well developed eyes, no hair follicles, & no external ear cartilage as consistent with most reptilian species. Since their means of reproduction is incompatible with our own, it is suggested that humans (women - Branton) may be fertilized by the grays by artificial insemination with human spermatozoa or perhaps they use the human uterus as an incubation chamber."

Note: Other indications are that the reptilians inject or encodify the human embryo with reptilian DNA during the early stages of development. Also, aside from the description given by Dale Russell to the effect that the ancient progenitors of the gray-type saurians may have had a type of 'ear', we presently know of only one other account describing a possible 'ear-like' appendage having been seen on a sauroid creature. This was described by a Mr. Brian Scott, who was allegedly abducted into an underground base beneath the Superstition Mts. area east of Phoenix, Arizona. He described these large, fearful creatures as having a type of 'flap' of leathery or 'crocodilian' texture which came down each side of their heads. It is uncertain however whether this was a type of ear-like appendage or not. These creatures according to Scott claimed to have a base in 'Epsilon Bootes' and worked with a smaller group of grayish white dwarfs of typical 'gray' description AS WELL AS WITH a group of 'transparent' entities who referred to themselves as 'the hosts', or the 'Ashtar' beings. Note the similarity between this description and John Foster's account in Nebraska's METRO-UPDATE. These transparent beings once told Brian that they were 'Beelzebub', and tried to convince him and his wife (who was once 'molested' by one of the infernal poltergeist-like creatures in her bathroom) to 'sell their souls' to them, and generally acted in a similar fashion as the malevolent beings typically described in connection with demoniacal possession cases.

As for the so-called 'hybrids', Hamilton's statements seem to be confirmed by others, including abductees, who have hinted that the 'hybrid' fetuses are actually conceived through human spermatozoa taken from men and ovum taken from women abductees, and that the fetuses are as we have stated somehow genetically altered with possible reptilian 'cells' or genetic coding being added. Many of the so-called hybrids however are nevertheless 'human', possessing human souls, and human blood - Branton).

Hamilton continues:

"...Alien vehicles are being tested at the alien physical technology center at S-4 at the Nevada Test Site. Alien vehicles are being replicated at Kirtland AFB & Sandia Laboratories & these replicas are referred to as ARVs (Alien Reproductive Vehicles). At least three of these vehicles are stored in hangers at Norton AFB, California. It is alleged that vehicle propulsion units were constructed by General Electric & composite materials were provided by Amoco. Alien vehicles generate an artificial gravity field which can be focused & intensified for high speed travel... Alien organisms and biological technology are tested (in the upper levels - Branton) at the underground biogenetic laboratories at Dulce, New Mexico. Alien genetic engineering, cloning, & cryogenic technology have been studied with a view towards 'enhancing' human genetics, deciphering the human genome, & gaining a biological advantage by ARTIFICIAL BIOLOGICAL ENGINEERING. Strange life forms have been bred in these laboratories..."

THE MOJAVE DESERT'S GREATEST SECRETS

Mr. Byron Carpedium, in a 'letter to the Editor' in the 'LEADING EDGE', dated February 18, 1990 presented some remarkable claims which we quote in entirety below:

"Dear Editor... As more and more information is beginning to surface concerning UFOs, super-technology, 'alien' cultures, abductions, multilevel coverups and conspiracies I see many different people trying to assemble data to get, or give, a better picture of what is really happening around us. Individually I do not believe that any ONE of us can gather ALL the facts, assemble them and expose it in a way that is palatable to Joe Citizen. COLLECTIVELY, however, I think that we can make an impact by increasing the total awareness of the entire population. This does not have to happen over a period of 10 or 20 years as would be done in a gradual acclimation program. It can be done in a relatively short period of time, if the proper steps are taken. Once the awareness or awakening process is complete, the individual must then decide whether or not to believe the information and the source of that information. Then the individual MUST act upon it in some form or fashion.

"The latter two steps can be done more efficiently in many ways. One possibility is to take some item or fact that most everyone agrees upon and then impart some new information about it to those interested about it. For example, if anyone saw the John Lear lectures in Houston last year or has seen the video tape, you saw Lear ask three questions at the beginning of the lecture: the third being 'How many of you think that Oswald shot Kennedy?' Naturally only a handful of people raised their hand. By this time Lear has gained the trust of his audience and has most everyone in agreement. Then he does not tell the audience, but instead shows the audience the Zapruder film showing W. Greer shooting the President. After this, convincing the audience of the rest is simple.

"The pieces are coming out now and need to be put together. Bill Cooper has gone several steps beyond Lear by tying things together on a global scale. Recently people with direct access to inside information are now corroborating what other researchers have long suspected.

"Evidence suggesting a secret project to fly 'alien' vehicles in Nevada to Alien/US/Soviet bases and operations on the moon are now some of the hot topics amongst UFOlogists and researchers. These are, for most people, ideas that are so far out that they cannot be believed. One of the reasons, I believe, for this attitude is the fact that VERY few people have ever researched anything having to do with the U.S. OFFICIAL space program, NASA, and it's relationship to the UFO coverup. If researchers, authors, lecturers, etc., would take the time to point out where NASA has suppressed, hidden and simply lied about information dealing with the U.S. space program people may consider these esoteric ideas more believable based on their new knowledge that the U.S. space program is not what it appears to be.

"MOONGATE by William Brian II is a good place to start. After that you can talk to people at NASA. Specifically people connected with the Department of Defense (DOD) missions. Many of these people, if willing to talk, will paint a very different picture of what is happening with OUR space program (remember, it is a civilian operation right??? Well, if you think it is, you had better look again).

"NASA was created on October 1, 1958. The main reason for NASA's creation was to capitalize on the military potential of space. A secondary reason was so that large sums of money may be diverted into 'black' projects which the public was to have no knowledge about. The plan was simple and quite easily accomplished. Money and manufactured items for top-secret or black projects can readily be allocated if they are hidden within our unclassified projects. Contractors and Subcontractors brought in by NASA have no idea where the money goes, what the parts they design and manufacture are really for and they almost never see the end project or result because everything is so compartmentalized at NASA.

"I am still in the process of gathering, verifying, and assembling this information so naturally I am interested in finding others who may be able to support or refute any of my findings. The following list of facts I have learned from several individuals who are working or who have worked or been linked with NASA in some way over the years. For obvious reasons I will not now use their real names. The list below represents some of the information from three people: one is currently working in DOD missions for NASA; another started working with NASA & DOD when JSC (Johnson Space Center) was built. He 'committed suicide' after the Space Shuttle Challenger was destroyed.

"The third is a scientist who has worked at NASA and other facilities. His work with Edward Teller (i.e. the inventor of the H-Bomb and alleged member of MJ-12 - Branton) is what is most known about this man:

"* There are buildings on the Moon.

"* There is mining equipment on the Moon.

"* Photos, NASA photos, do exist which clearly show both of these.

"* Hundreds, but probably thousands, of NASA photos have been tampered with. Specifically, by careful use of an airbrush, flying saucers and other UFOs can be removed, and then the photo is released to the public and/or press.

"* Film taken by astronauts clearly show UFOs, IFOs, Alien Vehicles, etc.

"* The NSA screens all photos before release to the public.

"* Everything that NASA has launched has been closely monitored by at least one 'alien' culture.

"* NASA knew about 'alien' activity on the Moon before Armstrong, Aldrin, and Collins ever set foot on it.

"* Edwin Aldrin at one point found evidence that we were NOT THE FIRST to arrive on the moon. After first seeing and then taking photographs of footprints in the lunar soil he then saw the beings that made the footprints (the report and transcripts of conversations between the astronauts were not clear if Aldrin had physical and/or mental contact with the entities).

"* Analysis of the footprint photos indicated that the beings that made them would have weighed (on Earth) 300-350 lbs. and would stand at least seven feet tall (which supported Aldrin's account).

"* Alien Vehicles flew within 50 feet of a U.S. space vehicle for one full Earth orbit and then the AV departed; again while Aldrin was present.

"* 'Buzz' Aldrin had a nervous breakdown because of these events and the pressure not to talk.

"* During the last successful mission before the Challenger disaster, NASA and the astronauts on board were warned directly by ETs of the impending dangers of space that they would meet (I have more details from multiple sources but still need confirmation on a few details. Do you know anything about this one?) [Note: Certain 'Ham' radio operators have allegedly recorded conversations from 'classified' frequencies between a Space Shuttle astronaut and Mission Control, making reference to an 'Alien Craft' which was following the Shuttle. Whether this story is legitimate or not remains to be seen - Branton].

"* There have been 22 deaths (many 'suicides') at JSC in Houston.

"* The Space Station project is nonexistent. It is a lie and will never be built. In reality the project is called the Space City.

"* No astronaut who has seen AVs or ETs is allowed to talk about it, even amongst themselves. If they do and are caught they may be fined, publicly humiliated, imprisoned, or have all pensions and future salaries taken away.

"* Voyager has been disabled. The pictures received from 'Neptune' in September of 1989 were not from the probe.

"* Galileo has been put out of commission and will not be allowed to complete its mission. The information being received from the probe indicating it's successful function is a deception by the 'aliens.' (Bill Cooper has stated that the Secret Government loaded Galileo with several pounds of plutonium, which 'they' intended to use to ignite the hydrogenic 'atmosphere' of Jupiter and thus create a nuclear reaction which would theoretically convert Jupiter into a small binary 'sun'. These occultists supposedly desired to 'create' this 'miraculous event' and call the new star 'Lucifer', as a SIGN announcing the 'New World Order'. If Cooper's and Carpedium's sources are correct, then NO WONDER an 'alien' race with possible bases on the Jovian moons would DISABLE such a presumptuous undertaking! - Branton).

"* NASA is a joke (i.e. in the words of one of the 'informants'.)..."

THE MOJAVE DESERT'S GREATEST SECRETS

The following submitted article allegedly appeared in 'SOVIET LIFE' magazine under the title; 'AMAZING CLAIM:'

"...A Soviet scientist who defected to the West said photographs taken by an orbiting satellite clearly show the ruined temples of a long-dead civilization - on the planet Mars!

"And LASER PROBES made by the secret Russian satellite revealed that the ruins littering the planet's surface ARE INCREDIBLY YOUNG by space-time standards (i.e. a few thousand years or less, or contemporary to the height of the Egyptian Empire as some researchers suggest!? - Branton).

"The 58-year-old scientist was a high-echelon member of an elite team that has worked together since 1961 when Vostok 1 carried Yuri A. Gagarin as the first man in space.

"But Russia's growing emphasis on the development of a nuclearized 'Star Wars' satellite system in space prompted him to flee Russia. He now lives under an assumed identity somewhere in Switzerland."

The following is from an 'add' introduction for Richard C. Hoagland's book 'THE MONUMENTS OF MARS: A CITY ON THE EDGE OF FOREVER':

"In 1976, NASA sent four Viking spacecraft to Mars, to photograph the planet and to set landers on its surface to test for the presence of life. On July 25, as part of the mapping sequence to select a suitable landing site, one of the orbiters photographed a peculiar-looking mesa resembling a human face a mile long. At the time the facial resemblance was dismissed by NASA as a trick of light and shadow. However, three years later, two computer scientists, Vince DiPietro and Gregory Molenaar, rediscovered the photograph in the National Space Science Data Center.

"Richard C. Hoagland, former Science Advisor to Walter Cronkite and CBS News, consultant for Cable News Network, and Editor of STAR AND SKY, was a member of the NASA press corps on that memorable day in July and is now in the forefront of the Mars investigation. Through careful analysis of a variety of photographs of the Cydonia region (in which the 'face' resides) and consultation with scientists and other professionals, he discovered the presence of other monuments and structures, including what is possibly an underground city in the style of Paolo Soleri's arcologies, plus a series of regular relationships and symmetries among the artifacts.

"In a wide-ranging and profound analysis of the 'Mars data,' Hoagland explains the importance of the 'face' and its implication regarding not only the past but future of the human species. As he himself writes: 'I realized I was looking at something that was either a complete waste of time, or the most important discovery of the twentieth century... There is no middle ground. It either is or is not artificial... If it is, it is imperative that we figure it out because... IT DOES NOT BE-

LONG THERE. Its presence, if it was made by someone, is trying very hard to tell us something extraordinary.'

"Does the 'face' summon us to Mars? Why is it OUR face? Why has NASA denied the existence of the artifact? What are the political implications of a Soviet-U.S. manned mission to Cydonia? Who were the 'Martians?' How does the existence of the 'face' change our entire history?

"The 30 SCIENTISTS, known as the Mars Investigation Group, think two photographs sent back from Mars in 1976 by the Viking space-probe indicate the existence of an ancient civilization, said Richard Hoagland, group member and science writer.

"The photos show what appear to be four huge PYRAMIDS lined up symmetrically with the face about 6 miles away, suggesting a parallel with Stonehenge, the ancient monument of huge stones in England, Hoagland said Thursday.

"'Geometrically, the face could be seen in profile [from the pyramids] as the summer solstice sun rose over it.'

"...Dr. C. West Churchman, a professor at the University of California at Berkeley and the group's principal investigator, said there are too many details pointing to the possibility of an extinct (? - Branton) Martian race.

"'It's hard to believe that all that symmetry could have been done by winds and sand as we know it on Earth,' he said. 'If it had just been the face, I would not have been that convinced. But the fact that these [pyramids] are lined up in a certain way with the face makes me inclined to believe that there was an ancient civilization.'

"The two Viking photographs were taken AT DIFFERENT TIMES of day, reducing the chance that the figures were illusions cast by tricky shadows, Hoagland said.

"The face, 1 mile long and 1 mile wide, appears to be looking toward the stars, he said."

Former Navy Officer William Cooper, mentioned above, claims to have seen top secret documents concerning UFO's and related events (having seen a UFO himself - which was of tremendous size and rose out of the sea in full view of his shipmates) during his involvement with Naval Intelligence. Here is his story:

"...There have been many related sequential coincidences all throughout my life, incidents that by themselves would have led nowhere. Statistically, the odds against the same or a related sequence of events happening to one individual are astronomically high. It is a series of incidents that have convinced me that God has had a hand in my life. I do not believe in fate. I do not believe in accidents...

"We have been taught lies. Reality is not at all what we perceive it to be. We cannot survive any longer by hanging onto the falsehoods of the past. Reality must be discerned at all costs if we are to be a part of the future. Truth must prevail in all instances, no matter who it hurts or helps, if we are to continue to live upon this earth. At this point, what we want may no longer matter. It is what we must do to ensure our survival that counts. The old way is in the certain process of destruction and a New World Order is beating down the door...

"I fear for the little ones, the innocents, who are already paying for our mistakes. There exists a great army of occupationally orphaned children. They are attending government- controlled day-care centers. And latchkey kids are running wild in the streets... and the lopsided, emotionally wounded children of single welfare mothers, born only for the sake of more money on the monthly check. Open your eyes and look at them, for they are the future. In them I see the sure and certain destruction of this once-proud nation. In their vacant eyes I see the death of Freedom. They carry with them a great emptiness—and someone will surely pay a great price for their suffering.

"If we do not act in concert with each other and ensure that the future becomes what we need it to be, then we will surely deserve whatever fate awaits us.

"I believe with all my heart that God put me in places and in positions throughout my life so that I would be able to deliver this warning to His people. I pray that I have been worthy and that I have done my job.

"THIS IS MY CREED - I first believe in God, the same God in which my ancestors believed. I believe in Jesus Christ and that he is my savior. Second, I believe in the Constitution of the Republic of the United States of America, without interpretation, as it was written and meant to work. I have given my sacred oath 'to protect and defend the Constitution of the United States of America against all enemies foreign and domestic.' I intend to fulfill that oath. Third, I believe in the family unit and, in particular, my family unit. I have sworn that I will give my life, if it is required, in defense of God, the Constitution, or my family. Fourth, I believe that any man without principles that he is ready and willing to die for at any given moment is already dead and of no use or consequence whatsoever. - William Cooper., August 3, 1990., Camp Verde, Arizona."

The following document was released by William Cooper to members of various UFO RESEARCH and PATRIOT RESEARCH organizations. The manuscript, which ties together certain aspects of the 'Secret Government' and the 'UFO Phenomena', was titled: THE SECRET GOVERNMENT (The Origin, Identity, and Purpose of MJ-12. May 23, 1989. Updated November 21, 1990):

"...I originally wrote this piece as a research paper. It was first delivered at the MUFON Symposium on July 2, 1989, in Las Vegas, Nevada. Most of this knowledge comes directly from, or as a result of my own research into the TOP SECRET/ MAJIC material WHICH I SAW AND READ between the years 1970 and 1973 as a member of the Intelligence Briefing Team of the Commander in Chief of the Pacific Fleet. Since some of this information was derived from sources that I cannot divulge for obvious reasons, and from published sources which I cannot vouch for...(this) must be termed a hypothesis. I firmly believe that if the aliens are real, THIS IS THE TRUE NATURE OF THE BEAST. It is the only scenario THAT ANSWERS ALL THE QUESTIONS and places the various fundamental mysteries in an arena that makes sense. It is the only explanation which shows the chronology of events and demonstrates that the chronologies, when assembled, match perfectly. The bulk of this I believe to be true if the material that I viewed in the Navy is authentic. As for the rest, I do not know, and that is why this paper must be termed a hypothesis. Most historic and current available evidence supports this hypothesis.

"During the years following World War II the government of the United States was confronted with a series of events which were to change beyond prediction its future and with it the future of humanity. These events were so incredible that they defied belief. A stunned President Truman and his top military commanders found themselves virtually impotent after having just won the most devastating and costly war in history.

"The United States had developed, used, and was the only nation on earth in possession of the atomic bomb. This new weapon had the potential to destroy an enemy, and even the Earth itself. At that time the United States had the best economy, the most advanced technology, the highest standard of living, exerted the most influence, and fielded the largest and most powerful military forces in history. We can only imagine the confusion and concern when the informed elite of the United States Government discovered that an alien spacecraft piloted by 'insect-like' beings from a totally incomprehensible culture had crashed in the desert of New Mexico (Note: Some have alleged that certain of the saurian grays appear 'insect-like'. Other say that there is a SEPARATE race of non-reptilian MANTIS or INSECT-like entities which have been seen working WITH the saurian GRAYS, apparently acting as their equals or overlords. Others sources such as researcher Ray Keller have mentioned another race, a genetic HYBRID race between the Reptilians and Insectoids. This race of alien 'mercenaries' were reportedly created in the Zeta Reticuli system as part of a Gray Empire agenda to obtain new genetic materials for their reptilian queen 'breeders' to assimilate, in order to 'upgrade' their genetic stock. An experimental hybrid Reptilian-Insectoid race which resulted from this genetic manipulation is said to reside en masse in the Bellatrix system of Orion, according to Keller. They are of course an extreme threat to the human race as a whole. The MANTIS like creatures themselves allegedly possess supernatural powers, have the ability to affect the weather, to project their conscious- ness into or 'possess' certain people, and there are some indications that they may have certain 'para-physical' characteristics. According to Kenneth Grant in his book 'OUTSIDE THE CIRCLES OF TIME' — Frederick Miller, Ltd., London. 1980; the O.T.O. [Ordo Templi Orientis] branch of the Illuminati believed that nuclear explosions, like those conducted within the Test Sites of New Mexico and Nevada, could be used to break open an inter- dimensional 'seal' which had been placed between our world and the dimension of an infernal alien race known as 'the Old Ones', a 'race' that had been imprisoned in a dimension called the 'abyss' eons ago. Grant states that Jack Parsons and L. Ron Hubbard assisted in a 1947 Crowleyan magical ritual in California designed to assist this release. - Branton).

"Between January 1947 and December 1952 at least 16 crashed or downed alien craft, 65 bodies, and 1 live alien were recovered. An additional alien craft had exploded and nothing was recovered from that incident. Of these events, 13 occurred within the borders of the United States, not including the craft which disintegrated in the air. Of these 13, 1 was in Arizona, 11 were in New Mexico, and 1 was in Nevada. Sightings of UFOs were so numerous that serious investigation and debunking of each report became impossible, utilizing the existing intelligence assets.

"An alien craft was found on February 13, 1948, on a mesa near Aztec, New Mexico. Another craft was located on March 25, 1948, in White Sands Proving Ground. It was 100 feet in diameter. A total of 17 alien bodies were recovered from those two crafts. Of even greater significance was the discovery of a large number of human body parts stored within both of these vehicles. A demon had reared its head and paranoia quickly took hold of everyone 'in the know.' The Secret lid immediately became a Top Secret lid and was screwed down tight. THE SECURITY BLANKET WAS EVEN TIGHTER THAN THAT IMPOSED UPON THE MANHATTAN PROJECT (which developed and tested the first Atomic Bombs - Branton). In the coming years these events were to become the most closely guarded secrets in the history of the world.

"A special group of America's top scientists were organized under the name Project SIGN in December 1947 to study the phenomena. The whole nasty business was contained. Project SIGN evolved into Project GRUDGE in December 1948. A low- level collection and disinformation project named BLUE BOOK was formed under GRUDGE. Sixteen volumes were to come out of GRUDGE. 'Blue Teams' were put together to recover the crashed disks or live aliens. The Blue Teams were later to evolve into Alpha Teams under Project POUNCE.

"DURING THESE EARLY YEARS THE UNITED STATES AIR FORCE AND THE CENTRAL INTELLIGENCE AGENCY EXERCISED COMPLETE CONTROL OVER THE 'ALIEN SECRET.' In fact, the CIA was formed by Presidential Executive Order first as the Central Intelligence Group for the express purpose of dealing with the alien presence. Later the National Security Act was passed, establishing it as the Central Intelligence Agency.

"The National Security Council was established to oversee the intelligence community and especially the alien endeavor. A series of National Security Council memos and Executive orders removed the CIA from the sole task of gathering foreign intelligence and slowly but thoroughly 'legalized' direct action in the form of covert activities at home and abroad.

"On December 9, 1947, Truman approved issuance of NSC-4, entitled 'Coordination of Foreign Intelligence Information Measures' at the urging of the Secretaries Marshall, Forrestal, Patterson, and the director of the State Department's Policy Planning Staff, George Kennan.

"The FOREIGN AND MILITARY INTELLIGENCE, BOOK 1, 'Final Report of the Select Committee to Study Governmental Operations with Respect to Intelligence Activities,' United States Senate, 94th Congress, 2nd Session, Report No. 94-755, April 26, 1976, p. 49. states: 'This directive empowered the Secretary to coordinate oversees information activities designed to counter communism.'

"A Top Secret annex to NSC-4, NSC-4A, instructed the director of Central Intelligence to undertake covert psychological activities in pursuit of the aims set forth in NSC-4. The initial authority given the CIA for covert operations under NSC-4A did not establish formal procedures for either coordinating or approving these operations. It simply directed the DCI to 'undertake covert actions and to ensure, through liaison with Senate and Defense, that the resulting operations were consistent with American policy.'

"Later NSC-10/1 and NSC-10/2 were to supersede NSC-4 and NSC-4A and expand the covert abilities even further. The Office of Policy Coordination (OPC) was chartered to carry out an expanded program of covert activities. NSC-10/1 and NSC-10/2 validated illegal and extralegal practices and procedures as being agreeable to the national security leadership. The reaction was swift. In the eyes of the intelligence community 'no holds were barred.' Under NSC-10/1 an Executive Coordination Group was established to review, but not approve, covert project proposals. The ECG was secretly tasked to coordinate the alien projects. NSC-10/1 & /2 were interpreted to mean that no one at the top wanted to know about anything until it was over and successful.

"These actions established a buffer between the President and the information. It was intended that this buffer serve as a means for the President to deny knowledge if leaks divulged the true state of affairs. This buffer was used in later years for the purpose of effectively isolating succeeding Presidents from any knowledge of the alien presence OTHER THAN WHAT THE SECRET GOVERNMENT AND THE INTELLIGENCE COMMUNITY WANTED THEM TO KNOW. NSC-10/2 established a study panel which met secretly and was made up of the scientific minds of the day. The study panel was not called MJ-12. Another NSC memo, NSC-10/5 further outlined the duties of the study panel. These NSC memos and secret Executive orders SET THE STAGE FOR THE CREATION OF MJ-12 ONLY FOUR YEARS LATER.

"SECRETARY OF DEFENSE JAMES FORRESTAL OBJECTED TO THE SECRECY. He was a very idealistic and religious man. He believed that the public should be told. James Forrestal was also one of the first known abductees. When he began to talk to leaders of the opposition party and leaders of the Congress about the alien problem he was asked to resign by Truman. He expressed his fears to many people. Rightfully, he believed that he was being watched. This was interpreted by those who were ignorant of the facts as paranoia. Forrestal later was said to have suffered a mental breakdown. He was ordered to the mental ward of Bethesda Naval Hospital. In spite of the fact that THE ADMINISTRATION HAD NO AUTHORITY TO HAVE HIM COMMITTED, the order was carried out. In fact, it was feared that Forrestal would begin to talk again. He had to be isolated and discredited. His family and friends were denied permission to visit. Finally, on May 21, 1949, Forrestal's brother made a fateful decision. HE NOTIFIED AUTHORITIES THAT HE INTENDED TO REMOVE JAMES FROM BETHESDA on May 22. Sometime in the early morning of May 22, 1949, agents of the CIA tied a sheet around James Forrestal's neck, fastened the other end to a fixture in his room, then threw James Forrestal out the window. The sheet tore and he plummeted to his death. James Forrestal's secret diaries were confiscated by the CIA and were kept in the White House for many years. Due to public demand the diaries were eventually rewritten and published in a sanitized version. The real diary information was later furnished by the CIA in book form to an agent who published the material as fiction. THE NAME OF THE AGENT IS WHITLEY STRIEBER and the book is 'MAJESTIC'. James Forrestal became one of the first victims of the coverup.

"The live alien that had been found wandering in the desert from the 1949 Roswell crash was named EBE. The name had been suggested by Dr. Vannevar Bush and was short for Extraterrestrial Biological Entity. EBE HAD A TENDENCY TO LIE, and for over a year would give only the desired answer to questions asked. Those questions which would have resulted in an undesirable answer went unanswered. At one point during the second year of captivity he began to open up. The information derived from EBE was startling, to say the least. This compilation of his revelations became the foundation of what would later be called the 'Yellow Book.' Photographs were taken of EBE which, among others, I was to view years later in Project Grudge. (Note: It has been alleged by many that the EBE's or Grays operate as part of a collective consciousness. Therefore the 'EBE' which gave the so-called 'revelations' must have been speaking for the alien 'collective', which must have had plenty of time to prepare its response to the inquiries of the Intelligence Officials. No doubt, these 'revelations' must have been delivered in such a manner as to FAVOR the cause of the EBE's themselves. - Branton)

"In late 1951 EBE became ill. Medical personnel had been unable to determine the cause of EBE's illness and had no background from which to draw... Several experts were called in to study the illness. These specialists included medical doctors, botanists, and entomologists. A botanist, Dr. Guillermo Mendoza, was brought in to try and help him recover. Dr. Mendoza worked to save EBE until June 2, 1952, when EBE died. Dr. Mendoza became the expert on at least this type of alien biology. The movie E.T. is the thinly disguised story of EBE.

"In a futile attempt to save EBE and to gain favor with this technologically superior race, the United States began broad- casting a call for help early in 1952 into the vast regions of space. The call went unanswered but the project, dubbed SIGMA, continued as an effort of good faith (Note: Apparently in this effort to kiss-up to a more technically advanced race of creatures these government officials forgot EBE's infernal 'TENDENCY TO LIE', and instead continued to believe what they WANTED to believe... that this was a sure may to satisfy their insatiable appetite for super technology, and that these creatures were benevolent - in spite of the fact that human body parts were found on board at least two of their craft. In our opinion these officials deserve whatever harmful actions may have been taken against them by the grays, as in the case of the 'betrayal' when the grays suddenly turned on our government and took control of the so-called 'joint operations' underground bases. The government was so blinded by their own lust for the personal power and profit which the aliens promised them, that they fell for the alien 'Trojan Horse' hook, line and sinker. As for the 'EBE' that Cooper describes, It is not certain whether this particular alien was one of the mantis-like 'Insectoids' or one of the gray 'Reptilians'. However the movie 'CLOSE ENCOUNTERS OF THE THIRD KIND,' which whitewashed the actual malevolent nature of the aliens to an incredible degree, depicted BOTH the small saurian 'gray' type beings AND the long- armed 'mantis' like creatures as working together. As we've said, it seems that the desire of the secret government to obtain occult- technology from these particular 'aliens' for entirely selfish purposes was one of their main motivations for establishing a WORKING contact with the saurian grays instead of with the more benevolent though protective human-alien races; even if it meant — as we shall soon see — the sellout of their fellow humans beings to obtain this. This 'forbidden fruit' of super- technology would apparently allow the recipients of the same to live like 'gods' over the rest of humanity - Branton).

"President Truman created the supersecret National Security Agency (NSA) by secret Executive order on November 4, 1952. Its primary purpose was to decipher the alien communications, language, and establish a dialogue with the extraterrestrials. The most urgent task was a continuation of the earlier effort. The secondary purpose of the NSA was to monitor all communications and emissions from any and all electronic devices worldwide for the purpose of gathering intelligence, both human and alien, AND TO CONTAIN THE SECRET OF THE ALIEN PRESENCE. Project SIGMA was successful.

"The NSA also MAINTAINS COMMUNICATIONS WITH THE LUNA BASE AND OTHER SECRET SPACE PROGRAMS.

"By executive order of the President, the NSA is exempt from all laws which do not specifically name the NSA in the text of the law as being subject to that law. That means that if the agency is not spelled out in the text on any and every law passed by the Congress it is not subject to that or those laws. The NSA now performs many other duties and in fact is the premier agency within the intelligence network. Today the NSA receives approximately 75 per cent of the monies allotted to the intelligence community. The old saying 'where the money goes therein the power resides' is true. The DCI today is a figurehead maintained as a public ruse. The primary task of the NSA is still alien communications, but now includes other extraterrestrial projects as well.

"President Truman had been keeping our allies, including the Soviet Union, informed of the developing alien problem. THIS HAD BEEN DONE IN CASE THE ALIENS TURNED OUT TO BE A THREAT TO THE HUMAN RACE (Note: Could this in part explain the sudden and unexpected 'fall' of the Soviet Union and 'Communism'? Although Communism still resides to a large extent in Red China and elsewhere, it's power has been greatly diminished in the Bolshevik states. The resulting international cooperation may be a two-edged sword, being either good or bad depending how it is proceeds. For instance a global system might involve INDUSTRIAL cooperation which could strengthen the planet against an alien threat on the one hand while still allowing nations to retain their political independence and cultural diversities; or on the other hand it could involve POLITICAL cooperation which may very well lead to a global consolidation of power and absolute dictatorial control of the world by one person or small group of persons, which would be devastating not only to individual liberties but also to the 'cultural diversities' which add variety to the human race. All nations might be pressured to give up their uniqueness in order to 'conform' to the one-world political 'beast', much as the Nazi S.S. attempted to make all Germans homogenized clones of themselves by forcing them to fall in line with the thinking, dress and behavior of the Nazi Party itself - Branton).

"PLANS WERE FORMULATED TO DEFEND THE EARTH IN CASE OF INVASION. Great difficulty was encountered in maintaining international secrecy. It was decided that an outside group was necessary to coordinate and control international efforts in order to hide the secret from the normal scrutiny of governments by the press. The result was the formation of a secret ruling body which became known as the Bilderberger Group. The group was formed and met for the first time in 1952. They were named after the first publicly known meeting place, the Bilderberg Hotel. That public meeting took place in 1954. They were nicknamed the Bilderbergers. The headquarters of this group is Geneva, Switzerland. The Bilderbergers evolved into a secret world government that now controls everything. The United Nations was then, and is now, an international joke (one might say that the Bilderbergers-Illuminati control the U.N. behind the scenes - Branton).

"Beginning in 1953 a new president occupied the White House. He was a man used to a structured staff organization with a chain of command. His method was to delegate authority and rule by committee. He made his decisions, but only when his advisors were unable to come up with a consensus. His normal method was to read through or listen to several alternatives and then approve one. Those who worked closely with him have stated that his favorite comment was, 'Just do whatever it takes.' He spent a lot of time on the golf course. This was not unusual for a man who had been career Army with the ultimate position of Supreme Allied Commander during the war, a post which had earned him five stars. The President was General of the Army Dwight David Eisenhower.

"During his first year in office, 1953, at least 10 more crashed discs were recovered along with 26 dead and 4 live aliens. Of the 10, 4 were found in Arizona, 2 in Texas, 1 in New Mexico, 1 in Louisiana, 1 in Montana, and 1 in South Africa. There were hundreds of sightings.

"Eisenhower knew that he had to wrestle and beat the alien problem. He knew that he could not do it by revealing the secret to Congress. Early in 1953 the new President turned to his friend and fellow member of the Council on Foreign Relations Nelson Rockefeller. EISENHOWER AND ROCKEFELLER BEGAN PLANNING THE SECRET STRUCTURE OF THE ALIEN- TASK SUPERVISION, which became a reality within one year. The idea for MJ-12 was thus born.

"It was Nelson's uncle Winthrop Aldrich who had been crucial in convincing Eisenhower to run for President. The whole Rockefeller family and with them, the Rockefeller empire, had solidly backed Ike. Eisenhower belonged heart and soul to the Council on Foreign Relations and the Rockefeller family. ASKING ROCKEFELLER FOR HELP WITH THE ALIEN PROBLEM WAS TO BE THE BIGGEST MISTAKE EISENHOWER EVER MADE FOR THE FUTURE OF THE UNITED STATES AND MAYBE FOR HUMANITY.

"Within a week of Eisenhower's election he had appointed Nelson Rockefeller chairman of a Presidential Advisory Committee on Government Organization. Rockefeller was responsible for planning the reorganization of government, something he had dreamed of for many years. New Deal programs went into one single cabinet position called the Department of Health, Education and Welfare. When the Congress approved the new Cabinet position in April 1953, Nelson was named to the post of Under- secretary to Oveta Culp Hobby.

"In 1953 astronomers discovered large objects in space which were tracked moving toward the Earth. It was first believed that they were asteroids. Later evidence proved that the objects could only be spaceships. Project SIGMA intercepted alien radio communications. When the objects reached the Earth they took up very high geosynchronous orbit(s) around the equator. There were several huge ships, and their actual intent was unknown. Project SIGMA and a new project, PLATO, through radio communications using the computer binary language, were able to arrange a landing that resulted in face-to-face contact with alien beings from another planet. The landing took place in the desert. The movie, 'CLOSE ENCOUNTERS OF THE THIRD KIND' is a fictionalized version of the actual event. Project PLATO was tasked with establishing diplomatic relations with this race of space aliens. A hostage was left with us as a pledge that they would return and formalize a treaty."

Note: The MELBOURNE SUN (Melbourne, Victoria, Australia), August 25, 1954 ISSUE, carried an article titled "THE NEW SATELLITES", which stated: "TWO meteors (asteroids?) had become satellites of the earth AND WERE REVOLVING WITH IT 400 to 600 miles out in space, the latest issue of the American Magazine 'AVIATION WEEK' said yesterday. The magazine said that the discovery of the satellites threw the air force into confusion this summer. Alarm over the sightings ended only after they had been identified as natural rather than man-made."

Another possibility may be that they were both 'engineered' natural objects such as hollowed-out asteroids taken from the asteroid belt, since it is unlikely that an alien race would attempt to move such objects between solar systems. The SIMULTANEOUS arrival of two or more large asteroids, combined with the fact that both took up a geosynchronous orbit (synchronized with the revolution of the earth in that they were positioned over a particular geographical area — orbiting with the rotation of the earth itself), would be an incredible coincidence indeed. In fact, the odds of even one extraterrestrial object not under intelligent control taking up a GEOSYNCHRONOUS orbit around the earth would be incredible in itself.

"In the meantime," Cooper continues, "a race of humanoid (Nordic-Blond? - Branton) aliens landed at Homestead Air Force Base in Florida and successfully communicated with the U.S. government. THIS GROUP WARNED US AGAINST THE RACE ORBITING THE EQUATOR AND OFFERED TO HELP US WITH OUR SPIRITUAL DEVELOPMENT. THEY DEMANDED THAT WE DISMANTLE AND DESTROY OUR NUCLEAR WEAPONS AS THE MAJOR CONDITION. THEY REFUSED TO EXCHANGE TECHNOLOGY CITING THAT WE WERE SPIRITUALLY UNABLE TO HANDLE THE TECHNOLOGY WE ALREADY POSSESSED. THESE OVERTURES WERE REJECTED on the grounds that it would be foolish to disarm in the face of such an uncertain future. There was no track record to read from. IT MAY HAVE BEEN AN UNFORTUNATE DECISION.

"A third landing at Muroc, now Edwards Air Force Base, took place in 1954. The base was closed for three days and no one was allowed to enter or leave during that time. The historical event had been planned in advance. Details of a treaty had been agreed upon. Eisenhower arranged to be in Palm Springs on vacation. On the appointed day the President was spirited to the base. The excuse was given to the press that he was visiting a dentist. Witnesses to the event have stated that three UFOs flew over the base and then landed. Antiaircraft batteries were undergoing live-fire training and the startled personnel actually fired at the crafts as they passed overhead... the shells missed and no one was injured (Note: These three craft were apparently from the orbiting 'gray' carriers that the 'humanoids' warned the government about. This 'meeting' apparently resulted in one of the major 'U.S. government - Gray' treaties. The fact that the startled gunners failed to destroy the alien ships may have been unfortunate, ironically, as such an event might have led to an abort of the so- called 'treaty' deals with the grays - Branton).

"President Eisenhower met with the aliens on February 20, 1954, and a formal treaty between the alien nation and the United States of America was signed. We then received our first alien ambassador from outer space. He was the hostage that had been left at the first landing in the desert. His name was 'His Omnipotent Highness Crilll or Krilll,' pronounced Crill or Krill. In the American tradition of disdain for royal titles he was secretly called 'ORIGINAL HOSTAGE CRILL, OR KRILL.' Shortly after this meeting President Eisenhower suffered a heart attack (the judgement of God? Incidentally, this egomaniacal 'alien' was also referred to as O.H. Krill, for short - Branton).

"Four others present at the meeting were Franklin Allen of the HEARST NEWSPAPERS, Edwin Nourse of BROOKINGS INSTITUTE (the Brookings Institute later became involved with the Montauk Project - Branton), Gerald Light of METAPHYSICAL RESEARCH fame, and CATHOLIC BISHOP MacIntyre of Los Angeles. Their reaction was judged as a microcosm of what the public reaction might be. Based on this reaction, it was decided that the public could not be told. Later studies confirmed the decision as sound.

"An emotionally revealing letter written by Gerald Light spells out in chilling detail: 'My dear friends: I have just returned from Muroc. The report is true — devastatingly true! I made the journey in company with Franklin Allen of the Hearst papers and Edwin Nourse of Brookings Institute (Truman's erstwhile financial advisor) and Bishop MacIntyre of L.A. (confidential names for the present, please). When we were allowed to enter the restricted section (after about six hours in which we were checked on every possible item, event, incident and aspect of our personal and public lives), I HAD THE DISTINCT FEELING THAT THE WORLD HAD COME TO AN END WITH FANTASTIC REALISM. FOR I HAVE NEVER SEEN SO MANY HUMAN BEINGS IN A STATE OF COMPLETE COLLAPSE AND CONFUSION, AS THEY REALIZED THAT THEIR OWN WORLD HAD INDEED ENDED WITH SUCH FINALITY AS TO BEGGAR DESCRIPTION. THE REALITY OF 'OTHER-PLANE' AEROFORMS IS NOW AND FOREVER REMOVED FROM THE REALMS OF SPECU-

LATION AND MADE A RATHER PAINFUL PART OF THE CONSCIOUSNESS OF EVERY RESPONSIBLE SCIENTIFIC AND POLITICAL GROUP. During my two days' visit I saw five separate and distinct types of aircraft being studied and handled by our Air Force officials — with the assistance and permission of the Etherians!

"'I have no words to express my reactions. It has finally happened. It is now a matter of history. President Eisenhower, as you may already know, was spirited over to Muroc one night during his visit to Palm Springs recently. And it is my conviction that he will ignore the terrific conflict between the various 'authorities' and go directly to the people via radio and television — if the impasse continues much longer. FROM WHAT I COULD GATHER, AN OFFICIAL STATEMENT TO THE COUNTRY IS BEING PREPARED FOR DELIVERY ABOUT THE MIDDLE OF MAY.'

"We know that no such announcement was ever made. The silence-control group won that day. We also know that two more ships, for which we can find no witnesses, either landed sometime after the three or were already at the base before the three landed. Gerald Light specifically states that five ships were present and were undergoing study by the Air Force. HIS METAPHYSICAL EXPERIENCE IS EVIDENT IN THAT HE CALLS THE ENTITIES 'ETHERIANS.' Gerald Light capitalized 'Etherians,' calling attention to the fact that these beings might have been viewed as gods by Mr. Light.

"The alien emblem was known as the 'Trilateral Insignia' and was displayed on the craft and worn on the alien uniforms. Both of those landings and the second meeting were filmed. These films exist today.

"The treaty stated that the aliens would not interfere in our affairs and we would not interfere in theirs. WE WOULD KEEP THEIR PRESENCE ON EARTH A SECRET. They would furnish us with advanced technology and would help us in our technological development. They would not make any treaty with any other Earth nation. THEY COULD ABDUCT HUMANS ON A LIMITED AND PERIODIC BASIS FOR THE PURPOSE OF MEDICAL EXAMINATION AND MONITORING OF OUR DEVELOPMENT, WITH THE STIPULATION THAT THE HUMANS WOULD NOT BE HARMED, WOULD BE RETURNED TO THEIR POINT OF ABDUCTION, AND WOULD HAVE NO MEMORY OF THE EVENT, AND THAT THE ALIEN NATION WOULD FURNISH MAJESTY TWELVE WITH A LIST OF ALL HUMAN CONTACTS AND ABDUCTEES ON A REGULARLY SCHEDULED BASIS.

"It was agreed that each nation would receive the ambassador of the other for as long as the treaty remained in force. It was further agreed that the alien nation and the United States would exchange 16 personnel with the purpose of learning of each other. The alien 'guests' would remain on earth. THE HUMAN 'GUESTS' WOULD TRAVEL TO THE ALIEN POINT OF ORIGIN FOR A SPECIFIED PERIOD OF TIME, then return, at which point a reverse exchange would be made. A reenactment of this event was dramatized in the movie 'CLOSE ENCOUNTERS

OF THE THIRD KIND.' A tip-off to who works for whom can be determined BY THE FACT THAT DR. J. ALLEN HYNEK SERVED AS THE TECHNICAL ADVISOR FOR THE FILM. I noticed that the Top Secret report containing the official version of the truth of the alien question, entitled project GRUDGE, which I read while in the Navy, was coauthored by LT. COL. FRIEND and DR. J. ALLEN HYNEK, WHO WAS CITED AS A CIA ASSET attached to Project GRUDGE — Dr. Hynek, the one who debunked many legitimate UFO incidents when he functioned as the scientific member of the very public Project BLUEBOOK. Dr. Hynek is the man responsible for the infamous 'it was only swamp gas' statement.

"It was agreed that bases would be constructed underground for the use of the alien nation and that TWO BASES would be constructed for the joint use of the alien nation and the United States Government. Exchange of technology would take place in the jointly occupied bases. THESE ALIEN BASES WOULD BE CONSTRUCTED UNDER INDIAN RESERVATIONS IN THE FOUR CORNERS AREA OF UTAH, COLORADO, NEW MEXICO AND ARIZONA, and one would be constructed in an area known as Dreamland (Note: Many sources allege that the reason the 'aliens' insisted on these underground bases beneath these particular areas was that 'they' in fact do not hail EXCLUSIVELY from other planetary bodies, but that they are originally from earth and have for centuries occupied deep cavern levels beneath the planet, and more recently beneath these areas of the southwestern U.S. The 'bases' then, which most in the government might believe are of exclusively human construction for use in 'joint' operations, would actually be 'covers' or 'fronts' for actual subterrean systems largely under the control of this saurian race. This would explain why many human workers in these 'joint' bases have been kept highly compartmentalized; why many do not realize what's taking place in the LOWER levels or even how many lower levels exist; why the 'security' increases enormously the deeper one descends into these underground bases; and why the human influence decreases and the saurian-reptilian-gray influence increases the deeper one descends into these underground networks - Branton).

"Dreamland was built in the MOJAVE desert near, or in, a place called Yucca. I cannot remember if it was Yucca Valley, Yucca Flat, or Yucca Proving Ground, but Yucca Valley is what I always seem to want to say. MORE UFO SIGHTINGS AND INCIDENTS OCCUR IN THE MOJAVE DESERT OF CALIFORNIA THAN ANY OTHER PLACE IN THE WORLD. So many, in fact, that no one even bothers to make reports. Anyone who ventures into the desert to talk to the residents will be astounded by the frequency of activity and with the degree of acceptance demonstrated by those who have come to regard UFOs as normal.

"All alien areas are under complete control of the Naval Department (although some may argue that they are only in control of the UPPERMOST levels of these 'bases' - Branton), according to the documents I read. All personnel who work in these complexes receive their checks from the Navy through a subcontractor. The checks never make reference to the government or the Navy. Construction of the bases began immediately, but progress was slow. LARGE AMOUNTS OF MONEY WERE MADE AVAILABLE IN 1957. Work continued on the Yellow Book.

"Project REDLIGHT was formed and experiments in test-flying alien craft was begun in earnest. A super-Top Secret facility was built at Groom Lake in Nevada in the midst of the weapons test range. It was code-named Area 51. The installation was placed under the Department of the Navy and all personnel required a 'Q' clearance as well as Executive (Presidential, called MAJESTIC) approval. This was ironic, due to the fact that the President of the United States does not have clearance to visit the site. The alien base and exchange of technology actually took place in an area code-named Dreamland above ground, and the UNDERGROUND portion was dubbed 'the Dark Side of the Moon.' ACCORDING TO THE DOCUMENTATION I READ, AT LEAST 600 ALIEN BEINGS ACTUALLY RESIDE FULL TIME AT THIS SITE ALONG WITH AN UNKNOWN NUMBER OF SCIENTISTS AND CIA PERSONNEL. DUE TO THE FEAR OF IMPLANTATION, ONLY CERTAIN PEOPLE WERE ALLOWED TO INTERFACE WITH THE ALIEN BEINGS, AND THOSE PERSONNEL WERE AND ARE WATCHED AND MONITORED CONTINUOUSLY.

"The Army was tasked to form a supersecret organization to furnish security for the alien-tasked projects. THIS ORGANIZATION BECAME THE NATIONAL RECONNAISSANCE ORGANIZATION BASED AT FORT CARSON, COLORADO. (Note: a new multimillion dollar N.R.O. facility, approximately a quarter of the size of the Pentagon itself, has also been constructed in northern Virginia - Branton) THE SPECIFIC TEAMS TRAINED TO SECURE THE PROJECTS WERE CALLED DELTA. LT. COL. JAMES 'BO' GRITZ WAS A DELTA FORCE COMMANDER.

"A second project code-named SNOWBIRD was promulgated to explain away any sightings of the REDLIGHT crafts as being Air Force experiments. The SNOWBIRD crafts were manufactured using conventional technology and were flown for the press on several occasions. Project SNOWBIRD was also used to debunk legitimate public sightings of alien craft (UFOs to the public, IACs - Identified Alien Craft - to those in the know). Project SNOWBIRD was very successful, and reports from the public declined steadily until recent years.

"A multimillion-dollar Secret fund was organized and kept by the Military Office of the White House. THIS FUND WAS USED TO BUILD OVER 75 DEEP UNDERGROUND FACILITIES. Presidents who asked were told the fund was used to build deep underground shelters for the President in case of war. Only a few were built for the President. Millions of dollars were funneled through the office of Majesty Twelve and then out to the contractors. It was used to build Top Secret alien bases as well as Top Secret DUMB (Deep Underground Military Bases) AND THE FACULTIES PROMULGATED BY ALTERNATIVE 2 THROUGHOUT THE NATION.

President Johnson used this fund to build a movie theater and pave the road on his ranch. He had no idea of it's true purpose.

"The secret White House underground-construction fund was set up in 1957 by President Eisenhower. The funding was obtained from Congress under the guise of 'construction and maintenance of secret sites where the President could be taken in case of military attack: Presidential Emergency Sites.' The sites are literally holes in the ground, deep enough to withstand a nuclear blast, and are outfitted with state-of-the-art communi- cations equipment. To date there are more than 75 sites spread around the country which were built using money from this fund. The Atomic Energy Commission has built at least 22 underground sites...

"Nelson Rockefeller was also given a second important job as the head of the secret unit called the Planning Coordination Group, which was formed under NSC 5412/1 in March 1955. The group consisted of different ad hoc members, depending on the subject of the agenda. The basic members were Rockefeller, a representative of the Department of Defense, a representative of the Department of State, and the Director of Central Intelligence. It was soon called the 5412 Committee or the Special Group. NSC 5412/1 established the rule that covert operations were subject to approval by an executive committee, whereas in the past these operations were initiated solely on the authority of the Director of Central Intelligence.

"By secret Executive Memorandum NSC 5510, Eisenhower had preceded NSC 5412/1 to establish a permanent committee (not ad hoc) to be known as Majesty Twelve (MJ-12) TO OVERSEE AND CONDUCT ALL COVERT ACTIVITIES CONCERNED WITH THE ALIEN QUESTION. NSC 5412/1 was created to explain the purpose of these meetings when Congress and the press became curious.

"MAJESTY TWELVE was made up of NELSON ROCKEFELLER, Director of Central Intelligence ALLEN WELSH DULLES (former President of the Council on Foreign Relations - Branton), Secretary of State John Foster Dulles, Secretary of Defense Charles E. Wilson, Chairman of the Joint Chiefs of Staff ADMIRAL ARTHUR W. RADFORD, Director of the Federal Bureau of Investigation J. EDGAR HOOVER, six men from the executive committee of the COUNCIL ON FOREIGN RELATIONS known as the 'Wise Men,' six members from the EXECUTIVE COMMITTEE of the JASON Group, and DR. EDWARD TELLER.

"The JASON Group is a secret scientific group formed during the Manhattan Project and administered by the Mitre Corporation. THE INNER CORE OF THE COUNCIL ON FOREIGN RELATIONS RECRUITS ITS MEMBERS FROM THE SKULL & BONES AND THE SCROLL & KEY SOCIETIES OF HARVARD AND YALE. The Wise Men are key members of the Council on Foreign Relations and also members of the ORDER OF THE QUEST known as the JASON Society.

"THERE WERE 19 MEMBERS OF MAJESTY TWELVE. THE FIRST RULE OF

MAJESTY TWELVE WAS THAT NO ORDER COULD BE GIVEN AND NO ACTION COULD BE TAKEN WITHOUT A MAJORITY VOTE OF TWELVE IN FAVOR, THUS MAJORITY TWELVE. Orders issued by Majesty Twelve became known as Majority Twelve directives.

"This group was made up over the years of the top officers and directors of the Council on Foreign Relations and later the Trilateral Commission. GORDON DEAN, GEORGE BUSH and ZBIGNIEW BRZEZINSKI were among them. The most important and influential of the Wise Men were JOHN MCCLOY, ROBERT LOVETT, AVERELL HARRIMAN, CHARLES BOHLEN, GEORGE KENNAN, and DEAN ACHESON. Their policies were to last well into the decade of the '70's. IT IS SIGNIFICANT THAT PRESIDENT EISENHOWER AS WELL AS THE FIRST SIX MAJESTY TWELVE MEMBERS FROM THE GOVERNMENT WERE ALSO MEMBERS OF THE COUNCIL ON FOREIGN RELATIONS. THIS GAVE CONTROL OF THE MOST SECRET AND POWERFUL GROUP IN GOVERNMENT TO A SPECIAL- INTEREST CLUB THAT WAS ITSELF CONTROLLED BY THE ILLUMINATI.

"Thorough researchers will soon discover that not all of the Wise Men attended Harvard or Yale and not all of them were chosen for Skull & Bones or Scroll & Key membership during their college years. You will be able to quickly clear up the mystery by obtaining the book 'THE WISE MEN' by Walter Isaacson and Evan Thomas., Simon and Schuster., New York. Under illustration #9 in the center of the book you will find the caption: 'Lovett with the Yale Unit, above far right, and on the beach: His initiation into Skull & Bones came at an air base near Dunkirk.' I have found that members were chosen on an ongoing basis by invitation based upon merit post-college and were not confined to Harvard and Yale attendees only. Because of this fact, a complete list of Skull & Bones members can never be compiled from the catalogues or addresses of the college segment of the Russell Trust, also known as the Brotherhood of Death, or the Skull & Bones. Now you know why it has been impossible to pinpoint the membership either by number or by name. I believe that the answer lies hidden in the CFR files, if files exist.

"A chosen few were later initiated into the secret branch of the Order of the Quest known as the JASON Society. They are all members of the Council on Foreign Relations and at that time were known as THE EASTERN ESTABLISHMENT. This should give you a clue to the far-reaching and serious nature of these most secret college societies. The society is alive and well today, but now includes MEMBERS OF THE TRILATERAL COMMISSION as well. The Trilaterals existed secretly BEFORE 1973. THE NAME OF THE TRILATERAL COMMISSION WAS TAKEN FROM THE ALIEN FLAG KNOWN AS THE TRILATERAL INSIGNIA. Majesty Twelve was to survive right up to the present day. Under Eisenhower and Kennedy it was erroneously called the 5412 Committee, or more correctly, the Special Group. In the Johnson administration it became the 303 Committee because the name '5412' had been compromised in the book 'THE SECRET GOVERNMENT.' Actually, NSC

5412/1 was leaked to the author to hide the existence of NSC 5410. Under Nixon, Ford, and Carter it was called the 40 Committee, and under Reagan it became known as the PI-40 Committee. Over all those years ONLY THE NAME CHANGED.

"BY 1955 IT BECAME OBVIOUS THAT THE ALIENS HAD DECEIVED EISENHOWER AND HAD BROKEN THE TREATY. MUTILATED HUMANS WERE BEING FOUND ALONG WITH MUTILATED ANIMALS ACROSS THE UNITED STATES. IT WAS SUSPECTED THAT THE ALIENS WERE NOT SUBMITTING A COMPLETE LIST OF HUMAN CONTACTS AND ABDUCTEES TO MAJESTY TWELVE AND IT WAS SUSPECTED THAT NOT ALL ABDUCTEES HAD BEEN RETURNED. The Soviet Union was suspected of interacting with them, an this proved to be true. THE ALIENS STATED THAT THEY HAD BEEN, AND WERE THEN, MANIPULATING MASSES OF PEOPLE THROUGH SECRET SOCIETIES, WITCHCRAFT, MAGIC, THE OCCULT, AND RELIGION. You must understand that this claim could also be a manipulation. AFTER SEVERAL AIR FORCE COMBAT AIR ENGAGEMENTS WITH ALIEN CRAFT it became apparent that our weapons were no match against them.

"In November 1955 NSC-5412/2 was issued establishing a study committee to explore 'all factors which are involved in the making and implementing of foreign policy in the nuclear age.' This was only a blanket of snow that covered the real subject of study, the alien question.

"By secret Executive Memorandum NSC 5511 in 1954, President Eisenhower had commissioned the study group to 'EXAMINE ALL THE FACTS, EVIDENCE, LIES, AND DECEPTION AND DISCOVER THE TRUTH OF THE ALIEN QUESTION.' NSC 5412/2 was only a cover that had become necessary when the press began inquiring as to the purpose of regular meetings of such important men. The first meetings began in 1954 and were called the Quantico meetings because they met at the Quantico Marine Base. The study group was made up solely of 35 members of the Council on Foreign Relations' secret study group. Dr. Edward Teller was invited to participate. Dr. Zbigniew Brzezinski was the study director for the first 18 months. Dr. Henry Kissinger was chosen as the group's study director for the second 18 months beginning in November 1955. Nelson Rockefeller was a frequent visitor during the study. (Note: as for Dr. Edward Teller, John Lear in his original 'Press Release' stated in reference to Dr. Teller's work with the 'Star Wars' or SDI Defense program: "...As these words are being written (June, 1988), Dr. Edward Teller, 'father' of the H-Bomb is personally in the test tunnels of the Nevada Test Site, driving his workers and associates in the words of one, 'like a man possessed'." - Branton)

"THE STUDY GROUP MEMBERS - Gordon Dean, Chairman; Dr. Henry Kissinger, Study Director; Dr. Zbigniew Brzezinski, Study Director; Dr. Edward Teller; Maj. Gen. Richard C. Lindsay; Hanson W. Baldwin; Lloyd V. Berkner; Frank C. Nash; Paul H. Nitze; Charles P. Noyes; Frank Pace Jr.; James A. Perkins; Don K.

Price; David Rockefeller; Oscar M. Ruebhausen; Lt. Gen. James M. Gavin; Caryl P. Haskins; James T. Hill, Jr.; Joseph E. Johnson; Mervin J. Kelly; Frank Altschul; Hamilton Fish Armstrong; Maj. Gen. James McCormack, Jr.; Robert R. Bowie; McGeorge Bundy; William A. M. Burden; John C. Campbell; Thomas K. Finletter; George S. Franklin, Jr.; I.I. Rabi; Roswell L. Gilpatric; N.E. Halaby; Gen. Walter Bedell Smith; Henry DeWolf Smyth; Shields Warren; Carroll L. Wilson; Arnold Wolfers.

"The second-phase meetings were also held at the Marine base at Quantico, Virginia, and the group became known as Quantico II. Nelson Rockefeller built a retreat somewhere in Maryland for Majesty Twelve and the study committee. It could be reached only by air. In this manner they could meet away from public scrutiny. This secret meeting place is known by the code name 'the Country Club.' Complete living, eating, recreation, library, and meeting facilities exist at the location (The Aspen Institute is not the Country Club).

"The study group was publicly terminated in the later months on 1956. Henry Kissinger wrote what was officially termed the results of 1957 as 'NUCLEAR WEAPONS AND FOREIGN POLICY,' published for the Council on Foreign Relations by Harper & Brothers, New York. IN TRUTH, THE MANUSCRIPT HAD ALREADY BEEN 80% WRITTEN WHILE KISSINGER WAS AT HARVARD. THE STUDY GROUP CONTINUED, VEILED IN SECRECY. A clue to the seriousness Kissinger attached to the study can be found in statements by his wife and friends. Many of them stated that Henry would leave home early each morning and return late each night without speaking to anyone or responding to anyone. It seemed as if he were in another world which held no room for outsiders.

"These statements are very revealing. The revelations of the alien presence and actions during the study must have been a great shock. Henry Kissinger was definitely out of character during this time. He would never again be affected in this manner, no matter the seriousness of any subsequent event. On many occasions he would work very late into the night after having put in a full day. This behavior eventually led to divorce.

"A major finding of the alien study WAS THAT THE PUBLIC COULD NOT BE TOLD. IT WAS BELIEVED THAT THIS WOULD MOST CERTAINLY LEAD TO ECONOMIC COLLAPSE, COLLAPSE OF THE RELIGIOUS STRUCTURE, AND NATIONAL PANIC, WHICH COULD LEAD TO ANARCHY (Note: This was no doubt based largely on the assumption that the existence of these 'aliens' could not be explained in terms of traditional Judeo- Christian religion, which conclusion might have been reached by many, especially in the face of the saurian grays' persistent attempts to hide their true reptilian nature as it relates to ancient Biblical history and prophecy. However, based on what we have already covered in this file, it is evident that such alien activity does in fact conform to Christian revelation and theology and was in fact prophesied in scriptural writings — the TORAH for instance — thousands of years ago. The real 'ignorance' would merely be an inability to properly interpret these ancient prophecies due to a lack of the foundational knowledge that is necessary to make such correct interpretations. Therefore such knowledge, if presented properly, would probably NOT bring about a collapse in the 'religious' world. Also, faith in the existence of an Almighty Creator-God of infinite power would likely deter the 'panic' and resulting economic collapse or anarchy which the 'Study Group' feared. It would be the hopeless non "religious" or "atheistic- humanist" segment of the population, who can put faith in non other than themselves, who would probably react most negatively to a potential invasion by a malevolent force outside this world. - Branton).

"Secrecy thus continued. An offshoot of this finding was that if the public could not be told, Congress could not be told. Funding for the projects and research would have to come from outside the Government. In the meantime money was to be obtained from the military budget and from CIA confidential, non- appropriated funds.

"ANOTHER MAJOR FINDING WAS THAT THE ALIENS WERE USING HUMANS AND ANIMALS FOR A SOURCE OF GLANDULAR SECRETIONS, ENZYMES, HORMONAL SECRETIONS, BLOOD PLASMA AND POSSIBLY IN GENETIC EXPERIMENTS. The aliens explained these actions as necessary to their survival. They stated that their genetic structure had deteriorated and that they were no longer able to reproduce. They stated that if they were unable to improve their genetic structure, their race would soon cease to exist. WE LOOKED UPON THEIR EXPLANATIONS WITH SUSPICION (Note: According to sources which we will quote later on, the actual purposes of the mutilations are far different from what these alien creatures allege them to be. Some groups connected to MJ-12 however seem to have fallen for this propaganda. For instance the top secret 'Yellow Fruit' unit working in Nevada has been, or at least were at one point, convinced that the 'grays' were incapable of reproducing themselves here on earth. In spite of 'their' allegations that the Grays or EBE's cannot reproduce, certain witnesses have alleged that the saurian grays are actually reproducing PROFUSELY within DEEP underground levels utilizing solar-heat 'egg' hatcheries, polyembryony tanks, cloning, etc. Also the body fluids, according to other sources, are not used exclusively for 'improving their genetic structure' but as sustenance or 'food' for the saurian grays, and possibly their 'Repton' superiors as well. Their claims to the contrary, as well as other allegations, should be studied in the light of their previous known "TENDENCIES TO LIE" - Branton).

"Since our weapons were literally useless against the aliens, Majesty Twelve decided to continue friendly diplomatic relations UNTIL SUCH A TIME AS WE WERE ABLE TO DEVELOP A TECHNOLOGY WHICH WOULD ENABLE US TO CHALLENGE THEM ON A MILITARY BASES. Overtures would have to be made to the

Soviet Union and other nations to join forces for the survival of humanity. In the meantime PLANS WERE DEVELOPED TO RESEARCH AND CONSTRUCT TWO WEAPONS SYSTEMS USING CONVENTIONAL AND NUCLEAR TECHNOLOGY, WHICH WOULD HOPEFULLY BRING US TO PARITY.

"The results of the research were Projects JOSHUA and EXCALIBUR. JOSHUA was a weapon captured from the Germans which was capable of shattering 4-inch-thick armor plate at a range of two miles. It used aimed, low-frequency sound waves, and it was believed that this weapon would be effective against the alien craft and beam weapons. EXCALIBUR was a weapon carried by a missile not to rise above 30,000 feet above ground level (AGL), not to deviate from designated target more than 50 meters, able to... penetrate '1,000 METERS OF TUFA, HARD-PACKED SOIL SUCH AS THAT FOUND IN NEW MEXICO,' carry a one-megaton warhead, and intended for use in destroying the aliens in their underground bases (Note: According to many sources, several of the 'alien' underground bases contain humans or human-souled- hybrids, and human captives both living and in cold storage, who have been the victims of alien abductions from surface and in some cases subsurface or extrasurface communities. Obviously, EXCALIBUR should not be used against such installations, but the surface-to-subsurface 'cavern' or 'tunnel' routes should be sought out and an underground invasion force should be utilized to destroy the aliens yet spare any surviving humans and take the bases intact. To do otherwise may be in essence 'sacrificing' innocent lives needlessly to get an advantage over the aliens, in which case we would prove ourselves to be little better than the alien-grays or sauroid reptilians themselves! In connection with the JOSHUA anti-spacecraft weapon, extreme caution should of course be used to distinguish BETWEEN human-occupied spacecraft and those craft utilized by the saurian grays, etc. - Branton).

"JOSHUA was developed successfully but never used, to my knowledge. EXCALIBUR was not pushed until recent years and now, we are told, THERE IS AN UNPRECEDENTED EFFORT TO DEVELOP THIS WEAPON. The public would be told that EXCALIBUR would be needed to take out Soviet underground command posts. We know that is not true because one rule of war is that you try not to destroy the leaders. They are needed to ensure peaceful transition of power and compliance of the populace to all negotiated or dictated terms.

"The events at Fatima in the early part of the century were scrutinized. ON THE SUSPICION THAT IT WAS AN ALIEN MANIPULATION, AN INTELLIGENCE OPERATION WAS PUT INTO MOTION TO PENETRATE THE SECRECY SURROUNDING THE EVENT. THE UNITED STATES UTILIZED ITS VATICAN MOLES AND SOON OBTAINED THE ENTIRE VATICAN STUDY, WHICH INCLUDED THE PROPHECY... The prophecy demanded that Russia be consecrated to the 'Sacred Heart' (of the Roman 'Madonna' - Branton). It stated that a child would be born who would unite the world with a plan for world peace and a false religion. The people would discern that he was evil and was indeed the Anti-Christ. World War III would begin (following the "Antichrist? - Branton) in the Middle East with an invasion of Israel of a United Arab nation using conventional weapons, which would culminate in a near holocaust. Most of the life on this planet would suffer horribly and die as a result. The return of Christ would occur shortly thereafter."

(Note: This 'prophecy' actually REVERSES THE SEQUENCE of events from the sequence in which they are given in the books of DANIEL and REVELATION, two major books describing Judeo- Christian end-time prophecy. For instance the prophecies in Daniel and Revelation [or for that matter all of the "prophetical" books, from ISAIAH to MALACHI] indicate that a period of time will occur when the following will take place within a SHORT SPACE: the mysterious disappearance of millions of people the world over; an invasion of Israel involving Arab and other allied armies - resulting in the nuclear[?] destruction of 5/6ths of the invading forces; the rebuilding of Solomon's Temple and the re- institution of animal sacrifices; and the rise of a COUNTERFEIT 'Messiah' FOLLOWING the attempted invasion of Israel by "GOG and MAGOG" who will apparently claim to be the returned Christ or God and will reign 3 1/2 years, at the end of which period his Evil nature will be apparent to all; The period between the battle of "Gog and Magog" and the time when the "Beast" implements the "Mark" is to be approximately 3 1/2 years, followed by another 3 1/2 years of horrible 'Inquisitions', at the close of which period the TRUE Christ or Messiah arrives at the battle of ARMAGEDDON with his armies of angelic light beings and 'regenerated believers' from the 'New Jerusalem' Command [to where most of those who had 'disappeared' were PHYSICALLY taken 7 years previous], the 'Command Center' of the Universe and headquarters of the Angelic Command who serve under Christ-Melchizedek. This incredible cosmic City reportedly entered the 3rd dimensional universe through the 'Eternity Gate' located in the Orion Nebula within the 'sword' of Orion, a fantastic nebula which actually lies far beyond the Orion open-cluster itself. According to insiders, electronic telescopes have actually seen this awesome sight, a multicolored 'star' which is reportedly now en-route to earth, and is due to arrive at the end of the next Millennium, which falls perfectly in line with the Book of Revelation description of the 'New Jerusalem'. Of all the worlds in the universe, according to revelation, the 'New Jerusalem' Command is to make its final resting place on planet earth once the Grand Drama or final Battle between universal Good and Evil is finally decided upon planet earth, which some "alien" sources have described as being the "psychic center of the universe". For some unknown reason, planet earth seems to be a universal "nexus", which is why it has been chosen as the final battleground in the Cosmic Conflict between the universal Legions of Light and the Forces of Darkness. As for the Fatima message, the fact that the 'aliens' REVERSED the sequence of these events may indicate that a COUNTERFEIT 'Antichrist' may rise before these events mentioned above take place -

and be labeled as such. When this 'False Antichrist' is taken care of BEFORE the Jerusalem invasion, the ACTUAL Antichrist who is to begin his tyrannical reign from Rome shortly INTO the 7-year "Tribulation" period FOLLOWING THE INVASION may then rise to power and not be suspected as much for what he/it is - Branton).

"When the aliens were confronted with this finding," Cooper continues, "they confirmed that it was true. The aliens explained that they had created us through genetic manipulation in a laboratory. They stated that they had manipulated the human race through religion, Satanism, witchcraft, magic, and the occult."

(Note: Similar 'revelations' were also said to appear in the so-called 'Yellow Book', which may in itself be a type of alien propaganda. Aside from outright deception the saurians-grays apparently utilize HALF TRUTHS as well. By telling people certain obvious facts such as the fact that 'they' were behind the Fatima manifestations and that they manipulate occult societies — possibly confessions made when they were "backed into a corner" with the facts — they apparently gain an element of human trust, through which they were or are able to convey other strategic, damning lies, such as the claim that they 'created us.' This lie alone could potentially destroy the desire within millions to resist these creatures, leading them to succumb to the demands of the aliens with the idea that it is futile to fight against their own 'creators.' Truth is useless unless it is believed and practiced IN FULL.

Salvador Freixedo, author of 'VISIONARIES, MYSTICS & CONTACTEES' — Arcturus Book Service — "...was a Jesuit for 30 years until, that is, he began to discover that the Roman-Church not only knew A LOT about unexplained phenomena, but that it USED PHENOMENA as a basis for exercising its stranglehold on the minds and spirits of 700,000,000 'faithful'".

Pope Leo XIII incidentally stated in 'THE GREAT ENCYCLICAL LETTERS', p. 304: "We hold upon this earth THE PLACE OF GOD ALMIGHTY." The question is... could the serpent race be getting a little help in it's attempts to deceive the masses from human collaborators, who are nothing more than 'dragons' in doves' clothing? (After all, do not the Jesuits themselves — the Gnostic serpent or dragon cult which established the Bavarian Illuminati, the Scottish Rite of Masonry and also helped to establish Hitler's SS — use as their emblem a white 'dove'? - Branton)

William Cooper continues:

"...The aliens showed a hologram, which they claim was the actual crucifixion of Christ. The Government filmed the hologram. We did not know whether to believe them.

"...A symposium was held in 1957 which was attended by some of the great scientific minds then living. They reached the conclusion that by, or shortly after, the year 2000 the planet WOULD self-destruct due to increased population and man's exploitation of the environment WITHOUT ANY HELP FROM GOD OR THE ALIENS.

"By secret Executive order of President Eisenhower, the JASON Scholars were ordered to study this scenario and make recommendations from their findings. The JASON Society CONFIRMED the findings of the scientists and made three recommendations called ALTERNATIVES 1, 2, AND 3.

"Alternative 1 was to use nuclear devices to blast holes in the stratosphere from which the heat and pollution could escape into space. They would then change the human cultures from that of exploitation into cultures of environmental protection. Of the three this was decided to be the least likely to succeed due to the inherent nature of man and the additional damage the nuclear explosions would themselves create. THE EXISTENCE OF A HOLE IN THE OZONE LAYER MAY INDICATE THAT ALTERNATIVE 1 MIGHT HAVE BEEN ATTEMPTED. THIS IS, HOWEVER, ONLY CONJECTURE.

"ALTERNATIVE 2 WAS TO BUILD A VAST NETWORK OF UNDERGROUND CITIES AND TUNNELS IN WHICH A SELECT REPRESENTATION OF ALL CULTURES AND OCCUPATIONS WOULD SURVIVE AND CARRY ON THE HUMAN RACE. THE REST OF HUMANITY WOULD BE LEFT TO FEND FOR THEMSELVES ON THE SURFACE OF THE PLANET. We know that these facilities have been built and are ready and waiting for the chosen few to be notified.

"Alternative 3 was to exploit the alien and conventional technology in order for a select few to leave the earth and establish colonies in outer space. I am not able to either confirm or deny the existence of 'batch consignments' of human slaves, which would be used for the manual labor as a part of the plan. The Moon, code-named ADAM, was the object of primary interest, followed by the planet Mars, code-named EVE. I am now in possession of official NASA photographs of one of the moon bases. I believe that the Mars colony is also a reality (Note: There are some who suggest that 'global warming' may not actually be taking place as believed, and that this 'scare' is based largely on computerized models or simulations which have not always coincided with actual temperature variations. Is it possible that the earth is attempting to 'heal' itself? Could it be that to some extent 'global warming' is more-or-less an 'excuse' that is being used to justify huge expenditures for subterran and exterran 'bases' for secret government use such as in the 'Alternative' scenarios? This is of course, even if true, no reason to destroy this planet, as pollution of the air, water and earth IS in fact something which could lead to an eventual environmental devastation of this Earth. - Branton).

"As a delaying action, ALL THREE ALTERNATIVES included BIRTH CONTROL, STERILIZATION, AND THE INTRODUCTION OF DEADLY MICROBES TO CONTROL OR SLOW THE GROWTH OF EARTH'S POPULATION. AIDS is only ONE result of these plans. It was decided BY THE ELITE that since the population must be reduced and controlled, it would be in the best interest of the human race to rid ourselves of undesirable elements of our society. Specific targeted populations included BLACKS, HISPANICS, and HOMOSEXUALS." (Note: It appears that when they made this decision the elite were on the verge of possessing the technology to solve the overpopulation, food and energy problems — even to the point of being able to transport excess populations to other planetary bodies if necessary. Apparently they opted for mass genocide instead, which they believed would keep the population to a manageable minimum, not wishing to give up the political and economic control which they possessed and which would to a large degree be lost if they openly gave this super-technology freely to the masses. Pro-abortion activist- leader and 'Planned Parenthood' founder Margaret Sanger betrays her own devotion to the Globalist genocidal policies and insensitivity to women's rights, especially NON-ARYAN women's rights — not to mention the constitutional rights to 'life, liberty and the pursuit of happiness' on the part of multi-millions of children — in the following words from her first book 'PIVOT OF CIVILIZATION'. In reference to free MATERNITY care for the poor she states: "Instead of DECREASING and aiming to ELIMINATE THE STOCKS that are most detrimental to the future of the race and the world it tends to render them to a menacing degree dominant." And in reference to her 'Negro Project' of the late 1930's, which aimed at recruiting black ministers, physicians and political leaders for the purpose of encouraging birth control and sterilization in the black community, Sanger wrote: "...We do not want word to go out that WE WANT TO EXTERMINATE THE NEGRO POPULATION, and the minister is the man who can straighten out that idea if it ever occurs to any of their more rebellious members." - Branton). Cooper continues:

"The joint U.S. and Soviet leadership dismissed Alternative 1 BUT ORDERED WORK TO BEGIN ON ALTERNATIVES 2 AND 3 VIRTUALLY AT THE SAME TIME.

"In 1959 the Rand Corporation hosted a Deep Underground Construction Symposium. In the symposium report, machines are pictured and described WHICH COULD BORE A TUNNEL 45 FEET IN DIAMETER AT THE RATE OF 5 FEET PER HOUR IN 1959. IT ALSO DISPLAYS PICTURES OF HUGE TUNNELS AND UNDERGROUND VAULTS CONTAINING WHAT APPEAR TO BE COMPLEX FACILITIES AND POSSIBLY EVEN CITIES. IT APPEARS THAT THE PREVIOUS FIVE YEARS OF ALL-OUT UNDERGROUND CONSTRUCTION HAD MADE SIGNIFICANT PROGRESS BY THAT TIME.

"The ruling powers decided that one means of funding the alien-connected and other 'black' projects was to corner the illegal drug market. THE ENGLISH AND THE FRENCH HAD ESTABLISHED A HISTORICAL PRECEDENT WHEN THEY EXPLOITED THE OPIUM TRADE IN THE FAR EAST AND USED IT TO FILL THEIR COFFERS AND GAIN A SOLID FOOTHOLD IN CHINA AND VIETNAM, RESPEC-

TIVELY.

"A young ambitious member of the Council on Foreign Relations was approached. His name was George Bush, who at the time was the president and CEO of THE OFFSHORE DIVISION OF ZAPATA OIL, BASED IN TEXAS. Zapata Oil was experimenting with the new technology of offshore drilling. It was correctly thought that the drugs could be shipped from South America to the offshore platforms by fishing boat, to be taken from there to shore by the normal transportation used for supplies and personnel. By this method no customs or law enforcement agency would subject the cargo to search.

"George Bush agreed to help, and organized the operation IN CONJUNCTION WITH THE CIA. The plan worked better than anyone had dreamed. It has since expanded worldwide. There are now many other methods of bringing illegal drugs into the country. IT MUST ALWAYS BE REMEMBERED THAT GEORGE BUSH BEGAN THE SALE OF DRUGS TO OUR CHILDREN. The CIA now controls most of the world's illegal drug markets.

"The official space program was boosted by President Kennedy in his inaugural address when he mandated that the United States put a man on the Moon before the end of the decade. Although innocent in its conception, this mandate enabled those in charge to funnel vast amounts of money into black projects AND CONCEAL THE REAL SPACE PROGRAM FROM THE AMERICAN PEOPLE. A similar program in the Soviet Union served the same purpose. IN FACT, A JOINT ALIEN, UNITED STATES, AND SOVIET UNION BASE EXISTED ON THE MOON AT THE VERY MOMENT KENNEDY SPOKE THE WORDS.

"On May 22, 1962, a space probe landed on Mars and confirmed the existence of AN ENVIRONMENT WHICH COULD SUPPORT LIFE (Note: Some may recall many years later when the first PUBLICIZED 'Viking' probe landed on the surface of Mars and began sending back pictures of a reddish-brown planet with a light blue sky. Immediately after this we were told 'oops,' the blue sky was just a mistake in the programming of the camera, which began sending the 'photos' back to earth in the wrong color. 'Fortunately' the problem was 'solved' and subsequent photographs appeared in which the sky was reddish-pink. - Branton). Not long afterward the construction of a colony on the planet Mars began in earnest. Today I believe a colony exists on Mars populated by specially selected people from different cultures and occupations taken from all over the Earth. A PUBLIC CHARADE of antagonism between the Soviet Union and the United States has been maintained over all these years IN ORDER TO FUND PROJECTS IN THE NAME OF NATIONAL DEFENSE WHEN IN FACT WE ARE THE CLOSEST ALLIES."

Note: An 'M.J.' of El Paso, TX sent a letter to 'World Watchers International' — Fall 1989 issue, p. 18 — concerning a woman he'd talked to who worked at JPL in Pasadena, CA., in 1962, as a classified 'photo interpreter'. Her husband also worked there designing domed structures capable of resisting 'gale-velocity winds' for 'colonies on the Moon, and then Mars!' Her husband was sent on a SUPER SECRET mission. Then one day she received word that her husband had died and no further details, then her 'Q' clearance was pulled. When asked of his fate she said with dead seriousness: "I think he was drafted to Mars!"

Frank Edwards, in his 'STRANGE WORLD' (Lyle Stuart Co., N.Y. 1964. pp. 329-330) gives the following revelations under the heading, 'THE MYSTERIOUS MOONS OF MARS':

"Now that man has tools which will enable him to obtain detailed information by near approaches to Mars, we may expect, within the next few years, to learn whether Mars is inhabited by intelligent beings, and, if so, what they look like and how they live. Among the factors which have focused so much of our time and talent on Mars are the two tiny satellites which orbit the planet where — prior to 1877 — no satellites had ever been seen before (In other words, about the time the canals of Mars were mysteriously starting to 'disappear', new satellites began appearing on the scene - Branton). The famous astronomers Herschel and Lasselle had excellent telescopes at their disposal — so good that they used them to DISCOVER THE MOONS OF URANUS. Yet neither these men, nor hundreds of other astronomers who observed the planets, were able to see any satellites around Mars. Then IN ONE WEEK in 1877, Asaph Hall found that Mars had TWO SATELLITES where none had been seen before. Furthermore, he found that the satellites were tiny but bright...brighter than the planet itself...as though they were made of some material other than that of Mars. It is also worth noting that not only do these two Martian satellites sweep around the planet at a very high speed but they travel in different directions... factors which had led to the suspicion that they are artificial. This is the theory advanced by Soviet astronomer I. S. Schklovsky, who points out that the Martian satellite known as Phobos exhibits a strange acceleration in its orbit, an irregularity which would be expected if the satellite were in reality a huge metal sphere that was hollow. The same difference in speed, however, would be impossible for a natural astronomical body. Therefore, says Dr. Schklovsky, at least one of the moons of Mars IS NOT A NATURAL OBJECT, but an artificial satellite placed in orbit around the 'red' planet in 1877, or shortly before that time. When we stop to think of the discovery of the Martian moons in 1877 — and of the mass of phenomena noted on our moon between 1879 and 1889 — the conviction develops that if we discover life on Mars...we may also discover that we are merely returning a visit."

Cooper continues:

"At some point President Kennedy discovered portions of the truth concerning the drugs and aliens. He issued an ultimatum in 1963 to Majesty Twelve. President Kennedy assured them that if they did not clean up the drug problem, he would. HE INFORMED MAJORITY TWELVE THAT HE INTENDED TO REVEAL THE PRESENCE OF (THE) ALIENS TO THE AMERICAN PEOPLE WITHIN THE FOLLOWING YEAR, AND ORDERED A PLAN DEVELOPED TO IMPLEMENT HIS DECISION (Note: One might consider this File and other present efforts to inform the public of the 'alien problem' as being nothing less than a Patriotic duty to fulfill the decree as set out by this former American President — the carrying out of an "Executive Order" is you will - Branton).

"President Kennedy's decision struck fear into the hearts of those in charge. His assassination was ordered by the Policy Committee and the order was carried out by agents in Dallas. President John F. Kennedy was murdered by the Secret Service agent who drove his car in the motorcade and the act is plainly visible in the Zapruder film. WATCH THE DRIVER AND NOT KENNEDY WHEN YOU VIEW THE FILM."

Note: On April 2, 1992, Geraldo Rivera in his television News magazine "NOW IT CAN BE TOLD", interviewed a Dr. Charles Crenshaw, one of the original doctors who worked on the body of President John F. Kennedy shortly after the assassination. Crenshaw claimed that he saw Kennedy's head wound and stated that Oswald could not have killed Kennedy as he was behind the President, whereas the fatal bullet wound came from the FRONT. Crenshaw claimed that the bullet entered from the front and exited from the rear of Kennedy's skull, leaving a large gaping wound 9-10 centimeters across. Although Texas law required an immediate autopsy in Dallas, the site of the crime, Crenshaw insisted that a swarm of Secret Service agents entered the hospital and demanded that the autopsy be performed out of state. Dr. Crenshaw stated on "NOW IT CAN BE TOLD" that several people he knew who had witnessed the President's wounds had died shortly afterwards under strange circumstances (Rivera documented over 100 mysterious deaths of witnesses, although Cooper claims "over 200 material witnesses" have died). Crenshaw believed that the 'official' photos taken at Bethesda Naval hospital showing no rear exit wound were tampered with and that the whole affair was covered up. If this is true then the two Mafia men behind the 'grassy knoll' would have been a BACKUP TEAM in case the Secret Service agent William Greer failed, and the CIA asset Oswald — with his carefully planted Communist ties — the PATSY or FALL GUY.

Cooper continues in his "SECRET GOVERNMENT" report by giving evidence that the so-called 'Zupruder' film of Kennedy's assassination shows that William Greer, the Secret Service agent who was with Kennedy in the car (Greer in the front seat, Kennedy in the back), quickly turned around and shot Kennedy in the front of the head just as Oswald and possibly others were firing. Cooper states:

"...You WILL have faith in your government if you learned that Greer killed

Kennedy ON ORDERS OF THE ILLUMINATI AND THAT IT HAD NOTHING TO DO WITH THE LEGAL, CONSTITUTIONAL GOVERNMENT. DID YOU KNOW THAT THE MAN WHO WAS IN CHARGE OF THE SECRET SERVICE AT THE TIME OF THE ASSASSINATION BECAME THE MAN IN CHARGE OF SECURITY FOR THE ROCKEFELLER FAMILY UP ON HIS RETIREMENT? Well, now you know. You should also know that BOB GRODIN (a reported CIA agent who Cooper alleges tried to prevent him from releasing the 'Zupruder' film publicly - Branton) IS A FRIEND OF LESLIE WATKINS, AND IT IS BOB GRODIN'S NAME THAT WATKINS USES AS THE ALIAS OF THE ASTRONAUT CITED IN 'ALTERNATIVE 003'. Did you know that when Ricky White made appearances on talk radio across the country to say that his father killed Kennedy, that Bob Grodin accompanied him? Did you know that every time a caller asked Ricky White a question, GRODIN ANSWERED FOR HIM? Do you really believe that is a coincidence? Ricky White's father did not kill Kennedy.

"...THE HEADQUARTERS OF THE INTERNATIONAL CONSPIRACY IS IN GENEVA, SWITZERLAND. THE RULING BODY IS MADE UP OF THREE COMMITTEES CONSISTING OF THIRTEEN MEMBERS EACH, AND ALL THREE TOGETHER COMPRISE THE 39 MEMBERS OF THE EXECUTIVE COMMITTEE OF THE BODY KNOWN AS THE BILDERBERG GROUP. The most important and powerful of the three committees is the Policy Committee. (It is more than interesting to note that the United States had thirteen original colonies and that 39 delegates from these colonies signed the Constitution after it was written and adopted in the first Constitutional Convention. Do you believe that is coincidence?) Policy Committee meetings are held on a nuclear submarine beneath the polar icecap. A Soviet sub and an American sub join at an airlock and the meeting is convened. The secrecy is such that this was the only method which would ensure that the meetings could not be bugged.

"...If the underground history is correct, ALIENS HAVE MANIPULATED AND/OR RULED THE HUMAN RACE THROUGH VARIOUS SECRET SOCIETIES, RELIGIONS, MAGIC, WITCHCRAFT, AND THE OCCULT. The Council on Foreign Relations and the Trilateral Commission are in complete control of the alien technology and are also in complete control of the nations' economy (Note: another interpretation would be that the draconian powers who influence the Trilaterals, CFR's, Illuminati, etc., CONTROL much of the economy and even the 'technology' THROUGH these secret societies. It is obvious that when dealing with this alien-reptilian race, 'they' do not give a person or a group of persons anything without getting something in return, namely their 'souls' or a certain amount of control over their thoughts, actions, emotions, will and so on - Branton).

"Eisenhower was the last President to know the entire overview of the alien problem. Succeeding Presidents were told only what Majesty Twelve and the intelligence community wanted them to know. Believe me, it was not the truth.

"Majesty Twelve has presented most new Presidents with a picture of a lost alien culture seeking to renew itself, build a home on this planet, and shower us with gifts of technology. In some cases the President was told nothing. Each President in turn swallowed the story (or no story at all) hook, line and sinker. MEANWHILE INNOCENT PEOPLE CONTINUE TO SUFFER AT THE HANDS OF THE ALIEN AND HUMAN SCIENTISTS. I have been unable to determine exactly what it is they are doing. MANY PEOPLE ARE ABDUCTED AND ARE SENTENCED TO LIVE WITH PSYCHOLOGICAL AND PHYSICAL DAMAGE FOR THE REST OF THEIR LIVES. Could this be a CIA mind-control operation? (Another possibility can be found in the account of the Barney and Betty Hill abduction. During hypnotic regression to bring out memories of the "missing time" the Hill's experienced, Barney Hill was quoted as saying in a very agitated and frightened voice that he had seen a "German Nazi" with evil looking eyes on board the alien craft, working with the "Grays" from Zeta Reticuli. This was WELL OVER A DECADE following the end of World War II. Harley Byrd, a former Pentagon employee who was also the nephew of Navy Rear Admiral Richard E. Byrd, insisted that his uncle was searching for a secret postwar Nazi base in Antarctica, and found it. In fact Admiral Byrd reportedly lost 4 planes in an air battle with top secret Nazi aerial disks which had been developed in secret underground bases in Germany during the war, and perfected in the hidden Nazi base in Antarctica. Harley Byrd believes that the Nazis are working with the Grays in an effort to gain dominance once again over the nations of the earth via abductions, implantation, techno-hypnotic programming, mind control, etc. An interesting CIA connection can be found in the secret "Operation Paperclip", which allowed at least a hundred Nazi SS war criminals into the U.S. and gave them influential positions within the CIA. If the Nazi's were the first modern political force to establish interaction with the Grays, and since CIA founder Allen Dulles was a former CFR president and thus member of the Bavarian [German] Illuminati, then it is no wonder why the fascist Trojan horse in American Intelligence known as the CIA, itself maintains an active interaction with the saurian Grays as well. - Branton)

"IN THE DOCUMENTS THAT I READ, 1 IN 40 HUMANS HAD BEEN IMPLANTED WITH DEVICES, THE PURPOSE OF WHICH I HAVE NEVER DISCOVERED. THE GOVERNMENT BELIEVES THAT THE ALIENS ARE BUILDING AN ARMY OF IMPLANTED HUMANS WHO CAN BE ACTIVATED AND TURNED UPON US AT WILL. YOU SHOULD ALSO KNOW THAT TO DATE WE HAVE NOT EVEN BEGUN TO COME CLOSE TO (technological - Branton) PARITY WITH THE ALIENS.

"...WE ARE BEING MANIPULATED BY A JOINT HUMAN/ ALIEN POWER STRUCTURE WHICH WILL RESULT IN A ONE- WORLD GOVERNMENT AND THE PARTIAL ENSLAVEMENT OF THE HUMAN RACE. This has been deemed necessary to solve the elemental question: 'Who will speak for planet Earth?' It has been decided that man is not mature enough in his 'evolutionary development' to be trusted to interact properly with an alien race (i.e. incapable of kissing-up to a grotesque race of reptilian beings without resisting? The hypocrisy here staggers the imagination - Branton). We ,already have enough trouble between the different human races, so what would happen if a TOTALLY ALIEN extraterrestrial race was introduced? Would they by lynched, spit upon, or shot? Would discrimination result in nasty encounters that would doom humanity as a result of the alien's obviously superior technology? Have our leaders decided to lock us in a playpen?

"...THE GOVERNMENT HAS BEEN TOTALLY DECEIVED AND WE ARE BEING MANIPULATED BY AN ALIEN POWER, WHICH WILL RESULT IN THE TOTAL ENSLAVEMENT AND/OR DESTRUCTION OF THE HUMAN RACE. WE MUST USE ANY AND EVERY MEANS AVAILABLE TO PREVENT THIS FROM HAPPENING."

Bill Cooper, in addition to the above, also released a document titled "SECRET SOCIETIES AND THE NEW WORLD ORDER", which was later included in his book 'BEHOLD A PALE HORSE'. In reference to the 'Cult of the Serpent' which he claims is headquartered in Rome, he states:

"...History is replete with whispers of secret societies... The oldest is the Brotherhood of the Snake, also called the Brotherhood of the Dragon, and it still exists under many different names. The Brotherhood of the Snake is devoted to guarding the 'secrets of the ages' and the recognition of Lucifer as the one and only true God... It's secret symbol is the all-seeing eye in the pyramid.

"...Houses of worship and sacrifice existed in the ancient cities. They were in fact temples built in honor of the many 'gods'... Most of the greatest minds that ever lived were initiated into the society of Mysteries by secret and dangerous rites, some of which were very cruel. Some of the most famous were known as Osiris, Isis, Sabazius, Cybele, and Eleusis. Plato was one of these initiates.

"...the documents that I read while in Naval Intelligence stated that Project GALILEO required only five pounds of plutonium to ignite Jupiter and possibly stave off THE COMING ICE AGE. Global warming is a hoax. It is easier for the public to deal with and will give the ruling elite more time before panic and anarchy replace government. The reality is that overall global temperatures are becoming lower..."

Cooper quotes from one (secret society) source:

"'The initiated elect communicate directly to gods (ALIENS) who communicate back to them... The elect are given knowledge of the Mysteries and are illumined and are thus known as The Illuminati or the Illuminated Ones, the guardians of the 'Secrets of the Ages.'"

"...Adam Weishaupt, a young professor of canon law at Ingolstadt University in Germany, was a Jesuit priest and an initiate of the Illuminati. The branch of the Order he founded in Germany in 1776 was the same Illuminati previously discussed. The Jesuit connection is important.

"...On the obverse of the Great Seal of the United States the wise will recognize the all-seeing eye and other signs of the Brotherhood of the Snake... The Brotherhood of the Snake is adept at throwing out decoys to keep the dogs at bay.

"...Allegations that the Freemason organizations were infiltrated by the Illuminati during Weishaupt's reign are hogwash. The Freemasons have ALWAYS contained the core of Illuminati within their ranks, and that is why they so freely and so willingly took in and hid the members of Weishaupt's group.

"...In 1826 an American Freemason wrote a book revealing Masonic secrets entitled 'ILLUSTRATIONS OF FREEMASONRY'. One of the secrets that he revealed is that the last mystery at the top of the Masonic pyramid is the worship of Lucifer... Morgan caused a small uproar against the Masons. The small uproar turned into a full blown anti-Freemason movement when the author, William Morgan, disappeared. Morgan had apparently been drowned in Lake Ontario.

"...Probably the most notorious Freemason lodge is the P2 lodge in Italy. This group has been implicated in everything from bribery to assassinations. P2 is directly connected to the Vatican, the Knights of Malta, and to the U.S. Central Intelligence Agency. It is powerful and dangerous... the Pope, John Paul II, has lifted the ban against Freemasonry. Many high- level members of the Vatican are now Freemasons (others allege that many 'secret' high Masons existed in the Vatican before the ban lifted, that in fact the Vatican controlled Masonry via the Jesuit-created Scottish Rite 'Illuminism', which in turn infiltrated Masonry, and that the former bans were merely smokescreens to hide the Scottish Rite-Vatican connection - Branton)... The 33rd Degree is split into two. One split contains the core of the Luciferian Illuminati and the other contains those who have no knowledge of it whatsoever.

"ALL of the intelligence officers I worked for while in Naval Intelligence were Masons.

"...1990 is the right time with the right leaders: ex-chief of the Soviet secret police Mikhail Gorbachev, ex-chief of the CIA George Bush, ex-Nazi cyanide gas salesman Pope John Paul II, all bound by an unholy alliance to bring in the New World Order.

"...REMEMBER — NEVER WORSHIP A LEADER. IF YOU WORSHIP A LEADER, YOU THEN NO LONGER HAVE THE ABILITY TO RECOGNIZE WHEN YOU HAVE BEEN DECEIVED.

"...Ex-President John Adams wrote to his successor, Thomas Jefferson: 'I do not like the re-appearance of the Jesuits. If ever there was a body of men who merited eternal damnation on earth... it is this Society...' Jefferson replied: 'Like you, I disapprove of the restoration of the Jesuits, for it means a step backwards from light into darkness.' (for more information on the Jesuits, see: Chick Publications., Box 662., Chino, CA 91710)

"...the heart of the Bilderberg Group consists of 39 total members of the Illuminati. The three committees are made up exclusively of members of all different secret groups that make up the Illuminati, the FREEMASONS, the VATICAN, and the BLACK NOBILITY. This committee works year round in offices in Switzerland.

(Note: William Cooper targets the MASONS. We must state however that Masonry was not always as it appears to be today. Several early Christian Patriots during the foundational period of the United States were part of a predominating YORK RITE of Masonry, which largely promoted PROTESTANT values and ethics, and fraternal brotherhood among members. Even at that time the JESUIT-spawned SCOTTISH RITE of Masonry was moving like a virus through the American fraternal lodges in an attempt to take them over from within. Today the Scottish Rite is becoming the predominant branch of Masonry in America. In fact, the Jesuit secret oath condones the absolute destruction of the world Protestant movement. This is interesting in that the Jesuit-created Scottish Rite has infiltrated America with the apparent intent of choking-out the York Rite, which was largely rooted in Protestantism - Branton)

"...In the Great Seal of the United States we see the ancient symbol of the Brotherhood of the Snake (or Dragon), which as you know is the all-seeing eye of the pyramid representing Lucifer..." Is it any wonder, then, that so many people claim that this symbol is used by the serpent race (the Grays) as well?

To sum-up what Cooper has said, then, let us quote from an article which appeared in 'INNER LIGHT' magazine, written by Sherry Hansen and Brad Steiger:

"...'the PROTOCOLS OF ZION were published as a deception (by the Russian Secret Police), to make people believe they had to worry about the Jews.'

"...'throughout history it has been a ploy of the Illuminati to dub anyone who told the truth as an anti-Semite or a Nazi. They only prove my point when they employ the same old tactics to shut people up and to intimidate them. They don't know what to do with me, because I don't intimidate and don't shut up.'

"Cooper states that he has traced the history of the nefarious Illuminati all the way back to the Ancient Temple of Wisdom in Cairo, long before the birth of Christ. 'The Illuminati exist today under many different names and many different occupations.' Cooper told us. 'They practice Hegalian conflict/resolution. They appear to oppose each other at the bottom ranks (like the 'apparent' conflict between socialist Freemasonry and fascist Romanism? - Branton), but at the highest levels they are actually organizing and controlling the conflict which they have created to produce the solution that they seek.

"'The Illuminati are extremely powerful, very wealthy men. They believe that they are the guardians of the secrets of the ages. They believe that the vast majority of people would not know what to do with the real knowledge and the real truth and the real science — and would, in fact, misuse them all. They further believe that everything that they do is for the ultimate betterment and survival of humankind — even if it means killing two billion people to reach their goal...'"

One possible area (aside from the so-called 'DREAMLAND' facility mentioned by William Cooper) which also lies within the Mojave Desert region and which also may connect to the alleged subsurface network is 'Iron Mountain', one of the peaks in the El Paso Mountains northeast of Mojave, California. There are many bizarre accounts connected with this mountain, which apparently got it's name in part from the many old iron mines which can be found there, along with numerous natural cavities which open out to the surface in many different areas. The area has allegedly been the site of certain activity concerning native American Indian occult practices, as well as the site of alleged secret government activity, some of which reportedly involves the observation and monitoring of strange creatures and/or automatons which are said to emerge from underground openings in the area on certain occasions. Just exactly what these 'creatures' are is uncertain, but some accounts indicate that they are dangerous! Could this also be a 'magnetic anomaly' zone due to the high iron content? There have been mysterious references to time-space windows in the area as well.

Flying Ace John Lear, in 'statements' released over Computer 'Bulletin Boards' devoted to researching the unknown (such as the PARANET BBS) has stated:

"...If the government won't tell us the truth and the major networks won't even give it serious consideration then what is the big picture, anyway? [Note: This was written before such programs as SIGHTINGS, ENCOUNTERS, UNSOLVED MYSTERIES, CURRENT AFFAIR, MONTEL WILLIAMS, NOW IT CAN BE TOLD and other TV programs DID in fact begin dealing with the UFO phenomena, abductions, and related phenomena in much greater depth - Branton], Are the EBE's, having done a hundred thousand or more abductions (possibly millions worldwide), built AN UNTOLD NUMBER OF SECRET UNDERGROUND BASES (Groom Lake, Nevada; Sunspot, Datil, Roswell, and Pie Town, New Mexico, just to name a few) getting ready to return to wherever they came from? Or, from the obvious preparations are we to assume that they are getting ready for a big move? or is (it) the more sinister and most probable situation that the invasion is essentially complete and it is all over but the screaming?

"A well planned invasion of Earth for it's resources and benefits would not begin with mass landings or ray-gun equipped aliens. A properly planned and executed invasion by a civilization thousands... of years in advance of us would most likely be complete before a handful of people, say 12?, realize what was happening. No fuss, no mess. The best advice I can give you is this: Next time you see a flying saucer and are awed by its obvious display of technology and gorgeous lights of pure color - RUN LIKE HELL! —June 3, 1988 Las Vegas, NV"

The above is just one excerpt taken from Lear's lengthy 'Press Release' describing recoveries of alien craft and their occupants, accounts which Lear claims to have learned from 'inside' sources. Lear has also stated:

"...In 1983 when the Grand Deception was discovered MJ-12 (which may now be designated 'PI-40') started work on a weapon or some kind of device to contain the EBE's which had by now totally infested our society. This program was funded through SDI which, coincidentally, was initiated at approximately the same date. A frantic effort has been made over the past 4 years by all participants. (The beginning of the "retaliation" projects apparently began in 1979, when the DULCE and DREAMLAND massacres reportedly occurred - Branton) This program ended in failure in December of 1987. A new program has been conceived but will take about 2 years to develop. In the meantime, it is absolutely essential to MJ-12 (PI-40), that no one, including the Senate, the Congress or the citizens of the United States of America (or anyone else for that matter) become aware of the real circumstances surrounding the UFO cover-up and (the) TOTAL DISASTER it has become."

In their QUARTERLY REPORT, July - September 1990, the 'Fund For UFO Research' (P. O. Box 277., Mount Rainier, MD 20712), related the following:

"Dear Supporter:

"I'm writing to you at a critical time in the history of the UFO movement. The issues contained in this letter are extremely sensitive, and so I would appreciate your confidentiality.

"Because of your support for scientific research into the UFO phenomena, I want to bring you up-to-date on recent events which may result in a resolution of the mystery of Unidentified Flying Objects.

"As you know, there is a great deal of interest currently in the apparent crash of one or more UFOs in New Mexico over 43 years ago. This event has become the most intensively- investigated — and best documented — case in UFO history.

"It came to the public's attention in 1980 with the publication of 'THE ROSWELL INCIDENT' by Charles Berlitz and William Moore. With the capable assistance of veteran UFO investigator and nuclear physicist Stanton Friedman, the authors documented that SOMETHING very unusual crashed in the New Mexico desert in July 1947.

"Friedman and Moore continued to follow up on new leads and uncovered new evidence following publication of the book. During the course of their research, they identified nearly 100 witnesses who had information about the event.

"However, the focus of their investigation changed with the release of apparently authentic documents outlining Operation Majestic Twelve, a TOP SECRET government research project initiated following the Roswell crash. The Fund for UFO Research awarded Mr. Friedman a $16,000 grant to investigate the documents, and his research into the MJ-12 matter inevitably turned up new witnesses in the Roswell event.

"In the meantime, Don Schmitt and Kevin Randle, under the auspices of the Center for UFO Studies, decided to reexamine the Roswell case and managed to bring the number of firsthand witnesses and sources of information to more than 200..."

In the May, 1989 issue of 'Leading Edge' (formerly 'Nevada Aerial Research') it was stated that: "...Information about underground bases at Edwards AFB (CA) are not new. Stories have circulated for years. There was the lady whose mother used to work at the cafeteria who overheard people talking about aliens and disks. The constant stream of construction materials going out to the end of the base, but nothing showed up on the surface. NASA has a large underground base that has been there for years.

"'Tube shuttles take personnel 50 miles to the other end of the base in the Tahachapi mountains. The underground base has been referred to as an underground city. It is even said that there are disks stored in glasslike enclosures under a vacuum to preserve them.'"

What may very well be a confirmation of the above appeared in the Dec. 1990 issue of a publication sent out by 'THE BORDERLAND SCIENCES RESEARCH FOUNDATION', which had for years been under the direction of Riley H. Crabb. The information was in the form of a letter which we quote here:

"...I spent the weekend with a 'recent' Edwards AFB workman and his wife — 'recent' because they are both repeat contactees and have become 'unmanageable' as the AFB management puts it. He was fired for blasting a Spybee with spray paint — which I find funny and as classic as the graffiti on New York subway cars.

"'You did it on purpose,' they told him, and they knew of course, because the Spybees are telepathic (i.e. capable of 'tuning in' to Extremely Low Frequency or 'ELF' electro- encephalographic neuro-brain wave patterns - Branton) as well as camera equipped. They also carry microphones. We were all laughing as he told us how the little spray-painted gold orb, blinded, went bouncing off walls and posts and was quickly withdrawn from its spy mission. He said Spybees are about the size of a basketball. They fly by antigravity all over any 'Above Top Secret' installation. They dart soundlessly everywhere and hover between workers, sometimes programmed to harass the guys for fun, like bumping them in the rear end.

"No person (that) he and his friends knew about there was allowed to say one word to another while on the job. They would test by trying to write to each other in the floor dust. Within two or three strokes a Spybee would whiz around the corner, lock on to and stop above the writing. His last comment was to write and draw a great big 'screw you'.

"His painting work was part of an ONGOING EXCAVATION beneath Edwards AFB on the high DESERT in California. He and his crew were always blindfolded and strip-searched before transit. They couldn't even have watches. BY TAKING TURNS COUNTING IN THE ELEVATOR GOING TO AND FROM THE WORK SITE, THEY ESTIMATED IT MUST BE SOME 9,000 FEET DOWN, AT LEAST TWO MILES, AND THE TRIP TOOK ABOUT 15 MINUTES.

"Management accused him of doing it on purpose, and they knew... 'No, no. The Spybee kept bumpin the back of my neck while I was sprayin. After one real hard knock I whirled around with the spray gun still goin.'"

"A prominent researcher with us that Saturday evening suggested, after careful questioning of the worker, THAT THE ELEVATOR ITSELF WAS ANTI-GRAVITIC, AS THERE WERE NO CABLES; SO THE ESTIMATED DISTANCE WAS AT BEST MINIMUM. ALL PRESENT CONFIRMED THE GOVERNMENT'S POSSESSION OF PLASMOLE TUNNELING MACHINES WHICH MELT A 50 FOOT HOLE THROUGH SOLID ROCK, AT A RATE OF ABOUT FIVE MILES PER HOUR.

"For part of the night we went 'foo chasing', their term for sightseeking UFOs. Tahachapi (is) where H. Hughes and Northrup Corporations and the USAF have just imported Delta Forces and fleets of black helicopters deployed by the government for top security events coverage. There is no doubt something major going on up there... even that night.

"The researcher and his team were hoping to see the 30- FOOT VERSION OF THE SPYBEES, as there are growing numbers of reports on these. THEY ARE DESIGNED TO FLY OVER YOUR HOUSE CARRYING SURVEILLANCE BEAMS FOR THOUGHT/EMOTION CONTROL AND BEHAVIOR MODIFICATION (Note: Since thoughts and emotions may be to some extent electromagnetic in nature, it may be possible for them to be manipulated by EM rays - Branton).

"...I often see Terra now as in near-final throes of exactly the H.G. Wells scenario where the unwilling and witless 90% of mankind inhabits a play-fantasy world on Earth's surface, while the split-off race of highly technical degenerates (in league with and/or controlled by the serpent race? - Branton), the Trogs, prey on them from underground..."

The following information was sent to us via a researcher who is investigating a continuous abduction of a young (at the time) nine-year-old boy in southern Nevada, who may have been taken to underground levels below that same area. Names, addresses and other details have been deleted on request to protect the privacy of the sources. We quote from a series of notes based on the young boys' experiences, exactly as they were sent to a member of "the Group", with our emphasis added:

1: The 'greys', he says they don't use words but communicate THROUGH him. THEY SHOW THEIR DISPLEASURE BY WRINKLING THEIR NOSES AND PURSING THEIR LIPS WITH A SLIGHT HISSING SOUND AT HIM.

2: HE SAYS HE FEELS LIKE HE'S BEING WATCHED WHEREVER HE GOES (Note: This is a very common observation made by people who claim to have experienced aerial AND/OR subsurface abductions or encounters with non- human aliens - Branton).

3: This is what they look like to him (a drawing was included depicting a traditional 'gray' with a somewhat 'wiry' build - Branton).

4: This is what the uniform they wear looks like to him. He says the box in the middle has different colored flashing buttons.

5: This is the large 'boat', A SORT OF FLOATING ISLAND HE WAS BROUGHT TO (Note: Some aspects of the abduction suggest that the young boy was taken to a large network of water-filled subterranean caverns - Branton). THERE WERE MANY 'HYBRIDS' ON IT ALSO.

6: These are the hybrids he sees. He says that they sit in a large circle holding hands. There is one small candle with a very large flame going. HE SAYS HE IS NOT AFRAID OF THE HYBRIDS.

(Note: These may have been so-called "hu-brids" with a human soul-energy "matrix". These according to different accounts are more or less 'slaves' to the grays and reptoids/ reptons from birth. Many of the women who claim to have been 'impregnated' during abductions and who have had their 'child' removed from them a few months into its term are allegedly carriers to these hybrids or hubrids, although it is possible that re-brids or 'hybrids' without a soul-matrix (more saurian than human) might be gestated in this manner also. The hu-brids are allegedly taken to underground bases beneath the surface of the earth and/or possibly installations on or below other planetary spheres. The ritual that the hybrids were apparently forced to undertake might be part of a psychic warfare operation against humans that their reptilian overlords are waging. It is interesting that Satanists-Illuminists have been known to gather in a circle and meditate on a candle flame in order to induce a state of astral projection, or projection of the spirit form (some have erroneously referred to is as "soul projection" - the "soul body" however can only separate itself from the physical form at death. - Branton)

"THERE IS A FEMALE (hu-brid - Branton) who BLENDS with him and he says it feels very peaceful and good. When asked if the greys were the only aliens he sees, HE DREW THE REPTILIAN, THESE ARE THE UNIFORMS ON THEM ALSO. HE SAYS THE GREYS COME TO GET HIM, BUT THEY FOLLOW THE LEADERSHIP OF THE REPTILIANS. HE CALLED IT A LIZARD. HE SAID HE SEES HUMAN BEINGS - ALIVE - HANGING FROM A WALL WITH NO EYES, OR MOUTHS LEFT.

"Please share with us your input on how to help this boy. We know what is happening here and we are ready and willing to do anything we have to. Love & Light, sincerely (Names deleted by request)."

The above is not, unfortunately, a singular case. MANY people are now coming forward with stories of alien abuse, or of being abducted to underground 'bases' controlled by small 'grayish' or large 'Reptilian' beings. In previously years most of these people have been terrified at the prospect of telling their stories, for fear of ridicule. Before the 'abduction' phenomena was widely known, many such people who spoke out about alien experiences actually ended up in psychiatric institutions, so there was at that time a definite danger of 'talking' too much about their horrifying encounters. Added to this is the official governmental denial of the phenomena, or even outright attempts to 'silence' those who knew too much for supposed "National Security" reasons (actually it was/is "Establishment Security" they were interested in). However at this point in time when radio, television and even motion pictures are giving the subject another (this time more respectable and honest) look, many more people are gathering the courage to come forward with reports of abductions by malevolent — or contacts with benevolent — 'aliens'.

In the hidden depths of the Nevada Military Complex a battle is raging. Few know just how long it has been going on. Apparently it began several years ago when the Nevada Test Site workers discovered vast subterranean cavities deep underground, "possibly" as a result of the underground nuclear blasts which had artificially excavated huge cavities deep below the surface.

This activity apparently corresponded with the same general time-period when the U.S. Secret Government was making deals with the 'Grays', establishing secret locations such as S-4 to study alien craft that had crashed, and constructing environmental enclosures for some of the 'few' alien beings that had been apprehended alive. Much of this activity allegedly took place and is taking place within the extreme high-security areas on and below the Nevada Military Complex.

However, the reports now coming out of the 'Complex' suggest that far more than just a 'few' of the alien grays, and even their reptilian overlords, are involved with the activities taking place in Nevada... more activity than even a few alien survivors of crashed disks could account for. Many accounts have spoken of vast caverns below the southern Nevada region which 'may' have been the ancient lairs of reptilian hominoids for decades or centuries. All the accounts point to only one possible conclusion: That the Test Site workers broke into the native habitat of these reptilian beings, or a system of caverns which the reptilians had taken control of in the recent or distant past. Possibly in an effort to prevent a unilateral warfare between the two expanding 'worlds', the secret government decided to establish a treaty with the saurian Grays (apparently the Grays tried to convince the human governments that they had "originated" from other-stellar regions — and that the humans had encountered one of their underground "bases" — in order to steer the humans clear of the fact that many of them were native to the Terran Subterranea. This may have been a half-lie, as the reptilians do reportedly have ancient facilities that they have established and entrenched on other planetary bodies).

Aside from establishing "treaties" with the extraterrestrial "Grays" that are apparently returning to their native planet, a secret treaty was also made with their counterparts in the so-called 'underground bases'. Most of the 'workers' would not be aware of the alien activity taking place in these extreme lower levels due to the higher security clearances necessary to enter or even KNOW of them. This could explain the confusion which seems to exist, and the comments made by workers, especially within the Nevada Military Complex, that everything is 'way out of control'.

It might also explain the comments made by others 'in the know' who have suggested that the government is in a panic since they have learned that the sauroid 'aliens from other stars' have infiltrated and undermined the surface of the earth without us even knowing it, and that this is why they are in such confusion, why they are rushing headlong to develop weapons such as 'Excalibur' to destroy subterranean alien strongholds, and so on.

In the movie 'THEY LIVE', which depicted an infiltration of human society utilizing underground 'bases' beneath major cities, one of the human resistance' members asks: "How LONG have they been here?" Later he comes to realize... "Maybe they've ALWAYS been here!" Perhaps the reason behind the supposed alien infestation and undermining of the underground systems below the surface of the earth could be explained by the possibility that they have ALWAYS been here, or have been for some time. Do not accounts of reptilian hominoids date back to prehistoric times when the dinosaurs walked the surface of the earth? Keep this possibility in mind when trying to fit the following revelations into your framework of reality.

Is it possible that a subterranean race — working closely with others of their kind which long ago left the earth for extraterrestrial realms — is staging (via subversion, implantation, disinformation, coversion, and infiltration) a takeover of human society FROM ABOVE AND BELOW?

One group that is allegedly tied-in with the inner workings of the government-alien interactions and/or conflicts are known as the 'Delta' Forces. The Delta's, some claim, have secretly been recruited by the secret government in order to perform certain functions in relation to the so-called 'joint-interaction' projects involving deep-level government organizations and the 'aliens' (saurian greys, etc.).

At the beginning of the 'interaction', the government was optimistic about their new-found alliance with an apparently benevolent race of nonhuman beings. When the government finally discovered the true nature of the grays; and the fact that they' were using the 'treaties' with the U.S. government merely as a means to further their infernal plans of bringing the human race under their control, then according to various sources 'all hell broke loose!' The government-CIA in their zeal to establish contact with what they hoped were technological 'saviors' from the stars, had 'bargained away' much of what they had, including much of the sovereignty of the United States and the World. When the 'Horrible Truth' was discovered it was too late, the aliens had already established too much control and their physical and occult conquests were increasing every day. And the Delta's were caught right in the middle.

The Delta Groups (or National Recon Group), wear the 'Trilateral' insignia, a black triangle on a red background. 'Delta' is also the fourth letter in the Greek alphabet, which has the form of a triangle. The symbol appears prominently in certain Masonic lodges, and is said to have had it's origin with the aliens (or serpent race).

The Delta Forces were the major group who, according to some sources, were involved in the attempted operation that was implemented to rescue several scientists who were being held captive within the deepest levels of the 'Dulce' complex below northwestern New Mexico. These workers had stumbled across the 'Horrible Truth', and according to reports over 66 persons, many of them Delta Forces, were slaughtered by the inhuman inhabitants and controllers of these lower levels. Others allege that Air Force Blue Berets were also involved in this conflict, which was later to become known as the 'Dulce Wars'. Exactly what part the Air Force Blue Berets played, however, is uncertain.

With this in mind, the reader might better understand the following revelations which were released by former Naval Petty Officer and Intelligence worker, William Cooper. On January 10, 1989, Mr. Cooper posted the following statement on a computer network devoted to the investigation of paranormal events:

"The following information was extracted from a rather long treatise/transcript/conversation between an individual and another who was assigned to DELTA SECURITY:

01: Delta security has a lot to do with inter-service projects.

02: The Trilateral insignia (alien) is valid and has been used to mark equipment.

03: 'The whole thing is grim and won't get any better.'

04: The Trilateral insignia has been seen on a disk at Edwards AFB, CA and Area 51 in NV.

05: There is a hanger at Edwards referred to as the Delta Hanger.

06: The Delta Hanger is on the North Base at Edwards.

07: You need a special badge to get near it. It is a red badge with a black triangle on the face of it and personal information on the back.

08: Disk in hanger at Edwards described as having insignia on the underside and on the top. It was about 50' in diameter, appearing like tarnished silver, about 15 to 18 feet thick. There were what looked like windows around the raised portion that were mostly described as rectangular. There was a groove around the disk about 4 feet from the edge all the way around. There was an area on the bottom that looked like vents or louvers.

09: When people assigned to Delta would break down and cry for no apparent reason, you would never see them again.

10: Apparently, the NRO (National Recon Organization) recruits for DELTA out of Fort Carson, Colorado.

11: Just about everyone assigned to DELTA are orphans, have no relatives, etc.

12: There are 'bounty hunters' connected with Dreamland.

13: If you work at Dreamland and go on leave or are not back on time they send 'bounty hunters' after you. That's where the 'visitors' live...there is an underground facility...

14: Area 51 is at Groom Lake in Nevada. The disks are flown there.

15: One of the craft looked like an upside-down diamond.

16: There is a radiation hazard apparent when some of the craft fly.

17: No one stays at Dreamland for more than a few months.

18: 'Everything is way out of control...'" (no longer under 'human' control? - Branton)

The following conversation, in relation to the Nevada Military Complex and the 'underground facilities', took place on the "Billy Goodman Happening" - KVEG Radio 840 AM, Las Vegas, Nevada, on November 19, 1989. It was transcribed by a Las Vegas resident.

Billy Goodman incidentally, has personally planned visits, in collaboration with KNBC Radio in Los Angeles, to observe the 'disks' which are being tested at Groom Lake. Goodman and others claimed to have seen these disks in operation, and back up these claims with video documentation. One such video shows a hovering object making a vertical ascent, stop in midair, make a horizontal traverse, followed by another vertical ascent. Something like this would be impossible for any conventionally known aircraft of the time to duplicate. Billy Goodman, who has since moved to another radio station in Los Angeles, has been very instrumental in getting the information out about the underground base at Site 51 (or

Area-51, the 'underground facility' where the 'visitors' live, according to Bill Cooper's source whom we've just quoted). In the following annotated transcript, the caller will be identified as 'C' and Billy Goodman as 'G':

G: Hi! Your on the Billy Goodman Happening on KVEG! Sir, what can I do for you tonight?

C: O.K. Are you ready? Hang on to your seats! Here goes! We are going 3,000 feet underground! O.K. We get to that point, 3,000 feet. We come out into a stainless steel atmosphere... and we come upon people that are ah... construction people... working people, and so forth that are supposed to be in that area. Then we come upon another people who push us into another little room. They tell us, "Do not come out of that area, until your told to." These guys are 6 minute marines, all right? They tell us, "If you do, you are going to get hurt!" OK? So we are construction workers!

G: Where are you working? Where is what you are describing to us.

C: On a certain test site!

G: A certain test site! Which one? You can't reveal which one?

C: We're kinda mixed up! We don't know what the hell is going on. We're making ah... good bucks... and everything has come down on us... and they are hurting us! OK? So we are contractors! We are workers! OK? So there's a person that I called and explained what is happening to me and they told me to call you and tell you! So, that is what I am doing right now! Calling you!

G: You presented it in a very odd way! First of all I didn't know if you were going to be serious or what! Are you saying to me that you are a construction worker and you had to go 3,000 feet under ground? First of all what would you be doing underground? Let me ask you that!

C: We are running lights and power.

G: And who assigned you this job?

C: It's through Reynold's Electronics. I have to say that because I get my pay check from someone else! (Note: Reynold's Electronics is a branch of "E.G. & G." Corporation which DOES IN FACT work with and contract through the Nevada and Utah Test Sites - Branton)

G: They tell you to put these lights underground?

C: Yeh, but there's more to it than that! I'm sort of afraid of expressing. Am I talking to you or what?

G: Yes, you are talking directly to me!

C: OK. You know some of the things that are happening, shouldn't be. It should be made public! The public should know what the hell is going on! And it scares the hell out of me. What is not being brought out you know? For example, can I give you an example? Here's an example! A few weeks back we were inside a certain cavern going through stainless steel halls, going north, and as we move along we are hanging lights. In the rooms are... they're like operating rooms. All of a sudden, off the elevator, our U.S. Marines come out, crash us down off our scaffold, pushing us down, and then into a room. This is taking a hell of a lot out of me to tell you this right now! The bosses come into the room and we're getting debriefed and all this kind of stuff and all of a sudden they are carrying fixed bayonets. Now I fought in Vietnam and I thought these guys were my buddies! Oh, no way! Forget it! These guys are from outer space! (Note: There is a slight possibility that the 'soldiers' which this man encountered were not 'human' marines, but we will deal with this bizarre possibility later on - Branton) These people brought these little characters on gurneys, OK? They had big heads and little bodies and they went into this little room. Then, behind them, these doctors in white coats and stuff! And we was really at ah... we didn't know what the hell was going on! We were shocked to hell! ...I was SCARED man!

G: Well, sure you didn't know what was going on and didn't expect it! I guess them handling you upset you first of all. Being man to man, you thought why should you treat me this way! And that's to be expected. As far as knowing where you are I have no idea.

C: I know where I was! I worked there every day! I keep a log and if someone asks me I know what's going on! I'm telling you man they're not telling us the truth. There is something damn wrong within our government. I only got a glimpse of this scientist on television (i.e. most likely referring to Robert Lazar - Branton), but I know he's not telling much of what he knows. I'm just a worker. A hammer and nail man. This guy's got more brains than I do, and would know more about it than I do. There's something INSIDE they aren't telling us!

G: OK. I understand that! Now what do you want us to do about it?

C: EXPOSE IT!!!

G: I think you've done that yourself, just now! Now you haven't told us your location and I think that's important so we have some idea where this is. I hope you understand at this moment...

C: I work at Mercury, Nevada and I'm the best electrician there. This is between you and me now. I don't want anybody else to know about this!

G: But your on the air Sir!

C: You mean somebody knows about this besides you and me?

G: But you are talking over the radio, Sir! Everybody, all over the West Coast that is listening has just heard you! So you've gotten your word out. Now let's see if anybody else knows about it. Maybe just maybe, we'll get some calls from some of the people that work with you.

C: Wait a minute! You mean somebody else knows about this beside you and me?

G: Now, this is a talk show, you called a talk show. I am over the radio - that's where you called!

C: OH, MY GOD!!!

G: Why, what's wrong with that? You called a talk show!

C: I thought I was just talking to you!

G: Now you said someone told you to call me. Was it someone you work with?

C: Yes.

G: Nobody knows who you are. You haven't said your name or anything! Now, let's see if anyone will back up your story!

C: But I didn't know other people would hear this. Now I'm scared for my life! There's tremendous stuff out there that's being hidden. It's being corrupted inside. It's being stashed away.

G: Well that's what we do here. We are trying to bring the information out, and it's people like yourself who are making that happen. They bring us information all the time! Are you trying to bring the information out yourself because you don't like what's going on?

C: I fear for my life because I've seen what happened. I fear for my life because the government is lying to me.

G: OK. Why do you fear for your life? Have you been threatened?

C: Before you even go down in the pit they threaten you! That is you tell anything of what you saw, you are dead!!!

G: But you're not saying more than what you saw. Is there anything else you want to say before we say thank you for calling?

C: Yes, one other thing. Whenever it gets down to the nitty gritty, it will be clear to the people, that what they are seeing on the news, is true! We've got six little bodies under ground, man!!!

G: Please keep in touch, OK? (end of transcript)

The reference to Reynold's Electrical, by the way, may be explained more fully in it's connection with E.G. & G., from the following reference which we quote, from an article that appeared in a newspaper called the REVIEW-JOURNAL, January 9th, 1990. This Associated Press article stated:

"Three Nevada-based EG&G companies employ most of the workers at the Nevada TEST SITE, the nations' nuclear proving grounds 65 miles northwest of Las Vegas.

"The companies employ 8,000 people: 1,500 at EG&G Energy Measurements Inc.; 1,000 at EG&G Special Projects; and 5,500 at Reynolds Electrical and Engineering Co."

Actually, present officials working at the Nevada Test Site are apparently, at least for the most part, refusing the advice of the FOUNDER of EG&G., Herald 'Doc' Edgerton, who once made the following statement at a meeting of the Archaeological Society of America:

"Work like hell, TELL EVERYONE EVERYTHING YOU KNOW, close a deal with a handshake, and have fun." Edgerton apparently was no supporter of 'official secrecy', yet many of those now involved in this company are being threatened to remain silent to the point of endangering their very lives if they speak out about what they have seen. Incidentally, Robert Lazar was hired by EG&G himself to work at the S-4 installation at Groom Lake. In fact, we will now relate another conversation which took place on the "Billy Goodman Happening" almost a week following the conversation which is recorded above. There are apparently SOME EMPLOYEES working at the Nevada Test Site, who ARE speaking out about what is going on there, like the one who called in to the Billy Goodman show on Nov. 24, 1989, possibly in response to the caller from Mercury, Nevada mentioned earlier, as well as in response to Bob Lazar's own experiences.

The person who transcribed this particular taped program indicated that they had missed the first 15 seconds or so of the callers conversation. This is NOT the same caller whose conversation we just described. In the following transcript, (C:) indicates 'Caller'; (G:) indicates Billy 'Goodman'; and (L.:) refers to Bob 'Lazar', who was Goodman's guest for that evening. Beginning with the 'Caller':

C: ...Well, we're kinda fed up with what's going on, right! And I mean nothing gets done without the ants! We are the ants! We are the construction workers, O.K.? We put things together and take them apart! You are the scientists (referring here to Robert Lazar - Branton). You do all the higher level of knowledge stuff, right? We do all the putting in this and putting in that: installing, construction and so forth! Well we heard about your situation, and it's going through a whole bunch of grape vines, O.K? It's coming together where people are meeting in small groups and they're trying to organize a support for you to back you up! Out of the meeting we had yesterday of 7 people, counting myself there are two that will come forward and support you! What they SAW, what they are INVOLVED WITH! The other guys are just scared to death and I'm a little scared myself, you know!

L.: Do these people work in area S-4?

C: Yeh, all over the area!

L.: That would be great!

C: Mostly UNDERGROUND! The deep sections of the area! The whole thing!

G: How do you feel Bob? Sounds like you are getting some support!

L: Yea, that's great! There's power in numbers!

C: We are trying to get things where it will be safe! You know what I mean Bob?

L.: Oh yeh, I do!

C: It's kinda hard to talk to you like this you know but the guys are for you! People are for you and everybody's wanted to do something a long time ago but nobody knew what they could do.

L.: Yeh, that was the consensus when I was down there! Everybody wanted to do something. I'm glad everyone has that attitude!

C: Yeh, you are probably the beginning of the first motion of the wheel you know! The first turn! The wheel is gonna turn faster and faster in order to get where we want to get to!

L.: Well hopefully that will be the case! Do you think these people would come forward if there was some sort of congressional amnesty for them?

C: I don't know but we all know a lot! We know our jobs well, like you do!

L.: I'm sure you do.

C: What we have to do is be firm about it, get to the point and say, "Hey, here's what's happening!" Why don't you tell the people what's happening? Why keep it a secret? Like before you walk into those hangers there. Somebody had to install this and install that! It's frightening. It scared the heck out of me. We got together out at Lathrup Wells and kicked it around. We B.S.'ed a little bit and said, "We gotta do something!" SO WE DID SOMETHING YESTERDAY. Like I said: there's only two of the seven of us who are willing to do something.

G: Sir, Sir! Is there anything we can do to help you in this matter? Is there anything the listening people can do? I know they are behind Bob Lazar 100%. I had him on here one night and there hasn't been one person by either mail, or by telephone, who has disputed what he has said! So they are behind him. Is there anything we can do?

C: Well you could form some kind of walk or picket! Or announce it on the street. Tell them we want to know! WE WANT TO KNOW!!!

G: When you say on the street, are you talking about downtown Las Vegas?

C: YES!

G: What do you think of that Bob? Do you think that would do anything?

L.: Certainly if these people come forward! They have a LOT to lose, if people start making a ruckus like that! They could lose their jobs right away! They talked about there being a ten year jail term and a $10,000 fine for divulging information like that! I mean they have a lot to lose! You might...

G: But you know something Bob? It's almost like...

C: We have the first amendment on our side!

L.: Yeh, you do but... have you thought about contact(ing) George Knapp? (of KLAS-TV, Las Vegas, who produced an entire series of UFO-based documentaries after Lazar came forward with his story - Branton) He's looking for anybody that is coming forward from S-4, and any surrounding areas having knowledge at all about that area or any of the flying saucer information! He's gathering all he can and doing a lot to try and expose it!

G: You might want to contact George! That might be a good idea! But I think there's another side to this. It's almost like they're not concerned any more about their jobs. They're more concerned about the Constitution! They're more concerned about Humanity! That's the impression I get!

L.: Yeh, you get that point but you have to feed yourself too!

G: Well you know, there are people that take chances in life, and sometimes they wind up with something better. Later on... down the line. You know what I'm saying? Someone like yourself. I'm not saying this would happen by coming forward, taking a chance, and all of a sudden, say, the government cut you off. You might get an offer for a better position. You follow what I'm saying? Because there are people who own the businesses that believe the way you believe. And I believe this! I hear this gentleman talking and it's happening more and more. There are people out there who would LOVE to come forward with information.

C: But somebody has to start it.

G: Right. And I think you've done that Bob! You started the ball rolling. I know you did. I think what is going to happen is the people who have been wanting to say something; this might be a relief for them. It's coming out and they won't have to keep it inside any more!

L.: That was the general consensus when I was out there.

G: Well obviously they want out too. They want to tell the truth.

C: Bob, did you have any work underground? IN THE TUNNELS?

L.: No! I have a friend whose dad worked on some of the drilling equipment! I know there's some tunnels down there!

C: There's more than just tunnels down there! There's everything you can imagine down there. I know cause we put it up!!! We installed. We did everything. I just want you to know that the M.W.s (Mercury Workers) are gathering together in small groups trying to put something together for you and contact you somehow to join you. If the people want to join us in a march or whatever it's going to be, that's what we're going to do!

L.: Oh! That's super!

C: So we're with you man!

G: Thanks for the call sir! Have a nice night. Bob, it sounds as though people are starting to come forward. (end of transcript)

Still on the subject of the strange events taking place in (and beneath) southern Nevada, we quote here part of a letter written by a subscriber to N.A.R. (Nevada Aerial Research - now Leading Edge Research), who made the following statements:

"...Bob Lazar, the scientist, was talking about riding in a bus with the windows blacked out and it brought back something an airline stewardess told me last summer (1989). She said, 'I'm trying to relocate to another part of the country right now. Once a week, I'm assigned to a flight that I hate! We only have Armed Forces officers on THIS flight. Before we take off, we are instructed to pull the window covers over the windows! After we take off, we circle widely, about 15 minutes (it would be unnoticeable to most people) - fly straight for 15 minutes, circle again about 15 minutes and then land. After we land the flight crew is ushered into a lounge. A half hour later we repeat the process back to Las Vegas. The people are all different on the return trip. We are told, 'Don't tell anyone about these flights!' I just can't stand the tension on this flight!' (Note: just what did she mean when she says the "people are different" on the return flight — different people or the same people with different personalities? - Branton)

"I think these trips are to Groom Lake!

"The jets are still swarming over the Blue Diamond area. It's VERY odd. I know in my heart that it's more than just practice flights!

"Something else very odd: (I think this might have something to do with the tunnels). The apartment complex where I work (fourplexes - 450 of them)... Two or three days ago the manager asked the maintenance men if any of them were doing any work in ONE of the buildings. Everybody said no. She said ALL 4 APARTMENTS in that building had called her and said that an explosion knocked all the pictures off their walls and broke them. No one else, from any other building felt anything. The man I said who saw the landing at Holloman beat a path to me to tell me about this. ...A Las Vegas subscriber."

In addition to this, here is another item which appeared in one of the NAR newsletters: "On November 25th (1990), television station Channel 8 in Las Vegas televised a two hour special on UFOs, Area 51, S-4 and the UFO coverup. It is revealed that some of the people who contacted Channel 8 had had their homes broken into in Las Vegas..." (could channel 8 have an "infiltrator" working among them? - Branton)

Also, the following information appeared in the NAR Newsletter, under the heading: "INTELLIGENCE REPORT" (also in reference to the UFO-Military connection):

"NRO - National Recon Organization: Based at Fort Carson, Colorado. Responsible for all alien or alien craft connected projects. Use unmarked black helicopters.

"DELTA - Security teams from NRO specially trained to provide tasked PROJECTS/LUNA security (MEN IN BLACK). This project is ongoing.

"BLUE TEAM - The first project responsible for reaction/ recovery of downed/crashed alien craft and/or aliens. This was an AF Material Command project.

"UFO sightings of craft accompanied by black helicopters are REDLIGHT assets that originate at Groom Lake (Dreamland), Area 51 north of Las Vegas.

"...PROJECTS: BLUE TEAM, SIGN, GRUDGE, AQUARIUS, SIGNA, PLUTO, SNOWBIRD, LUNA, GABRIEL, EXCALIBUR (1988)... (Note: These are some of the 'secret projects' allegedly relating to the U.S. Government's interaction with the UFO phenomena. Further details on these projects are available from Leading Edge Research., P.O. Box 481-MU58., Yelm, WA 98597. Although L.E.R. carries much documentable information from very reliable sources, the reader should be warned that they also carry some 'occult channeled' information which may be of an extremely dubious nature, information that CANNOT be physically substantiated. But the 'documentation' it does carry is extensive and very well compiled - Branton).

The 'INTELLIGENCE REPORT' segment in NAR-LER also revealed the following information concerning former Naval Officer Bill Cooper:

"Bill Cooper recently received some strange phone calls in which the following statements were made by the caller:

"'I called to tell you that you are wrong about the alien base. LUNA is the name of the base on the far side of the moon. The earth base is called Dreamland.

"'You are in over your head. Would you like to end up in an asylum? If you continue your activities you will meet me sooner than you think. You should know who I am.'

"Bill Cooper has some comments. We will print them:

"'When I released PUBLIC 02.DOC (release of info on computer bulletin board) my purpose was to expose the documents and information released by William Moore et al as being fraudulent and misleading. MAJESTIC TWELVE is an advisory team of scientists who's only purpose is to evaluate information and make recommendations. The information gathered by the control group MAJI is released to MAJESTIC TWELVE when study is needed. MAJESTIC TWELVE has never been the whole truth. MAJI is the MAJESTIC AGENCY FOR JOINT INTELLIGENCE and has total control of information and interface with the aliens in dealings with the United States government. Some of the documents released by Moore were changed from the original with the deliberate intent to mislead UFO researchers. I believe that the government is behind the whole thing. The rest of the documents are deliberate frauds. MAJIC is the highest security classification in the nation...'" (Other 'Above Top Secret' security classifications reportedly include the "Q", "E", "MJ" and "ULTRA" classifications - Branton)

The following information from William F. Hamilton III appeared in "UFO UNIVERSE" and describes further details on the 'Yellow Fruit' account, including claims which YF made over the air during the few 'interviews' in which he took part on KVEG Radio's Billy Goodman talk show:

"...Yellow Fruit revealed that A CONFLICT WAS GOING ON BETWEEN THE BENEVOLENT ONES and THE EBE's and that now the benevolent ones had gained the upper hand at Dreamland where he said a contingent of 37 benevolent ones were stationed and where 3 EBE's were held in captivity.

"Bizarre! Science Fiction? Yellow Fruit knew a lot about the test site area. I resolved to go to the location he gave of the EBE installation in Deep Springs, California and then on to visit Pat at the Rachel Bar & Grill to make contact with Yellow Fruit (the name for the first level of security force at Area 51 and also the name of an old Army-CIA unit). The second level of security he called 'Sea Spray' and intimated that you would have an encounter of the unpleasant kind if you ever met with them.

"Callers to the Billy Goodman Radio Happening had already organized trips to mile-marker 29 1/2 on highway 375 where a dirt road left the highway to intersect the road to Dreamland. There was a heavy black mail box on this road which identified it. I got to Rachel early one October morning and left my card with Pat at Rachel's Bar and Grill to pass on to Yellow Fruit. She knew him by sight. I then inspected the dirt roads where people stood to observe the test flights. I had already interviewed four witnesses by phone who testified that they had seen UFOs over the Groom Mountains on certain nights in the same area they were seen by John Lear. I made a second trip to the area in late October where a public group visited Rachel and that is when I saw the mysterious Yellow Fruit in the cafe. He later called me on the phone. I left him with a copy of my book, 'Alien Magic' and he remarked on the research I had done concerning the search for underground bases.

"According to Yellow Fruit and others there are underground bases and tunnels that conceal the activities of the aliens and secret government projects..."

The following is an excerpt from an article which appeared in a UFO-related publication. We do not know exactly who the author of the article is, but we relate the excerpt as it was sent to us:

"...Lear directed my attention to a large map of Nevada, which delineates all the areas which civilian maps coyly leave as uncharted military preserves. 'Right in the very center is a place called Area 51. It is our most secret complex. There are 1900 people there — it takes presidential clearance to work there — and they're ferried in by aircraft in the morning and taken out about 5 o'clock in the evening. They have nothing to do with the saucers. The people who work on the saucers go up later in the afternoon, and go home about midnight. The saucer facility is called S-4.' S-4 is in the southwest corner of Area 51.

"Unfortunately, this facility — and a similar setup near Dulce, New Mexico

— may now belong to forces not loyal to the U.S. Government, or even the human race. 'It's horrifying for us to think that all the scientists we think are working for us are actually controlled by the aliens.'

"Here, Lear seems to contradict himself. He speaks of 'aliens,' plural, in a controlling capacity, whereas previously he noted but one survivor, kept as captive. He resolves this conflict by describing an alleged landing at Holloman Air Force Base on April 24, 1964 — our first 'diplomatic contact,' as it were, with the visitors (Note: In addition, this writer does not take into account the apparent SUBTERRANEAN connection and origin of many of the 'alien' beings, which has been alleged by many sources and which WOULD explain the large alien influence or presence in Nevada and elsewhere - Branton). According to Lear and other sources, the 1973 Robert Emenegger documentary 'UFOS: PAST, PRESENT AND FUTURE' presented a thinly-fictionalized version of this event; government contacts allegedly provided the filmmakers actual footage of the meeting, which, alas, was withdrawn at the last moment for as-yet unspecified reasons.

"'A deal was made with them in the latter part of the 1960s (Note: As we've indicated earlier, this might have been a 'revisioning' of an earlier treaty, as certain sources claim that these treaties go back to the 1930's, if not earlier. Some of those involved in this 'deal' may have had good intentions, since the Grays presented themselves as evolved 'space brothers' who only wanted to help us. John Lear even alleged that huge underground bases were constructed with the 'help' of the Grays, yet when completed, the Grays did an about face and took control of not only the lower levels of these bases but also the mechanisms which were supposedly given to the government as part of the 'deal'. This is about the time that the 'wars' began within the subterranean system itself, near the time when the so-called 'Grand Deception' of the aliens was discovered - Branton).

"'In exchange for technology, we would cover up the existence of the aliens.' Apparently this agreement — engineered by an arm of government so covert that even the President may not be on the 'need to know' list — also sanctioned the abduction of humans, which the aliens rationalized as an ongoing monitoring of a developing civilization. We asked only for a list of the abductees.

"In 1973, the deal soured. 'Hundreds of people — thousands — were being abducted that weren't on the list. In 1978-79, there was an altercation between us and the aliens, in which they killed 44 of our top scientists, and a number of Delta forces who were trying to free them. I'm not sure where this altercation occurred — it could have been Dulce (probably Dulce, as the term 'Dulce Wars' — which has been referred to by different sources — would seem to indicate. Also, there is some confusion as to the "66" and "44" numbers. Paul Bennewitz says that 66 Special Forces were killed in an attempt to set free some of our scientists from the "aliens" that had taken them captive, whereas 44 escaped. Whether the 44 were storm-troopers or scientists is uncertain, although most sources state that the scientist did NOT make it out alive. Bennewitz claims that the "44" did not die but escaped instead. Since some report that the scientists were NOT set free it may have been that 100 special forces were sent in — 66 of them being killed in the attempt and 44 escaping the alien counterattack - Branton), or it could have occurred in Groom Lake (Robert Lazar has stated that a similar confrontation between the aliens and human Security DID occur in the bases below Groom Lake - Branton.) This battle, Lear claims, left us bereft of our own facilities; ever since, we have attempted to create a counterforce to meet the alien challenge." (In other words, the 'aliens' invaded and took control of the underground bases — probably from BELOW — and killed many of the TOP SCIENTISTS in America, destroying much of 'our' ability to defend ourselves, at least technically, from their ongoing incursions - Branton)

"...The Strategic Defense Initiative was one such scheme. 'SDI, regardless of what you hear, was completed two years ago; that was to shoot down incoming saucers. The mistake was that we thought they were coming inbound - in fact, they're already here. They're in underground bases all over the place.' It seems that the aliens had constructed many such bases without our knowledge, where they conduct heinous genetic experiments on animals, human beings, and 'improvised' creatures of their own devising.'"

The following information was released by Leading Edge Research and describes some additional details concerning the serpent race/greys based upon the findings of several researchers who have pooled their investigations in order to find out more about this apparent enemy or nemesis to humankind. The following scenario emerged from this cooperative effort (emphasis ours - Branton):

"NOTES ON ALF (Alien Life Forms): Term used by the government to describe the Greys in terms of being a MALEVOLENT life form. The deal with the Greys is that their field around their body is different (from) ours to the point where merging of the fields ends up creating physical symptoms (the 'body terror' mentioned by people like Whitley Strieber). The field around them is in direct opposition to ours. IT IS AN ANTI- LIFE FIELD... THEY ARE EXPERTS OF MANIPULATION OF BOTH THE HUMAN BODY (THROUGH MANIPULATION OF THE FIELDS) AND THE HUMAN MIND. THEY REQUIRE BLOOD AND OTHER BIOLOGICAL FLUIDS to survive. THEY ABDUCT HUMANS AND ANIMALS IN ORDER TO ACQUIRE THESE FLUIDS (VAMPIRIAL in nature - Branton). They implant small devices in the brain which potentially GIVES THEM TOTAL CONTROL AND MONITORING CAPABILITY. These devices are very difficult to detect. The analysis of the devices by technical staff has produced a description that involves use of crystalline technology combined with molecular circuitry and these ride on the resonant emissions of the brain and the various fields of the human (body). Information is entrained on the brain waves. It appears that all attempts to remove the implants

(1972) have resulted in the death of the human. They perform surgery and other operations on human subjects. These abductions continue to be an ongoing matter. A list of abductees is provided periodically to MAJI, although IT IS KNOWN THAT MANY MORE ARE ABDUCTED THAN ARE REPORTED... Various descriptions of the ALF's relate the following characteristics: Between 3 to 5 feet in height, erect standing biped, small thin build, head larger than humans, absence of auditory lobes (external), absence of body hair, large... eyes (slanted approximately 35 degrees) WHICH ARE OPAQUE BLACK WITH VERTICAL SLIT PUPILS, ARMS RESEMBLING PRAYING MANTIS (normal attitude) which reach to the knees, long hands with small palm, CLAW-LIKE FINGERS (various number of digits - often two short digits and two long, but some species have three or four fingers), tough gray skin WHICH IS REPTILIAN IN TEXTURE, small feet WITH FOUR SMALL CLAW-LIKE TOES... a non-functioning digestive system; TWO SEPARATE BRAINS; movement is deliberate, slow and precise; ALIEN SUBSTANCE REQUIRES THAT THEY MUST HAVE HUMAN BLOOD AND OTHER BIOLOGICAL SUB- STANCES to survive. In extreme circumstances they can subsist on other (cattle, etc.) animal fluids. Food is converted to energy by Chlorophyll, by a photosynthetic process (this supports results gained from autopsies at 29 Palms underground base where it was seen that their 'blood' was greenish and the tissue was black). Waste products are secreted through the skin. The two separate brains are separated by mid-cranial lateral bone (anterior and posterior brain). There is no apparent connection between the two (could one be an 'individual' brain while the other works as part of a 'collective consciousness'? - Branton). Some autopsies have revealed a crystalline network which is thought to have a function in telepathic (and other) functions which help to maintain the group consciousness between members of the same species. Functions of group consciousness in this species does have a disadvantage in that decisions in this species comes rather slowly as the matter at hand filters through the group awareness of those who must make the decision..."

The above description fits almost perfectly with the description of the 'UFO occupants' witnessed by police officer/patrolman Herb Shermer. Shermer described these creatures which he swore he encountered outside of Ashland, Nebraska, shortly after midnight on December 3rd, 1967:

"...They were from 4 1/2 to 5 1/2 feet tall. Their uniforms were silver-gray, very shiny. Their suits came up around their heads like a pilot's cap. On the right side of their helmet's they had a small antenna, just above where the ear would be. Their chests were bigger than ours, they were built very wiry and muscular. Their eyes were the one thing I will never forget... THE PUPIL WENT UP AND DOWN LIKE A SLIT. When they looked at me they stared straight into my eyes. They didn't blink. It was REAL uncomfortable. Their noses were flat, their mouths looked more like a slit than a regular mouth..."

The fact that the pupils of the creatures encountered by Shermer were 'slit-like' would indicate that the creatures were most likely reptilian-saurian in nature, as most snakes and lizards, etc., have vertical-slit pupils. The reptilian connection which we make with the creatures encountered by officer Shermer is not based solely on his testimony alone, but on the other testimonies of various persons who have also encountered creatures similar to the ones just described. Many of these accounts give a more definite link — between the ancient reptilian-saurian race which disappeared from the surface of this planet ages ago — and the nonhuman UFOnauts encountered by literally tens of thousands of individuals the world over.

QUEST INTERNATIONAL (c/o 15, Pichard Court., Temple Newsam., Leeds, L515 9AY., ENGLAND U.K.), a major British UFO research organization consisting mainly of retired Police, Security and Military personnel, is presently investigating what may well be the most documentable case of the crash-retrieval of an unidentified flying disk to date.

On the 7th of May, 1989, NORAD installations allegedly tracked an unidentified object as it entered African airspace. The South African Air Force is also said to have tracked the craft by radar, traveling at a calculated speed of 5746 nautical miles per hour. The incident was related by a South African Intelligence Worker, who along with documentation of his military position, also sent secret files and transcripts to two QUEST INTERNATIONAL investigators, Tony Dodd and Henry Azadehdel, telling of the event. Also, several RECORDED telephone conversations with high-ranking military and government officials were obtained which strongly suggest that 'something' did in fact happen over South African terrain. Some of these recorded conversations involved military officials in South Africa who strongly reprimand the intelligence-worker-turned-informer over the phone. This was due to the fact that the informer had left South Africa for Britain, where he stayed at the house of the researchers, and then later went into hiding.

QUEST INTERNATIONAL director Graham W. Birdsall has stated that the documentation and the individuals involved in the incident are of such a nature that the event must have taken place, or the International Intelligence Community is collectively perpetrating a hoax of incredible magnitude concerning a crashed and recovered flying disk. Birdsall strongly suspects that the incidents did take place, due to the weight of evidence. Following is part of a word-for-word transcript given to the researchers by the informant, which he alleged was taken from the actual top secret report of the initial tracking of the object:

"...The object entered South African air space at 13.52 GMT. Radio contact was attempted with object, but all communications proved futile. As a result two armed Mirage fighters were scrambled. A short time later the object suddenly changed course at great speed which would have been impossible for conventional aircraft to duplicate.

"At 13.59 GMT, Squadron Leader —— the pilot of the fighter reported that they had radar and visual confirmation of the object. The order was given to arm and fire the experimental aircraft- mounted Thor 2 laser cannon. This was done.

"Squadron leader —— reported that several blinding flashes emitted from the object which had started wavering whilst heading in a northerly direction. At 14.02 it was reported that the object was decreasing altitude at a rate of 3000 feet per minute. Then at speed it dived at an angle of 25 degrees and impacted in desert terrain 80 miles north of the South African border with Botswana, identified as the central Kalahari desert. Squadron leader —— was instructed to circle the area until a retrieval team arrived. A team of Air Force Intelligence Officers, together with medical and technical staff were promptly taken to the area of impact for Investigation and retrieval. The findings were as follows:

1) a crater 150 meters in diameter and 12 meters in depth.

2) A silver colored disk shaped object 45 degrees embedded inside of crater.

3) Around the object sand and rocks were fused together by the intense heat.

4) An intense magnetic and radioactive environment around the object resulted in electronic failure of air force equipment (causing the crash of one Air Force helicopter).

5) The object was eventually moved to an Air Force Base for further investigation.

6) The terrain of impact was filled with sand and rubble to disguise all evidence of the event having taken place..."

The report indicated that a hydraulic type landing gear was fully deployed, suggesting that electronic malfunction had caused the object to crash, probably due to the Thor 2 laser cannon having been fired at the craft. While the team observed the object at the Air Force Base a loud sound was heard. It was then noted that a hatch on the lower side of the craft had opened slightly and appeared to be stuck. This opening was later forced with the use of hydraulic pressure equipment, at which point two humanoid entities in tight fitting grey suits emerged and were promptly apprehended. The report stated that the entities were of the following description (emphasis ours - Branton):

"HEIGHT: 4-5.5 ft.; COMPLEXION: Greyish blue - skin texture smooth, extremely resilient; HAIR: Totally devoid of any bodily hair; HEAD: Oversize in relation to human proportions. Raised cranium with dark blue markings around head; FACE: Prominent cheek bones; EYES: Large and slanted upwards towards side of face. NO pupils seen; NOSE: Small consisting of two nostrils; MOUTH: Small slit devoid of lips; JAW: Small in relation to human proportions; BODY/ARMS: Long and thin reaching just above knees; HANDS: CONSISTING OF 3 DIGITS, WEBBED,

CLAW-LIKE NAILS; TORSO: CHEST AND ABDOMEN COVERED WITH SCALY RIBBED SKIN; HIPS: Small narrow; LEGS: Short and thin; GENITALS: NO EXTERIOR sexual organs; FEET: CONSISTING OF THREE TOES, NO NAILS AND WEBBED. NOTES: Due to AGGRESSIVE NATURE of humanoids, no samples of blood or tissue could be taken (One humanoid ATTACKED DOCTOR causing DEEP SCRATCHES ON FACE AND CHEST). When offered various food, refused to eat... One way passage has been requested for both humanoids to Wright Patterson Air Force Base USA for more advanced investigation and research..."

Many of the details regarding these 'humanoids' are actually very similar to other branches of the reptilian race as it has been described by other witnesses. It appears as if the 'serpent race' is composed of several different branches or types, much the same as dogs and other animals retain their distinction but are composed of several different 'types' or 'branches'. Commonly known reptiles are devoid of bodily hair, have prominent cheek bones, large slanted eyes, small openings in place of ears, 3-digit webbed hands and feet — except in the case of snakes, etc., which lost use of their limbs through atrophication over 1000's of years, — have claws, are covered with 'scaly' ribbed skin, and have no external reproductive organs, being egg-layers, and are aggressive and predatory in nature.

The top-secret document indicated that the passage of the object and creatures would be implemented on the 23rd of June, 1989 to Wright Patterson AFB. Actually, sources DO indicate that Wright Patterson DID IN FACT GO ON RED ALERT on that date. Subsequent documents supplied by the Intelligence source to QUEST INTERNATIONAL indicate that the creatures seemed to have a strong connection with the SAURIAN race which existed in ancient times. The exact wording of one particular document which is now in the hands of QUEST INTERNATIONAL is as follows:

"All informations found aboard alien spacecraft concerning the evolution of alien life forms indicates to an evolution similar to that which we find on Earth PRIOR TO THE EXTINCTION OF THE DINOSAURS... (the findings indicate) a high degree of ADAPTABILITY. Further physiological and psychological studies performed in South Africa and in the United States points to a simple and complex structure of behavior. It would seem as if these lifeforms CAN NOT FUNCTION INDEPENDENTLY WITHOUT GROUP INTELLIGENCE AND IDENTITY TOGETHER WITH A CENTRAL COMMAND. According to additional informations found aboard retrieved craft a separate race is designated superior by them. CONCLUSION: An in-depth study and analysis of the psychological makeup and behavior prediction is advised. Studies performed on two alien life forms captured has proven that they cannot act independently from own acquired intelligence without access to communication, orders and instructions from a hierarchy or central command..."

THE MOJAVE DESERT'S GREATEST SECRETS

Three different aspects of the South African affair in fact coincide very closely with what other sources have revealed concerning these reptilian-saurian or 'alien' creatures:

1) Numerous sources indicate that the saurioid 'grays' are the lower echelon of a hidden reptilian hierarchy, and that the other race which is considered to be superior is saurian-reptilian and hominoid as well, although they are a different and larger 'branch' of the serpent race. They resemble "lizard men" of a somewhat similar appearance to the RAPTORS depicted in the movie JURASSIC PARK, yet of a more hominoid mutation or appearance than those depicted in the movie;

2) Many other sources state that the serpent race, saurians or reptilians operate on a 'collective consciousness' level as if the individual alien beings are — to put it in one perspective — individual 'cells' in an immense mind or body of a single immense creature. Actually there seems to be a COMBINATION of both individuality AS WELL AS 'collective consciousness' operating in these entities;

3) The description of the 'aliens' as well as the electromagnetic nature of their craft corresponds exactly with descriptions given in THOUSANDS of separate reports of this nature.

The Intelligence Officer who contacted QUEST INTER- NATIONAL and provided them with the information, claims he did so out of concern for the security of the human race as a whole, and although he was pressured into signing a 'National Secrecy Act' form he believes that he would be guilty of treason against the human race if he did not disclose what he knew, and what the governments were trying to hide.

It is remarkable that the majority of the nonhuman occupants which are reported in connection with these AERIAL craft are said to be REPTILIAN or SAURIAN in nature, especially in light of such prophecies as the one given in Revelation chapter 12, which reads:

"...And there was WAR IN HEAVEN: Michael fought against THE DRAGON; and THE DRAGON fought and his angels... and the GREAT DRAGON was cast out, that OLD SERPENT, called the Devil, and Satan, which DECIEVETH the whole world..."

One of the 'phenomena' which we have mentioned earlier has taken place in several different parts of the world, but most prominently along the Continental Divide region of the U.S.

Since the late 1960's, bizarre animal (especially cattle) mutilations have been on the increase. Numerous accounts claim that these mutilations were performed with laser-fine surgical precision, with cuts so precise (down to the separation of the molecules themselves) that they could not have been accomplished by the conventionally known technology of the time. Eyes, colons, reproductive organs, etc., are very often reported as having been removed in such a manner as if part of a rehearsed process being carried out in widely scattered locations. The blood is almost always described as having been drained with no resulting vascular collapse (also impossible with the conventional technology of our society at the time). In most cases no tracks or markings in the ground have been discovered, which is another mystery that investigators for a large part have been unable to explain; but in the few cases where markings have been seen, the investigators consistently report the existence of strange 'tripod' or 'crop-circle' marks in the ground, nothing else. Another strange phenomena surrounding these mutilations is the fact that predatory birds and other animals which have fed off the carcasses of the mutilated animals have often been found lying dead nearby. It is even reported that in some cases maggots have refuse to touch such carcasses. Again, the reason is unknown. Just who or what is mutilating these animals? The "Mutilation" phenomena was at its height from the mid-1970's to the late 1980's. In the mid-1990's the mutilations seem to have had a major resurgence, especially throughout the Rocky Mountain states. In the Vol. 5, No. 4, 1990 issue of "UFO" Magazine (pp.16-17), Linda Moulton Howe, in her article, "THE HARVEST CONTINUES: ANIMAL MUTILATION UPDATE" made some very remarkable observations concerning the mutilators themselves. She wrote:

"In 1989, there were so many cattle mutilations in southern Idaho that Bear Lake County Sheriff Brent Bunn told me: 'We haven't seen anything like this since the 1970's.' Sheriff Bunn sent me 16 neatly-typed 'Investigation Reports' about cattle mutilations that had taken place in his county between May and December. Over half occurred in a remote valley called Nounan. Only eighty people lived there. Ranching is their main income source, and cattle are precious. Disease and predators are old and well-understood enemies. What descended on Nounan, Idaho in the summer and fall of 1989 was not understood — and it scared people.

"'Bloodless cuts — that's what bothers people,' officer Greg Athay wrote in his mutilation report,' There were no visible signs of the cause of death. It appeared that only the soft tissues (nose, lips and tongue) were gone off the head and four nipples off the bag. Again there was no blood on the hair and ground.'"

Howe described another incident which took place in this region during the same time-period. This series of mutilations involved mostly cattle, over half of which were young calves:

"...One mutilated calf, found December 24 (1989), north of Downey, Idaho, was found lying on its back with the naval, rectum and genitals neatly cut out of the steer's white belly. No blood was found anywhere. The steer was taken for an autopsy to Dr. Chris Oats, D.V.M., at the Hawthorne Animal Hospital. Dr. Oats checked all the vital organs and was unable to determine the cause of death. During the autopsy, a sharp cut was found in the right chest area, and Dr. Oats also discovered that a main artery had been severed under the chest wound.

"She was surprised that 'the steer had lost a large amount of blood, but (she) could not understand where it went to.' There was no blood on the steer or on the ground. Dr. Oats also determined that the steer had not been dragged by the neck or tied up around the feet."

Linda Howe also confirmed the fact that strange aerial disks have often been reported in connection with the mutilations:

"...Throughout the history of the animal mutilations, since 1967, there have been numerous eyewitness accounts of large, glowing disks or 'silent helicopters' over pastures where dead animals were later found. One Waco, Texas rancher said he encountered two four-foot tall, light green-colored 'creatures' with large, black, slanted eyes, carrying a calf which was later found dead and mutilated. In 1983, a Missouri couple watched through binoculars as two small beings in tight-fitting silver suits worked on a cow in a nearby pasture. The alien heads were large and white in color. Nearby, a tall, green-skinned 'lizard man' stood glaring with eyes slit by vertical pupils like a crocodiles..."

On Oct. 20, 1991, California researcher Michael Lindemann, founder of 'The 20/20 Group' (3463 State St., Suite 264., Santa Barbara, CA 93105), gave a lecture before a large crowd of interested investigators which seems to confirm much of the information which appears above. Mr. Lindemann began his report by saying:

"...How many of you saw the program on CBS Network on May 17th (1991) called 'ABDUCTION'? It was narrated by James Earl Jones. It was really quite a remarkable program, it took the subject of abduction absolutely seriously. This was prime time network, CBS. Of course FOX (network) has done a number of other programs and there have been some out standing UFO segments on 'UNSOLVED MYSTERIES'. But last night, maybe even a little more remarkable than the FOX 1-hour special, was what came on the news right after. Because in the Fox Network news program that followed in the 10 o'clock segment there was a hard news story about the allegation that the United States government is 'doing business' with greys. I have never seen anything like it... it was a very impressive indication of the way in which this subject is suddenly becoming O.K. to talk about. That says to me there has been a switch 'at the top'...

"In our conversation today I use two terms... and the first of these terms is 'government'. We speak of the government as if it is a single thing. It is hardly that. It is actually a hodgepodge of...power-struggling people, but I would like to break it up into two main categories, and that is: 1) The government that we consider to be our duly constituted, our elected and appointed representatives who attempt as best they can to run a semblance of order or Federal government which follows the dictates of the constitution of the United States. The constitution is, after all, a darn good piece of paper, it is one of the best ever written... If only our government were capable of behaving in even...a resemblance of what is intended in the constitution, probably few of us would have a great deal to gripe about...

"Now that they've failed to do that is not only because they are fallible humans, but also because they are undermined by another government. There is indeed another government operating and that government has immense power and operates primarily behind the scenes. And some other researchers have called it the 'secret government', some have called it the 'high cabal'. And it is a group of people, a very elite group, nonelected, self-appointed people who guide the evolution of (government) policy from behind the scenes. These are people who transcend partisan politics, indeed who transcend the rule of law, and have no thought whatsoever toward the dictates of the constitution.

"These are people who regard themselves as the only true guardians or crafters of geopolitical reality. And they regard us, indeed they regard elected officials as 'mere mortals'. These people are the self-appointed 'OLYMPIANS'. They have done many things in the name of an agenda which is their own, that we would consider appalling and reprehensible. Indeed things that are criminal, but they're more than criminal because they have sapped and usurped the rights and privileges and the possibilities of our future. These people are running a kind of 'end game' right now. They are trying to determine how 'they' will survive the end time... whether that endtime comes as a kind of biblical apocalypse or...as the catastrophic collapse of the environment... the (so-called) 'population bomb' and all the other things... whether it comes as a collapse of the banking-system which looks to be only days away, or the collapse of the rest of the world's economy — there are many things that could get us.

"These people in effect are building their own version of 'Noah's Ark'. And that 'Noah's Ark' they're building is underground. Underground bases, indeed all over the world, but particularly here in the United States. Huge underground bases that have actually festooned the underground geography of our continent in a way that would probably stun and shock you. But they even have an underground government, because you see when the government topside is no longer functional because a nuclear bomb lands on Capital Hill, or whether it comes simply because the chaos has reached a point where they must abandon ship, there is preparation as there has been for decades for continuity of government; all the computers, all the personnel are currently in place and operating around the clock. Yes, they are there friends, we have another government in waiting, a government that you never authorized, that you never said we would pay for, that has cost a CALLOSAL FORTUNE, but it's there underground, ready to take over. And indeed, here in our area, I have focused on the Lancaster (CA) area as an example of one of the many... but even in Lancaster in particular, we know for certain are huge underground bases. These are not only places where incredible research is underway but also places where people will go to live when the 'bleep' hits the blades as they say.

"And, these are places that are capable of supporting on an ongoing basis some tens of thousands of people. And so across the country it may be possible to 'save' an 'elect' remnant of some hundreds of thousands of people who will be the 'cream' of the civilization that is meant to survive the apocalypse or the downfall... or whatever it is that's out there getting us. Us 'mere mortals' will have to fend for themselves. The expectation is, part of the end game is, (that those on the surface) will eventually fight each other into a draw or will die of exhaustion or starvation or brutality. And that eventually the 'mere mortals' will (destroy) themselves and rid the world of excess population, so that the 'cream', the 'remnant' will come forward and claim their 'rightful' place... I must say that there is an immense amount of evidence which does support this exact scenario.

"Let's talk about the term 'aliens', because there are those who claim that there are 'aliens' among us... There are at least... three kinds of aliens represented in the evidence available to us... (he explains these as those presently inhabiting other planetary bodies such as the greys; those hidden among us such as human-like beings who inhabit underground, undersea and in some cases other-planetary regions yet who often walk unnoticed in our societies; and paraphysical entities who inhabit another 'dimension' other than the one we see with our physical sight - Branton) and I think the evidence is very strong that there is a profound 'alien' presence among us... these are people who are here, beings who are here, in large numbers...

"But there is this government that has known about the alien presence for a long time, a government that has been playing an 'end game'. A government that has an agenda of concealment and control, that is operated by terror. In Lancaster, that agenda of concealment and control is what I call the 'Lancaster Syndrome'. It produces strange distortions in many peoples lives... First let me tell you about a man who sits today in Pierce County jail outside of Tacoma, Washington. This man's name is Michael Riconosciuto..."

Lindemann states that Riconosciuto formerly worked for a corporation called Wackenhut which provides special security protection for high-security areas such as the Nevada Test Site. Michael R. claims that the real reason he was sent to jail was because he swore out an affidavit against the Dept. of Justice. In that affidavit he explained that the U.S. Dept. of Justice had 'swindled' the private company INSLAW out of a proprietary software called PROMIS. This software was a database designed to track special groups of people according to various characteristics. It was a very powerful, very capable database. INSLAW developed this in the early 1980's and took it to the Dept. of Justice thinking it would be a good law enforcement software. The software would be most useful in helping to track terrorists and other troublemakers. Certain men within the Justice Department realized that if they could get control of the software, according to Michael R., they could sell it to other countries and make huge profits.

"So the Dept. of Justice allegedly made a deal with the INSLAW Corp. for an exclusive on the PROMIS software, and then they drove INSLAW into bankruptcy by refusing to pay. Lindemann continues:

"The amazing thing is that they were caught. And in 1988 BARONS magazine in the April 4th (1991) issue... contained this fairly astonishing piece of news: 'Presiding judge in the bankruptcy hearing was judge George Basing.' According to BARONS, Judge Basing had found that the justice dept. had personally propelled INSLAW into bankruptcy in an effort to steal its PROMIS software through 'Trickery, deceit and fraud.' On Feb. 2, 1988, Basing ordered the justice dept. to pay INSLAW about 6.8 million dollars (no doubt to be ultimately financed by the friendly American taxpayer - Branton). He postponed at that time a decision on punitive damages which could run as high as $25,000,000. And as it happens, all of that is all in appeal. The justice dept. was not at all pleased with that ruling. It does state that justice is in a sorry state in America. If you didn't know that already, I hope this helps you to understand."

Michael was responsible for doing the modifications on the PROMIS software before selling that software to the Canadian government after it was 'stolen' from INSLAW, and so he had an inside track on this information, Lindemann stated.

"He explained that the Dept. of Justice, among other things, prevailed on him in Feb. of this year (1991) NOT to offer his information in the ongoing lawsuit. One Dept. of Justice official by the name of Peter Videnicks stated that IF he would cooperate with this request they could promise him certain benefits..." (including an assurance of a favorable outcome in a prolonged custody battle between Michael R. and his ex-wife).

According to Michael R., the Dept., of Justice "'...also outlined specific punishments that I could expect to receive... if I did cooperate with the House Judiciary Committee!'

"Now this is just an indicator," Lindemann states, "that the Dept. of Justice definitely has it's own idea of the meaning of justice."

Michael Riconosciuto went ahead and swore out an affidavit against the Justice Dept. alleging grand larceny against the INSLAW Corp. Lindemann stated that none of the threatened punishments ever came about as they found an easier way to frame him, "...that is, they busted (framed) him for drugs, and now he sits facing a possible life sentence in the Pierce Co. Jail. But because of that he's very, very scared because he knows now that these guys will take-him-out whenever they darn well feel like it. And so he's talking, he's talking in every way he can... In particular we wanted to ask Michael R. something about some of the things going on at the underground bases. I'd like to read you just a little bit of what Michael Riconosciuto told us recently about that. I asked him, what did he know about the underground bases in the Lancaster area. I'm going to quote now our conversation:

"He said, 'Well, there's extensive stuff in... I call it the 'Edwards position', and then at Nellis over in Nevada, and at the Nevada Test Site.' Then he went on to say, 'Last summer I had a group of guys bagging a whole bunch of files and records, and some equipment out of Wackenhut and they had a helicopter loaded to the nuts and they got shot down before they could get out of there.'

"I don't know how many of you noticed,' Lindemann continues, "but there was an article in the LOS ANGELES TIMES, the 24th of July of this year - FATAL COPTER CRASH AT THE NUCLEAR TEST SITE PROBED. This was the most serious accident which had ever occurred in the history of the Test Site. Five people were killed when this helicopter went down, and the FAA and the DOE and the National Transportation and safety board all converged on the Nuclear Test Site to figure out what brought this copter down. But you may be ASSURED that they will never tell you because it was SHOT down by Wackenhut, and it contained two pilots and 3 Wackenhut personnel according to the article in the L.A. TIMES.

"I said, 'I heard about that. Are you saying that that was a group of, let's say, renegades from the inside who were trying to bolt for the blue and WACKENHUT shot them down? Is that your allegation?' And he said,

"'Yep!'

"And I said, 'Is there anything more that you can say about this?' He said:

"'Not on the phone.'

"I said, 'Were you aware of that before it happened?'

"He said, 'Yes. I told a handful of people that we were hoping to get a big stash of stuff out of there.'

"I said, 'Were they trying to get out of Nellis?'

"He said, 'No, not Nellis, off the Nuclear Test Site.'

"And the information they were trying to get out, what did it pertain to?'

"And he said, 'Guess! I don't even want to talk about it. The worst!'

"And I said, 'The very worst, huh?'

"And he said, 'yep'.

"Now I don't know of the 'very worst,' do you? I mean I'm not really sure, but it seemed to me, judging from other things that we had talked with Mike about and some of the other things that we've heard from witnesses in the underground bases... the 'very worst' could be one of two main possibilities in my book... The very worst #1) Really nasty, scary alien stuff. The very worst #2) Really nasty, scary bio-tech... bioengineering stuff. There's all kinds of genetic engineering, some of which has to do with the 'creation' of biological warfare agents, some of which has to do with the 'creation' of strange bacteria, and perhaps new strains of chimpanzees and (perhaps) people. There are very, very weird experiments going on, and I thought, 'O.K., fine, maybe one or the other of those things.'

"But our conversation continued and it leaned in one direction, so let's just see what he had to say next.

"I said, 'One of your associates seemed to indicate that there was technology operating that would have the appearance of flying saucers, but be absolutely terrestrial. Can you comment on that?'

"And he said, 'Sure, we had some propulsion devices that were, let's say, rather astounding.'

"I said, 'Is this stuff operational?' And he said 'Oh, yes, it's operational.'

"I said, 'O.K., so there are vehicles. Would you say that they belonged in the arsenal, or are they part of a sort of gee- whiz lunatic fringe of science?'

"And he said, 'Oh no, they're part of the arsenal. It's not lunatic fringe stuff, it's all well-funded, it's all very real. I've worked on portions of it, I've worked on teams that have worked on this stuff, and I've seen with my own eyes. The only thing that I have been shielded from, is any REAL (alien) contact. That I've never been brought directly in contact with, in fact, that part has been minimized to me.'

"And I said to him, 'In the way you've said that, I get the impression that you assume that there are extraterrestrials (i.e. 'aliens') around.'

"And he said, 'I have no direct knowledge of that, O.K.? That's all. There's alot of strange technology, there's alot of extra-heavy security, O.K.? Anybody who breeches a certain point of security is instantly dead or disappears.

"I said, 'Are you saying that given all the other indiscretions you've shown over the years, that this one would be worst?'

"And he said, 'Yes, I would say so.'

"I said, 'really?'

"He said. 'Yes, Yes! It's like those people who were leaving the Nuclear Test Site, they were summarily blown out of the sky.'

"Now, Michael knew (he was talking on a prison telephone - his phone was tapped) indeed, that people who talk too loud, in too much detail about the actual 'alien' situation are liable to run into severe problems. Being that he's already in prison and a sitting duck, he's obviously very careful with his words. But we have talked with some other people who have been more forthright about what they have actually seen in the underground bases.

"One of our sources is a construction worker. He came out of Vietnam, he was a very decorated Special Forces soldier. Among other things he got the Congressional Medal of Honor. And because he was special forces in the Vietnamese war, when he came back stateside he was offered all kinds of bizarre jobs in top security. He felt that those would be too restrictive so he went into construction instead. But because of his military record he had an inside track on a security clearance. He wound up doing construction in the underground bases.

"Now you see, the underground installations are built just like a building is built. You know, you've got to do electrical conduit, you've got to paint the walls! Whose going to do it? It's not going to be the Secretary of Defense. It's going to be a guy like our guy! It's going to be like this fellow whose got a Congressional Medal of honor and now does special electrical conduiting underground. So he's told us what he saw.

"There's a facility called Haystack Butte, it's on the Edwards (AFB) reservation... (Note: At this point Lindemann shows the audience a map of the area encompassing Edwards AFB, the city of Lancaster and Palmdale to the south — which is the sight of 542 where the B-2 bomber is assembled, along with alot of other secret aircraft. All of the major aircraft and aerospace companies are located in this area, among other sites. It also showed the Tahachapi facility west of Lancaster, nicknamed the 'Ant Hill', which is administered by Northrup and which is rumored by some to house underground 'disk' hangers for wingless aircraft built by the Secret-Government-Military-Industrial establishment. In the southeast corner of Lindemann's map the Tejon ranch was visible, which is a large cattle ranch that goes up into the area of the Tahachapi range to the southeast of Bakersfield, California. He also pointed out an extensive underground facility maintained by MacDonnell Douglas, and the Helendale Facility administered by Lockheed. In this same general area is Haystack Butte which is 'jointly' administered, with North American Rockwell involved as well - Branton).

"So what we have here is a situation where you've got our major aerospace companies heavily implicated. I mean this is what is meant by the Military-Industrial Complex. These companies are HEAVILY implicated in super, super secret projects, and at the very top they're all cooperating together. All the 'bidding wars' and every thing that you see are like mid- level smoke and mirrors. But at the very top we're talking about projects that are conducted by all these different people pooling their resources, pooling their information, and indeed pooling their money, which comes in incredible profusion from the Black Budget.

"How many of you have seen the book 'BLANK CHECK'?... It is not a UFO book. I strongly recommend that you read the book 'BLANK CHECK' so that you can understand something about how these projects are funded without your say-so, indeed without the say-so of Congress. Most citizens don't know for example that the National Security Act of 1947 made it illegal to ever say how much money is spent on the CIA; indeed all of our tremendous alphabet soup collection of Intelligence Agencies. Whether your talking about the CIA, or the NRO, or the NSA or the DIA, etc., all of them are in the same category.

"You cannot say how much these things cost. All you can do if you want to find out is add-up the numbers on the Budget (which at this writing is at a deficit of well over 4 TRILLION dollars, a large portion of which may have been spent on construction for the 'underground nation' - Branton) that aren't assigned to anything that actually means anything. There are these huge categories that have tens of billions of dollars in them that say nothing but 'Special Projects...' And every year the Congress dutifully passes this bloated budget that has some $300,000,000,000 or more with HUGE chunks of cash labelled like that — 'Special Projects,' 'Unusual Stuff.' - Ten billion dollars. O.K., well where does the 'unusual stuff' money go? Well, it DOES go to 'unusual stuff', that's for sure, and one of the places it goes is...into the underground bases. Indeed TIM said recently since the publication of his book (BLANK CHECK)... MORE Black Budget money goes into underground bases than ANY OTHER kind of work.

"Now I don't believe that 35 billion, which is the approximate size of the black budget money that you can find by analyzing the budget, I don't think that comes CLOSE to the real figure because there is absolutely unequivocal evidence that a great deal of additional money was generated in other ways, such as the surreptitious running of guns and drugs. And one wonderful example of that is coming to light with the B.C.C.I. scandal which I hope you've heard of... a number of very high-ranking American officials are caught in the undertoe of the BCCI tidal wave... Even though these guys are tying to pull 'fast ones' on an immense scale they are getting caught. These things don't always work. Indeed they are very, very vulnerable.

Indeed this whole 'end game' is very vulnerable and that's why they feel it requires such secrecy. The American people wouldn't stand for this stuff if they had the information, and that's the reason why we have to get the information out and take it seriously because it really is a matter of OUR money and OUR future that's being MORTGAGED here.

"But my friend who worked in the underground bases, who was doing sheetrock was down on, he thinks, approximately the 30th level underground... these bases are perhaps 30-35 stories deep ('ground-scrapers' as opposed to a 'skyscrapers' - Branton). As I say they are not just mine shafts, these are huge, giant facilities... many city blocks in circumference, able to house tens of thousands of people. One of them, the YANO Facility (we're told... by the county fire dept. director, the county fire dept. chief who had to go in there to look at a minor fire infraction) there's a 400-car parking lot on the 1st level of the YANO Facility, but cars never come in and out, those are the cars that they use INSIDE.

"O.K., so... a very interesting situation down there. Our guy was doing sheetrock on the 30th floor, maybe the 30th floor, underground. He and his crew are working on a wall and right over here is an elevator door. The elevator door opens and, a kind of reflex action you look, and he saw three 'guys'. Two of them, human engineers that he'd seen before. And between them a 'guy' that stood about 8 to 8 1/2 feet tall. Green skin, reptilian features, extra-long arms, wearing a lab coat, holding a clipboard...

"I tend to believe that story because, first of all because we have other stories like it, but more importantly because he walked off that job that very day. And he was getting paid a GREAT deal of money... If your basically a sheetrock kind of guy, if you can do sheetrock in a place like that then you get paid way more than standard sheetrock wages, you can count on it.

"So, he walked off that job. His buddy on that same crew turned into an alcoholic shortly after. This is an extremely upsetting thing. You know, it wasn't like this alien jumped out and bit his head off or anything, it was just standing there for a few minutes, the doors closed. He has a feeling that that elevator was malfunctioning, otherwise he never would have seen that except by accident.

"In another incident though... at the China Lake Naval Weapons Station, up here at China Lake... near Ridgecrest... they were working there on the China Lake Naval Weapons Station and walked by a hanger... They walked by a hanger as they were headed for their trucks to leave for the day. And they had parked their trucks in an unusual place, a place they didn't normally park, because it was an extremely hot day and they wanted to keep the trucks out of the sun. So the Security had given them permission to park the trucks in a place that wasn't normal. So they walked by a hanger that they didn't normally walk by, and they looked in, just kind of glanced in, and saw inside a couple of grays working on something. And of course they were, you know, astonished... And an MP came running over and said: 'Hey, you can't be here! What are you doing here?' And they said: 'Well, Security said we could park our trucks here.' And (the Security Guard) says: 'Well that's fine, but you get out of here because you'll get yourself killed!' So they left. But one of the young guys on that crew couldn't leave well enough alone. The guy we've been talking to said, 'Look, I know what you saw, I know what I saw. I know what we saw at Haystack (Butte), it's all for real, I know what's going on, but don't be a stupid jerk. Leave it alone!'

"This kid didn't leave it alone, and very shortly thereafter he was booted off the base, and three months later he was dead under mysterious circumstances. Now of course we can't say that he died 'because' of this. There's a disturbing pattern of people dying however when they see things they're not supposed to... Michael Riconosciuto makes it very clear in his statement to us that if you go past a certain point your dead or disappear, just like that. We've heard that time and time again. Indeed there are a great many people on the 'inside' who are making it clear that they would love to flee, people like these people that apparently were blown out of the sky, the Wackenhut garbage. These are trained (mercenaries) who have seen things they cannot stand, things that turn their stomach, things that make them want to grab evidence and flee for their lives. And they were blown out of the sky, probably by something equivalent to a stinger missile or something like that. And there are lots of people who want to get out.

"Just an example of the way these people talk, one of them said to us, 'I would trade my $100,000.00 a year salary for a job at McDonald's if I could get out alive. There's a certain despair there, a certain feeling of entrapment. You see there are the people who know what's going on and who have created this agenda and have 'bought-into' it entirely, they are enrolled in it, and they believe that they are indeed the 'Olympians'. They have to employ lots of normal humans like us to do the sheet- rocking, to do the grubwork, and those people are in a very bizarre catch-22, because they are given the promise of a salary that they never believed possible. You know... they're going to paint walls all day and they're going to take down a hundred grand a year, this is unusual. That's the upside of the deal. The down side of the deal is (you know, and they make it very clear)... all these people who get these high security clearances are subjected to INCREDIBLY intimidating indoctrination and intimidation processes... they really do subject these people to tremendous pressure, tremendous intimidation, indeed they do inflict great violence on people (on whom) they 'need' to. They make 'examples' of people..."

In one sense then, there is a growing division taking place between the Constitutionalists of America and the 'Alien' controlled segments within the underground bases. This would also include their human 'pawns' who will apparently do anything, even murder their fellow human beings, in order to continue receiving the technological 'benefits' from their alien masters, to whom they have 'sold' themselves and whose agenda of control and subversion they are serving, whether knowing or unknowingly.

The following is a transcript of parts of a speech presented by Norio F. Hayakawa, director of the CIVILIAN INTELLIGENCE NETWORK, at the 11th 'LOS ANGELES WHOLE LIFE EXPO' held at The Los Angeles Airport Hilton Convention Center on November 16 and 17, 1991. The transcript from which we will quote is a revised and expanded version of the address written on June of 1992 and is titled — 'UFO'S, THE GRAND DECEPTION AND THE COMING NEW WORLD ORDER':

"...AREA 51 is located in the northeastern corner of a vast, desolate stretch of land known as the Nevada Test Site (a large portion of which includes the Nellis Air Force Test Range) but has practically nothing to do with underground nuclear testing. It is located approximately 125 miles north-northwest of Las Vegas and consists of Groom Lake and the Papoose Lake Complexes. The presently expanding eastern portion of the latter complexes is known as the S-4 site.

"This entire area is under the strictest control of Airspace R-4808N (with unlimited 'ceiling'), prohibiting any entry therein of air traffic, civilian or military, unless special clearance for such entry is secured well in advance. By land, the area is meticulously patrolled 24-hours a day by several tiers of external security even through it is conveniently covered by the... Jumbled Hills (north of the Papoose Lake area), making it virtually impossible for anyone to see the facilities without first climbing atop the hills of the rugged mountain range which became off-limits to the public since 1985.

"The main external perimeter security is now being handled by Wackenhut Special Securities Division, part of the operations of Wackenhut Corporation, a worldwide semiprivate security firm based in Coral Gables, Florida which has an exclusive contract with the U.S. Department of Energy and handles not only the perimeter security at the Nevada Test Site but also at many other secret facilities and sensitive installations throughout the U.S., and U.S. interests worldwide, including ground-level perimeters for several large underground facilities in and around Edwards Air Force Base in Southern California.

"It is also important to mention that dozens of unmanned, miniature-sized remote-controlled automatic security vehicles constantly patrol the immediate perimeters of the S-4 Site, located around (and presently expanding particularly towards the eastern portion of) Papoose Lake. These automatic, miniature- sized four-wheel vehicles have been produced by Sandia Laboratories of Albuquerque, New Mexico exclusively for the Department of Energy.

"The outer northeastern perimeters of this area located in the Tickaboo Valley come under the geographical jurisdiction of Lincoln County and are relegated to the Bureau of Land Management (B.L.M.). Yet it is considered highly unadvisable for anyone to even enter the main country dirt road, known as the Groom Road, which begins its southwestern extension towards Groom Lake from a point midway between mile marker 34 and 33 on Highway 375, and leads to the guard shack located two and a half miles northeast of the Groom Lake complexes.

"The first line of exterior security forces (dressed in military- type camouflage uniforms but with no insignia of any kind whatsoever) consists of the GP patrols (the 'Groom Proper' patrols, in Bronco-type four-wheel drive vehicles) who sometimes drive around at night with their lights off on various country dirt roads adjacent to the outer demilitarized zone, intimidating any civilian vehicle that tries to enter those access roads (off of Highway 375) located on public land. The GP patrols themselves (part of Wackenhut Special Securities Division), however, are strictly ordered to avoid any direct contact with civilians. They are only instructed to radio the Lincoln County Sheriff immediately should anyone be spotted driving on any of those dirt roads. The most common radio frequency used between Security Control and Lincoln County Sheriff's patrols is 138.306 MHZ.

"...The only area 'allowed' by the Sheriff for such curiosity seekers to 'congregate' is an open area near a black mailbox located at the south side of Highway 375 between mile marker 29 and 30. Even then, the Sheriff patrol will routinely stop by during the evening to check on the cars parked at the mailbox area.

"Moreover, it is our understanding, based on information provided by a highly reliable source connected to a special U.S. Navy SEAL operations center, that the mailbox area is constantly being monitored by high-powered, state-of-the-art, infrared telescopes set up at a facility known as Security Control high atop Bald Mountain (10 miles west of the area), the highest peak in the Groom Mountain Range.

"...It was precisely at 4:45 a.m. on the morning of Thursday, April 16, 1992, that an NBC news crew, dispatched to the area to report on the landing of an alleged super spy-plane known as Aurora on Groom Lake, accidentally succeeded in videotaping the first flight (which we have been calling the 'Old Faithful') of [a] mysterious object while standing at the mailbox area and looking due south toward Jumbled Hills. The footage, taken with a night-scope vision camera, was broadcast nationally on NBC Nightly News with Tom Brokaw on April 20, 1992. The NBC News reported that it had videotaped a test flight of a new U.S. aerial craft that had definitely defied the laws of physics, and that the news team may thus have taken the first glimpse of the other 'deep black' projects (aside from the Aurora project) being conducted within the confines of the top-secret facility.

"Also in regards to the ongoing program, it is to be noted that usually a day or two prior to significant test flights (i.e., only if the test flight is a significant one, by whatever measure known only to the installation) a vehicle-traffic counter is laid on Highway 93, at approximately a mile and a half north of Ash Springs, right before the juncture of Highway 375. The other counter is set up about a half mile or so west upon entering Highway 375. The obvious question is: in such desolate, less-traveled areas of Nevada, why should there be such traffic counters installed on undivided, lonely highways? It is now my belief that the number of cars being registered that head out west on Highway 375 at such times (particularly in 'clusters', such as caravans) is relayed to several of the security posts at AREA 51, including the main observation post high atop the previously mentioned Bald Mountain. However, it is very possible that they may now have more sophisticated devices for registering the number of vehicles going through the area.

"The February 21, 1990 expedition was instrumental in the subsequent production of a two-hour documentary program entitled 'Saturday Super Special' televised throughout Japan on March 24, 1990 which was seen by more than 28 million viewers on prime time. The entire program dealt with AREA 51 and also the crew's pursuit of an alleged biogenetics laboratory thought to be located just outside of Dulce, a tiny town in northwestern New Mexico, about 95 miles northwest of Los Alamos.

"...The U.S. Naval Research Laboratory...seems to have a Parapsychology Research Unit that coordinates its research activities with DARPA (the Defense Advanced Research Projects Agency). It is my understanding that some of their activities conducted under the auspices of the Office of Naval Intelligence are being held at locations such as AREA 51.

"ELF (extremely low frequency) wave-emitting devices, scalar machines, electromagnetic beam weapons and highly-defined holographic projections are just a few examples of the many new types of mind-control 'weaponry' that the government seems to have developed in the past three decades or so. Newest researches on special types of hallucinatory and memory- tampering drugs are part of a growing 'arsenal' that the U.S. Naval Intelligence boasts to have developed in its own Parapsychology- Mind Control Unit.

"According to recent information provided to me by a highly reliable informant within a special operations group of the Department of the Navy, two of the most widely used devices will be R.H.I.C. (Radio Hypnotic Intra-Cerebral Control) and E.D.O.M. (Electronic Dissolution of Memory). The first of the two, Radio Hypnotic Intra-Cerebral Control, calls for the implantation of a very small, electronic, micro-radio receiver. It acts as a Stimulator which will stimulate a muscle or electronic brain response. This, in turn, can set off a 'Hypno-programmed' cue in the victim or subject, which would illicit a preconditioned behavior. The second one, Electronic Dissolution of Memory, calls for remotely-controlled production within the brain of Acetyl-Choline which blocks transmission of nerve impulses in the brain which results in a sort of Selective Amnesia. According to this source, in the hands of certain units within the intelligence community both of these methods are ALREADY BEGINNING TO BE USED!

"An amazing article appeared in the Los Angeles Times on May 12, 1992 announcing that Caltech scientists have recently discovered and confirmed the presence of 'tiny magnetic particles in the brains of humans, similar to those that have heretofore been found in other animals.' (L.A. TIMES, Section A, page 3). According to the Caltech researchers, it is now an undeniable fact that every human brain contains a tiny natural magnetite particle, even from the time of conception. Could the government, particularly the U.S. Naval Research Laboratory, have known this fact for a long time? The answer definitely seems to be in the affirmative! (Note: Perhaps the 'Philadelphia Experiment', described in Charles Berlitz' book of the same name, had an adverse affect on the 'electrochemical' or 'magnetite' particles in the brains of the experimental subjects. Could this explain why so many of them allegedly went insane after the 'tests'? - Branton)

"It is interesting also to note that as of this writing, many strange, turquoise-colored antenna-towers with triangular configurations on top, are beginning to be constructed along key areas near the freeway systems of many U.S. cities, particularly proliferating the Los Angeles and Orange County areas of California. According to several reports, these antenna-towers are presently being used as relay towers for the increasing networks of cellular telephone systems being operated by such firms as Pacific Bell and Telesis.

"Yet the most interesting aspect of the constructions of these strange antenna-towers is that there are increasing reports that the Department of Defense is somehow involved in this operation. The frequency waves being utilized in the cellular telephone communications are, according to several researchers, strikingly close to the range of frequency waves used in several ELF emission and microwave experiments of the U.S. Naval Research Laboratory as well as D.A.R.P.A., the Defense Advanced Research Projects Agency.

(Note: non-digital cellular telephone conversations can be easily intercepted. This writer has succeeded in listening in on cellular conversations by scanning through the upper frequencies of the UHF band on a normal television set! So then, along with the 'mind control' capabilities, it is evident that cellular phone conversations have also been heavily monitored by Military Intelligence - Branton) Will these towers be utilized throughout the nation?

"...A large underground genetics laboratory is thought to be located just outside of Dulce, a tiny town in the midst of the Jicarilla-Apache Indian Reservation located about 95 miles northwest of Los Alamos and 100 miles east of sinister-sounding Highway 666, the only stretch of highway in the U.S. with that designation and the only highway that links the four states of Arizona, New Mexico, Colorado and Utah.

"Perhaps it may just be a pure 'coincidence' that this highway, befittingly named Highway 666, which originated in southeast Arizona and goes up north, cuts into northwestern New Mexico, right near the Four Corners area — an area that happens to have one of the most consistently concentrated UFO sighting reports in the country since around 1947... This entire Four Corners area, especially northwestern New Mexico and southwestern Colorado also has had some of the most concentrated reports of unexplained cattle mutilations in the nation during the late seventies and early eighties. Was something covertly taking place in those areas?

"Even though we could not locate the alleged underground genetics laboratory in Dulce when the Nippon Television crew and I visited the area in late February of 1990, I had several opportunities to interview scores of local residents there that admitted that nightly appearances of mysterious lights (occasionally accompanied by unmarked black helicopters) — darting over, into and out of nearby Archuleta Mesa and Archuleta Mountains — were quite common during the late seventies and early eighties.

"Many of them even claim to have spotted, on many occasions, military-type trucks and jeeps as well as government vans passing through Dulce and loitering around nearby mesas. Occasionally even black limousines carrying what appeared to be 'CIA' agent-types were claimed to have been sighted 'loitering' around the foothills of 'other' nearby mesas.

"We must bear in mind that the Dulce area is only 95 miles northwest of Los Alamos. Los Alamos National Laboratory is one of the top U.S. research laboratories specializing in the study of the human genome. Also it is a vital center of the government's SDI research and development programs. Just about a hundred miles southeast of Los Alamos is Albuquerque, New Mexico's largest city, and more significantly, a city where Kirtland Air Force Base is located right next to the sensitive Manzano Storage Facility, a top-secret underground military facility. Sandia Corporation, one of the nations top-secret government contractors specializing in top military-industrial projects is also located in Albuquerque.

"As far as advanced biotechnology is concerned, I have no doubt that a microchip implantation technology is being perfected in which tiny microchips could be implanted in our circulatory systems, vital organs and tissues if need be for whatever purpose the future may 'require'. It is my conclusion that a large-scale research has been completed by the government (with possible assistance from 'outside' sources) within the last 20 years or so utilizing tens of thousands of cattle in the Southwest to conduct this covert experiment. Only recently has science proven that cow hemoglobin could be substituted (by utilizing a special purification system) with human blood in situations of 'unforeseen national emergencies.'

Researcher David L. Dobbs of Cincinnati, OH., described the following 'resume of report received... after the MUFON 40-meter net on April, 5, 1980.':

"...Mike (DELETED), Iowa (DELETED), stated that during the period 1961-63 he performed radio maintenance at the atomic proving ground. He also did some top-secret radio work for the Air Force at times. The U-2 was developed here.

"'Area 51' was located 60 miles due east of the base camp, behind a mountain range separating it from Yucca Flat. Here a secret operation was performed under unbelievable security precautions known as 'Project Redlight.' A UFO which had been shipped from Edwards AFB was flown here. It was not conventionally powered, but was SILENT in operation. Mike assumed that this was the disc recovered intact and shown in the UFO movie reported by radar technicians. Security in Project Red Light was so strict that no one stayed there more than six months. Mike did not see this movie himself, however.

"While on vacation, he saw a story in Reader's Digest at his parent's home which told of a UFO exploding over the test site in 1962 while being flown. This would have been a recent story at the time. Mike is aware of the conventionally-powered disc built by the Air Force which was publicized. We both feel that this may have been a cover-up for the real project which he describes. He also heard the stories about parts from a UFO which could not be duplicated successfully by aerospace contractors on the west coast, and many of the rumors about UFOs which have emanated from Nellis AFB. Incidentally, Nellis AFB operated 'Area 51' where he says the UFO was flown.

"This information has bothered him for 20 years, and he wonders if it might be possible for documentation regarding 'Project Red Light' to be obtained under the Freedom of Information Act."

According to various sources, 'Area 51' in Nevada, where the S-4, Groom Lake, or Dreamland complexes are located, is the same area where the Stealth Bomber, SR-71, 'Star Wars' or SDI Technology, and all manner of aerospace hightech had been developed and tested; these include CIA experiments and tests. Other names for the 'Dreamland' complex include: 'The Ranch' or 'The Skunk Works'. This is where Francis Gary Powers, who flew the ill-fated U-2 spy plane mission which was shot down over Russia (where Powers was held prisoner for some time), was trained. Incidentally, there are also rumors that the vast caverns which have been excavated by the underground nuclear blasts in the adjacent Nevada Nuclear Test range, have been and are being connected by underground tunnels and used for top secret purposes. If this is the case one may wonder how the problems of radiation residue were solved... [via 'clean' nuclear blasts?]

Referring to the subsurface regions, we quote now from yet another item that appeared in the N.A.R. newsletter, which was titled, 'IS INNER EARTH RESEARCH HAZARDOUS TO YOUR HEALTH?':

"An observation has recently been made that most of the outstanding inner earth researchers have died of heart attack (Note: Heart attack is reportedly one weapon or method of psychic attack that is recognized by those occultists who are familiar with 'voodoo' or 'psychic' warfare. Heart Attacks of this nature are allegedly induced by the use of intense TERROR that is 'projected' against individuals by the initiators of such attack. It is alleged that hominoid nonhuman beings such as the serpent races might have the ability to direct psychic attacks against human beings via the use of black magic, witchcraft or sorcery. It is interesting that there have been very few if any UFOlogists, etc., who claim to have taken up a devout 'Christian' lifestyle, who have physically suffered the 'negative' side of UFO research — including encounters with MIBS, abductions, paralysis, heart attacks or other FEAR-ORIENTED forms of victimization. This suggests that a deep FAITH in the Creator may neutralize the FEAR that the aliens seem to depend on as their major "weapon" in their psychic attacks against humankind, making the 'believers' impervious to their otherwise destructive influences -

Branton). Surely, this is beyond a simple coincidence. GRAY BARKER, DICK SHAVER, and JOAN O'CONNEL [New Atlantean Journal] are but a few (also, researcher CHARLES MARCOUX - Branton). Locally, there are several inner earth researchers who are very notable in their persistence.

"Lew Tery, who has recently relocated to Utah, was the foremost local proponent of (the) geomagnetic vortex/UFO connection theory. Lew was instrumental in the discovery of underground tunnel networks in the Las Vegas area, one of them being between the base of Boulder Dam and Jumbo Peak, where there are two mines whose owners view 200' diameter disks on a frequent basis. At one point, Lew offered to set up an interview with these miners. Alas, Mr. Tery is not to be found.

"A local Henderson resident, who shall remain nameless, has been into inner earth research for years. This person has been hounded and chased due to intimate knowledge of inner earth tunnels in the local area.

"There is obviously something here that some people wish to protect. Something to hide. Many seem to know what it is, and they speak cautiously about REPTILIAN HUMANOIDS and the SERPENT RACE, which are two subjects which seem to be surfacing again. Response to local television and radio programs featuring JOHN LEAR have been overwhelming. A recent lecture in Las Vegas drew over 700 people.

"According to some sources, the 'Greys' are the lower level of a bigger scenario that involves this reptilian race..."

The following is a transcript of a letter which was sent by John Lear to researcher TAL LeVesque. The letter, dated October 6, 1990, states:

"Dear TAL... Many thanks for your recent, very interesting letter. I showed it to Bob (i.e. Lazar - Branton) and he thinks we are both crazy. He does not believe that Dulce exists. Bob went through extreme brainwashing at S-4 so I can understand his feelings. About the time that he was brainwashed, maybe a little before, he told me that Dulce was mentioned up there once or twice in conversations that he was not part of...but that he overhead. Since that time he has forgotten even that part. Since I know Dulce exists, what Bob thinks does not affect me in the least.

"A source of mine that is a security guard at the test site tells me that currently there are 5 types of aliens there: The Greys, the Orange, the reptilians, the ones that look like [the aliens] in the movie 'V' and the ones that look so ugly that they take your breath away until you get used to looking at them.

"I now believe that a very large Saucer crashed near Sedona, possibly 2 years ago and is in the process of being retrieved in sections, as it is too big to remove in one piece.

"The recent stories in Aviation Week, I believe, are attempts to buy more time, to mislead the public and to confuse the issue (Note: Lear is here referring to the article in the Oct. 1, 1990 issue of AVIATION WEEK AND SPACE TECHNOLOGY, titled "Secret Advanced Vehicles Demonstrate Technologies For Future Military Use". The article referred only to the fairly well-known super- advanced jets being tested in Nevada, giving the impression that these may explain all of the 'UFO' sightings in the area - Branton).

"Again, I appreciate very much your fascinating letter and look forward to more information on Dulce... With much respect and admiration... JOHN LEAR."

In connection with the subject of this File, that is the 'invasion' of an alien race from above and below utilizing mind-bending techniques, psychological warfare, mind control and implantation, we will quote from Brad Steiger's 'THE UFO ABDUCTORS' (1988., Berkley Books., N.Y.):

"In 1969 I and my research associates... Loring G. Williams and Glenn McWane, were bombarded with the claims of dozens of contactees who said that they had had an implant left somewhere in their skulls, usually just behind the left ear. These contactees/abductees came from a wide variety of occupations, cultural backgrounds, and age-groups.

"We employed private detectives and medical doctors... in an attempt to learn what archetype had been fed into their particular group consciousness. We never found any implants that were detectable to X rays, but our hypnotic sessions turned up an incredible amount of fascinating, albeit bizarre, information about underground UFO bases, hybrid aliens walking among us, and thousands of humans slowly turning into automatons because of readjusted brain wave patterns.

"...Dagmar and Carl R. have a farm in northeast Iowa about forty miles from the Mississippi River. One night in August of 1982, Carl observed what he called at the time a 'lantern in the sky' that hovered over him while he was working late in the field...

"In October that year, while Carl was working late in the field preparing for the annual corn harvest, he was startled to see the glowing 'lantern' return to the sky above him. It appeared to be the same object that he had seen in August.

"Although he tried to remain oblivious to the object, it seemed to be hovering above him, even following him up and down the corn rows. He became nervous and disconcerted and went back to the farmhouse, where he asked Dagmar to come out and witness the strange object.

"Dagmar was able to see the object, too, and they stood and watched it for several minutes before it suddenly moved high into the night sky and then sped off at a great rate of speed in a westerly direction.

"About three the next morning, Carl was awakened by the sound of cattle bellowing nervously in the stockyard. As he got out of bed and looked out the bedroom window, he saw a disk- shaped object hovering above the barnyard. It was glowing in a kind of greenish color..."

Following this, the couple was 'tranquilized' by the object or its occupants somehow, possibly by some kind of intoxicating, pacifying or stimulating ray which apparently induced a drugged or trancelike electrochemical reaction in their brains and bodies, after which they were taken by some entities. A conventional 'abduction' sequence ensued, similar to that described by so many thousands of others. Steiger related the couples' afterthoughts concerning their abduction by 'smallish' large-eyed beings "with only nostril openings (rather than a pronounced nose) and with tight, expressionless lips."

Steiger continues:

"While the young Iowa couple can remember no further UFO interaction since that particular autumn, they both admit to being nervous about having another encounter. Carl, especially, feels that he was used. Dagmar speculated that bits of her skin tissue might have been removed in the examination, and although she does not claim to be an expert in such matters, she wonders if enough of her body could be cloned in a way to interact with whatever embryo or fetus might have been fathered by the semen that was taken from her husband (Note: Dagmar claimed that during one part of the 'examination' a needlelike object was stuck into her abdomen. Many believe that this is one process by which the 'entities' extract ovum from human females - Branton).

"Not wanting to sound like victims of some science fiction thriller, the young couple have theorized that they might have been used in some strange program of creating hybrid beings. Perhaps, they suggest, Carl's semen was used to impregnate an alien female or an Earth female, who is somehow influenced by and under the control of alien beings. In either event, they are uncomfortable with the experience and with the memory of the encounter. Both of them feel as though they may have been used in ways opposed to their normal expression of will.

"Dagmar has gone even farther in her speculations by suggesting that if bits of her body could have been used to create a clone and if Carl's semen could somehow be used at a future time to impregnate such a clone, then alien beings could be breeding their own brand of humans as part of an organized program to create an army of humanlike robots that would be totally under control of aliens in their master plan to conquer Earth.

"UFO investigator Richard Siefried was told by Pam Owens that she was taken aboard a UFO on November 25, 1978, while she was expecting a child. She was nineteen at the time, and she had no memory of the abduction until she was hypnotically regressed. Then she was able to give full and fascinating details of her encounter.

"Mrs. Owens told Siefried that she was paralyzed and able to move only her eyes. She lay helpless on a table and stared up in terror at two weird-looking creatures.

"According to Mrs. Owens, their heads were hairless, oversize domes, their eyes were big and sunk back in their skulls. The greenish skin covering their bodies was coarse. Each hand had four fingers that she described as being twice as long as a human's. And to her terror, one of those strange hands was holding a long silver needle, preparing to plunge it into her stomach..."

Dr. Clifford Wilson [M.A., B.D., Ph.D.], in his book "UFOS... AND THEIR MISSION IMPOSSIBLE" (Signet Books., N.Y.) presents his own 'intelligence' or research concerning the on- going invasion/infiltration of our society by alien powers:

"...Not only have many seen UFOs, but there is also a growing army of those who claim to have had actual contact with UFO occupants. An authoritative, and possibly conservative, estimate is that there are 50,000 silent contactees in the United States alone.

"It could well be there are thousands of people who do have information and are not prepared to reveal it because of threatened consequences to themselves. Possibly many do not know they have that 'knowledge' because they themselves gained it in a hypnotic state.

"HYPNOTIZED SLAVES AWAIT A SIGNAL - Nations could be conquered by the infiltration of agents into government seats of authority, and it is surely more frightening to think that mankind could be overcome and even destroyed by programmed men and women from within their own ranks. If there is indeed a final confrontation approaching, an army of people could be involved. They could be ready to take action which they themselves do not even anticipate, but yet with no option but to obey because they have been conditioned to obey, at a given signal.

"We are not alone in suggesting this dreadful possibility. To quote John Keel once again:

"'We have no way of knowing how many human beings throughout the world have been processed in this manner, since they would have absolutely no memory of undergoing the experience, and so we have no way of determining who among us has strange and sinister 'programs' lying dormant in the dark corners of his mind.

"'Suppose a plan is to process millions of people and then at some future date trigger all of those minds at one time? Would we suddenly have a world of saints? Or would we have a world of armed maniacs shooting at one another from bell towers?'

"If Armageddon, to which the Bible points, is indeed a final battle in which human and nonhuman forces alike wage that dreadful conflict to the death, this sort of 'programming' is a real possibility, and it appears to be proceeding at breakneck speed across the whole of the world. It is reported that the term 'Armageddon' has been used in a message to a contactee and other 'end of the world' messages have been given. Is there a desperate preparation for a last-ditch stand by the forces of evil, a final attempt to thwart the plans of the Holy God against Whom they have rebelled? Bible history gives many examples where Satanic forces have attempted completely to destroy God's plans that would result in total blessings for man. There has continually been a diabolical scheme to bending minds by deceitful assurances and 'brainwashing.' Posthypnotic suggestions, with in-built commands for action to be triggered at a given signal, would fit the general pattern of rebellion consistently seen in the Bible records.

"A FRIGHTENING PROSPECT - The prospect if frightening. It is entirely possible that by posthypnotic suggestion a whole army of people could suddenly find themselves willing slaves of intelligent beings who care nothing for the welfare of those slaves, or of the world itself as we know it. If there is some great super- plan of a spiritual counterattack to reach its culmination in Armageddon, it could well be that (this) army of slaves will be available to obey orders, without even knowing beforehand that they have been inducted into the armed forces of what the Bible refers to as the principalities and powers.

"The indications are that even children are at times utilized for the implementation of the plans of these evil powers. That possibility is illustrated by the following incident.

"On December 12, 1967, Mrs. Rita Malley was driving along a public highway to her home at Ithaca, New York, with her five- year-old son Dana in the back seat of her vehicle. At about 7:00 P.M. she suddenly realized that a red light was apparently following her, and as she was moving above the speed level, her first reaction was that she was about to be pulled over. She looked through her window and found that it was not a police car behind her but an eerie flying object, moving along above the power lines at the left of her car. Then she found she no longer had control of her vehicle, and shouted to her son to brace himself. However, he remained motionless as though he were in a trance.

"A white beam of light flashed down from the vehicle overhead, then she heard voices that sounded weird, broken, and jerky. She herself became hysterical, but through it all her son took no notice whatever of her cries. The radio was not on, but she heard those voices tell her that at that moment a friend of hers had been involved in a terrible accident some miles away. The next day she found that this was indeed true. The voices also told her that her son would not remember anything that had happened. The ordeal was terrifying to Mrs. Malley herself, and for some time afterward whenever she remembered the episode she would break down sobbing.

"...It would seem possible, then, that pliable children are especially useful for the purposes of these beings. Many children have been used as tools so that men and women would believe in these beings who have a plan whose totality has not yet been revealed.

"...These incidents are not limited to children. Mrs. Ralph Butler was watching flashing lights outside Owatonna in Minnesota one night in November, 1966. She was with a friend, and suddenly her friend became immobile, with her head dipped down. Mrs. Butler herself heard a voice talking to her, but soon the ordeal was over. However, when the two friends tried to discuss the incident later, both found they immediately suffered blinding headaches. Mrs. Butler also told of hearing strange voices on her radio, and of having peculiar visits from 'air force officers.' This pattern is reported by many who claim to have been contacted by UFO personnel.

"The Butler family have experienced various poltergeist phenomena since that 1966 experience — glass objects moving around and breaking without any known cause, strange noises being heard throughout the house, even telephones and television sets being strangely interfered with (Note: Such activity often occurs during UFO encounters where there seems to be a COLLECTIVE involvement of paraphysical 'Poltergeists' or 'Infernals', Reptilians, and possibly 'controlled-cybernetic' Men In Black — such activity as is typical of the malevolent powers that have allegedly established bases or 'empires' in systems such as Alpha Draconis, Epsilon Bootes, Altair Aquilla, Zeta Reticuli, Bellatrix Orion, and Rigel Orion as well as their Solarian-subTerran counterparts - Branton).

"This sort of activity has followed many other supposed saucer sightings. The similarities between the stories are of such a nature as to cause surprise at first — someone temporarily in a trance, men posing as air force or other officials, those men being slight in stature with dark olive skins and pointed features, and the contactees having dreadful headaches, hallucinations, and nightmares. Some of them have gone into trances and have temporarily become mediums through whom strange voices could be heard...

"A TAKEOVER ATTEMPT? — Is there to be an attempt at a takeover? There surely are limitations to the life-giving powers of these UFO creatures... Man is the master of the ANIMALS, and despite seemingly way-out theories, such as monster INSECTS waiting to attack us, in fact man is still able to control the LESSER creatures... (Note: That is unless man accepts the propaganda and lies of the such lesser 'beasts' as the serpent races, etc., such as their claim that they created us genetically and are therefore our 'gods'. IF man believes such trash then he WILL NOT try to resist and appropriate the God-given dominion over these 'beasts' which the Creator has given to MANKIND. Not all, but MUCH of the power that the 'aliens' wield over humanity is the power that WE ourselves have capitulated or yielded to them, if we are to trust the Judeo-Christian version of history as a reality - Branton).

THE MOJAVE DESERT'S GREATEST SECRETS

"EVIL FORCES ARE REAL - Even apart from my strong Christian beliefs, and my acceptance of the Bible as the revealed Word of God, I would have no doubt whatever as to the fact of spiritual beings, evil forces, and phenomena that cannot be explained by purely physical, psychical, or psychological concepts.

"If there is truth in this hypothesis, preparations would be going on — just in case these overheard futurist interpretations happened to be correct..."

On July 30, 1992, radio announcer and reporter for RADIO FREE AMERICA, Anthony J. Hilder, sent the following letter to Patty Cafferata., Lincoln County District Attorney., Pioche, Nevada 89043., 702-962-5171. Several dozen copies were sent by Hilder to other researchers as well as several activist, political, legal, media, patriot, congressional, and (real) 'National Defense' officials:

"Dear Mrs. Cafferata: I am calling on the Attorney General of the State of Nevada to initiate an immediate 'FULL SCALE' Grand Jury Investigation into the activities of the Wackenhut S.S., your office and the Lincoln County Sheriff's Department. The reason for the urgency of this action is because of the rapidly increasing number of 'LIFE THREATENING' situations CREATED by unidentified paramilitary personnel who operate under the color of law to harass, intimidate and suppress the constitutional rights of many hundreds of American citizens and Japanese nationals who come to view the Unidentified Flying 'Saucer-Shaped Disks' being tested over your county.

"It is my prayer that with the prodding of the people and the press that the Attorney General will launch 'this investigation' in time to avert one of these innocent individuals from being murdered by that paramilitary mob or winding up as a permanent prisoner in one of the 'strange' underground 'experimental laboratories' below Dreamland and S-4 within the Nellis Test Range.

"During my conversation with you on the afternoon of June 6, I made repeated attempts to acquire the names of six individuals who were arrested last month by the Lincoln County Sheriff's Department somewhere in the Tickaboo Valley. As a reporter, I sought your professional cooperation. I did not get it.

"Not only did you refuse to reveal the names of those arrested and their 'alleged' violation of law — you continually badgered me for my home address, phone number and specifically just what radio stations would be broadcasting the story. Could it be that you wanted to 'cover-up' the story? As I stated, I simply wanted to cover the event.

"I am curious as to the reason you would attempt to prevent the media from reporting the arrest. Obviously you didn't want me to contact those people for their side of the story before their arraignment. Is there something you fear from honest disclosure? What is it that you don't want to know? Could it be that these arrests were illegal?

"Did the Sheriff's Department violate 'the constitutional rights' of these citizens, Mrs. Cafferata? Has it become the policy of Lincoln County Sheriff's Department WITH YOUR APPROVAL and under the color of law, to 'HARASS AND INTIMIDATE' the curious onlookers who come to your county to sit beneath the stars in the high desert, hoping to see and possibly photograph the strange and 'alien lights' in the night sky for which that region has now become famous? Is this a crime in Nevada? One might wonder if Lincoln has now become the first county in a 'Hitlerian Superstate' of a NEW WORLD ORDER — where freedoms are suppressed and terror tactics are 'public policy'?

"...It's definitely not a TOP SECRET that what's going on within the bowels of those underground bunkers at S-4 and Area 51 in the Nellis Test Site is 'ABOVE TOP SECRET". Obviously there's something very strange going on out there that the 'BLACK PROJECT BOYS' have to hide regardless of what it costs. If the public were to become aware of what these 'Dr. Strangelove's' were 'creating' in those underground laboratories — I believe the world would be shocked and horrified beyond all belief.

"Need I remind you that it is your responsibility as District Attorney of Lincoln County to UNCOVER — NOT COVER UP crimes that are being committed in your county. Other questions arise. Is there a dereliction of duty by the District Attorney's office? Do you have a conflict of interest? And for whom do you serve?

"I am deeply concerned as is the American Civil Liberties Union in seeing that the constitutional rights of all Americans who live in or pay a visit to Lincoln County are PROTECTED — NOT VIOLATED by the WACKENHUT S.S. (Security Service), your Sheriff's Department, or anyone else.

"Correct me if I am wrong, but at one time or another did you not take some sort of oath to uphold and defend the Constitution of the United States? Or is the Lincoln County District Attorney EXEMPT from upholding such 'antiquated trivialities' as the United States Constitution?

"Would you be willing to share with me information as to how and why the Wackenhut S.S. is ALLOWED by your office under the color of law to STOP, INTIMIDATE AND HARASS 'sightseers' on PUBLIC land? Are they 'ABOVE THE LAW'? Are they IMMUNE TO PROSECUTION?

"What law is it that allows the WACKENHUT S.S. to drive unlicensed vehicles on county roads in the state of Nevada at speeds far exceeding the posted limit? Does your office now allow them to search sightseers' vehicles without warrants? Maybe some judge in Lincoln County issued them 'POCKET WARRANTS'? And if so, what judge has the legal authority in this country to issue such 'invisible warrants' to the WACKENHUT S.S. or any other PARAMILITARY MOB? What law gives you the legal authority to allow the WACKENHUT S.S. to stop, interrogate and intimidate sightseers, tourists, campers and naturalists? Or for that matter, do they need ask your permission at all? Are they a law unto themselves?

"Are these 'HITLERIAN HARASSERS' CIA, NSA, 'Black Project', U.N. or paramilitary personnel? Just where is the law in Lincoln County? Asleep? Or do you simply WINK YOUR EYE at all those Orwellian incidents?

"The obvious collusion between Wackenhut and the Sheriff's Department necessitates that these questions be asked. It has become EVEN MORE NECESSARY to prevent our freedoms from disintegrating — that these questions be answered.

"Who are these men who stand behind LOADED FULLY AUTOMATIC WEAPONS, show NO IDENTIFICATION, wear camouflaged clothing, DISPLAY NO BADGES, wear no emblems, drive unlicensed vehicles and who show no warrants when they stop and interrogate American citizens on American soil? They demand to see identification, social security cards, driver's licenses, take pictures of the sightseers, record their conversations, search their cars and write down the license plate numbers for 'her files' just like in Nazi Germany. They have even on occasion drawn their weapons and aimed them at American citizens — with what can only be described as INTENT TO KILL — should the 'sightseers' not instantly obey their commands. Surely you must be aware that all this is taking place on public 'taxpayer owned' land in your county. Why are you allowing this, Mrs. Cafferata?

"Who are these paramilitary people that you seemingly protect from prosecution? Under whose authority do these NEOFASCIST FORCES operate? Yours? MJ-12? Some cryptic banking cartel? The Skull and Bones? The Jason Society? Global 2000? The Tri-Lates? I know it's not the Boy Scouts, Mrs. Cafferata. Just who is running the show?

"I doubt seriously that the average citizen of Lincoln County who pays your salary has any idea what's going on. I feel quite certain that the residents of Rachel, Pioche and Alamo haven't secretly met with you in some obscure smoke-filled back-room to persuade you to make sure that the WACKENHUT S.S. remains 'immune' from criminal prosecution.

"I don't quite understand why you're doing what you're doing or rather NOT DOING. Does somebody have some sort of hold on you? Does some 'secret society' pay for your cooperation? or are you and the Sheriff's Department just working with the Wackenhut S.S. VOLUNTARILY, without pay?

"In Nazi Germany, Hitler had a quasi-government group called the S.S. Beyond their borders, they called the collaborators WAFFEN S.S. They were authorized by the Fuhrer to operate 'BEYOND THE LAW'. Is this the case in Lincoln County? Has the Wackenhut S.S. replaced the WAFFEN S.S.?

"Under what law have you allowed unmarked black helicopters to buzz, harass and threaten the lives of tourists in Lincoln County? If these aircraft are not, by the law, allowed to threaten the lives of people who come to Tickaboo Valley 'to see the sights', then why hasn't your office prosecuted these criminals? Are they above the law? Or has 'SELECTIVE PROSECUTION' replaced CRIMINAL JUSTICE in Lincoln County?

"Are you ready to testify in a court of law that you are 'unaware' that BLACK HELICOPTERS have been swooping down upon innocent travelers — in an attempt to scare them or try to kill them?

"...If you don't recollect any such incident, let me remind you but one. Norio Hayakawa, Gary Schultz and a party of sightseers were buzzed by an unmarked helicopter — in a LIFE- THREATENING MANNER in May of 1991.

"Under what law do you allow such outrage to occur over Lincoln County roads? Have you bothered to even so much as 'discuss' this attack with those who authorized it? Why haven't they been brought to court to explain their OFFENSIVE ACTION taken against those innocent, unarmed people? Did you make NO ATTEMPT WHATSOEVER to prosecute the perpetrators of that crime? Might I remind you that it occurred over a Lincoln County road, which is under your jurisdiction?

"...On March 26 of this year Norio Hayakawa and Shinichiro Namiki were stopped by Undersheriff Gary Davis and Deputy Sheriff Doug Lamoreaux, at which time their camera equipment was 'FORCIBLY CONFISCATED' on public land by these TWO ARMED MEN. In years gone by this was considered HIGHWAY ROBBERY. Under what law do you justify such outrage now? or is theft now legal in Lincoln County?

"Is it not incumbent upon you to at the very least bring Lamoreaux and Davis up before a judicial hearing in front of an unbiased judge? In case you've lost their numbers, Mrs. Cafferata, you can reach Undersheriff Davis at 702-725-3447 and Deputy Sheriff Lamoreaux at 702-725-3645 in their off-hours when they might be more inclined to give some straightforward answers about this outrageous behavior.

"I realize that you are at the very least angered by my inquiries. If your arrogant attitudes towards this reporter is any example of how you slip, slide, duck and hide from inquiries by others in the Fifth Estate — you must hold those of us in the media with very deep disdain. Your attitude reminds me of Richard Nixon. He had a similar attitude towards the free press, but you are in good company — so did Adolph Hitler.

"This country has been very good to me, Mrs. Cafferata. I owe a great debt to our forefathers who had the courage to stand up and speak out against tyranny imposed upon them by King George. They had to fight for the freedom we enjoy in this greatest nation on earth. So I am not about to remain silent, turn my back and do nothing as you would prefer me to do while I see our constitutional rights that they FOUGHT and died for twisted and turned by the knaves of Lincoln County law enforcement.

"I realize that you are paid handsomely to do and say what you do, Mrs. Cafferata. I have no problem with you making money, just as long as you don't 'sell out' our freedoms to obtain your fortune. Our freedoms are not for sale and we are not willing to see you surrender them to some 'Neo-Fascist' NEW WORLD ORDER. I fear that if your belligerent behavior is allowed to remain UNCHALLENGED in Lincoln County, Nevada may well be on its way to becoming Nazi-ized.

"I thank God that we still have freedom of speech and expression in this country. In the Commu-nazi nations of this world I would be investigated and subject to arrest for daring to make such inquiries of even a tank-town backwoods bureaucrat. Up until recently in the Soviet 'SLAVE SYSTEM' the KGB would concoct evidence against individuals like Solzhenitzen who dared to bring to light the grizzly Hitlerian horrors happening in the Gulag Archipelago.

"As deeply as you might be in 'COVERING' for those who are 'COVERING UP' the Nightmares at Nellis, I believe that you will soon discover that the overwhelming majority of those who receive this letter are far more dedicated to 'UNCOVERING CRIMES' being committed against American citizens in your neck of the world — than you will be in prosecuting crimes committed in Lincoln County.

"Incidentally, irrespective of how 'new' you might think that President Bush's NEW WORLD ORDER is, his 'presidential proclamation' is definitely not new. Adolph Hitler used the exact same words to describe 'his plan' for Global Government some fifty years ago. Now Bush claims he wants to accomplish it 'IN A KINDER AND GENTLER WAY.' But that's just on TV — for the mindless masses. For your edification THE NEW WORLD ORDER is the title of Hitler's second book......the first one was MEIN KAMPF. It served the Fuhrer and his Fascist followers who justified the INHUMAN WRONGS of 'HUMAN RIGHTS' committed throughout Europe. This included justification for Dr. Joseph Mengele's monstrous 'MEDIAL EXPERIMENTS' that were performed on the unsuspecting population in order to develop a MASTER RACE.

"Of course there's a difference between Bush and Hitler's phraseology. Hitler talked about a THOUSAND-YEAR REICH. Bush talks about a THOUSAND POINTS OF LIGHT.

"I know that it shatters your senses for someone like myself to suggest that 'GENETIC ENGINEERING' and 'MEDICAL EXPERIMENTS' could be going on in the miles of tunneled underground facilities at S-4 and Groom Lake — and that history could be repeating itself, yet this topic has come up repeatedly over the past year — from 'several sources'.

"I recall one case in point when the Lincoln County Sheriff's Department picked up a young black woman named Trassie Wingfield who was wandering about in the Tickaboo Valley one night near the perimeter of the base. As I understand it she's in the Navy and is stationed out of Hawaii. She claimed to have been abducted and brought to 'the facility' twice for 'medical experiments'. Did your office investigate her charges? And if not, why not?

"According to the FBI and Department of Justice records, well over 300,000 children end up MISSING AND UNACCOUNTED FOR in this country every year. Where do you think these 'MILK CARTON KIDS' disappear to, Mrs. Cafferata? Certainly they can't all get swallowed up in the inner cities or wind up in shallow graves off lonely backwoods roads or served up on the table of some psychopathic cannibal.

"In Bill Hamilton's book 'COSMIC TOP SECRET' there may be an answer to this question. In it is described a literal Hitlerian 'hell under the earth' which was created at a TOP SECRET- BLACK PROJECT base called Dulce. That one is located in New Mexico, not far from the Los Alamos National Laboratory. I have enclosed two pages from Hamilton's book for your review. Though I suspect you will — I pray that you don't — take these murderous matters lightly.

"I have recently heard stories of people who, under hypnosis, have described in nightmarish terms what goes on in these God-forsaken underground facilities like DREAMLAND. Based upon what I have heard, I can only describe the 'HELL-HOLES' as 'FRANKENSTEIN FACTORIES'. According to my sources, these laboratories are run by a small army of I.G.O.R.S. (the Invisible Government's Robotons) who follow 'the party line' as did their Nazi predecessors who ran the Hitlerian Hospitals at Auschwitz and Dachau.

"I don't know what Hitlerian horrors are happening out there with PROJECT REDLIGHT but I feel it's imperative to ask the Attorney General of the State of Nevada to appoint a special (independent, non-government) investigative team to uncover just what kind of 'experimentation' is going on in the underground facilities at S-4 and Groom Lake (if these biogenetic experiments are taking place in United States territory, should not they be subject to the same Federal regulations that all of the other Medical Institutions are subject to? - Branton). The country has the right to know if the missing 'MILK CARTON KIDS' are being used for 'genetic engineering' and if adult 'abductees' are used for mutation experiments and body parts.

"I would think that if you refuse to cooperate with such an investigative team or to even address this issue — one might conclude that you, like your predecessors, are following close to 'the party line'.

"A final question about 'THE FINAL SOLUTION', Mrs. Cafferata. As you know, Adolph Hitler was reported to have ordered HIS I.G.O.R.S. to gas millions of innocents in 'death camps' like Auschwitz and Dachau 'TO CLEANSE' the world of the Jewish problem. Did you ever ask yourself what happened to those atomic scientists in Germany who were developing the A-Bomb and the dozens of doctors who conducted those medical experiments on human beings? Is it merely coincidental that there exists many thousands of Malthusian Minded Men who openly accept 'MASS MURDER' as necessary to bring about a NEW WORLD ORDER? These Orwellian ONE WORLDERS working within the Bush 'Black Projects' believe that the world's population has to be reduced by 1,2500,000,000 people by the year 2000 (25%). If you don't believe, there are madmen with this mind-set... Read GLOBAL 2000's MASTER PLAN.

"These Malthusian men have the minds of monsters. They use 'controlled conflicts' (war), 'bacteriological warfare' (AIDS), sterilization, mandatory abortion and 'weather modification' to create droughts that result in mass starvation. To achieve their 'end objective' for global government upon the ashes of all national-sovereignty they are willing to mass-murder millions. That requires, of course, the 'cooperation' of officials like you, Mrs. Cafferata, to follow 'the party line'.

"I know it's very hard for you to accept, even in your wildest thoughts, that an AMERICAN AUSCHWITZ could exist UNDER American soil. I bet it's even harder for you to conceive that it could be fully functioning in Lincoln County. Are you willing to testify in a court of law that it doesn't exist there, Mrs. Cafferata?

"During the Third Reich even 'the party liners' who lived around 'the death camps' were reluctant to believe that 'their government' could commit such horrendous crimes as were discovered after the invasion of Germany. Yet, although they heard faint screams in the far distance and cries for help — they SHUT THEIR EARS TO IT. Even though they saw carloads of people by the thousands going into the concentration camps — and none return — THEY SHUT THEIR EYES TO IT. Even when they saw billows of smoke belch from the bowels of the burners and smelt the stiff strong stench of burning flesh — THEY SHUT THEIR SENSES TO IT. And, in spite of the fact rumor had it that 'unspeakable horrors' were going on in the 'killing camps' - THEY SHUT THEIR MINDS TO IT.

"Those that asked local government officials, like yourself, WHAT WAS GOING ON were told that it was all 'TOP SECRET' and involved 'NATIONAL SECURITY'.....and NOT TO QUESTION AUTHORITY. Then one day when the war came to a close and the truth was unearthed, the 'party people' acted shocked when it became public that millions had been mass-murdered. They just couldn't believe that genocide, infanticide and homicide could have been not only allowed but carried out to the last deadly detail by other 'party liners' in the government who just went along...... saw nothing, said nothing and did nothing.

"When it came time for the TRIAL at Nuremberg, Mrs. Cafferata, the 'Vun, Vurid, Vurkers' who ran the killer concentration camps at Auschwitz and Dachau — 'CLAIMED INNOCENCE'. Even those 'party people' who shoved and shoveled their victims into those carnivorous crematoriums - 'CLAIMED INNOCENCE'. THEY SAID THEY WERE JUST OBEYING ORDERS. They said they were merely carrying out the MASTER PLAN — for the Master Race.

"I am not accusing you of any crime, Mrs. Cafferata. It is possible that you could just be so inordinately apathetic or just so blindly obeying orders that you cannot see, or simply refuse to open your eyes to what's going on. Or do you 'CLAIM INNOCENCE', Mrs. Cafferata? The Attorney General's office will be the judge of that. It is the A.G.'s responsibility to determine if any crimes have been, or are now being committed or allowed 'to be committed' by your office. Ultimately, any decision with regards to the 'wholesale abuse of the law' is made by the prosecution who tries the case, be it in a court of law or before the bar of public opinion..."

"Sincerely, Anthony J. Hilder - RADIO FREE AMERICA"

Perhaps those of us who read these words should heed the battle-cry of the Jews when they say: "NEVER AGAIN!!!"

In the early 1990's an avowed high-level Intelligence Worker in the U.S. Government who refers to himself only as "Commander X", for his own protection, 'spilled the beans' on a key secret concerning the interaction and conflict taking place below the Mojave Desert, against the Gray Empire which had entrenched itself in the subterranean levels of the Southwest:

"The underground...base outside of Dulce, New Mexico, is perhaps the one MOST FREQUENTLY referred to. It's existence is most widely known, including several UFO abductees who have apparently been taken there for examination and then either managed to escape or were freed just in the nick of time by friendly...forces.

"According to UFO conspiracy buff and ex-Naval Intelligence Officer Milton (William) Cooper, '...a confrontation broke out between the human scientists and the Aliens at the Dulce underground lab. The Aliens took many of our scientists hostage. Delta Forces were sent in to free them but they were no match for the Alien weapons. Sixty-six people were killed during this action. As a result we withdrew from all joint projects for at least two years...'

"CENTURIES AGO, SURFACE PEOPLE (some say the ILLUMINATI) entered into a pact with an 'Alien nation' HIDDEN WITHIN THE EARTH." Commander X alleges. "The U.S. Government, in 1933, agreed to trade animals in exchange for high-tech knowledge, and to allow them to use (undisturbed) UNDERGROUND BASES, in the Western U.S.A. A special group was formed to deal with the 'Alien' beings. In the 1940's 'Alien Life Forms' (ALF) began shifting their focus of operations, FROM CENTRAL AND SOUTH AMERICA, TO THE U.S.A.

"The CONTINENTAL DIVIDE is vital to these 'entities.' Part of this has to do with magnetics (substrata rock) and high energy states (plasma)... This area has a very high concentration of lightning activity; underground waterways and cavern systems; fields of atmospheric ions; etc..."

The following is taken from an article by 'TAL' LeVesque, titled 'THE COVERT RETURN OF AN ALIEN SPECIES OF REPTILIAN HERITAGE - THE DULCE BASE,' which appeared in a mailer-newsletter distributed by researcher Patrick O'Connel:

According to TAL, ages ago "...a CONFLICT with other beings (ELs) destroyed most of their (Reptilian) civilization, which forced some into DEEP CAVERNS & others to LEAVE EARTH (to Alpha Draconis and/or Altair in the constellation Aquila, which in ancient lore was associated with evil reptilian creatures)... The conflict is a Species War, between the Evadamic Seed & the 'Serpent' (draconian) Seed."

(Note: Researcher Maurice Doreal claims that this "conflict" took place between giant humans or 'ELs' working with PRE- NORDICS based in the Gobi region of Asia several thousand years ago, and Reptilian hominoids based in Antarctica! - Branton)

"Under cover of darkness, with bases hidden inside the earth, this nocturnal invader has chosen to reclaim what was once theirs & use it (and us) as a staging area in their ancient conflict with the 'ELs'. (Note: That is, the reptilians wish to 'reclaim' that which they WANT US TO BELIEVE was once theirs. The 'ELs' are the so-named EL-der race, a humanlike culture tied into the Evadamic heritage yet who have attained or retained a very tall physical stature, in some cases being twice as tall as the average 'International' or 'surface' Terran. Because of their physical differences, they have chosen to inhabit exterran, subterran, and according to some other dimensional realms so as not to induce irrational fear or worship of themselves by their more diminutive human cousins - Branton)

"Humans with alien brain implants (the 'zombies') have been programmed to help overthrow Mankind in the NEAR FUTURE. The 'Reptoids' are even able TO TRANSFORM THEMSELVES INTO BEINGS WITH HUMAN CHARACTERISTICS & FEATURES. The planet Earth is being stressed so that human resistance will be minimal, during the overt takeover & control of Mankind.

"It started as a 'joint interaction program.' An Alien Species wanted to 'share' parts of it's advanced technology with certain humans in KEY POSITIONS OF POWER within government, military, corporations, 'secret societies', etc... The population as a whole began to be manipulated into the 'Alien Agenda'... they wanted TOTAL CONTROL of us!"

(Note: When this was written, the real name of the 'source' of information described in the following paragraph was with- held and known only as "T.C." or "Thomas C.". We have now been authorized to reveal the full name of the former Dulce Base worker as being Thomas Edwin Castello, who possessed a LEVEL-7

"ULTRA" security clearance within the Dulce facility, and who was in fact a head of Security within the underground installation. There are unconfirmed reports that Thomas Castello, after years in hiding, has finally passed away in Costa Rica. Whether or not his alleged death had anything to do with his intimate knowledge of the underground bases, is not known - Branton)

"...T.C (had) seen tall Reptilian Humanoids at the base. This is interesting to me because in 1979 I came face-to-face with the over 6 foot tall 'Other' Species (REPTOIDS) which materialized in our home! They took blood from my wife (who is an Rh-negative blood type); & her daughter, who was 1500 miles away.

"...We all came to know that the 'Visitors' were here to stay. We also learned how the Reptilian Race was RETURNING to Earth & the 'Greys' — who are mercenaries — WERE BEING USED to interface (with) & manipulate humans. Their DEMONIC AGENDA was to keep earth surface (mankind) CONFUSED & unaware of their true nature & potential... ALSO (to conceal) THE KNOWLEDGE OF VAST & VARIED CIVILIZATIONS LIVING WITHIN THE EARTH.

"The Fantastic Truth was made to seem a fantasy, a legend, a myth, an illusion! The REPTOIDS are RETURNING to earth to use it as a staging area, in their ANCIENT CONFLICT with the Elohim (the Creator and the Angelic forces as described in Revelation chapter 12, who are not to be confused with the 'ELs' with whom the Reptilians are ALSO in conflict - Branton). The ADAMIC Race has underground bases within Mars... they are a 'Warrior Cult' culture.

"...There is a vast network of Tube Shuttle connections under the U.S., which extends into a GLOBAL SYSTEM OF TUNNELS & SUB-CITIES... Note: They (reptilians) DO NOT consider themselves 'Aliens'... they claim Terra (3rd from the Sun) was their home before we (humans) arrived. (Note: The saurian grays may have originated on earth and 'developed' or 'mutated' from the early bipedal saurioid species, yet there is much evidence that their 'claim' that this is 'their' planet is merely propaganda designed to convince the human race that they or we must surrender this world to their control - Branton).

"...As a species," TAL continues, "the reptilian heritage beings (the Greys, Reptoids, Winged Draco with 2 horns - the classic stereotype of the 'Devil')... are highly analytical & technologically oriented. They are seriously into the sciences of automation (computers) & bioengineering (genetics)! However, their exploits in these areas has led to reckless experimentation, WITH TOTAL DISREGARD FOR ETHICS (moral standards) AND EMPATHY. This is also true of MANY OF THE HUMAN BEINGS WORKING WITH THEM!."

TAL then describes something which might seem unbelievable if it weren't for the fact that dozens of other sources tend to confirm it. This discovery was allegedly one of the REAL reasons for the incitation of the 'Dulce Wars':

"...LEVEL #7 is the worst. Row after row of 1,000's of humans & human-mixture remains in cold storage. Here too are embryos of humanoids in various stages of development. Also, many human childrens' remains in storage vats. Who are (were) these people?"

The sources for these incredibly disturbing allegations aside from Thomas Castello himself, according to TAL, included:

"...people who worked in the labs, abductees taken to the base, people who assisted in the construction, intelligence personnel (NSA, CIA, etc.), and UFO-Inner Earth researchers." This information, TAL states, "is meant for those who are seriously interested in the Dulce base. For YOUR OWN PROTECTION, be advised to 'USE CAUTION' while investigating this complex."

The 'Symbol' for the Dulce Base that is worn on many of the workers there, allegedly consists of an UPSIDE-DOWN triangle or pyramid with an upside-down 'T' superimposed over it. William Hamilton added a few comments in his book 'COSMIC TOP SECRET', concerning studies of the carcasses of mutilated cattle found near Dulce, New Mexico. These include:

"...Schoenfeld Clinical Laboratories in Albuquerque analyzed the samples (of the affected hides of cattle studied by Gomez and Burgess) and found significant deposits of potassium and magnesium. The potassium content was 70 times above normal.

"...Level 1 (of the Dulce base) contains the garage for STREET MAINTENANCE. Level 2 contains the garage for TRAINS, SHUTTLES, TUNNEL-BORING MACHINES (or what former Dulce-base worker Thomas Castello refers to as the "terrane drive" - Branton), AND DISC MAINTENANCE.

"...The Greys and reptoid species... have had ancient CONFLICTS with the NORDIC humans from outer space societies, and may be staging here for a future conflict."

Penny Harper, in the January 1990 issue of 'WHOLE LIFE TIMES', wrote an article in which she referred to the UFOlogist and prominent physicist Paul Bennewitz:

"Paul Bennewitz — whereabouts unknown (Note: A search of a major laser-disc U.S. telephone database in 1993 revealed only one listing for 'Paul Bennewitz' — at 120 E. Pebble Beach Dr., Tempe, AZ 85282 — telephone #602-966-5704. This may or may not be the 'Paul Bennewitz' in question - Branton). Paul was a scientist investigating an abduction case. A woman and her son drove down a road in the southwest, the woman witnessed aliens mutilating a calf. The aliens captured both mother and son, taking them into an underground installation." The woman saw many frightening things, apparently much of it similar to what abductees Christa Tilton, Judy Doraty and others had witnessed, yet they — mother and son — also saw, according to Penny Harper: "...human body parts floating in a vat of amber liquid. After a horrifying ordeal, the woman and her son were taken back to their car. Bennewitz was able to determine that there is a secret 'alien' base beneath Dulce, New Mexico. He wrote 'The Dulce Report' and sent it to the civilian UFO group called APRO (i.e. Aerial Phenomena Research Organization). Bennewitz was then committed to the New Mexico State Hospital for the mentally ill where he was given electroshock 'therapy.' When he was discharged, he publicly stated that he would not have anything to do with UFOs. He is a recluse today, but still alive, last I heard."

Again, we quote from Commander X, who has stated:

"...From my own intelligence work within the military, I can say WITH ALL CERTAINTY that one of the main reasons the public has been kept in total darkness about the reality of UFOs and 'aliens', is that the truth of the matter actually exists TOO CLOSE TO HOME TO DO ANYTHING ABOUT. How could a spokesman for the Pentagon dare admit that five or ten thousand feet underground EXISTS AN ENTIRE WORLD THAT IS 'FOREIGN' TO A BELIEF STRUCTURE WE HAVE HAD FOR CENTURIES? How could, for example, our fastest bomber be any challenge to those aerial invaders when we can only guess about the routes they take to the surface; eluding radar as they fly so low, headed back to their underground lair?

"...the 'Greys' or the 'EBEs' have established a fortress, spreading out to other parts of the U.S. via means of a vast underground tunnel system THAT HAS VIRTUALLY EXISTED BEFORE RECORDED HISTORY..."

The following account, concerning an area in THE MOJAVE just east of BISHOP (OWENS VALLEY), CALIFORNIA, was related by Val Valerian in his 'LEADING EDGE' Newsletter, Dec. 1989 - Jan. 1990 issue. The article, titled: 'DEEP SPRING'S, CALIFORNIA', stated:

"Deep Springs, California is an area that is becoming known as the site for very strange events. According to the information released both on the air on KVEG-AM and from other sources, the area is full of strange people wandering around in black suits. There have also been rumors that there is an underground facility in the area. Checking with gravity anomaly maps proved that there are large cavities under the ground in that area. The wildest claims relative to the area have stated that alien lifeforms are being released there... Deep Springs Lake has been probed and it appears bottomless. Divers have traveled along an underground river 27 miles toward the Las Vegas area before having to turn around." (This 'river' would probably have been a 'partially' water- filled passage with a large stream or river flowing through it, rather than an entirely underwater system, since 27 miles of travel through entirely underwater passage would most likely be entirely out of the question, with present diving technology - Branton).

The following list of 'entity types' or 'aliens' comes from the anonymous Intelligence worker 'Commander X', as he received them from John Lear and other 'inside' sources:

"THREE TYPES OF EBE'S (GRAYS): GRAY-1 — 3 1/2 feet tall. Large head. Large slanted eyes. Worship technology. Don't give a damn about mankind. GRAY-2 — Same type, different finger arrangement, slightly different face. More sophisticated than Gray-1... May not need secretions (large- nosed or large-muzzled grays? - Branton). GRAYS: Same basic type. Lips thinner. More subservient to other two grays.

"BLONDES, SWEDES, NORDICS: Known by any of these monikers. Similar to humans (although it is unknown as to whether they are related to any of the nationalities mentioned). Blond hair, blue eyes. Will not break (so-called) 'universal law' of 'noninterference' to help us...

"INTER-DIMENSIONAL: Entity that can assume various shapes... (also include fallen angelics or poltergeists. These often apparently utilize androidal forms to operate in the 'physical' realm, temporary energy forms, forms constructed from restructured physical matter, or even physical biological 'shells' constructed from 'mutilated organs' and other materials, etc. - Branton)

"HAIRY DWARF'S: Four feet tall, 35 lbs. Extremely strong. Hairy (possibly a degenerate branch of the humanoid Sasquatch - Branton).

"VERY TALL RACE: Look like humans but seven or eight feet tall. United with Blondes.

"HUMANS APPEARING SIMILAR TO BLONDES SEEN WITH GRAYS: ...Child-like mentality.

"MIB'S: (Men In Black). Wear all black. Sunglasses. Very pale skin. Do nor conform to normal accepted patterns; Extremely sensitive to light..."

Researcher Val Valerian has quoted various 'inside' sources who claim that the Grays are able to use organs taken from mutilated victims to construct physical 'shells' for their invisible or nonphysical (demoniacal-poltergeist?) masters, allowing them to operate in the physical. In apparent confirmation, 'Commander X' shows how the Saurians might be able to 'create' such biogenetic forms:

"...What the government didn't realize was that they (the Grays) planned to abduct tens of thousands of individuals, plant monitoring devices in their brains, and program them with specific series' of responses to direct commands.

"The EBEs — also behind our backs — began to mutilate cows and other animals because they wished to use their tissues TO CREATE A GENETICALLY ADVANCED RACE OF FLESH AND BLOOD ROBOTS. When the government realized what the EBEs had in mind, and wanted to back out of their agreement, THE 'ALIENS' TOOK OVER SEVERAL UNDERGROUND BASES WHERE THEY HAD ALREADY INSTALLED UNDERGROUND LABORATORIES."

On p. 109 of John Keel's book 'THE MOTHMAN PROPHECIES', we read the following concerning an even more alarming possibility in regards to the reptilian threat:

"...I am an amateur herpetologist and once kept three-fanged cobras in my New York apartment... until my concerned neighbors squealed to the Board of Health. SOME OF THE DESCRIPTIONS OF THE (alien) ENTITIES IMPRESSED ME AS RESEMBLING SOME KIND OF REPTILE RATHER THAN HUMAN MAMMALS. I didn't mention the reptile notion to anyone. But on July 24, Lia (an alleged alien tied-in with the Men In Black - Branton) visited Jane (a contactee) and refused to talk about anything but eggs. She took some eggs from Jane's refrigerator and sucked out the contents like a reptile! Jane was perplexed by this exhibition and called me soon afterward." And on pp. 176-177 of Signet's 1975 paperback edition of 'MOTHMAN PROPHECIES', in reference to this same 'contactee' Keel states:

"...Meanwhile, Jane's phantom friends were visiting her daily and helpfully giving her surprising information about my own 'secret' investigations. My interview with the Christiansens of Cape May, and the details of their pill-popping visitor, Tiny, was then known only to a few trusted people like Ivan Sanderson. But on June 12, Mr. Apol and his friends (including the creature referred to above which called itself 'Lia' - Branton) visited Jane when she was alone in her house and asked for water so they could take some pills. Then they presented her with three of the same pills, told her to take one at that moment, and to take one other in two days. The third pill, they said, was for her to analyze to assure herself it was harmless. They undoubtedly knew she would turn it over to me. Two hours after she took the first pill she came down with a blinding HEAD ache, her eyes became bloodshot, and her vision in her right eye was affected. When her parents came home they expressed concern because her eyes were glassy and her right eye seemed to have a cast. The sample pill proved to be a SULFA DRUG normally prescribed for infections of the urinary tract..." The possible significance of the 'Sulfa' drugs will become apparent later on in this File.

In early 1992 the UNIVERSAL Company's Debut Network aired a made-for-TV version of John Carpenter's movie 'THEY LIVE', which was based on the premise of an alien race of bulge- eyed (one might imagine saurian-reptilian?) creatures that had infiltrated human society, disguised as humans, and which were in the process of subtly taking control of powerful social, media, economic and political positions. They were assisted by a small group of 'human power elite' who through subliminal 'mind control', hidden frequency transmitters, television propaganda, etc., helped to keep the masses in a constant state of semi- consciousness. Those who had not caught-on to the alien conspiracy went about their business in a slightly catatonic state sufficient to keep them 'blind' or 'asleep' to the point that the aliens and their subversive activities remained just outside of their conscious perception. It is interesting that John Carpenter (not to be confused with the well known MUFON investigator) depicted the attempts of the aliens to "annihilate" human consciousness as a means to minimizing human resistance, by destroying individual creativity and programming all human "cattle" to conform to the dictates of the alien intruders. All of this without humanity even being aware that they were the mind- slaves of an alien force which they were "programmed" to believe did not exist.

Also in the movie, secret subliminal messages were broadcast throughout all levels of society via all branches of the media, keeping the sleeping masses in a constant state of tranquilized apathy and subservience. A HORRIFYING prospect to say the lest. Also in the movie, the aliens utilized 'joint' underground bases beneath major cities which were more-or-less the back-stage of the alien control scenario.

Incidentally, Disneyworld in Florida contains an underground tunnel network with hidden entrances. The employees of the park use these as a 'back stage' — dressing rooms, employee indoctrination centers and other facilities necessary to keep up THE ILLUSION of 'Disneyworld'. This is of course all innocent enough, yet John Carpenter in his movie reveals the idea that the huge underground 'bases' beneath major cities are being used as 'back stages' in order to keep an infinitely more diabolical 'illusion' going, with the help of power-elite who are assisting in the covert subjugation of the masses for personal gain. The movie 'THEY LIVE' was based on the short story by Ray Nelson, 'Eight O'Clock in the Morning'. One might wonder where Nelson got the inspiration for his story, especially when we realize that the subject of the story and the movie itself is very similar to events which — according to numerous sources — are actually taking place, if we are to accept the MANY accounts which appear in this and other Files.

Also, in the movie it is the Judeo-Christian element which first 'wakes up' to what is going on, and who begin the revolutionary 'resistance' movement in order to destroy the stranglehold of the aliens upon human society... Could this scenario be somewhat prophetical as the book of Matthew (13:24-28) seems to suggest?

(Note: There have been similar reports as the above emerging from the Dugway Test Site on the Salt Flats of western Utah, just across the border from the Nevada Military complex. In fact there are allegations that much of the joint Alien-Illuminati activity which originated within the Nevada Military Complex has now moved into the underground facilities which have and are being constructed beneath Utah and Idaho, now that the Nevada activity has been the subject of wide exposure by the media. There is one reported case where a worker at the Dougway Test Site claimed to have seen a man temporarily transform into a reptilian while he was changing a tire, but the most interesting case was that of a woman, "Barbara", who worked in the small town of Dougway as a hair dresser. She worked on many of the base personnel there. On one occasion a customer who was a high-ranking military officer at the base came in. While she was working on his 'hair', she noticed a brief transformation during which she saw the officer turn into a "reptilian" creature. K.S., a Salt Lake City based UFOlogist, claims that during an "Open Mind" UFO gathering in the early 1990's, "Barbara" alleged that while working at Dougway she heard "rumors" that "reptilian humanoids" were operating "all over" the base. Another former Dougway worker, Ray White, who was a top secret courier, stated that during his work at the base [1960's-1970's?] he witnessed an experiment where an object was "teleported" from one room to another. He also noticed that high-ranking Russian officers sometimes visited the base. He also claimed that some of the "people" that he met there were NOT human. When asked what he thought they were, he did not know, but he did mention that top secret research into advanced robotics was being carried out at the base - Branton)

Researcher Val Valerian has, incidentally, described a very similar event. Valerian has researched alien phenomena and interaction with human beings since 1969. He spent 18 months in Southeast Asia from 1970-71 as a combat photographer, where he saw much UFO activity. After spending four years in England from 1980 to 1984 he gathered all the top research at his disposal and released what became known as 'The Krill Papers,' forerunner of the 381-page book, 'The Matrix', published in 1987. He began networking with researchers worldwide and started an organization known as Nevada Aerial Research Group.

Between 1988 and 1989 he functioned as Nevada State Section Director for MUFON. In 1990 he was appointed interim Associate Director for UFO Contact Center International and was a member of the Aerial Phenomenon Research Organization. In 1988 NAR began issuing a small newsletter detailing research findings. By 1990, this newsletter became known as 'The Leading Edge' and has grown to a monthly 100-page publication. The massive 581 page work entitled MATRIX II was released in 1990. In April of 1991, NAR moved to Washington State and was renamed as 'Leading Edge Research Group'. Valerian has a degree both in Civil Engineering and Psychology and had significant input into Nippon Television investigations on alien activities, the research that stimulated the production of the 1989 KLAS award-winning program entitled 'UFO'S: THE BEST EVIDENCE'.

F. W. Holiday, in his book 'THE DRAGON AND THE DISK' (W.W. Norton & Co., Inc. New York, N.Y. 1973) relates some unusual facts concerning the relationship between serpent or 'dragon' legends and the modern 'UFO' phenomena:

"...Satanism — that is to say the religion of the dragon... seems to have been contemporaneous in BABYLON and Bronze Age Britain. In both countries it was probably practiced by minority groups and became official only in times of decadence.

"When Cryus occupied Ur...a form of dragon-worship seems to have been in vogue. The priests of this cult escaped the Persians by fleeing north with their PONTIFF (or 'PONTIFEX MAXIMUS', a position which has allegedly been secretly held in an unbroken chain from Babylon up to modern times - Branton) into the mountains of Asia Minor. They finally came to rest at a place called Pergamos in Lydia (western Turkey) and there set up a religious centre which became known as 'Satan's seat'. St. John said: 'And to the angel of the church of Pergamos, write: These things saith He [God] which hath the sharp sword with two edges [judgment and mercy]: I know they works, and where thou dwellest, EVEN where Satan's seat is...'

"The ROMANS also knew about Satan's seat AND ANNEXED IT INTO THEIR EMPIRE IN 133 B.C., after the death of Attalus III, the last of the Pergamite kings. About this period A PLAGUE BROKE OUT IN ROME and prayers were offered to the Roman 'gods' in vain. It was decided, therefore, to appeal to Satan at Pergamos.

"The symbol of the cult was A SERPENT and a special ship was sent to Lydia TO TRANSPORT THE GOD TO ROME. (Most likely a depiction or "idol" representation of the "god", in that idols among early pagans were indistinguishable from the so-called "gods" themselves - Branton) There it was installed as a deity with great pomp. The disease had probably run its course and the resulting improvement in public health was attributed to Satan. The new religion was so popular that snakes of inoffensive species were allowed to glide around at parties — at least so Seneca says. In HISTORIA AUGUSTA they are called DRACUNCULI or little dragons.

"The Aesculapian Serpent — as the 'god' was called — is shown on a carving at Pompeii and is unlike anything known to herpetologists. It had vertical humps and snaillike horns, exactly like the monsters (sea serpents - Branton) of Scotland and Ireland. A bronze Urarian cauldron in Rome carries the erect head and neck of the creature modeled in the round. It is hideous. It has a shovel-like mouth, bulging eyes and tentacles or sensory organs hanging on each side of the face.

"No-one, of course, thought that snakes were dragons. The malignant Great Serpent of Babylonia was TYPHON or Teitan, Satan, the author of wickedness...

"Politicians, however, never look a gift-horse in the mouth as long as it produces results. After giving the Roman people carnage in the guise of circus entertainment, there was no reason for the EMPERORS to shrink from a little devil-worship. Even the national flag was given the treatment. Ammianus Marcellinus describes the standard 'PURPUREUM SIGNUM DRACONIS'. And when Julius Caesar appeared in full regalia as the PONTIFEX MAXIMUS he was dressed in reddish-purple robes the same as the Pergamite dragon-priests. The reader can trace the rest of the story in Gibbon's 'RISE AND FALL OF THE ROMAN EMPIRE'.

"DRAGON-WORSHIP PERSISTED LONG AFTER CHRISTIANITY (and also 'Catholicism?' - Branton) HAD BEEN PROCLAIMED. Tertullian complained: 'These heretics magnify the serpent to such a degree as to prefer him even to Christ himself; for he, they say, gave us the first knowledge of good and evil.'

"...there is a case to be argued that monsters and U.F.O.s are in some way linked. Abnormal chains of causation tending to frustrate inquiry into the nature of the phenomena have been reported in both cases. John A. Keel, an American journalist who has been delving into the mystery for over thirty years, talks about a 'conspiracy'. He warned me: 'Proceed with great caution in your Loch Ness work. We are caught up in a series of games which must be played by "their" rules. Anyone who tries to invent his own rules, or breaks the basic pattern, soon loses his mind or even his life.' (This might apply in many cases, except of course in the case of those who are working for and 'on the side' of a power much 'greater' than the draconian forces that are apparently working behind much of the 'UFO' and creature' events. When Jesus sojourned in this world, for instance, he condemned the serpent race as being in league with the fallen archangel Lucifer-Satan, and promised his followers that they would have supernatural power and authority over these 'serpents' if only they would put their trust in Him. - Branton). Those who think that this is dramatic and absurd may care to remember the words of St. John:

"'And he doeth great wonders, so that he maketh fire to come down from heaven on the earth in the sight of men and deceiveth them that dwell on the earth by THE MEANS of those miracles which he had power to do in the sight of the BEAST.'

"'The beast' that performed these miracles was what the Jews called 'The Shining One', 'The Great Serpent' and 'Satan'. If this is the underlying truth of the phenomena then Keel's warning is by no means too strong."

In relation to the above, during the Dark Ages of Roman Rule, early 'Dracologists' documented many accounts of battles between knights and dragons or winged and limbed serpents. This "infestation" as it was called by the early chroniclers, was allegedly halted with the advent of the spread of Christianity, and the "worms" as they were often referred to were forced to retreat back into the underworld — from which they had emerged — by the valiant Christian Knights such as St. George and Lancelot, who vanquished the beasts at every turn.

In 'POPULAR SCIENCE', March 1990 issue, p. 24, we read of an apparently quite intelligent, predatory lizard which constantly walked upright on two legs in a remarkable humanlike manner, counter balanced by a tail. This lizard, in fact, may have been the original ancestor of all the reptilian species throughout this world (and beyond?). If left to it's 'natural' course (of not so much 'evolution', but rather 'mutation') over the years, according to some paleontologists, a race of creatures such as described below might have — through natural selection and environmental adaptation — become more intelligent and 'hominoid' in nature. As its brain and physical form 'developed', and it's limbs became stronger through 'survival of the fittest', the 'tails' of such a predatory race may have become atrophied [as the 'limbs' became atrophied in snakes, a reptilian branch that apparently 'mutated' in the opposite direction]. The article states:

"The oldest known dinosaur, HERRERASAURUS... (was) a flyweight when compared with some of its ponderous descendants. HERRERASAURUS weighed perhaps 300 pounds and stretched a mere six to eight feet long. It had enormous claws and small forelimbs, showing that it spent much time ambling on two legs. It also had a peculiar, double-hinged jaw... that allowed it to clamp down on wriggling prey. And its teeth were finely serrated. These characteristics...clearly mark HERRERASAURUS as an active flesh eater.

"The site of the fossil find (of the remains of this saurian - Branton), the Ischigualasto Formation in northwestern Argentina, is the only area in the world where there are no gaps in the fossil record across the time zone being investigated."

In reference to the discoveries made by researcher Paul Serano — a paleontologist at the University of Chicago, who with colleague Alfredo Monetta discovered some remains of the bipedal saurioid lizard near San Juan, Argentina — the article states:

"Serano says that the very first dinosaur should have lived at the time of the rock layer containing HERRERASAURUS, but that climate and geological factors combined to keep any fossils from being preserved there.

"'We'll have to concentrate above and below that zone,' says Serano, 'Fortunately, those layers are very good. It's likely we'll be able to find more interesting fossils there.'

"The paleontologist won the $500,000 Packard Foundation Award last October, which he says will enable him to continue on the track of dinosaurs."

The following is apparently a description of the nefarious activities of the saurian 'Grey' entities, which was submitted to us along with a miscellaneous collection of UFO data by a Mr. Ray White. We do not know it's original source, other than the apparent fact that the information seems to be based on the revelations of a certain 'abductee', and begins by making reference to the greys as being:

"...eaters of souls — harvest(ers) of souls — placed in huge globular depositories — something extracted, as hemoglobin is extracted from blood — some residue buried in a graveyard not on this planet... couldn't move or speak — couldn't move head — tunnel vision — everything blurred except straight ahead — they have rank — like an army but not the same — you know by the way they 'talk' to each other — thumb, 3 fingers, perhaps 1 very small — suction pads on tips of fingers — our eyes do not pick up the real color of their skin, only a colorblind person would see their skin as it really is — she saw them as grayish green — their skin is not their true skin — it is like a shield they use, a protective covering (Note: In a similar manner Kenneth Ring, Ph.D.. in his book 'THE OMEGA

PROJECT' — William Morrow & Co., N.Y. 1972., states that, based on abductee reports, the 'opaque black' eyes of most of the 'Grays' may also be artificial 'coverings' - Branton) — their perception of pain is different from ours — one had compassion (Note: In most cases the only 'greys' described as having 'compassion' are the so-called 'hybrids', most of which are actually HUMANS conceived from human semen and ova taken from abductees, yet which have been 'genetically altered' through biotechnology and/or artificial post- natal gene-spicing with the 'aliens' or other life-forms. Just as the 'greys' are allegedly part of a lower saurioid hierarchy, the 'hybrids' or 'hubrids' are reportedly the slave-workers who work under them - Branton), others did not — ship blended into rock — total camouflage — HAVE INSTRUMENTS THAT CAN CAMOUFLAGE SHIPS AS [like?] ARMY VEHICLES — when she entered the ship, at first she thought that she was going into a cave in the rocks — they take off your clothes right away, without your realizing they have done it — they have a section strictly for men, another strictly for women — they did not understand her menstruating — she had to explain menstrual periods to female alien — cure of cancer in spices and roots — deformed babies in some sort of liquid — some E.T., some human, some E.T./ human, some deformed baby animals — failed experiments — they HAVE NOT yet had luck in interbreeding with us — offspring survive a certain amount of time, but then die — their metal different from ours, soft but not soft (?) — they don't understand how we bruise so easily, the softness of our skin — they were interested in soft spot at top of skull — they told her about her family history, going way back, ALWAYS the terrible things, traumatic childhood memories, few seconds each, the things she had blocked out, NEVER the happy memories — they can't understand why we aren't more advanced than they are — we limit ourselves — block knowledge out — ringing in ears both on and off ship — calf alive but frozen — different types of samples of animal life — they give birth through naval, not vagina — UBAN — Starmaster 12' tall — Night of Lights when everyone will see it — the whole world."

On Oct. 16th, 1992, FOX Network's 'SIGHTINGS' documentary described several abduction experiences involving 'grays' and larger 'Reptilian' entities. One woman alleged that during one encounter with the reptilian 'greys' she saw a 'preying mantis' type of creature working WITH the saurian greys and which seemed to be the leader. It had HUGE black eyes and even through the woman despised the greys she felt an even stronger disgust and hatred for that particular creature. This is not the only case where reptile-saurian 'predators' and Insectoid 'parasites' (as some have referred to them) have been seen working together.

Just what are these 'Mantis' like creatures that have been seen WORKING WITH the greys-reptilians? Some have suggested that they are an extreme mutation of the reptilian race, while others suggest they are interdimensional entities of insectoid configuration. John Lear has alleged that one of the first crash-retrievals of an unidentified aerial disk involved these 'mantis-like' creatures which were found on board. However he also states that within a short period following the incident ALL of the high government officials who investigated that particular case died under mysterious circumstances. Such a 'coincidence' may seem sinister if not demoniacal in nature. Like the reptilians themselves, these 'Mantis' like creatures have usually been described as being deadly and very deceptive and abusive. It seems as if they operate on an equal basis, and in some cases a superior basis to the so-called 'Reptilian' AND saurioid 'Gray' alien groups and possibly the pterodactoids or so-called 'Mothmen' as well.

One source, although unconfirmed, 'claimed' to have seen huge 'Mantis-like' creatures in a cavern deep below a drill-shaft south of the Kokoweef mountain area near the Mojave Desert. The account, rather obscure in some details, was related by way of a Mr. 'Stolz' who knew some individuals who were involved in modern attempts to break into Earl Dorr's legendary 'underground grand canyon' or river of gold beneath Kokoweef peak. It is uncertain whether the man in question was lowered down the hole or whether he allegedly saw the creatures via camera equipment that was lowered down the drill-shaft.

In his book 'THE SERPENT AND THE SATELLITE' (Philosophical Library, New York), author F. Alfred Morin reveals on page 343:

"...In the Jewish legends the serpent is sometimes described as a modified reptilian humanlike creature indicating that this description was also gradually evolving into the symbolism of wickedness or Satan into the image and likeness of a man."

The LEADING EDGE RESEARCH GROUP, P.O. Box 481-MU58., Yelm, Washington 98587., published the following 'advertisements' or introductions for two of their publications. Although these publications contain some 'occult-channeled' metaphysical information of a rather unsubstantiated or subjective nature, other informations arrive from more down-to-earth (and thus more substantiating or objective) sources. The first add is as follows:

Valerian, Valdamar. MATRIX II: THE ABDUCTION AND MANIPULATION OF HUMANS USING ADVANCED TECHNOLOGY. 3rd Edition. Updated with New Material. LEADING EDGE RESEARCH GROUP, 1991, 8 1/2 x 11, Velo-Binding, 660 pages, 1400 line-item index. Its first two editions sold out planetwide as of June 1990. It is rumored that some alien species have secured a copy, and the US Government has also apparently acquired it. The original MATRIX, issued in 1988, set the stage for this incredible piece of work... The book, now in its 3rd edition, updated in July 1991, encompasses an incredible range of data which includes precedental research on human abduction by both government and off-planet forces — material that other authors will not speak of and what publishers will not allow themselves to print.

After the book was released, other researchers began to catch on to what has been occurring. Val Valerian weaves a wide range of interrelated material into a literary experience that will rock you to the core of your being — Included within the book is... data and updates on underground bases at Dulce and the Nevada Test Site, a large number of illustrations, maps and charts detailing activity sites, underground installations and tunnel networks, commentary by John Lear, Robert Lazar and a host of other top-notch researchers. Valerian takes us through the whole gambit of how, why, and by whom humans are manipulated, information about government connections to the abduction process, post-abduction problems, and things that the abductee can do.

The book is the first to adequately relate research on memory functions relative to the abduction process, virtual reality machines and Reichian programming, and mind control by human and alien manipulators. It also discusses the abduction of human children and how to handle adjustment of the child to the experience, multi- generational scenarios and cases, human multidimensional anatomy and how it can be manipulated by technology, and elements of advanced technology possessed by the government. There is more information about the various species known as the Greys in MATRIX II than there has been (or probably ever will be) published anywhere... There is additional data on the Reptilian species who are dominant over the Greys, and what they may have planned for humans in the coming years. There are overviews of the processes and rationale for implanting humans, as well as cross-sections and technical data gleaned from extracted alien implants during 1991. Electronic space societies (which the Earth will become in the near future) are discussed.

The book has an incredible spectrum of information about alien influence on human society, historical facts that are hard to come by, and much much more. There is just so much data in this book that it would take pages and pages to describe it... The book is the death- knell for the planetary domination-based control systems — the whole domination/control game and its accompanying social manifestations (and what is ultimately behind them) are exposed for all to see. MATRIX II and the research of Valerian and others he includes in his book also spells the end for "classical Ufology" with its attendant "Ufologists", "experts", and most of the "UFO organizations" that are here today. It also exposes techniques that intelligence and security forces use to have influence over people and teaches you why they are doing it. Through the book, we can see how alien interaction has affected wave after wave of civilization on this planet, injecting elements of adverse technology and mind control, and how the suppression of human awareness is being performed and supported. MATRIX II is an absolute MUST to have in your library — you might throw all your other books on the subject away. LEADING EDGE RESEARCH also offers on a regular basis, the 100-page newsletter, THE LEADING EDGE. MATRIX II is $52,50, postpaid.

And then the following 'add', which may seem rather confusing at first, however when compared with the rest of this File as a whole, one will begin to see how the following information corroborates with that which other sources have related:

ORION BASED TECHNOLOGY, MIND CONTROL AND OTHER SECRET PROJECTS — A SERIES OF CONDUCTED INTERVIEWS, 53 pg, $8.00:

This 53-page report was constructed from over 9 hours of video interviews, personal interviews and individual commentary. It is structured in an open question-answer format in such a way that the identities of the different parties are protected. This was requested by several of the parties in order to permit this piece of work to be done and disseminated. It took approximately 20 hours of work to create the report, which contains information about some of the following topics: The Philadelphia Experiment, or Project Rainbow, Phoenix Projects 1-3, origins of the Radiosonde and connections with the work of Wilhelm Reich, government weather control programs and hidden agenda, the Montauk Mind Control projects, the deliberate murder of thousands of American children in mind control research and time tunnel experiments, government time-tunnel projects and operational procedures, how Nickola Tesla and Von Neumann contributed to these projects, the "martyrdom clause", mind control by individual signature, technical ways to produce planetary holograms and Maitreiya effects... government rationale and plans for the confinement camps and slave labor, Project Dreamscan, Project Moonscan, the Airborne Instrument Labs, Project Mindwrecker, the alien group known as the Kondrashkin and their interaction with US Government mind control programs, the Kamogol II and Giza Groups, the negative Sirians, Soviet scalar weaponry, Orion Group manipulations... telepathy producing drugs and their use and suppression, the FAA and zero-time generators, technical spin-offs from the Philadelphia project, the International Aerospace Alliance, cross-section of implant device, Wilhelm Reich and mind control, Reichian Orgastic-type programming and its use by the US Government and Sirians, the Psi-Corps, Alien soul-trading, Montauk and the aliens from the Antares system, the Leverons... the US Government and the Greys, electronic life support systems of the Reptilian Humanoids, new life form masses over the poles and their relation to yearly outbreaks of flu-like disease, AIDS and Fort Detrick (NSA), Maglev trains and the US underground tunnel network, the missing human genes, buried spacecraft and alien technical archives under the Giza pyramid, the coming new money, the "Black Nobility", Nordic and human copper based blood systems and physiology, the technology of cloning and development of synthetic humans and political replacement programs, the Middle East situation, Congressional awareness of drug and alien agenda, the MIB, the US Army and the black helicopter forces, government mobile mind disruption technology, nature and purpose of the Orion Group, fourth density transmutation of the human race, geological changes, Sirian Mind Control technology, and more, along with illustrations gleaned from witnesses with photographic memory and a lot of courage.

Again, in reference to the 'serpent races', John A. Keel, in his book 'OUR HAUNTED PLANET' (1968. Fawcett Publications., Greenwich, Conn.) has stated:

"...The parahuman Serpent People of the past are still among us. They were probably worshipped by the builders of Stonehenge and the forgotten ridge-making cultures of South America.

"...In some parts of the world the Serpent People successfully posed as gods and imitated the techniques of the super- intelligence. This led to the formation of pagan religions centered around human sacrifices. The conflict, so far as man himself was concerned, became one of religions and races. Whole civilizations based upon the worship of these false gods rose and fell in Asia, Africa, and South America. The battleground had been chosen, and the mode of conflict had been decided upon.

"The human race would supply the pawns. The mode of control was complicated as usual. Human beings were largely free of direct control. Each individual HAD TO CONSCIOUSLY COMMIT HIMSELF TO ONE OF THE OPPOSING FORCES...

"The main battle was for what was to become known as the human soul.

"Once an individual had committed himself, he opened a door so that an indefinable something could actually enter his body and exercise some control over his subconscious mind. (According to Judeo-Christian teaching, THIS would either be the incorruptible Spirit of the Messiah or the soul-destroying spirit of anti-Christ, the serpent, Satan, etc. Just as nature hates a vacuum, so does the human soul and spirit. In other words, what Keel is saying is that the human spirit cannot work entirely of it's own volition, but must serve as a channel or a vessel of a 'higher power', whether that power is good or evil. The act of 'free will' which is given to man is a 'choice' over which of these powers to submit to or serve, and to accept personal responsibility for that choice. It is the greatest presumption to believe that finite beings like ourselves can choose to be neutral in this ancient battle between the Angelic forces of Light and Life, and the fallen demoniacal powers of Darkness and Death. Neither side will allow for 'neutral territory', in this case human souls, because the stakes in this Cosmic Conflict are too high - Branton).

"...the Serpent People or OMEGA Group, attacked man in various ways, trying to rid the planet of him. But the super- intelligence was still able to look over man... God worked out new ways of communication and control, always in conflict with the Serpent People."

The mysterious "government insider" whose books have been published by Tim Beckley's Abelard Press of New York, "Commander X," related a very interesting incident which involved the subterranean mega-complex beneath Dulce, New Mexico. The story he tells might turn out to be an important part of the overall puzzle in connection with that which has previously been related. One of the many accounts concerning this particular alien 'stronghold' — an underground empire which is apparently attempting to spread it's borders to the Mojave, where 'they' have met resistance from relatively more benevolent human forces — was related by this anonymous Intelligence Worker, who states:

"...In another case an old illustrator, John D., does very painstaking work, but during his being on active duty at Dulce he began to act very queerly. He would write letters to the President informing him of a plot underway to undermine the government, and to sabotage the base. He began to draw pictures of American flags, beautifully executed. He drew strange designs of mechanical devices, began to visit the library and bring back books on physics and advanced electronics. He hardly knew how to spell the words.

"He would patiently explain something of a very technical nature which he shouldn't have understood. When asked what he was raving about and why he was causing trouble by writing the President, John D. would say that he had been 'sensitized.'

"'Last year when I was sick (John D. explained), the doctor on the base gave me sulfanilamide. There is a fifth column in this country that is tied up with aliens. Selenium is being slipped into SULFA DRUGS, and this selenium lodges in the bones and makes the body receptive to extremely short waves, those in the wave band of the brain. Similar to the waves that can be detected by the encephalograph. About 300,000 people in this country have been sensitized, and at least seven secret radio stations have been set up in this country, and they are broadcasting to these sensitized persons, instructing them in the best way to perform acts of sabotage against our planet.'"

These claims as given by the Dulce worker, John D., are incredible indeed, and could easily be dismissed as the ravings of a madman, IF NOT FOR THE FACT THAT many others are saying basically the same thing, that there is a movement underway to bring the minds of the masses under the subjection of some alien force, whether through implantation or other means, and that these alien powers from all indications intend on bringing humanity under their control through such manipulations.

Why would the "controllers" use the United States as the major target of their activity? We believe that this is due to the fact that the United States is a place that was originally intended by it's 'founding fathers' to be a refuge for peoples from all nations to come and work out their collective destinies free from the restrictions of prejudice and dictatorial or tyrannical rule — a land where all people could express their creativity and individual destinies without interference. This was their "intention", however it is obvious that the "dream" has not been fully realized because of collective and governmental compromise of the principle that "all men are created equal". The United States, nevertheless, is unlike any other single nation. It is a "melting pot" and a place where not only international human societies on the surface CONVERGE and intermingle in a dramatic way, but apparently where human societies beneath or beyond the earth converge as well. For instance, according to various accounts, most non- surface human societies who are aware of earth have their representatives walking among us in our society (and to a lesser extent, other nations throughout the world).

There is even the possibility presented by some accounts, however strange as this may seem, that the sauroids or reptilians themselves have their own chameleon-like (human-appearing) "representatives" walking among us, infiltrating our society, for the most part unknown for their true nature. We have mentioned a few cases previously, however there is another account of a 'chameleon' entity which may have attempted to infiltrate the Pentagon itself, in an effort to seize information about U.S. plans for 'Star Wars' or SDI technology. The unconfirmed account alleged that such a creature was in fact apprehended after a 'contact lense' it was wearing, while posing as a high military officer, fell out, revealing a strange eye-arrangement and a vertically-slit pupil. The creature was apprehended and studied, and found to possess a reptilian internal makeup! The apartment where the creature was staying was searched and numerous copies of sensitive documents relating to SDI were discovered within, information which 'it' was apparently sending on to it's superiors.

The U.S., then, seems to be in essence a 'World Scenario', if not a 'universal' scenario in miniature and therefore the 'Conspiracy' sees it as a most valuable 'prize'. Therefore it would probably not be too 'far out' to suggest that the war between the human and serpent races from all three 'realms' CONVERGE in the United States and, to be more exact, within the vicinities of Mt. Archuleta near Dulce, New Mexico (a MAJOR earth-base of the Reptilian Empire); the Panamint Mountains of California (a MAJOR earth-base of the Nordic Federation); and the real 'hotbed' of INNER-Planetary and CYBER (electronic) warfare, the Nevada Test Site.

Linda Dudar of Washington, New Jersey [whose letter appeared in a UFO research journal, and was later reprinted in Val Valerian's 'LEADING EDGE' magazine] made the following unusual allegation:

"...I liked the story of the silver B-B (TSB, Feb. 1990 issue). I also had one. I was about 9 years old when it started to bother me. I don't know when I got it, but it was under my skin on my midriff section, just below my right ribs. I went to the doctor and he sent me to the hospital to remove it. I saw when he put it in the tray — a little silver ball about 1/4" around, maybe smaller. I also still have the scar.

THE MOJAVE DESERT'S GREATEST SECRETS

"Dr. Mundy, a therapist who speaks about contactees (and abductees - Branton), told us at a workshop one night about these silver B-Bs. Apparently they are/were a communication/ tracking device. The ball was not given to me. The hospital kept it. Dr. Mundy told us that during this time period, the 1950's, the government informed all doctors and hospitals to be on the alert for these B-Bs."

During the 'contactee' era of the late 1950's and early '60's a man by the name of Mel Noel made the rounds of the UFO circuit describing his experiences as an Air Force 'line pilot' whose top secret mission involved the photographing of UFO's (both visible and 'cloaked' craft — radar directing and infrared film being used for the latter). These encounters usually took place over the Rocky mountains of Utah and Idaho, according to Noel, and throughout the years 1953-54. One of Noel's lectures was delivered during that period to a huge crowd at the Giant Rock UFO Convention held in the Mojave desert near Twenty Nine Palms, California.

For several years 'Mel Noel' was out of the news, until in the early 1990's that is, when he reappeared stating that 'Noel' was merely a pseudonym, and implying that because of greater present-day awareness of the UFO phenomena he could more easily use his real name of 'Guy Kirkwood'. Kirkwood later appeared on the premier 'UFO CONTACT' episode of the Fox Networks 'SIGHTINGS' series, in the early 1990's. Kirkwood described an almost identical account as was given by 'Noel'.

Kirkwood's (or 'Noel's') commanding officer during the operation had allegedly established radio contact with the human occupants of alien craft, who were rather attractive in appearance and could even pass themselves off as Americans if they were to walk the streets of any large city. His Commanding Officer later claimed that he had physical contacts with these craft. These humanlike aliens claimed during a 'radio conversation' (between themselves and the Commanding Officer — a conversation which Noel and his three copilots were allowed to listen in on) that 'they' were from underground cities beneath other planetary bodies in the Sol System, AS WELL AS from underground cities within the earth itself. They claimed that these colonies or societies were affiliated together through a Central 'Tribunal' on or below the moons of Saturn.

In Kirkwood's own words, in reference to this communication:

"...they referred to, they made the statement that our scientists had made statements based upon theories that LIFE CANNOT AND THEREFORE DOES NOT EXIST ON THE OTHER PLANETS IN THIS SYSTEM, AND THEY SAID THAT THEY WERE CONFIRMING THOSE STATEMENTS. HE SAID, 'LIFE DOES NOT AND CANNOT EXIST ON THESE OTHER PLANETS; IT'S ALL INSIDE THE PLANETS, IT'S ALL IN THE INTERIOR, JUST AS THE HOUSE OF THE LORD. THIS IS THE HOUSE OF THE LORD WE LIVE IN, THE INTERIOR OF THE PLANET..."

Kirkwood also stated:

"...They went into a number of other things that may or may not be important; by discussion with legal advice, much of this, I CAN ONLY DISCUSS ABOUT 10 PER CENT OF WHAT TOOK PLACE."

This last statement probably had something to do with his security clearance. However, one of the most interesting things about the case was that almost a month after Kirkwood's Commanding Officer informed him and his friends that 'he' was being allowed to join the aliens' society, his plane disappeared off the eastern coast without a trace. Kirkwood/Noel is convinced that 'they' took him. At one point during the 'Contactee' period 'Noel' even claimed that he could arrange 'for rides' on UFO's, suggestive that he might have had later physical encounters with these space beings. Researcher John Keel once had dinner with 'Noel' in a restaurant in New York City, and Keel noticed that 'Noel' did hang around people and especially women who were very 'exotic' looking, and Keel was convinced that their conversation was being monitored, possibly by CIA types.

In the mid-1980's a Canadian woman by the name of Joan Howard wrote a privately published book, titled "THE SPACE - OR SOMETHING - CONNECTION". We refer to it here because it dealt with some experiences which she, or rather her husband, had shortly after she came to America from Britain. In fact Joan devoted an entire chapter to her husbands account, which involved some incidents that took place while he was doing some field work for a certain company, which required a great deal of activity in the out-of-doors. During his employment with this company, 'they' (he and his co-workers) had to travel through some relatively unpopulated terrain in West Virginia, particularly in the regions between Newville in Braxton county, and Helvetia in Randolph county, or rather the general region in and around the northern part of Webster county.

During their travels through the forests and wilderness, and the rolling hills-mountains of West Virginia, he had encountered some very strange things, and heard accounts of strange cavern- related experiences from the locals. At one point, he claimed, their group ran across what appeared to be a pipe sticking up from the ground far from the nearest town. There was no other sign of civilization or anything man-made for miles in either direction, yet here was this large pipe or tube sticking straight up from the ground. But the most remarkable thing was that a flame was shooting out of the pipe as if it were burning some type of gas. They never found out just what it was. Also, in this same general area, they explored caverns which contained some very strange things. One of the caverns had strange hieroglyphic-like writing on it's walls, and others claimed that they heard what sounded like faint voices, and also machinelike sounds moving underground, as if they were emanating from beyond the walls of the caverns, or from their unexplored depths. Two men, he claimed, bedded down one night in front of a certain cave which contained a very deep, unexplored chasm some ways inside. The next morning one of the men woke up and found that his partner had disappeared, and no trace was ever found of him. This particular cave by the way had been known as a place of unusual happenings, and a place to stay away from. Some even went so far as to call it 'Satan's Lair'. Whatever the case may be, it may provide an answer to the man's disappearance. One of the most remarkable accounts that Joan's husband heard involved a man who claimed that, while exploring the labyrinthine depths of a particular cavern in the area, he had suddenly come face to face with a woman. She was attractive yet completely devoid of hair (such as someone who might have been subjected to radiation poisoning?). The woman, who spoke a language completely foreign to the man, tried for some time to communicate. After they found that they were not getting anywhere, they departed and went their separate ways.

Joan Howard also claims to have had contacts with dwarfish beings since she was a small child, although her experiences make it unclear whether these 'occupants' were human or not. She does state however that 'poltergeist' type manifestations often accompanied her UFO experiences, suggesting that the occupants — whether humanoid or saurioid, were involved with the darker side. She did warn potential researchers to be suspicious of ANY alien group which might attempt to contact them; encouraged them to PROVE if their claims are true; and always to keep "...a cold, keen, analytical mind."

Stan Deyo was one of many Air Force cadets during the 1960's who dreamed of serving his country as an Air Force pilot. That was until Deyo learned that something strange was going on in the Air Force Academy where he was stationed. The anonymous Intelligence Community insider, 'Commander X', relates:

"...Because of what he discovered while an unwilling 'guinea pig' in certain experiments that were secretly being conducted by a covert organization working within the military, Stan Deyo had to flee the United States for a new home half way around the world. Running as far as he could, the bearded scientist ended up in Perth, Australia, where he surfaced to tell his incredible saga of a conspiracy so sinister that it doesn't seem possible that something like this could actually transpire in the birthplace of George Washington, Abe Lincoln or John F. Kennedy.

"Deyo had enlisted into the United States Air Force and was sent for special training to the highly prestigious Air Force Academy located in Colorado Springs, Colorado.

"'...We were the elite from all over America, especially selected for a secret purpose we knew nothing about,' he told PEOPLE MAGAZINE, an Australia weekly news magazine not to be confused with the celebrity profile magazine of the same name published in the U.S.

"'They got control of our minds when we were asleep and fed us the most advanced physics for months on end. Then some of us began to realize something was happening to our minds and we rebelled.

"'After two years, they failed the entire class — 180 of us. We knew too much. I'm speaking out now because I believe the world should know what they are up to, as well as for my own protection.'

"As Deyo explains it, the Sixties were a turbulent period even as far as the U.S. government was concerned. For some unexplainable reason, Stan Deyo found himself along with his classmates in the middle of an 'intelligence war' between the FBI and the CIA, with the CIA bound and determined to keep the lid on a brand new form of technology directly related to UFOs.

"The CIA in conjunction with military-industrial 'big business' has for a period of several years been in collusion, Deyo alleges, on findings that center around the development of a type of disk or saucer-shaped, antigravity machine that originated out of 'alien' technology. According to Deyo's scenario, the U.S. is worried that sooner or later they will run out of conventional fuel sources and that the 'elite' and powerful will need a revolutionary technology in order to survive (and no doubt maintain their control over the populations of the earth). So they contacted General Electric, Sperry Rand and Bell Aircraft to spearhead a drive to develop this new technology, which can whirl a disc-like craft through interplanetary space at thousands of miles a second using the minds of the craft's crew members to navigate the Earth-made UFOs. This is where Deyo's training was supposedly to come in handy. Because of his intelligence level, he was to be made one of the ship's pilots as soon as his mental capabilities had been 'stretched' through hypnosis and an advanced form of electronic 'mind control'.

'Commander X' continues:

"...One of the most astounding things Deyo said — and this was almost ten years ago (i.e. around the late 1970's and early '80's - Branton) — was that he felt one of the staunchest supporters of this radically new antigravity technology was none other than the late William P. Lear — John Lear's father!

"At the time, Lear Sr. was quoted by the Associated Press as having said: 'I can't help but feel flying saucers are real, because of numerous manifestations over long periods of time with many simultaneous observations by reliable observers.' — And this is the clincher: 'THERE ARE NOW SERIOUS EFFORTS IN PROGRESS TO PROVE THE EXISTENCE OF ANTI-GRAVITATIONAL FORCES AND TO CONVERT ATOMIC ENERGY DIRECTLY TO ELECTRICITY...'

Commander X continues:

"For those who hold suspicions that John Lear might — at least sometimes — be responsible for dealing from the 'bottom of the deck' — providing as much in the way of 'disinformation' as valid 'information' — we can't help but theorize about the significance of the above quote attributed to his father, and the possibility that some of what John Lear is telling us is meant to steer our attention toward 'aliens', rather than look right under our very noses at an Earthly technology that may be advanced beyond what we are currently taught is achievable through modern day science.

"We wonder if perhaps there isn't to be found substantiation behind the rumor that Lear Aircraft Company (a firm that John's dad founded) is directly involved in some sort of research and development project(s) involving antigravity and the manufacturing of UFOs made right here on Earth.

"One possible scenario is that John Lear found out about this Top Secret project — perhaps while eavesdropping — and this is his way of 'spilling the beans' without implicating his father or anyone else as the source."

In 1990, researcher Val Valerian released a peculiar document which was sent to him by another researcher. The document is actually a list of several military personnel. However, the strange thing about this document was the title-heading.

Some researchers believe that within the deepest levels of the government is an on-going 'covert space program' utilizing some very remarkable aerospace and propulsion technologies. However, the very nature of this program, the clandestine (and possibly illegal) means by which it is funded, as well as the possible means by which they came across this 'technology', has apparently led the 'Secret' Government into keeping these activities one of the world's top secrets, and apparently they have enforced this cover-up, as John Lear says, with 'deadly force'. Perhaps one of the most important reasons for the secrecy, according to some, is that SOME groups within the secret government have allegedly — in the face of 'superior alien technology' — 'surrendered' to a malevolent alien race and have become their 'agents' on earth.

Is it also possible — as many researchers and prominent military, government and industrial personnel are actually confirming — that the 'secret government' is utilizing this advanced super-technology (which they have hidden from the public) to carry out a clandestine space program involving not only manned FLIGHTS to the moon, but also manned BASES on the moon and, some claim, even Mars as well? There appears to be enough mounting evidence to cause the public to at least consider the possibility of these claims. Actually, if one carefully examines all of the various claims and how they merge together in synchronicity, and if one studies the various theories and arguments concerning Einstein's 'unified field' theory and the apparent underlying connection between electromagnetism, gravity waves, and other 'unified field' forces, such a scenario involving a fleet of top secret government antigravity craft would not be outside the realm of possibility.

The document referred to above contains in the title heading both the terms 'Starfleet International' and 'United Federated Planets'. Why would such a statement appear on a MILITARY document? Could it be that, although perhaps somewhat presumptuously, a secret group of 'astronauts' constantly travel back and forth from ultra-secret bases on or below the earth, the moon, and mars; and have in anticipation of an ever-growing interplanetary network named this organization 'Starfleet International' and/or the 'United Federated Planets'?

Val Valerian gives the following 'introduction' and story behind the document:

"...Researcher George Andrews forwarded this puzzle to us. From the introduction, it might seem that this thing was complete bunk. There it might have stayed, except that WE TRACED 11 PEOPLE ON THE LIST TO ACTUALLY BEING IN THE MILITARY. What does it mean?"

The following introduction is given by George Andrews:

"A friend who wishes to remain anonymous, who lives in a large city, recently woke about 3 A.M. with a strong but apparently irrational impulse to get dressed and to go to an all- night photostat place. As she was entering, she noticed a man dressed in a Navy officers uniform who was just leaving, who threw some papers into the trash barrel near the door. She made her copies and was about to leave and had another impulse to retrieve what the Navy officer had thrown away. She came up with these pages. Under normal circumstances, the news that the United States Navy has a flying disk named the U.S.S. Excalibur (and U.S.S. Concord? - Branton), operated by a crew of four, would be cause for celebration... however (unless) this achievement is the result of the collaboration of the 'Greys'..."

Andrews goes on to suggest that they might, because of their collaboration with the 'Greys', be forced to take part in offensive attacks against the 'Blonds', who have allegedly had ancient conflicts with the Greys.

The introduction goes on to state that those names which appear with an (x), are people who have actually been traced to the military. Take special note of names like Ferguson, Caskey, Taylor, Burrall, Stevens, and Miller — which are repeated more than once throughout the list. Possible signs of Nepotism?

George Andrews suspects that 'Starfleet International' consists of human-military personnel only, while the 'United Federated Planets' may somehow tie-in with the nonhuman entities' such as the 'Serpent Race' or the 'Greys'. However, Andrews' theory that THIS particular Governmental establishment has collaborated with the Grays is yet to be confirmed.

There is a possibility that the UFP involves interaction with the 'Federated' human cultures in this small corner of the galaxy. Let us hope that this is the case, IF the following information is true. There is evidence in fact that certain 'Constituted Government' officials (who are loyal to the American- Constitutional 'Republic') — as confirmed by Guy Kirkwood and others — have secret 'alliances' with the 'Nordics'; whereas the 'Secret Government' collaborators (who are loyal to the Bavarian- Roman 'Empire') tend to collaborate with the saurian Grays, etc. Below is a reproduction of the document:

UNITED FEDERATED PLANETS
STARFLEET INTERNATIONAL
U.S.S. CONCORD NCC-1989
CREW ROSTER

CREW MEMBER	SF EXPIRATION	SERV. NUMBER
COL. MIKE FERGUSON (SFC ST./MC)	JUNE 1990*@	SCMC-8901-0002
LT. LAURA FERGUSON (SFC)	JUNE 1990@	SCM-8901-0007
LCDR. HARLAN STEVENS (SFC)	SEP. 1989@	SCSS-8906.23
ENS. REBECCA BURAND (SFC)	SEP. 1989@	SCS-8902-0004
MAJ. MIKE WEST (SFC STAFF/MC)	UFP ONLY	SCMC-8901-0004
LT. KATRINA CASKEY (SFC)	NOV. 1989@	SCE-8906-0005
2LT. BOB BURRALL (SFMC)	NOV. 1989@	SCMC-8906-0003
CMDR. BOB TOMPKINS (SFC)	DEC. 1989@	SCE-8906-0002
SGM. RAY CHAMBERS (SFMC)	DEC. 1989@	SCMC-8903-0008 (x)
ENS. RON CASKEY (SFC)	JAN. 1990@	SCSY-0906-0005
LT. DEBRA MCCLARY (SFC)	JAN. 1990@	SCSS-8906-0004 (x)
MSG. IVAN GOODMAN (SFMC)	JAN. 1990@	SCMC-8904-0001
CS. CRYSTAL FERGUSON (SFC)	JAN. 1990@	SCM-8906-0011 (x)
MDSM. PHILIPPE BEAUDETTE (SFC)	JAN. 1990@	SCM-8906-0009
A-ENS. EVERETT NEW (SFC)	FEB. 1990@	SCE-8906-0007
MSG. JOHN HIGGINS (SFMC)	FEB. 1990@	SCMC-8906-0010 (x)
WO3. DOUG TAYLOR (SFMC)	MAR. 1990@	SCMC-8906-0001 (x)
CS. ROSE TAYLOR (SFC)	MAR. 1990@	SCS-8906-0012
SP1. AMANDA TAYLOR (SFC)	MAR. 1990@	SCMC-8906-0001 (x)
A-ENS. KELLY MADDOX (SFC)	MAR. 1990@	SCSS-8906-0008
RADM. ANNE MILLER (SFC STAFF)	MAY 1990*@	SMC-8901-0006 (x)
LTJG. SHAREN BURRALL (SFC)	MAY 1990@	SCSS-8906-0014
WO4. CHUCK GRAHAM (SFMC)	MAY 1990@	SCMC-8906-0001 (x)
PO1. DEAN KING (SFC)	MAY 1990@	SCO-0906-0015 (x)

PO. CHUCK STEVENS (SFC)	MAY 1990@	SCE-0906-0015
SP1 WILLIE STEVENS (SFC)	MAY 1990@	SCE-8906-0017
LTJG. JASON MARRS (SFC)	JUN 1990@	SCO-8906-0018
LTJG. CHARLES FINCH III (SFC)	UFP ONLY	
LTJG. JAMES CABANISS (SFC)	UFP ONLY	SCS-8908-0004
WO. TERRY MILLER (SFC)	UFP ONLY	SCS-8908-0004 (x)
WO. DEANNA WINSLETT (SFC)	UFP ONLY	SCM-8907-0005
SFC. RICHARD PARKER (SFMC)	UFP ONLY	SCMC-8907-0004 (x)
WO. STEVE WILKES (SFC)	UFP ONLY	
LT. RUSSELL NATES (SFC)	UFP ONLY	SCSS-8908-0006
WO. SHELLEY SAVAGE	UFP ONLY	SCM-8907-0006
CPL. CHUCK FAIR	UFP ONLY	SCMC-8908-0005
CPL. JON PLANT	UFP ONLY	SCMC-8908-0007
WO. KARREN SULLIVAN	OCT 1990@	SCC-14522-12
WO. KELLY SPANGLER	OCT 1990	SCC-14508-12

PAGE TWO U.S.S. CONCORD NCC-1989 CREW ROSTER@

LTJG. JANET KELLEY SCC-

CPL. MARCUS MALONE UFP ONLY SCMC-

WO. ALEN SHERWOOD	UFP ONLY	SCO-8908.02
CS. KAHUNA KITE	UFP ONLY	SCE-8908-0003
SPEC. VINCENT LIN	UFP ONLY	SCE-8906.23
WO. GLEN LOWE	UFP ONLY	SCM-8907-0002
WO3. MIKE WIER	UFP ONLY	SCMC-

* DENOTES VICE FLEET ADMIRAL FOR UFP
@ DENOTES DUAL MEMBERSHIP IN UFP AND STARFLEET

* DENOTES VICE FLEET ADMIRAL FOR UFP
@ DENOTES DUAL MEMBERSHIP IN UFP AND STARFLEET

(Note: In the original document, 4 of the above names were indicated as being members of the crew of the 'U.S.S. EXCALIBUR')

PEA Research (105 Serra Way., Ste. 176., Milpitas, CA. 95035) made the following comments in one of their 'Files' (which consist of collections of large amounts of documents and research related to UFO's):

"...Ramifications of MJ-12.

"If the U.S.A.F. test-flew a disk and was successful, what's to prevent them from using the same saucer to transport men and materials to the moon and mars? They would also be in a position to exploit the archeological artifacts of the pyramids and sphinx in the valley of Illysium on Mars. Also they could recover artifacts of previous races on the surface of the moon. With the aid of NASA satellites they could map and mine the rare earth (Moon, Mars) minerals at the expense of the tax payers while at the same time claim that we have nothing better in our technology than space shuttles (rocket power).

"If the Canadian Geomagnetic project was successful with their free-energy geomagnetic motor, then why haven't we seen free-energy engines for the home and auto instead of hearing about oil shortages?

"If the President of the USA is allowed only certain appointed staff by the Constitution and Congress - are the members of MJ-12 outside of the limits of the Constitution or did Congress give the President the power to set up a Secret Government (nonelected) without the public right to vote on this choice of the governing of the various military and nonmilitary branches of the united states?

"When the MJ-12 use non-appropriated funds for their Secret operations are they using money from the Black Budget? If so, when did we cast a vote stating that ANY branch of the Government can use the taxpayers money without giving an account or being held accountable for it?

"When MJ-12 refuse to grant FOIA requests because of National Security reasons, is it because the USA won't be secure against foreign earthly powers, alien powers or against the wrath of a misled and deceived United States public (the Voters)?

"Can laws be passed to Guarantee that various branches of the Government will be held accountable for (the) shredding of classified documents? How about passing laws to guarantee stiff jail sentences for underlings (secretaries, lower rank personnel) that carry out the command to shred confidential files?

"If the top of the mountain is corrupt, what about the foundation that was later raised under it. If a Secret Government is illegal, what about all of the secret projects it started and maintains control of? It's one thing to classify advances in technology as SECRET, but it's quite different to classify nonelected government as SECRET. When that non-accountable Government (non- accountable by reason of being SECRET) passes military laws that affect all branches of Government (military and nonmilitary) are the laws legal or non Constitutional?

"If the JMP (Justice for Military Personnel) letter is true, are the actions of the CIA legal as used AGAINST citizens of the USA? Isn't the purpose of the CIA to protect citizens AGAINST foreign threats?

"If the MIBS exist according to the documents, what has happened to the

Conscience of the Military Personnel that carry out false ID missions against private citizens? Why are Military Personnel carrying out higher up orders to impersonate branches of Government they neither represent or have Rank in? Is this patriotism or blindness?"

In the April, 1963 issue of SEARCH Magazine, Will Carson and Jeannie Joy, in their regular column 'PRYING INTO THE UNKNOWN', related the following incredible story, which involved an apparent encounter with an unknown race below the MOJAVE Desert region:

"It has always been a mystery to us in the first place how Mr. and Mrs. P.E. can find and afford the time to do the sort of things most of us only dream of doing. After knowing them for more than fifteen years, it is inconceivable to suspect their integrity or sanity - and yet they impose the following excise upon our credulity...

"While exploring for petroglyphs in the Casa Diablo vicinity of BISHOP, CALIFORNIA, Mr. & Mrs. P.E. came upon a circular hole in the ground, about nine feet in diameter, which exuded a sulfurous steam and seemed recently to have been filled with hot water. A few feet from the surface the shaft took a tangent course which looked easily accessible and, upon an impulse with which we cannot sympathize, the dauntless E.'s, armed only with a flashlight, forthwith crawled down into that hole.

"At a depth we've failed to record the oblique tunnel opened into a horizontal corridor whose dripping walls, now encrusted with minerals, (and) could only have been carved by human hands, countless ages ago - of this the E.'s felt certain. The end of the short passage was blocked by what seemed to be a huge doorway of solid rock which, however, wouldn't yield. The light of their flash was turned to a corner where water dripped from a protuberance - which proved to be a delicately carved face, distorted now by the crystallized minerals, and from whose gaping mouth water issued.

"As Mr. and Mrs. E. stood there in silent awe - wondering what lay behind that immovable door - the strangest thing of all happened...but our chronology will not be incorrect if we wait till they return to the surface before revealing this, for now the water began gushing from the carved mouth and from other unseen ducts elsewhere in that cave and rising at an alarming rate!

"They hurried to the surface, and in less than half an hour there was only a quite ordinary appearing pool of warm mineral water on the desert floor.

"'Do you know,' Mrs. E. said to her husband, 'while I stood down there I heard music - the strangest, most weird music I'd ever heard. But it seemed to come from everywhere at once, or inside my own head. I guess it was just my imagination.'

"Mr. E. turned pale. 'My God,' he said; 'I thought it was MY imagination, but I heard it, too - like music from some other world!'

THE MOJAVE DESERT'S GREATEST SECRETS

"Why do they call that rock formation near where the E's had their strange experience Casa Diablo - the Devil's house? And why did the Indians name that area Inyo - dwelling place of the great spirit?"

The following is a quote from Matt Spetalnick's article "IS ANYBODY OUT THERE? NASA LOOKS FOR REAL ET'S", in REUTERS Magazine, Oct. 5, 1992:

"At least 70 times scientists have picked up radio waves that bore the marks of communication by beings from other worlds, but they were never verified, [Frank] Drake said."

Through proposed projects such as SETI [Search For Extraterrestrial Intelligence], which involves large arrays of Radio Dish receiving mechanisms to 'tune in' to cosmic radio waves, Drake and others hoped to contact outside intelligences. However, if the incidents related by Forest Crawford earlier in this File are correct, this has already occurred. If our tax dollars are going toward other SETI type 'experiments', chances are that the public will NOT and NEVER be officially told of the outcome, if they [once again] receive signals from other nearby stars. Such a disclosure might threaten the psychological "control" which the (secret) government has imposed on the nations. THE SECRET GOVERNMENT DOES NOT WISH TO ALLOW PLANET EARTH TO BECOME A MEMBER OF A BENEVOLENT FEDERATION OF HUMAN WORLDS, as the Federation policies would certainly condemn the horrendous power-games which the Illuminati has used for centuries to keep mankind in its stranglehold of slavery. The Illuminati will only ally themselves with aliens (such as the REPTILIAN/GRAYS and some branches of the ASHTAR/ASTARTE network which has collaborated with the ILLUMINATI, NAZIS and GRAYS in the past) that share their desire to wield absolute god- like empirical control of the planet. It is very likely that Frank Drake was somehow sold-out to the Bavarian-Roman-Gray (Illuminati "Serpent Cult") Combine, when we consider his complicity with the International UFO coverup.

Incidentally, another possible use of radar-dish antennas has been suggested by K.S. of Salt Lake City, Utah, who allegedly talked to a man who was involved in setting up top secret underwater radio dishes for secret government projects. He claimed that many of these dishes were used to communicate with "our" bases on the moon and mars. If this is the case could the SETI program be, to some extent, an extension of this?

Death Valley, California and the Mojave Desert region, as we have indicated earlier, has been the sight of numerous UFO sightings in the past. Some regard it as no less that a doorway into another world.

The Paihute Indians as we have also related, tell of a race of Grecian or Egyptian-like people with white robes, sandals, and long dark hair held back with a band, who thousands of years ago arrived in North America in large rowing-sailing vessels. The Paiutes say that when Death Valley was still part of an inland sea connected to the Pacific ocean through the Gulf of California, these "Havmusuvs" discovered an underground cavern system within the Panamint mountains adjacent to the west edge of Death Valley, and within these vast caverns they built their civilization. To briefly review the Paihute account:

The legend says that these ancient people landed their ships near or just below large 'quays' or 'doors' high up the eastern slope of the Panamints. However after centuries the lake eventually dried up and disappeared, and as a result of this they developed new methods of reaching the world beyond. This, the Paiutes say, was when they began to experiment with the construction of silvery 'flying canoes'. Whether there is any connection with the following account is uncertain, but in 1905 an 'airship flap' was observed throughout southern California. On August 2, 1905, J. A. Jackson, "a well-known resident of Silshee," was out at 1:30 in the morning when a bright light appeared in the sky and headed for him. According to an account published in the Brawley, California, NEWS on Aug. 4, 1905:

"He watched it closely until behind the light there appeared the form of an airship, apparently about 70 feet in length, with a searchlight in front and several other lights aboard. The mysterious machine appeared to be propelled by wings alone and rose and fell as the wings flapped like a gigantic bird. Apparently there was no balloon attachment as is usually the case with airships.

"Mr. Jackson, being close to the home of W.E. Wilsie, woke him up in time to see the lights of the machine before it disappeared.... The same night, H. E. Allatt, postmaster at Imperial, was awakened from sleep by a bright light shining into his room. There was no moon, the light was thought to be fire, and Mr. Allatt rose to investigate, but no fire was found. Looking at his watch, the time was discovered to be 1:30 o'clock (a.m.), and it is believed that the brilliant light was caused by the searchlight from this mysterious airship."

A craft of almost identical description was reported only 4 years later in the Dec. 15, 1909 issue of the Arkansas GAZETTE:

"A. W. Norris of Mabelvale, road overseer of District No. 8, is of the opinion that an airship passed over his residence at about 10 o'clock Monday night (December 12). Mr. Norris states that he was standing in his doorway when a strange light appeared, apparently about 300 feet above him, traveling south at a rapid rate of speed and disappeared a moment or two later in the darkness. He said that the light had the appearance of a searchlight similar to those used on automobiles, and IT ROSE AND FELL like a bird in flight. The night was cloudy, which precludes the possibility of the light having been a star or any atmospheric phenomena."

Air ships of this description were apparently common following the turn of the century, but few if any of this particular type of craft have been reported after the period just described (1900-1910, etc.).

THE MOJAVE DESERT'S GREATEST SECRETS

Just because an 'airship' appears over California or Arkansas does not necessarily indicate that the airship was native to either one of those areas. However, there are nonetheless many evidences, as indicated elsewhere in this File, that the Mojave Desert—Panamint Mountains — Death Valley areas were apparently (in ancient times) a 'cradle', possibly one of many, for an early civilization which later developed an advanced form of technology; and having done so in relative secrecy, they were unhindered by the 'uncivilized' tribes outside of their domain who continued in their relatively ignorant lifestyles.

Perhaps the most remarkable confirmation of this appears in Bourke Lee's biography 'DEATH VALLEY MEN' [MacMillan Co., New York. 1932], which also dealt with alleged caverns WITHIN the Panamint Mts. region. If indeed the Panamint mountains are an ancient 'doorway' to an advanced and hidden HUMAN civilization, then one must recognize that it—as well as any of it's 'NATIONAL TREASURES'—should be (as should be ANY NATIONAL BORDER ON THE FACE OF THE EARTH) considered the legal territory of those who have possessed it since ancient times. "Borders" need not be entirely horizontal, but they can be vertical as well. Unwelcome intrusions into such an 'undiscovered country' might be dealt with as in ANY OTHER nation on earth, and one should approach such territories with caution. UNLIKE other areas where subterranean and malevolent antihuman or 'reptilian' activity is alleged to exist, the independence and national sovereignty of those subsurface regions where hidden HUMAN colonies reside should be honored as one would honor ANY national border on the face of the earth.

Even if an archeological discovery is found which belonged to the ancestors of an ancient culture which STILL EXISTS, that discovery should be the property of that culture alone. One of the arguments FOR making public sensitive information on various exterran and subterran cultures would be to protect those HUMAN cultures from the secret governments machinations, by bringing international public support in favor of that hidden culture and its right to maintain their sovereignty and independence (if the secret government knowingly violates another "countries" rights, every other independent country in the world would feel threatened as well). And in the case of the various hidden underground centers utilized by the reptilian grays, the public knowledge of this would be necessary to maintain the "national security" of each independent nation which might otherwise be "infiltrated" via implantation, or other forms of mind control (which inevitably leads to other forms of control — political, spiritual, educational, economical, etc.). Even IF various subsurface human cultures were driven out of their underground homes by nonhuman malevolents, AND if those territories are somehow regained in a possible future counter-invasion against the reptilian incursions, then those territories should STILL rightfully and legally belong to or returned to the human cultures who formerly possessed them.

Supposing there IS a counter-invasion in the future, there would no doubt still be much territory left over once the reptilians are driven out and/or destroyed, territory which might NOT be 'claimed' by a cave-dwelling tribe, colony or culture. Such underground systems could then be claimed by an outside government if they felt the need to expand their own 'territory'. According to some accounts, the U.S. government does know about many such underground systems and having found many of them unoccupied in past explorations, have claimed them for their own.

Unfortunately, even in the case of smaller underground repositories of ancient artifacts, there are indications that many ancient treasures have been 'melted down' by prospectors, tomb robbers, etc., in order to gain the metal value of the gold, silver and other precious metals, out of which the ancient artifacts were formed, in order to PREVENT the state from taking 'their find' away. In doing so, such plunderers have destroyed the immense historical and archaeological value of such treasures in exchange for the 'relatively' pitiful metallic value. Many of the ancient Egyptian treasures fell prey to such vandals and 'grave robbers' in ancient times. Even if one does not agree with the religious symbolism's behind such artifacts, their historical and archeological value makes them nevertheless worthy of preservation. The only reason that 'King Tut's' treasures have made such an impact (even though he was a minor 'king'), is that these treasures were among the VERY FEW which were not discovered by grave robbers and melted down for their metal content.

There is no telling how much HISTORICAL INFORMATION about ancient cultures has been forever lost by such careless actions. Hopefully humankind has reached the point of maturity where the discovery of such treasures in the future will result in a cooperative scientific study of the ancient artifacts for the benefit of all, rather than the violence, death and betrayal which has often resulted in the past through the mistakes of selfish treasure hunters fighting each other for the 'booty'. According to some accounts many of these ancient sites still await discovery, finds which may make King Tut's Tomb look insignificant by comparison.

As we have implied, just as one should honor the ancient archaeological SITES of existing cultures, in the same way one should honor the national sovereignty of another human CULTURE itself. To fail to do so would be in essence to THROW AWAY any 'legal' argument a nation might have FOR the protection of their own national sovereignty (CASE IN POINT: the reptilian or 'Draconian' Empire with it's major earth-center in the "Bhoga-vita" complex below India, and the human 'Illuminati' empires on and beyond earth — which apparently have a secret alliance with each other — have so interfered in the sovereignty of nearly EVERY nation on earth, and have done so to the point that they can no longer legally claim any rational defense against ANY nation which would decide to abuse THEIR 'sovereignty'. The Reptilian empire is of course a problem in itself, having been at war (via overt attacks or covert manipulation - against the majority of humanity in, on, and above earth) since ancient times and apparently, from the accounts given throughout this and other files, does not even acknowledge humankind's right to this planet, nor even their 'right' to exist).

Paihute Indian legends say that the 'People of the Panamints' long ago left their ancient city within the mountains of California and moved most of their civilization into still deeper cavern levels, AND (according to still other accounts) to colonies beyond the confines of planet earth itself. Although these 'Havmusuvs' may be 'benevolent' in comparison to some cultures inhabiting the surface of the planet, they nevertheless — according to the documentation in this and other databases — have the ability and technology to defend their 'borders' and their loved ones from any potential enemy..

In his chapter 'OLD GOLD' the author of 'DEATH VALLEY MEN', Bourke Lee, relates the allegedly-true account of two prospectors who claimed to have discovered this ancient, abandoned 'city' within huge caverns inside the heart of the Panamint mountains. Take special note of the INCREDIBLE similarity between this account and the one given to the Navajo Oga-Make by an old Paihute sage, as recorded in the article 'TRIBAL MEMORIES OF THE FLYING SAUCERS'. We will take up the story where two Death Valley residents by the name of Bill and Jack are having a conversation with two prospectors, 'Thomason' and 'White', from whom the author 'apparently' learned the details of the following discussion, if not present at the discussion himself:

...Thomason looked from Jack to Bill and asked, 'How long have you men been in this country?'

Jack spoke before Bill had a chance. 'Not very long,' said Jack quietly. Bill glanced curiously at Jack but said nothing. If Jack thought that 30 years was not very long, that was all right with Bill.

Thomason said, 'I've been in and out of the Death Valley country for 20 years. So has my partner. We know where there is lost treasure. We've known about it for several years, and we're the only men in the world [?] who do know about it. We're going to let you two fellows in on it. You've been good to us. You're both fine fellows. You haven't asked us any questions about ourselves, and we like you. We think you can keep a secret, so we'll tell you ours."

Jack blew smoke and asked, "A lost mine?"

"No, not a mine," said Thomason. "A lost treasure house. A lost city of gold. It's bigger than any mine that ever was found, or ever will be."

"It's bigger than the United States Mint," said White, with his voice and body shaking with excitement. "It's a city thousands of years old and worth billions of dollars! Billions of Dollars! Billions! Not Millions. Billions!"

Thomason and White spoke rapidly and tensely, interrupting each other in eager speech.

Thomason said, "We've been trying to get the treasure out of this golden city for years. We had to have help, and we haven't been able to get it."

"Everybody tries to rob us," put in White. "They all want too big a share. I offered the whole city to the Smithsonian Institution for five million dollars — only a small part of what it's worth. They tried to rob us, too! They said they'd give me a million and a half for a discovery that's worth a billion dollars!" he sneered. "I had nothing more to do with them."

Jack got up and found his plug of tobacco. He threw away his cigarette and savagely bit off an enormous chew. He sat down and crossed his legs and glowered at White as he worked his chew into his jaw.

Bill's voice was meek as he asked, "And this place is in Death Valley?"

"Right in the Panamint Mountains!" said Thomason. "My partner found it by accident. He was prospecting down on the lower edge of the range near Wingate Pass. He was working in the bottom of an old abandoned shaft when the bottom fell out and landed him in a tunnel. We've explored the tunnel since. It's a natural tunnel like a big cave. It's over 20 miles long. It leads all through a great underground city; through the treasure vaults, the royal palace and the council chambers; and it connects to a series of beautiful galleries with stone arches in the east slope of the Panamint Mountains. Those arches are like great big windows in the side of the mountain and they look down on Death Valley. They're high above the valley now, but we believe that those entrances in the mountain side were used by the ancient people that built the city. They used to land their boats there."

"Boats!" demanded the astonished Bill, "boats in Death Valley?"

Jack choked and said, "Sure, boats. There used to be a lake in Death Valley. I hear the fishing was fine."

"You know about the lake," Thomason pointed his blue chin at Jack. "Your geology would tell you about the lake. It was a long time ago... The ancient people who built the city in the caverns under the mountain lived on in their treasure houses long after the lake in the valley dried up. How long, we don't know. But the people we found in the caverns have been dead for thousands of years. Why! Those mummies alone are worth a million dollars!"

White, his eyes blazing, his body trembling, filled the little house with a vibrant voice on the edge of hysteria. "Gold!" he cried. "Gold spears! Gold shields! Gold statues! Jewelry! Thick gold bands on their arms! I found them! I fell into the underground city. There was an enormous room; big as this canyon. A hundred men were in it. Some were sitting around a polished table that was inlaid with gold and precious stones. Men stood around the walls of the room carrying shields and spears of solid gold. All the men — more than a hundred — had on leather aprons, the finest kind of leather, soft and full of gold ornaments and jewels. They sat there and stood there with all that wealth around them. They are still there.

They are all dead! And the gold, all that gold, and all those gems and jewels are all around them. All that gold and jewelry! Billions!" White's voice was ascending to a shriek when Thomason put a hand on his arm and White fell silent, his eyes darting about to the faces of those who sat around the table.

Thomason explained quietly, "These ancient people must have been having a meeting of their rulers in the council chamber when they were killed very suddenly. We haven't examined them closely because it was the treasure that interested us, but the people all seem to be perfect mummies."

Bill squinted at White and asked, "Ain't it dark in this tunnel?"

"Black dark," said White, who had his voice under control again. His outburst had quieted him. "When I first went into that council room I had just some candles. I fumbled around. I didn't discover everything all at once like I'm telling you. I fell around over these men, and I was pretty near almost scared out of my head. But I got over that and everything was all right and I could see everything after I hit the lights."

"Lights? There were lights?" It was Bill asking.

"Oh, yes," said White. "These old people had a natural gas they used for lighting and cooking. I found it by accident. I was bumping around in the dark. Everything was hard and cold and I kept thinking I was seeing people and I was pretty scared. I stumbled over something on the floor and fell down. Before I could get up there was a little explosion and gas flames all around the room lighted up. What I fell over was a rock lever that turned on the gas, and my candle set the gas off. That was when I saw all the men, and the polished table, and the big statue. I thought I was dreaming. The statue was solid gold. It's face looked like the man sitting at the head of the table, only, of course, the statue's face was much bigger than the man's, because the statue was all in perfect size, only bigger. The statue was solid gold, and it is 89 feet, six inches tall!"

"Did you measure it," asked Jack, silkily, "or just guess at it?"

"I measured it. Now you'll get an idea of how big that one room — the council room — is. That statue only takes up a small part of it!"

Steady and evenly, Jack asked, "Did you weigh the statue?"

"No," said White. "You couldn't weigh it."

Bill was puzzled. "Would you mind telling me how you measured it?" asked Bill.

"With a sextant," said White. "I always carry a sextant when I'm on the desert. Then if I get lost, I can use my sextant on the sun or moon or stars to find myself on the map. I took a sextant angle of the height of the statue and figured it out later."

"A sextant," said Bill, frowning heavily.

Jack said, "It's a part of the church, Bill. Never mind that.... Tell us some more about this place. It's very interesting."

Fred Thomason said, "Tell them about the treasure rooms."

"I found them later." White polished his shining pate with a grimy handkerchief. "After I got the lights going I could see all the walls of this big room and I saw some doors cut in the solid rock of the walls. The doors are big as slabs of rock hung on hinges you can't see. A big rock bar lets down across them. I tried to lift up the bars and couldn't move them. I fooled around trying to get the doors open. I must have been an hour before I took ahold of a little latch like on the short end of the bar and the great bar swung up. Those people know about counterweights and all those great big doors with their barlocks — they must weigh hundreds of tons — are all balanced so that you can move them with your little finger, if you find the right place."

Thomason again said, "Tell them about the treasure."

"It's gold bars and precious stones. The treasure rooms are inside these big rock doors. The gold is stacked in small bars piled against the walls like bricks. The jewels are in bins cut out of rock. There's so much gold and jewelry in that place that the people there had stone wheelbarrows to move the treasure around."

Jack sat up in sudden interest. "Wheelbarrows?" he asked...

"We don't know how old they are," said Thomason, "but the stone wheelbarrows are there."

"Stone wheelbarrows," marveled Jack. "Those dead men must have been very powerful men. Only very strong men could push around a stone wheelbarrow loaded with gold bars. The wheelbarrows must have weighed a tone without a load in them."

"Yes," said Thomason, slowly, "the wheelbarrows are stone and of course they are very heavy—"

"But they're very easy to push around even with a load in them," White explained. "They're scientific wheelbarrows."

"No," objected Jack in a low tone of anguish.

"Yes," insisted White, pleasantly sure of himself. A small boy could fill one of those stone wheelbarrows full of gold bars and wheel it around. The wheelbarrows are balanced just like the doors. Instead of having the wheel out in front so that a man has to pick up all the weight with his back, these wise people put the wheel almost in the middle and arranged the leverage of the shafts so that a child could put in a balanced load and wheel the barrow around."

Jack's heart was breaking. He left the table and threw his chew out the door. He went over to the stove with his cup. "Anybody want more coffee?" he asked. No one did.

Bill studied Thomason and White for several minutes. Then he asked, "How many times have you been in this tunnel?"

"I've been there three times," said White. "That's counting the first time I fell in. Fred's been in twice; and my wife went part way in the last time we was in."

Mrs. White stroked her blond hair and said, "I thought my husband was romancing when he came home and told me what he found in the mountains. He always was a romancer. I was sure he was just romancing about this city he said he found. I didn't believe it until they took me into it. It is a little hard to believe, don't you think?"

Bill said, "It sure is." Jack stirred sugar into his coffee and sat down at the table again. Bill asked, "Did you ever bring anything out of the cave?"

"Twice," said Fred Thomason. "Both times we went in we filled out pockets with gems, and carried out a gold bar apiece. The first time we left the stuff with a friend of ours and we went to try and interest someone in what we'd found. We thought the scientists would be interested or the government. One government man said he'd like to see the stuff and we went back to our friend to get the gold and jewels and he told us he'd never seen them; and dared us to try to get them back. You see, he double crossed us. We were in a little trouble at the time and the loss of that stuff just put us in deeper. We couldn't get a stake because we were having hard work making anyone believe us. So we made another trip out here for more proof. That time we brought out more treasure and buried it close to the shaft entrance to the underground city before we went back to the Coast. I persuaded some university officials and some experts from the Southwest Museum to come out here with me. We got up on the Panamints and I could not find the shaft. A cloudburst had changed all the country around the shaft. We were out of luck. The scientists became unreasonably angry with us. They've done everything they can to discredit us ever since."

Jack watched Thomason and White across the rim of his coffee cup. Bill said, "And now you can't get into your treasure tunnel. It's lost again. That's sure too bad."

Thomason and White smiled. "We can get in all right," said Thomason in a genial voice his cold eyes did not support. Mrs. White smiled confidently and her husband bobbed his head. Thomason went on: "You've forgotten about the old boat landings on the Death Valley side of the Panamint Mountains. All we have to do is climb the mountain to the openings where the galleries come out of the city on the old lake shore. Do you know the mountains along the west side of Death Valley?"

"I've been down there," said Bill.

Thomason turned to White: "How high do you think those galleries are above the bottom of Death Valley?"

White said, "Somewhere around forty-five hundred or five thousand feet.

You looked out of them; what do you think?"

"That's about right," agreed Thomason. "The openings are right across from Furnace Creek Ranch. We could see the green of the ranch right below us and Furnace Creek Wash across the valley. We'll find those windows in the mountains, all right."

"You goin down there now?" asked Bill.

"That's it," said White. "We're through with the scientists. We tried to make a present of our discovery to science because we thought they would be interested. But they tried to rob us, and then they laughed at us and abused us..."

Saying thanks and farewell the treasure hunters left, promising to return, and drove in their car down to Emigrant Canyon towards Death Valley. Later that same afternoon Bourke Lee, the author of DEATH VALLEY MEN, allegedly met the three of them on the floor of the valley. Their car was parked beside the road between Furnace Creek Ranch and the Salt Beds. The men were patching a tube. They did not need any help, so he wished them well and said goodbye and went on towards the southern part of the barren valley. He never saw Fred Thomason, Mr. White nor his wife again, and ten days later when he again visited Bill Cocoran and Jack Stewart they told him that they hadn't seen them since either. When another week went by and the proprietors of the 'lost city' did not appear, the author and Bill made a trip down into Death Valley in their car and took along a pair of field glasses, hoping to see some sign of the explorers or of the 'windows' or 'quays' allegedly hid among the shadows of the eastern slope of the sun- blistered Panamints. They failed to find any sign of either.

As we have indicated, there are many who suggest that Nevada rather than New Mexico may be the 'center' of subsurface 'alien' activity in America. This may be true in the sense that the major 'conflict' or 'interaction' zone between Evadamic (Govt.- Nordic) and Draconian (Gray-Reptilian) forces seems to exist below the Great Western Deserts of southern California, Nevada and western Utah. The military installations in this region are also, according to many sources, heavily involved in the alien scenario, for either good or evil.

Whereas the 'front lines' so-to-speak may exist below the 'test' ranges of Nevada and adjacent states, the 'center' of reptilian activity itself seems to be Mt. Archuleta, N.M. and the 'Four Corners' region.

The American Center of the various subsurface human cultures seems to be the Cascade-Sierra Nevada ranges (especially between Mt. Shasta and the Panamints) even though some suggest that, at least in the past — as in the case of the U.S. Govt. itself — 'some' of the human groups below the California region made the tragic mistake of opting for a policy of 'appeasement' rather than 'retribution' in dealing with the serpent race. This does not necessarily mean that this policy continues widespread today, although the Mt. Lassen region is reportedly a strong center of current 'collaboration' between exterran/subterran reptilian grays AND above ground/subterranean branches of the human Illuminati.

The following account which appeared in the Winter '92 issue of 'FAR OUT' Magazine, in an article by H. Leo O'Neal titled 'THE LEGEND OF THE DEATH VALLEY MUMMIES', was apparently an attempt to classify the following tale as 'fantasy' even though the author of the article does admit that SEVERAL people (witnesses) have reportedly been in these ancient chambers below the Mojave, mentioned in the story.

These (more) recent events surrounding the Death Valley catacombs, mentioned in the article, are as follows. We ask the readers simply to make their own determination as to the authenticity of the account based on other similar reports which we have related earlier.

In 1946, Dr. F. Bruce Russell, a retired Beverly Hills physician, struck of a conversation with a Mr. Howard E. Hill in the city of Los Angeles. Russell informed Hill that in 1931, while sinking a shaft in a claimsite of his in Death Valley, he broke through to an underground cavern. After finding some lights he entered and found himself in a cavern with two passages, one heading 'left' and the other 'right'. Exploring the left-hand passage he came to a cave-in, some 25 yards from the entrance shaft. The right-hand path however continued at a steep angle downward for about a quarter of a mile. Although some of the passages seemed natural, others appeared to have been expanded by artificial means, but all of these went off in several directions. One tunnel eventually led to a large room, and this room also had branch tunnels leading off in all directions. Laid out in this chamber were 3 'mummies' and several strange artifacts, some of which appeared 'Egyptian' while others were more 'American Indian' like in construction. The strange and shocking thing about the mummies however, according to Russell, was that many of them were nearly 8 foot long or tall! He described the underground system as a kind of 'underground city'.

The inhabitants must have been very advanced, Russell concluded from what he observed, and he was certain that the find was much more important than the famous King Tut's Tomb itself. Following the passages he eventually discovered other openings to the surface, but most of these were in obscure places, yet all that he explored were within 7 miles of the 'shaft' through which he had first entered the underground complex.

Eventually, Russell discovered 32 caves in all throughout the area. Although he could not prove it, since many of them had collapsed, he supposed that many of them might have at one time connected with the underground system. These 32 caves were all within 180 SQUARE miles of each other, and were located in Death Valley and the extreme southwest region of Nevada.

He also stumbled across a large chamber which he referred to as the 'ritual hall', and which contained strange markings and symbols. Another tunnel, according to Russell, went from this room to another underground hall where well-preserved bones of dinosaurs, sabre-toothed tigers, mastodons and other extinct animals were displayed in hollowed areas along the walls.

In 1946, after years of private investigation and secrecy, Russell decided to exploit the find. After gathering a group of potential investors he held a meeting in which he displayed some of the artifacts which he had taken out of the underground system. Mr. Hill was invited to the meeting provided that he could help out as an investor. He accepted the invitation and attended the meeting. The company was called 'Amazing Explorations', and the 'Investors' meeting took place at a suite in Beverly Hills, although all of the investors were sworn to absolute secrecy. Hill and the rest of the investors were taken, after this meeting concluded, to the underground complex itself, to where Russell returned the artifacts which he had displayed to the investors as he was convinced that the protected atmosphere of the caves would preserve them. The group was taken into the cavern in which the 'bones' and the 'temple' were located. According to witnesses, it was "chock full of bizarre artifacts of all kinds." Russell told them that they could look but not touch, as he realized the necessity of preserving such a find in its original condition, both for archaeological as well as monetary reasons.

On August 4, 1947, Howard Hill, acting as spokesman for 'Amazing Explorations', issued a brief statement to the press announcing the discovery. The story received minimal coverage, to his surprise, and only appeared in a few newspapers in which the story was 'balanced' with very derogatory and skeptical statements from the 'scientific' community.

After this, a live press conference was planned, in which Russell planned to display a skeleton and/or several artifacts which would "convince even the most skeptical reporter." And from that they could discover for themselves the reliability of the find. For this, Russell had to return once again to the caves to retrieve the necessary artifacts. He also planned before leaving or shortly after his return to open a bank account at Barstow bank to deposit investment capital. Russell left for Death Valley but was never seen again. His CAR was later discovered with a busted radiator in a seldom travelled part of Death Valley. Although some suspect that he left with the money of the investors, this is unlikely since the investors' money which he possessed at the time was not nearly enough to warrant his disappearance, or the discontinuance of plans to commercialize the site as one of the wonders of the world, and the potential wealth that this might bring.

The investors attempted to relocate the underground chambers that Russell had shown them, but claimed that they could not remember the exact route since they did not pay much attention to landmarks on the first trip, and besides this, the shifting sunlight and shadows and the uniformity of the vast landscape made that difficult. So ended the brief but interesting events surrounding what might have turned out to be one of the most popular wonders of the world, a 'potential' Federally-protected museum invaluable to archeologist, anthropologist and historian alike, as well as millions of potential tourists. In spite of the corroborating "circumstantial" evidence for the existence of these ancient ruins, this "world" (or perhaps its present for former inhabitants?) seems to continually resist all efforts of us "outsiders" to probe its secrets in any dramatic way, at least (perhaps) until its "protectors" feel that we are ready to discover these historical treasures. Perhaps the "greed" that such treasures often arouse in human hearts is in itself the very force that prevents their acquisition. Perhaps when we set our hearts to search for Truth — not for our own personal greed or profit, but for the benefit of all humanity — perhaps only then will the TRUTH make itself available to those who are "ready" to receive it.

The following letter was sent to researcher Tim Beckley, and confirms much of the information which has been 'surfacing' in recent years:

"...I enjoy your magazine very much. Thank you for such a fine publication. I have seen UFOs, and it seems after you have seen one you're never the same. I separated from the U.S. Air Force in December of 1987. In the Air Force I was a 'Security Specialist.' It was my duty to safeguard Top Secret aircraft, weapons and equipment. I also guarded nuclear warheads. I was stationed at David-Monthan A.F.B. in Tucson, Arizona. In January of 1987 I was training in the desert for a Desert Survival Course. This area is between Indian Springs, Nevada and Las Vegas, Nevada. It is known as Silver Flag Alpha. There is a huge mountain range and on the other side of this range lies the 'Area 52', also known as 'Dreamland.'

"I asked an instructor what would happen if somebody went over the ridge. He said, 'No one can make it over that ridge,' and then gave me a foxish grin. One night about 0300 hours I was sitting in my foxhole gazing at the stars when a white light rose over the ridge. It performed two vertical loops then shot up into the sky at a speed you would not believe. Also it didn't make any noise.

"After separating from the Air Force I stayed in Tucson for 19 months. During this time my best Air Force buddy received orders for 'Area 52.' I told him to stay in touch. He called one day and told me he DIDN'T LIKE the assignment. I asked him about 'Area 52' and he said he wasn't at liberty to discuss it. He did say he was stationed at Nellis A.F.B. Nevada and forced to live off base. He said an Air Force vehicle would pick him up and transfer him to 'Area 52' where he would spend 48 hours in an underground complex. After 48 hours he was then returned to his apartment for 48 hours off time. I asked him what kind of things he had seen. He only said don't be surprised if one day we are living in space. After this we talked about normal guy stuff. I never have heard from him since, which is PECULIAR. I wonder if the Air Force had his apartment phone tapped? - Steve

Blankenship - Somerset, TX."

The January, 1957 issue of FATE magazine, p. 10, carried an account of the following strange discovery:

"Dear Douglas, Ga., in Coffee County, workmen of the Head Well and Pump Company were drilling a 145-foot deep hole on the property of Mr. and Mrs. Earl Meeks, seven miles from Douglas. They stopped drilling when an unusual noise began to come out of the hole.

"It was a roaring sound, SOMETHING LIKE AN UNDERGROUND RAILWAY. As soon as they heard it, the drillers stopped. Driller Scott Dinking said he never heard anything like it before — not in 27 years in the business.

"Joe Sports of the Associated Press went out to look at the hole. He found it was making so much noise that the Meeks had covered it partially by a plank because it kept them awake as night.

"Sports noticed that AIR WAS BEING PULLED INTO THE HOLE BY A KIND OF SUCTION. He lighted a match atop the hole — the smoke was drown downward. Sports borrowed a mirror and reflected light so he could see the bottom. He saw water down there. It all 'looked' quite and peaceful."

The following passages are quoted from the Greek philosopher Seneca's classic ten-volume NATURALES QUAESTIONES (QUESTIONS OF NATURE), Vol. II, pp. 99-105, 151-157 (English translation by Thomas H. Cocoran, Ph.D.., Harvard University Press, Cambridge, Mass., & William Heinmann Ltd., London. 1972). Seneca begins by postulating that:

"...rivers are no less existent under the earth merely because they are not seen. You must understand that down there rivers as large as our own glide along, some flowing gently, others resounding in their tumbling over the broken ground. What then? Will you not equally allow that there are some lakes underground and some waters stagnating there without exit?

"...Throughout the entire earth, one of them says, runs many different kinds of water. In some places there are perpetual rivers large enough to be navigable, even without the help of rains.

"...Moving air in the lower region inside the earth bursts the atmosphere, which is thick and complete with clouds, with the same force that clouds in our part of the world are usually broken open.

"...Now permit me to tell you a story. Asclepiodotus is my authority that many men were sent down by Philip (i.e. Philip II of Macedon, 382-336 B.C., the father of Alexander the Great who according to Diodorus opened several new mines - ed) into an old mine, long since abandoned, to find out what riches it might have, what its condition was, whether ancient avarice had left anything for future generations. They descended with a large supply of torches, enough to last many days. After a while, when they were exhausted by the long journey, they (after breaking into vast cavities - ed) saw a sight that made them shudder: huge rivers and vast reservoirs of motionless water, equal to ours above ground and yet not pressed down by the earth stretching above, but with a vast free space overhead.

"I read this story with great enjoyment. For I realized that our age suffers not from new vices but from vices that have been handed down all the way from antiquity, and it is not our age that avarice first pried into the veins of earth and rock searching for treasure poorly hidden in the darkness.

"...Even before King Philip of Macedon there were men who followed after money down into the deepest hiding-places and, of upright and freeborn spirit as they were, let themselves down into those caverns where no difference between night and day reaches.

"...What powerful necessity bent men down, man ordinarily erect to the stars, and buried him to the bottom of the innermost earth so that he might dig out gold, no less dangerous to search for than it is to possess? On account of this he dug shafts and crawled around the mud-smeared, uncertain booty, forgetful of day, forgetful of the better nature of things from which he had turned himself away.

"...They dared to descend to a place where they found a strange order of things, layers of earth hanging overhead, dead winds in the darkness, dreadful springs of water flowing for no man, and a night other than our own, and perpetual. Then, after doing these things, they fear the Underworld!"

The following appears on p. 169 of Daniel Cohen's book 'THE ANCIENT VISITORS' (Doubleday & Co., N.Y. 1976):

"...For centuries hell was a very real and tangible place found somewhere underground. The 'entrance to hell' has been located countless times. Usually it was found in the country of one's enemy.

"There were serious and scholarly speculations about huge underground caves. One seventeenth-century scholar said that dragons lived in underground caves, and that is why we saw so few of them. Siberian tribesmen who found the frozen remains of woolly mammoths, assumed that they were the remains of creatures that lived in a subterranean world. The Siberians could not conceive of extinct animals that had lived thousands of years ago, but vast underground worlds came quite naturally to them. According to legend, dwarfs lived in underground caves, and most accounts placed the realm of fairies under the earth as well."

In reference to the 'caverns of hell' or 'Hades', this belief pre- dates Christianity itself and can be traced back to ancient Greece. The Greeks spoke of 'Hades' as a vast series of deep caverns, some containing frozen conditions while others filled with smoking flames. The real tormentors of Hades however were the fallen angels of ancient tradition, who are said to torment all souls that enter here. Also traditionally, over the entrance to Hades can be read the words "ABANDON ALL HOPE, ALL YE WHO ENTER HERE". Hades is said to be the center of the

Satanic Kingdom established by the fallen archangel Lucifer after his failed coup de'etat against the throne of the Creator. It is said to contain vast fortresses created by his infernal followers over the eons, possibly created of insubstantial or etheric 'matter'.

As one descends through the caverns of Hades, according to Greek tradition, things only become worse, until at last one reaches the realm of 'Tartarus' itself. Tartarus, according to the Greeks, is "as far below Hades as Hades is beneath the earth". It is a great "chasm" in the extreme depths that is diffused throughout the entire earth. The Christian Bible refers to Tartarus as the 'Bottomless Pit'. 'Bottomless' might indicate an absence of gravity and a sense of eternal 'falling' for those unfortunate enough to enter therein. Apparently physical life could not possibly exist there because of the suffocating heat and darkness, and the lack of oxygen which must instantly be consumed by the volcanic flames of terrifying realm. The Bible also adds that there is a third level to 'Hell' called Gehenna, or a 'lake' of boiling magma or fire... a place almost too horrifying to imagine.

This certainly does not conflict with present geological theory concerning the interior of the earth, which is said to increase in temperature as one passes the crust, the moho, the upper and lower mantle and finally the outer and inner molten core. However there is another 'theory' as to the configuration of the center of the earth, one which is steadily growing in popularity. This theory states that the earth is more like a gigantic "geode" with a hollow interior. In this case the "hollow" would not coincide with the "bottomless" pit simply because the "inner surface" pushes out- ward as opposed to the inward gravitational push of the outer surface. However, if one were standing on the inner surface they would not drift off to the center of the planet because they are attached or drawn to the inner surface, not gravitationally but through centrifugal force (the same force that one can see at work in a washing machine as the "spin" cycle pushes everything against the inner surface, leaving a "hollow" center). Several people in the past have proposed this theory, among them Edmund Halley after whom "Halley's" comet is named; Capt. John Cleves Symmes whose writings actually inspired a government expedition to the North Pole — as the theory states that the entrances to the inner hollow exist somewhere near the north and south poles; and Cotton Mathers who was a central figure in the "Salem Witch Trials". Also, countless science and fantasy fiction writers have used this theme in their writings, some of the more well-known authors being Edgar Rice Burroughs and Edgar Allen Poe.

If such a concavity exists, then how would the traditions of Hades, Tartarus and Gehenna fit in to this new cosmography of a "Geoditic" planet? One possibility is given by Dr. Hank Krastman, who claims that he was shown an underground city below the Grand Canyon area by a blond-haired, blue-eyed "Hopi" Indian. This city was connected to its counterpart on the inner surface of the earth's (alleged) concavity, a city of Grecian-like architecture called PALATKWAPI. In 1994 researcher B. Alan Walton sent Krastman a letter in which he posed the following questions:

"...Have your Hopi sources mentioned anything about the nature of the earth BETWEEN the outer and inner (hollow) crusts? I am particularly interested in learning of conditions within the terminal zone where gravitational "pull" and centrifugal "push" cancel each other out. My "theory" is that there would be no gravity, and thus vast cavernous spaces. I would guess that this would also include a chaotic environment similar to the Greek tradition of Tartarus or the "Bottomless" (non-gravitational) Pit where earth-material, magma, various chemicals and gases are being slammed together in weightlessness by the rotational movement of the earth itself, causing an inferno-like region where physical life could not exist, as it (apparently) does on the inner and outer crusts of this giant "geode" known as earth."

Hank Krastman's response, dated 11-27-94, was as follows:

"...The nature of the Earth between the outer and inner Earth is molten Lava type rock... When I walked on the inside of the Earth it was the same gravity pull, no difference, however the Air machines powered by the eternal Sun, the sky is blue without any clouds 24 hours a day (Note: the logistics of an internal "sun" at the center point, as suggested by several earlier theorists, would seem to violate the laws of physics when compared to the mass necessary for a "sun" or "star" to gain nuclear fusion ability — or whatever process is at work. Perhaps the "sun" that is described is actually a "focal point" of the electromagnetic currents passing through the earth, similar to the pinpoint of light that can sometimes be seen in the center of a spherical crystal. - Branton).

"The INFERNO region does exist in cavities between the two worlds. If you saw the Movie STARGATE it is similar going through the gate to the inner world."

Elsewhere Krastman stated that when he was transported to the interior surface from the underground city below Arizona it was at the "speed of light", suggesting that instantaneous travel was and is accomplished between the two worlds via time-space windows, or teleportation rather then via tunnels that pass through the "infernal" zones. Depending on the source, the distance between the outer and inner surfaces may be anywhere from 500 to 1500 miles!

In the Book of Revelation as well as other sections of Judeo- Christian scripture there is a prophetic event described which some refer to as the 'rapture' (the word doesn't exist in the Bible although the 'concept' does). This event is said to coincide with the disappearance of deceased Christian believers from their graves. Since certain (nonhuman) alien species have been known to 'counterfeit' divine or 'Biblical' events through the application of high occult-technology, is it possible that this prophetical event of the 'rapture' may also be 'counterfeited' for some psychological or manipulative purpose?

THE MOJAVE DESERT'S GREATEST SECRETS

The following incident was reported in the Oct. 1964 issue of SEARCH magazine, by Will Carson in his column 'PRYING INTO THE UNKNOWN':

"A GRAVE MATTER — J.E. was born in Spain, to which country her late parents originally had immigrated from what was then called Bohemia. Their native village has long since been submerged by the waters of a hydroelectric project — all of which pretty well obliterates our chances of pinpointing the exact time and date. But as J.E. recalls her parents relating many times, one day all the graves in the cemetery behind the now vanished village were found to be empty, but there were no mounds of dirt beside each grave. Upon further investigation the excavations proved to be apparently bottomless!

"Authorities were never able to solve the mystery, and finally (since it was impossible to refill the graves) they were boarded over and sealed with mortar and a high stone fence built around the area."

The following is from an add describing a book written by 'Michael X' (no relation to 'Commander X'), titled 'WE WANT YOU — HITLER ALIVE', published by UFO Review., Box 753., New Brunswick, NJ 08903:

"DID HITLER CAPTURE ALIEN CREW & BUILD HIS OWN FLYING SAUCER? Here is proof Hitler escaped death, and tried to reorganize his mighty forces at the South Pole in underground bases...

"Here also are clear—close up—photos of Hitler's own secret flying disks which he hoped would someday enable him to rule the world.

"Discussed for the first time is the mysterious 'Mr. Michalek' who had toured Europe telling of his contacts with aliens and the establishment of the majestic government of the 'World Republic of Earth,' and how both Moscow and Washington would be 'wiped out' if they did not 'give in' to other worldly advice. Was he speaking on behalf of the Fuhrer?"

In reference to any possible International counteroffensive against the 'Grays', some have suggested that the 'threat' will be used by the Illuminati as an excuse to unite the world together in a one-world government. If in fact the Korean and Vietnam wars were 'orchestrated' by the Serpent Cults as some have suggested, is it not likely that a United Nations-backed counteroffensive against the grays will result in the same type of no-win war with an eventual loss on our side? Especially if the 'One Worlders' are collaborating with the Grays and Reptons?

Perhaps it would be best for each individual nation to deal with the reptilian infestation or undermining of their own countries in their own way, without the help of a 'World Militia', or keep the battle at a 'grass roots' level? Global COOPERATION on an ECONOMIC level might be tolerated by freedom loving peoples, but Global CONTROL on a POLITICAL level definitely will not be! A world 'Federation' may be maintained without surrendering all national sovereignties to a one-world political force (namely, the NEW WORLD ORDER). Those extraterrestrials who profess the need for a One World Government on earth as a prerequisite to join their Alliances or Federations should realize that the cultural diversity on Earth is unique in the universe, and therefore a 'unique' answer to the problem should be suggested, namely that they attempt to align themselves with the governments of individual sovereign nations, and offer them memberships within their Confederations, rather than wait for the world to turn into a global police state.

The one-world Republic that 'they' so desperately seek could just as easily become a one-world dictatorship that would be controlled by despots, allied to the Grays for instance, who might bear animosity to the Federation(s). On the other hand if an individual nation were to become a member of such a Federation, they could enjoy the benefits of such cooperation. Such a plan must include the promise of the Federation(s) to come to the aid of that nation in a DEFENSIVE manner if it is being threatened by another nation, especially one backed by an opposing interstellar group. But such an agreement must absolutely prohibit any type of OFFENSIVE attack on the part of the host nation across its borders and a strict compliance with an inter- national noninterference policy. It goes without saying that, for instance, such a nation would have the right to root-out any subsurface "base" utilized by parasitical groups such as the grays that are being used as centers of abduction, mutilation, implantation and other such activities AGAINST the inhabitants of that nation. The Federation is fully justified in admitting individual nations into its fold, and this should not be misconstrued as a violation of their "Prime Directive", ESPECIALLY since the reptilian grays have already established their own destructive alliances with various national governments throughout the world. In light of this such a plan is the ONLY way that the Federations, Alliances, etc., can salvage their own interests for the future of planet earth.

Now to continue with the subject of how individual nations are responding to the reality of alien contact, the Oct-Nov. issue of NEXUS Magazine related the following information in an article titled 'UK RADIO PROGRAMME ON UFO COVERUP':

"...The following is an example of what one can pick up off the computer networks. The network in this case is called EarthNet, run by Pegasus Networks based in Byron Bay (P.O. Box 201., Byron Bay NSW 2481).

** Topic: Aliens from outer space... **

** Written 12:14 am, Aug. 5, 1991 by huw in peg:sci.astro **

"'I recently heard a Radio One program in the UK that contained an interview with a leading proponent of the popular 'US Government has aliens locked up and is experimenting with their space planes' conspiracy theory. However this particular individual sounded very reasonable, did not make any outrageous claims, and further had some interesting facts to disclose. In particular he mentioned several verifiable facts which I would like some follow up on:

"'Rockwell International and NASA were planning a *massive* joint exhibition of space exploration this year (1991) but it was delayed inexplicably until 1992. In the *official* prospectus for this exhibition, one of the exhibits was clearly stated to be 'an extraterrestrial spacecraft'. When asked about this by various individuals, all enquiries were referred by NASA to the US DoD. An unnamed Pentagon spokesman speaking off the record is meant to have indicated that they 'had a number of such space vehicles to choose from...'

"'The Pentagon also held a press conference to deal with press inquiries on this matter — and refused to answer any questions. In fact reporters later said that the Pentagon had asked most of the questions, and they all pertained to 'what would be the public reaction if...'.

"'The guy on the radio program referred extensively to two NASA consultant engineers who claimed to have worked on alien spacecraft studying propulsion systems for NASA — both had high level security clearances in the States...'"

Tim Beckley's UFO REVIEW [issue #37] carried the following article by the editor titled 'ET SAUCERS VS. EARTH MADE UFOS'. We quote excerpts here beginning with a reference to researcher William Cooper:

"...(William Cooper) will, he says, 'prove once and for all that the Secret Societies, NOT our [Constitutional] government, murdered President Kennedy as a sacrifice to the ancient god Baal in an outdoor temple.' Cooper will also [in future lectures] 'explain the true meaning of the movie 2001 as a message of the secret societies to their followers, and will show a first-generation color copy of the Zapruder film with all the previously missing frames...'

"THE 'Antigravity' WORLD OF VLADIMIR TERZISKI:

"...According to Terziski, the Nazi's were building flying saucers that took them to other planets even before the start of World War II. Being a Slav, Vladimir says he cannot but have the 'utmost revulsion towards everything Hitler's racial and political philosophies stood for,' and it is because of his revulsion he decided to look into various 'black technologies' developed by THE NAZIS, whom he now believes were secretly backed by the sinister Illuminati operating way behind the scenes (Note: As can be seen elsewhere in this File the 'link' between the Illuminati and the Nazi's seems to have been the gnostic Jesuit and Thule Societies - Branton).

"In his vast collection of photos and other documents, Terziski has many pictures and drawings of the various disk-shaped craft constructed by the Nazi scientists that were powered by Schauberger turbines and Kohler TACHYON magneto-gravitic drives (all based upon free energy or antigravity principles). Actually, Vladimir says that we've known all about antigravity for a long time and that THE BRITISH (Marconi Group) MAY ACTUALLY HAVE LANDED ON THE MOON

A CENTURY AGO, AND EVEN THE VATICAN HAS A GROUP OF SCIENTISTS WHO ROCKET OFF INTO SPACE FROM SOUTH AMERICAN BASES FROM TIME TO TIME.

"Meanwhile, deep underground at Area 51's 'Dream Lab' in the Nevada desert, a renegade branch of the CIA — protected by a private security SS-like police force that the Illuminati supplies — is constructing their own fleet of 'flying saucers' utilizing Hitler's forbidden technology..."

Elsewhere in this File we have written of the alleged 'Federation' which loosely ties together such human colonies as those in TAU CETI, EPSILON ERIDANI, the TAYGETA and other systems of the PLEIADES, VEGA in LYRA, various colonies in the HYADES, the alleged SOLARIAN Tribunal on the moons of SATURN, ALPHA CENTAURI, various cultures from the ANDROMEDA constellation, the KOLDASIAN and other systems from the DAL or antimatter universe, and the 'UMMITES' in WOLF 424 [all of which have been repeatedly described by numerous and apparently separate 'contactees]'. One additional allegation is that the 'UMMITES', a 'Scandinavian' appearing race who live on a planet with a magnetic field much more intense than that of earth, have apparently made contact with scientists associated with the French and Spanish governments. It is interesting that M.K. Jessup's annotated version of the 'CASE FOR THE UFO' contains comments by alleged members of an ancient terran race who have access to inter- planetary craft technology.

These have stated that France, for instance, has been the subject of much interest among certain ex-terran cultures because of it's unique social atmosphere. The UMMITES allegedly come from the star system we know of as Wolf 424, a star which they themselves refer to as IUMMA. Their 'insignia' resembles an 'H' with an extra vertical 'bar' in the middle and the four corners of the 'H' tapered into an outward curve. This symbol has been PHOTOGRAPHED on the underside of some UFO's which have been encountered in the 20th century. Also the UMMITES speak of themselves as belonging to a large 'Federation' of planets, possibly consisting more or less of the interstellar regions described above. They seem to have a particularly strong alliance with the Oriental-like Vegans, who are a remnant of the ancient Lyran civilization that gave rise to the present human cultures in the Pleiades.

The following are several abbreviated excerpts taken from 'THE OMEGA PROJECT", by Kenneth Ring, Ph.D.. (William Morrow & Co., N.Y. 1972). The following points were brought out in the book:

——Most abductions (possibly between 60%-80%? - Branton) are conducted by the 'greys' of traditional description.

—— Many state that their experiences are often 'dreamlike' yet with evidence suggesting real events.

—— The 'greys' (and in some cases black creatures in 'capes' that act as 'guards' during the painful and terrifying 'medical operations') have a way of 'blurring' their faces in the minds of the abductees, so that the abductee cannot later recall what the aliens' 'face' looked like.

—— Many abductees experience sleeping problems (not to mention severe social-relational-sexual problems) after being abducted by the saurian or reptilian grays, and these problems often last for years afterwards.

—— Some abductees who resist are 'shocked' repeatedly with an 'electric gadget' which may induce paralysis and/or unconsciousness.

—— A majority of the 'greys' seem to be of the grey-white variety, some with opaque 'black' eyes and some with vertically slit (snake or lizard-like) pupils.

—— Some of the greys are described as 'sinister', and one abductee stated that when she was taken "one alien was by my head and attempted to frighten me with his large eyes," as three other creatures mechanically performed painful operations, unheeding of her terrified cries to make them stop. She (Clair Chambers) stated that "In my many encounters where I have always been kidnapped from my home, the aliens have shown no compassion. I have several times felt them exhibit FEAR when I have hit them as they do feel FEAR... their reaction behavior patterns do NOT indicate an intelligence as high as I would expect from their technology (Due to their "collective- consciousness" nature? - Branton)... these experiences have been dreadful, terrifying, and I would like them to stop!" (Note: Four separate doctors have confirmed various wounds and injuries in Clair Chambers which she insists resulted from the abductions).

—— Some 'greyish' aliens, with 3-digit fingers, have been described as being 7 ft. tall (Reptons? - Branton). One woman who was abducted by them felt as if the creatures wanted her to have the IMPRESSION that they were 'friendly', but after being returned to her car from which she was abducted "I then broke to pieces as my whole body shook uncontrollably. I cried 'OH GOD, WHY ME?' I couldn't calm myself as I cried like a baby..."

—— A woman with an M.S.W. [degree?] (who was at the time of this revelation 51 years old), stated:

"...The first experience was when I was a child of about 5. For years I had a RECURRING 'dream' of standing beside a field WHEN A HOLE OPENS UP IN THE GROUND in front of me. The dream ends with me looking into the hole. I was just standing there looking at the hole. Under hypnosis I [recall that I] stepped into the hole and walked down a short tunnel. The tunnel widened into a small waiting area where there was a bench just at the right height for a 5 year old. I sat down and waited. A tall black 'featureless' being came through a doorway, walked to me and held out his hand. I took his hand and went back through the doorway with him. He placed me on a table that appeared to be about 3 to 4 feet high. He laid me on my back and took one big hand and held my upper body flat on the table. The other beings were behind him looking at instruments on the wall. I was held this way for several minutes. When the being turned to look at the other two, it was as if he lost CONTROL over me and I jerked out from under his hand, fell off the end of the table and ran for the door. When I got to the door, I knew I wasn't 'supposed' to go any further. I stopped and turned around. The being who had been holding me came to me, took hold of my left arm and looked into my eyes. I was looking at where the eyes should be on a HUMAN, BUT I don't REMEMBER actually SEEING eyes. I feel something was communicated, but I don't know what."

—— The author states that some of the large opaque-black 'eyes' seen by many abductees, after being taken by the greys, seemed to have been 'coverings' for real 'eyes' which they felt might have been hidden behind or inside of what might have been artificial opaque-black visual coverings. At least this was the 'impression' that some abductees had.

The following article, 'THE INCREDIBLE REVELATIONS OF DR. KUEPPERS', by Helga Morrow, also appeared in UFO REVIEW - issue #37, with the following heading: "He Escaped From Nazi Germany At The Height Of World War II And Came To America To Work For The U.S. Military On Top Secret Projects Involving Invisibility, Time [Manipulation], Anti-Gravity Research And Teleportation:

"Editors Note: The following is a highly-abbreviated account of Helga Morrow's recollections of her late father, Dr. Fred A. Kueppers, a German-born engineer who defected to the U.S. during World War II...

"[Helga's Story] 'I have learned from various sources that my father was one of the scientists who worked on the Philadelphia Experiment; had invented the timing device for the A-bomb; had been chosen by the bomb scientists to represent them to Harry Truman, asking him NOT to drop the bomb; had invented the mathematical formula that brought the astronauts back; had designed the miniaturized electrical system of Sputnik, the first space launching; had worked on Project Blue Book/Black Book, UFOs; had initiated the use of aluminum wiring to replace the heavier wiring in World War II planes; had worked with mind warfare, using psychics to communicate with astronauts in case communication systems failed; and had trained extraterrestrials to fit into human society.

"'My head spun; in it wheels were turning, and a thousand things began to make sense. Suddenly the things my father had told me in my childhood and youth snapped into place. It was as if nineteen years after I attended my father's funeral, I began to know him for the first time as only a few others knew him — a man who, for obvious reasons, could never be mentioned in public records, but who had clearly deserved such recognition for the valuable service he had given the nation. My mind began to go back to my earliest remembrances...

"'When I was in the second or third grade, I watched him hang up an award from RCA in his room. I asked, 'Why did you get this award?' He told me it was too lengthy to go into. I said, 'Try me!' and he did. He said it was an award for an experiment in time, and then proceeded to put two ashtrays on his bed, and through simple gestures and explanations, show how two objects could transpose in time and return the same way. Then he took me into the cellar, where he put some steel shavings in a cigar box with a large U-shaped magnet taped underneath. He gently tapped the steel shavings, and to my amazement, two distinct series of concentric circles gradually appeared! He then simplified this by saying that if one could transpose these circles, one could transpose time [or 'bend' time such as to speed it up or slow it down, or even stop it altogether? - Branton]. He said that alien spacecraft were partly moved by 'reverse magnetism.' He showed me how to get this effect by holding two opposite magnets.

"'I never forgot this lesson. And this was BEFORE anyone really talked about flying saucers. I was Daddy's confidant. I never discussed this information with anyone; he had sworn me to secrecy.

"'My father was not home much — only several times a year. He was completely focused on his work, so normal family life was difficult for him...

"'Daddy was a popular innovator in many fields of science and technology. All his patents became the property of either the company that employed him or the U.S. Government [Such patents, which have been established by various scientists working in antigravity research, allegedly exist in the patent offices for all to see, IF they only knew how and where to find them - Branton].

"'The third winter of 1961 before he died (February 12, 1962, Lincoln's birthday), my father confided many things to me. He told me that what he was about to tell me was bizarre, unbelievable and might sound absolutely crazy. I was 27 at the time, and thought he had gone off the deep-end (my mother had always thought so). Daddy assured me that by the time I reached 55 or so, all these bizarre statements that he was about to make, as well as everything he had ever explained to me when I was a child, would come back to me and make sense.

"'He told me that he had three months to live. 'They' had given him three months to conclude his personal affairs, he said. I asked, 'Who are they?' He said I wouldn't understand. So I realized that I was taking my last walk with him through Guilford. He turned around to see if he was being followed, as always, aware of intrusion. He confided that he had not only been on the moon but INSIDE it, and that he had both spoken to and trained extraterrestrials who looked like us to blend into human society. He had been in spaceships and had traveled in space.

"'He told me of the riots where we would kill or be killed in a period of racial intolerance that would occur around 1966 — which is now history. He told me that red-baiting propaganda was a lie to keep humanity occupied with worry over 'fighting communism.' And that in reality the two nations were great friends;

Russian scientists got along well with their American counterparts and worked amiably together. The Russian 'threat' was nothing but B.S. and a distraction for the public.

"'In the meantime, there were alien bases all over the world and on the moon. He said that whoever controls the moon can target anyplace on Earth; no place would be safe. Therefore, Russians and Americans must remain friends or eliminate each other. He told me he had worked with Tesla, Einstein, Von Broun, Von Neumann and many others.

"'My father broke down and cried when I visited him that Christmas. He said, 'If you only knew the real truth!' But as long as I didn't I was safe, he said. He seemed a frightened man alone with his thoughts, afraid to speak out, trusting no one. He rarely spoke on the phone (our phone had always been tapped) and always thought he was being followed.

"'My father died in the hospital in the arms of a nun, we were told. When my mother wanted to send flowers and candy to this unknown nun, she was told that there had been no nun in his room (though we had seen her) at the time of his fatal 'heart attack'. She couldn't be traced. At his funeral, I saw two Secret Service men at his coffin (wearing the obvious trench coats)...

"'There was something strange about the body in the coffin. I always remember my father's hairy arms and hands. But there was NO HAIR ON THOSE HANDS! His face felt like cold stone, and it had so much makeup that it looked like wax. Was it really my father in the coffin? If so, why had his grave 'disappeared' when I looked for it in the family plot in 1985 — a plot that dated back hundreds of years? There was no trace that it had ever existed; there were no grave records!

"'And then on May 30, 1962, several months later, he materialized before me and told me he was not dead but only in 'another dimension IN TIME!' I felt his suit, smelled his Molle shaving cream — and his weight pushed down the mattress on my daybed. He was wearing his usual conservative grey suit; I even felt the material as I touched his knee. He told me to continue his work, but not call on him unless absolutely necessary, as appearing to me was painful. He said that he would make himself known to me 'at the crossroads of my life' to help me (and he has kept his promise).'"

Based on other accounts, "another dimension in time" would probably indicate that the dimension into which he had been "phased" was and is a dimensional 'branch' off from the main- stream multidimensional reality that is visible to us. Since time, space and matter are all integral parts of the unified field, it has been theorized that another dimension "in time" — for instance a dimension in which the time-flow is accelerated (one of 'their' days may equal one of 'our' hours, for instance) — would also include a spacial and molecular shift as well. This could be perceived either as 'entering' another dimension or simply as a 'phasing' of an individual to the point that he or she begins to 'perceive' and become part of a dimension that was always there yet one which they could not comprehend or interact with until they were 'tuned in' to it on the molecular level. This dimension would be invisible to most of those within the 'mainstream' of reality, and we would be invisible to them to some extent (possibly an extent which is determined by the depth of the molecular-time-space phasing).

Returning to the subject of alien activity, in particular the 'Grays', there are those who believe that such activity has some apocalyptic and theological significance. Could such activity have been prophesied in ancient spiritual texts?

Leviticus 26:22 (in the TORAH or OLD TESTAMENT) relates a strange warning, possibly directed against those nations who tend to ignore the command of the Almighty or the Creator to live together in brotherly love... Could this be a prophecy of a coming invasion of alien 'beasts' such as the Grays? The Torah describes the serpent race as 'beasts' in Genesis chapter 3, although it also makes it clear that these reptilians were by far the most superior, "subtle" and intelligent members of the entire 'animal' kingdoms. We quote this passage as follows (see also: Amos 9:2-3):

"I WILL ALSO SEND WILD BEASTS AMONG YOU, WHICH SHALL ROB YOU OF YOUR CHILDREN, AND DESTROY YOUR CATTLE, AND MAKE YOU FEW IN NUMBER, AND YOUR [HIGH] WAYS SHALL BE DESOLATE."

George Adamski, the 1950's "contactee" and alleged Rosicrucian, was one of several who claimed to have had contacted Aryan-like saucer pilots during that time period. One little known fact about his contact in the Mojave desert was that one of the 'footprints' left by the 'man' he encountered in his initial experience revealed some strange symbols which had apparently been impressed into the ground from the sole of the aliens' shoe. One footprint showed two depiction's of a 'swastika'. One interpretation is that the saucer pilots encountered by George Adamski and other contactees such as George King, George Van Tassel, George Hunt Williamson (apparently these "E.T.s" have an affinity for those bearing the name "George" - Branton), Howard Menger, Mel Noel, and others are not Germans in the true sense of the word. It is believed by some however that the Germans have for centuries been doing business with a race of ancient ARYANS — possibly tied-in with the ancient Aryans who occupied India several thousand years ago — or "Arriani", who are part of a high-tech society based in underground cities near the North and South poles. German occultists in fact have been known to sabotage polar expeditions of other nations long before the beginning of World War I. These "Aryans" may have assisted the Germans with their technology during World War II, although it is uncertain whether or not they actually agreed with or support- ed Adolph Hitler's racist genocidal policies. These "Arriani" seem to have some connection with the so-called "Tribunal" on Saturn, which may explain why plans discovered for Nazi flying disks revealed one design that was an EXACT DUPLICATE of the so- called "Venusian" design described and photographed by Adamski.

In his book 'MESSENGERS OF DECEPTION' (Bantom Books, 1980), Jacques Vallee relates some disturbing connections between fascist politics and some of the early 'contactees' of California. According to Vallee, Adamski had prewar ties with American fascist leader William Dudley Pelley, who was interned during the war. Contactee George Hunt Williamson (whose real name was Michael d'Obrenovic) was associated with Pelly's organization, 'Soulcraft', in the early fifties. Other associates of Williamson during the great era of the 'flying saucers' were such contactees as John McCoy and the two Stanford brothers, Ray and Rex. Pelley, who died in 1965, was the leader of the 'Silver Shirts', an American Nazi group which began it's activities about 1932. It's membership overlapped strongly with Guy Ballard's 'I AM' movement based at Mt. Shasta. It was about 1950 that G.H. Williamson began working for Pelley at the offices of his 'Soulcraft' Publications, in Noblesville, Indiana, before moving to California, where he allegedly witnessed Adamski's desert contact in 1952, with a 'Venusian with long blond hair.'

Former 'Dulce' worker Thomas Castello, who was previously alleged to have worked as a top secret photo analyst for the Air Force, reported seeing a photo of a 'disk' with a swastika on it's side!

In all fairness, as we have suggested, it is possible that those who contacted Adamski were not 'Nazis' as we know them. Perhaps Adolph Hitler took an ancient and already existing symbol as some suggest and corrupted it with his own malevolent occultic philosophies. Then again, many of the claims made to Adamski do not ring true with many scientific UFOlogists, such as the allegation that the surface of Venus is just as temperate and mild as the earth itself, and so on. Could those who contacted Adamski have been using Venus as a 'cover' to hide their true place of origin (perhaps Antarctica) as other researchers have suggested?

As for the swastika itself, the Hopi Indians of northwest Arizona and the ancient Hindus, for instance, were apparently using it thousands of years before the Nazis began to... and some suggest that German occultists may have borrowed the symbol from them.

The following report appeared in the Sept. 1966 issue of FATE, pages 25 and 28:

"FROM 'DOWN UNDER' — We suspect this story may be a hoax but we can't resist reporting it. We have TWO DIFFERENT clippings from Darwin, Australia, concerning the discovery of animal flesh, hairs and hide during a well-drilling operation at a depth of 102 feet.

"An experienced well driller, Norman Jenson, was boring for water 15 miles from Killarney homestead, about 350 miles south of Darwin. He had penetrated seven layers of limestone, clay, red soil and sandstone when, at 102 feet, the bit of the drill struck something soft and quickly dropped to 111 feet.

Jensen thought the drill had penetrated an underground water course and lowered a pump to make tests. His pump brought to the surface a bucketful of what he believed to be flesh, bone, hide and hairs. Jensen told Constable Roy Harvey he never had seen anything like this before. Some of the material was given to chickens at Killarney station. They ate it, apparently without ill effect. Several days later the rest of the matter HAD NOT putrefied, although it had been left EXPOSED in the open air.

"Dr. W. A. Langsford, Northern Territory Director of Health in Darwin, stated that microscopic examination revealed the material to be hair and tissue. Samples were to be forwarded to forensic laboratories in Adelaide for further tests. There is even a possibility, he said, that the matter is HUMAN.

"Possibly romancing, Australians report that for many years overland drovers have DISLIKED TAKING CATTLE ALONG THAT PART OF THE ROUTE because of FREQUENT STAMPEDES."

One might wonder if the 'material' allegedly recovered from the well might have been from a 'Sasquatch' like creature or an animal unknown to us. It would seem logical for living matter, once dead, to remain 'relatively' free from putrefaction for long periods of time within the cool and unchanging environment of an underground cavern system as opposed to the often hot, degenerating and debilitating environment on the surface. Could a type of natural 'mummification' have also taken place underground, possibly explaining why the hair and flesh had not putrefied after several days?

According to William Hamilton, John Lear revealed an incident concerning an older gentleman who is known only as Mr. 'K', whose son was being held captive in an underground base in Utah. This son formerly worked in the Dulce base in New Mexico and possibly was transferred to the base in Utah via an underground route. When contacted about the incident, Mr. Lear had this to say:

"...The son, whose father I met and who passed away several years ago is apparently being held in a base near or around Sleeping Ute Mountain [Utah]. I don't remember how I came by that information but it had to do with some research I was conducting in a search for the Project Blue Light base near Delores (which I never found)."

Native 'Indians' of Alaska refer to a benevolent tribe who long ago disappeared underground into vast underground chambers below the mountains north of the town of Tanana. Occasionally, tradition holds, a young member of one of the villages on the surface would become overly discouraged by their life in the world above, and would make a journey in search of these caverns and their peaceful inhabitants, and disappear into the underground land where they would enjoy a more fulfilling life.

It would be very encouraging if most of the accounts of subsurface colonies were of this genre. A few centuries ago this might have been the case, but the infestation and undermining of the continents by so-called "draconian" forces and the mercenary "gray" species that work for them, has reportedly increased dramatically — especially during the last few centuries — to the point that their influence may be dominant in the subterranean world. However it is encouraging that in the latter part of the 20th century the reptilian advances seem to have halted in several areas of the world as indicated by the numerous 'standoffs', and in some cases reptilian forces have apparently been driven back and defeated as more and more humans refuse to give up their ground, having become aware of their malicious intent as well as the propaganda and deceptions which the aliens have in the past used as effective tools of conquest on their part.

Some researchers have stated that there are some governments which are considering possible overt military action against the serpent races (or 'Grays', 'EBE's', 'ALF's' etc., as they are also known) if such becomes necessary. Covert military action has allegedly been initiated in the past, with mixed results.

The alleged interception of a reptilian-controlled aerial craft in South Africa could be considered a victory, whereas the 66 CIA-trained Delta Force and Blue Beret special forces, casualties in the "Dulce Wars" (and God only knows how many 'casualties' in the way of the human abductions and mutilations, the knowledge of which allegedly attributed in part to the 'Wars') beneath the Archuleta mesa in New Mexico, could be considered a defeat.

If or when such action is taken it would be very wise to consider the need for what we may call an "occupational force". To illustrate, let's use the Middle East crisis of the early 1990's as an example, without going into whether the economic motives for the counteroffensive were commendable or not.

In that case we had a small relatively undefended country by the name of Kuwait. Having become apathetic to the Iraqi- Babylonian threat, this small nation in essence let their guard down, "fell asleep" under the influence of their wealthy, materialistic and extravagant lifestyle, and in such a 'drunken' state lost their vigilance against any possible enemy who might try to overtake them.

Taking advantage of the relatively undefended borders, Iraqi troops swiftly moved in and took control of the nation, looting and pillaging, and in some cases gang-raping woman and little girls in front of their families, following which the entire family was often murdered.

Unable to defend themselves, they petitioned a much more powerful force, the United States and the Allied Coalition to help them fight the battle. The rest is history.

After the Allies drove modern 'Babylon' from Kuwait (Saddam Hussain made no secret of the fact that he identified himself with the first Babylonian king Nebuchadnezzar, and was in the process of rebuilding the ancient city of Babylon), an "occupational force" was left by some of the Allies, as well as the now much-more-vigilant Kuwaites.

After this enemy (not necessarily the Iraqi soldiers themselves, but the mad dictator who drove them to their deaths by the thousands and whom many of them secretly resented) was cast out, this "occupational force" was necessary to defend the region from a possible re-invasion. If such an occupational defense force once again became non-vigilant and let down it's guard, then there is a chance that the former invaders would regroup their forces and re-invade the land, possibly with even greater fury, not willing to make the same mistake as before.

In the same manner, if an overt attack against the reptilian invaders is undertaken, it would serve little purpose in the long run to destroy multitudes of them physically and IGNORE the NEED for their human victims (victims of subtle alien occult- technological mind manipulation) to be delivered from their "Post-Traumatic Stress" and other psychological, emotional and physical problems that were the direct result of alien interference in their lives. The need for psychological and spiritual 'de- programming' (as well as the safe removal of implants and sub- conscious "programs" injected through hypnotic indoctrination) would be paramount!

Since the serpent races rely on demoniacal energy and assistance to empower their activities, they seek to destroy man's connection or relationship with Almighty God, the ONLY one powerful enough to protect and defend man from this reptilian influence — a force which would otherwise seek to conquer and control all of creation using all of the deception, confusion, subtlety and cunning at it's disposal.

God is not going to FORCE man to trust in Him, since we all have the free choice to determine our own destinies (and in fact if God only created a race who had no free will, but followed His every dictate robotically, then the human 'soul' or 'personality' as we know it would not exist).

On the other hand, we MUST realize that man is like a living 'temple' created to magnify his Creator. If there is no 'light' in the temple, then darkness must reign within it, but where the light exists, darkness vanishes.

There is no 'middle' ground. One cannot expect to defeat these 'dragons' of deception nor the poltergeists or infernal supernatural entities that motivate them, while at the same time refusing to abide in the LIFE or LIGHT of God. If we were to destroy most of the reptilian influences and temporarily cast them out of their trenches (so to speak) and at the same time refuse to establish an "occupying force" in the form of divine dominion in our own personal lives as a nation, then the reptilians may regather their infernal forces and return in even greater force the next time, intent on learning from the 'mistakes' of their last defeat.

Several 'abductees' have allegedly be taken during the night by GOVERNMENT officials by way of anything from flying disks, pickups, or even jet aircraft. One couple, referred to in a book titled 'INTO THE FRINGE', by Karla Turner, Ph.D., (Berkley Books, N.Y. 1992) described such an abduction which they shared one night. They were 'drugged' and put into a type of dreamlike trance and then taken via pickup to a remote swamp-like area. The next thing they remembered was descending through some type of tube only to find themselves walking through a musty underground cavern filled with various machines similar to those one might find in a factory. They were escorted into a room which resembled a 'saloon'. The husband later felt as if this atmosphere may have been specifically designed to reinforce the 'dreamy' quality of the experience. However, the husband began to come out of the 'trance', at which point a man (like an Army Sergeant) noticed him and became very upset and emotional. He began asking the husband questions about his abductions by the Grays (the couple did recall such abductions, which were shared with other people, some of whom they claimed were in the underground military installation that same night). The Military officer wanted to know what the Grays had told them, what their plans were, and so on. When the husband refused to answer him the Officer lost control and became very emotional, DEMANDING to be told what the grays were doing, treating him more-or-less like a collaborator with an enemy power rather than as a victim of an abduction.

If the (Constitutional) Government is going to such lengths to find out what is going on, then they must not have all of the answers. Unfortunately many abductees are seen as possible 'collaborators' by various segments of the U.S. Military, and the fault for this probably lies with them as well as with the abductees, being that the Constitutionals through their own apathy had in the past allowed the secret government, particularly the CIA, to drag them into the 'game'. The Air Force for instance must have been deceived by the CIA as to the true nature of the Grays, and it has only been in recent decades that they have come to realize the full truth, and therefore explaining the present 'Intelligence War' between the two Intelligence agencies — Naval Intelligence's "COM-12" which supports a counteroffensive against the Gray Empire and the pro-Gray CIA-NSA "AQUARIUS" agency — both of which are fighting for control of the Nevada Military Complex, the underground bases, the Wackenhut technologies, the Intelligence Network (especially MJ-12), and the U.S. Government itself.

Hopefully in the future the 'elected' government and the abduction VICTIMS will be able to put aside their paranoia of each other (no doubt fueled by alien propaganda), and work together for each others mutual benefit AS THEY DID DURING THE GENESIS OF THE AMERICAN REPUBLIC. At this point it is obvious that if they don't learn to work together and RESPECT each other (the Government respecting the public's right to Constitutional Freedom and the Public respecting the Constitutional government's duly elected authority), little will be accomplished in the way of defending ourselves from the alien vermin who infest and undermine the nations of our world.

First we must make a distinction between the Constitutionally ELECTED open government and the National Socialist IMPOSED secret government. To put it simply, the UNITED NATIONS who betrayed America during the Korean and Vietnam wars is the ENEMY WITHIN that must be thrown out of America. If they desire a world dictatorship (for that is exactly what they are promoting, in spite of the 'benevolent world government' tripe that they have been spouting for years), then they can go do it some- where else. As for the United States of America, we have our own historical document upon which this great nation was founded — The "DECLARATION OF INDEPENDENCE"!

The following account was revealed by writer and UFO investigator Preston Dennet, in an article titled: 'EXPOSED: PROJECT REDLIGHT'. In his article, which originally reached several thousand readers, he reveals the following information which supports the allegations of William Cooper, John Lear, Michael Lindemann and several others:

"...Tom's story began in high school. He was very bright and had received an exceptionally high score on the Scholastic Aptitude Test. In fact, his scores were so high, it caused some attention to be paid to him. It seemed that the United States Government was very interested in Tom and wanted him to work for them. He had no idea then what his high scores were going to cost him.

"Government officials first approached Tom's parents, and asked them if they would allow their son to work for the government. When Tom's parents gave their consent, Tom was approached and given an offer he couldn't refuse. In exchange for his services, he would receive a Top Secret security clearance to match a ridiculously large salary. His job was to conduct research in a Top Secret underground base in Alaska.

"Tom accepted the offer and went directly out of high school and into government service. He told everyone that he was stationed at a base in Nevada — but this was only a cover story. In reality Tom spent only the weekends in Nevada. On weekdays he flew by private military jet to a Top Secret Government base in Alaska.

"The base was an eight story building located almost totally underground. The base financed itself by setting up the world's leading drug smugglers. Officials would arrest the drug smugglers, confiscate all the money and drugs, and then turn around and sell the drugs to another smuggler — whom they would then proceed to arrest and confiscate. It sounds like a strange way to finance a scientific-military research base, but it is obviously very profitable. Although not strictly legal, such practices could be justified in the name of National Security (at least in some minds).

"Tom reported that the base was mainly a research station that nabbed up some of the best scientific minds in the country, and had the latest technology for advanced research. There were three major areas of research of which he was aware.

"Firstly, the base researched and developed biological weapons, which, as Tom said, made all other weapons seem like childsplay.

"Secondly, the base researched and developed electronic sensory and detection devices that allowed telescopic sight through solid objects, such as walls.

"Thirdly — and most importantly — the base researched and developed electromagnetic propulsion devices — flying crafts which needed no fuel other than the Earth's magnetic field on which to operate. According to Tom, the ships look like UFOs, and are able to hover silently, and move at astonishing speeds. As Tom says in his own words, 'Some of the UFOs seen over Alaska are probably ours.'

"Tom didn't say exactly what his job at the base entailed, but he did say that the security was extremely high. Every week he was subjected to a horrible ritual. Due to the nature of his job, everything about him had to be known. He would be taken to a special room where he was dosed with Sodium Pentothal and put into a hypnotic trance. For a period of a couple hours, he would be interrogated into every aspect of his life for the past week. Every detail would be laid bare to make sure that there were no security leaks. This agonizing ritual was repeated every week as long as he was at the base. There were no exceptions.

"Tom evidently got out of the business after several years as the lifestyle was too harsh. Since he left the base he has been, and still is, under close monitoring by the government. After his release from the base, he was offered several extremely high-paying jobs by some of the country's leading corporations. Tom declined these offers and pursued a more modest job and lifestyle.

"So closes Tom's story, which alone could be easily dismissed. But in league with those collected by other researchers, it seems evident that the government is in possession of UFOs, and are in fact, flying them around!"

The following article comes from the 'TC TECHNICAL CONSULTANT', Nov.-Dec., 1991 issue:

"The death of a journalist in West Virginia, plus the jailing of an alleged CIA computer consultant in Washington State may be elements of a much wider scandal that could have serious implications for the Bush White House in 1992.

"What started out as an investigation of an apparent case of pirated software has grown to be a project involving hundreds of journalists all over the world.

"The dead journalist, Joseph Daniel 'Danny' Casolaro was found dead August 10th in a motel room in West Virginia. His wrists were slashed seven times on each wrist and a suicide note was found nearby. The only manuscript of his book, with accompanying notes, WAS MISSING.

"The book, provisionally titled 'The Octopus', was meant to be an explosive expose of misdeeds by the Justice Department under the Reagan administration. Time Magazine also reported that Casolaro's research centered on gambling and attempted arms deals at the Cabazon reservation near Indio (California - Branton).

"Indeed, the scope of Casolaro's investigation was so large that any one of a large number of areas of research could have been the trigger for a possible hit.

"While authorities declared his death a suicide, his relatives definitely stated that Casolaro's mental state was sound, indeed upbeat, after the completion of his book.

"Casolaro started his work nearly two years before, investigating the bankrupting of a small computer software company called Inslaw, allegedly by the U.S. Justice Department. INSLAW, a company headed by Bill and Nancy Hamilton of Washington D.C., had developed a package known as PROMIS — short for Prosecutor's Management Information System — to act as a case management tool for the Justice Department's unwieldy work load.

"Inslaw President Bill Hamilton (NOT to be mistaken for the well-known UFO researcher - Branton) has claimed that Ed Meese associate EARL BRIAN was given control of pirated versions of the PROMIS software by Meese to sell back to different U.S. government agencies for great profit. Two courts have so far agreed with Hamilton, awarding an 8 million dollar judgment, but a higher court of appeal has quashed the award and the verdict, declaring that it was not the jurisdiction of the lower courts. As of October 9, the case has moved into the realm of the Supreme Court.

"EARL BRIAN OWNS UNITED PRESS INTERNATIONAL (UPI) and FINANCIAL NEWS NETWORK (FNN).

"According to a Washington man, who claims to have modified the Cobol-based software for the CIA and other intelligence agencies, the software was a reward for Earl Brian's role in arranging the so-called 'October Surprise' gambit, the alleged conspiracy to withhold the American hostages in Iran until after the 1980 election which saw Carter removed from power. The 'October Surprise' scandal has taken some time to emerge.

"In a Paris meeting, President Bush (at the time Ronald Reagan's Vice Presidential running mate - Branton) is alleged to have met with Ali Akabar Hashemi Rafsanjani, the speaker of the Iranian Parliament, Mohammed Ali Rajai, the future President of Iran and Manucher Ghorbanifar, an Iranian arms dealer with connections to Mossad, according to Navy Captain Gunther Russbacher who claims to have flown Bush, William Casey — the CIA chief — and Donald Gregg, a CIA operative to that location. Russbacher, who made these allegations in May is now in jail on Terminal Island, convicted on the charge of impersonating a U.S. Attorney.

"The Washington man is MICHAEL RICONOSCIUTO who is now waiting for a trial in a Washington jail on conspiracy to sell drugs charges, charges which Riconosciuto claims are manufactured. Indeed, the charge made against Riconosciuto were made one week after Riconosciuto authored and signed an affidavit describing his role in modifying the pirated software.

"The affidavit also claimed that he had been contacted by phone and threatened by PETER VIDENIEKS, a Justice Department employee and Customs official, who Riconosciuto alleged had intelligence ties, as to the possible consequences of his going public with certain information.

"According to Riconosciuto, Videnieks was a frequent visitor to the Cabazon Indian reservation near Palm Springs and visited with tribal manager, John P. Nichols. Nichols was in essence Riconosciuto's boss in a number of enterprises conducted on reservation land and the PROMIS modification was just one of these projects. According to Riconosciuto, in an interview with T.C. conducted from jail, the PROMIS software was modified to install a backdoor access for use by American intelligence services. The software was then sold to 88 different countries as a sort of 'Trojan horse' package enabling us to access their intelligence systems. According to Riconosciuto these countries included Iraq and Libya.

"Correspondence between Nichols and other companies, if authentic, indicates that Riconosciuto's claims of his expertise in the area of electronics and armaments appear to be true. Marshall Riconosciuto, Michael's father, is a reputed former business partner of Richard Nixon.

"According to Riconosciuto, the fuzzy status of reservation land as 'sovereign' allowed elements of the CIA and organized crime to conduct business uniquely.

"Among the projects worked on during this time were joint projects with WACKENHUT, a company loaded with former CIA and NSA personnel and business ventures with the Saudi Arabian royal family and other unusual projects.

"A joint venture with Southern California Edison will soon be generating power for biomass drawn from local waste outlets. Biological warfare projects were investigated with Stormont laboratories looking into the creation of 'pathogenic viruses' and enhanced fuel-air explosive weapons (which) were created and tested in league with Meridian Arms at the NEVADA TESTING RANGE which matched the explosive power of nuclear devices.

"These enhanced weapons gained their power from polarizing the molecules in the gas cloud by modification of the electric field, a technology developed from exploring Thomas Townsend Brown's suppressed work, a knowledge which Riconosciuto claims he gained from working at LEAR in Reno, Nevada.

"Riconosciuto is said to have worked on the enhanced fuel- air explosive weapons with Gerald Bull of Space Research Corporation. Bull, now deceased, later became an arms advisor to Saddam Hussein. It is said that HUSSEIN POSSESSES THE FAE TECHNOLOGY.

"In July, Anson Ng, a reporter for the Financial Times of London was shot and killed in Guatemala. He had reportedly been trying to interview an American there named Jimmy Hughes, a one-time director of security for the Cabazon Indian Reservation secret projects.

"In April, a Philadelphia attorney named Dennis Eisman was found dead, killed by a single bullet in his chest. According to a former federal official who worked with Eisman, the attorney was found dead in the parking lot where he had been due to meet with a woman who had crucial evidence to share substantiating Riconosciuto's claims.

"Both Eisman's and Ng's deaths were declared suicides by authorities.

"Fred Alvarez, a Cabazon tribal leader who was in vocal opposition to the developments on the reservation, was found shot to death with two friends in 1981. Their murder remains unsolved.

"The leader of the House, Thomas Foley, announced last month that a formal inquiry will be initiated into the Inslaw case. Foley appointed Senator Terry Sanford as co-chairman of the joint congressional panel. Prior to his election, Senator Sanford was the attorney representing Earl Brian in his 1985 takeover bid for United Press International and was instrumental in appointing Earl Brian, a medical doctor, to the board of Duke Medical School, of which Sanford is President.

"However, despite repeated requests from journalists to produce photographs showing Riconosciuto together with Brian, and requests to produce his passport showing his alleged trip to Iran, he has not yet done so. Also Riconosciuto failed to be able to describe Peter Videnieks to CNN's Moneyline program, claiming a medical condition prevented him from remembering clearly.

"This led one former intelligence operative to speculate that we may be witnessing a very sophisticated intelligence operation being played out in public.

"Former F.B.I. Special Agent, Ted Gunderson, speaks for Riconosciuto's credibility. Gunderson, who lives in Manhattan Beach, has worked with Riconosciuto for many years in his capacity as private investigator.

"Together, according to Gunderson, they were responsible for thwarting a terrorist operation during the Los Angeles Olympics. According to Gunderson, Riconosciuto was well known in certain circles as a genius in almost all sciences.

"The so-called drug operation broken up in Washington State was an electrohydrodynamic mining operation claimed Gunderson, using Townsend

Brown technology. A videotape viewed by this journalist revealed metallic powders and apparent processes unrelated to drug manufacture. Indeed, a government analysis of soil samples revealed the absence of drug contamination, but a high concentration of barium. Barium is often found in high voltage related work.

"Unsubstantiated information from an intelligence source claims that the current situation is the visible effect OF A WAR CURRENTLY GOING ON IN THE INTELLIGENCE COMMUNITY between a group centered in the CIA called Aquarius (around a powerful center known as MJ-12) and a group known as COM-12 centered around Naval Intelligence. COM-12 is reputedly trying to sustain a rearguard action to sustain and preserve constitutional government and is deliberately LEAKING INFORMATION damaging to the former group." (Take note of William 'Bill' Cooper's pro-constitutional, anti-MJ/12 writings and his past association with high levels of Naval Intelligence - Branton)

In the same publication, same issue, there appeared a small article just following the one quoted above. Written by Thomas Zed, the article, titled "WACKENHUT'S CONNECTION WITH THE BLACK PROJECT WORLD", stated:

"The Wackenhut company has a very close connection to the world of BLACK BUDGET PROJECTS. Besides being connected with the Cabazon venture mentioned in this issue it is also responsible, according to jailed computer consultant Michael Riconosciuto, FOR THE SECRET PROJECTS BEING UNDERTAKEN IN DULCE, NEW MEXICO where the JICARILLA INDIAN RESERVATION IS BEING SIMILARLY USED. (Note: The Underground Labs near Dulce are alleged to be tied-in with the Department of Energy, Rand Corp, DARPA, Los Alamos Labs, MJ-12, the CIA and other 'secret government' controlled military- industrial-intelligence organizations. It is believed to be the largest underground 'joint-interaction' Illuminati/Alien laboratory of it's kind in the United States, and possibly the world - Branton)

"After sending two of my colleagues there recently AND RECEIVING CONFIRMATION THAT THERE WAS A TOP SECRET MILITARY TYPE INSTALLATION I decided to call the newspaper office and make an educated bluff.

"I identified myself as a freelance reporter from Los Angeles — and told the newspaper that I was doing a story on the Cabazon reservation biological warfare projects that had been undertaken there on behalf of the CIA. I told her that I had heard that there were similar things being done in Dulce and would like to know what was going on.

"The official I spoke to BECAME FRIGHTENED and said, 'I can't talk to you about that! It would be very unprofessional of me to talk to you about that. You'll have to speak to the President of the tribe.' She then hung up.

"I have yet to call back and ask the President of the tribe, but will report on that in the next issue.

"Wackenhut is also responsible for security of a lot of UNDERGROUND FACILITIES in California and Nevada, including the notorious S-4 or Area 51 in Nevada where Townsend Brown flying disk technology (written about in a T.C. recent issue) has been flying and developing for decades.

"A recent helicopter crash at the area, where two pilots and three security guards from Wackenhut flying in a Messerschmit BO-105 helicopter were killed was not at all accidental claimed Riconosciuto, who said that the individuals aboard the helicopter were traveling with sensitive documents.

"Groups are now investigating Riconosciuto's claims."

'Commander X', the 'anonymous' Intelligence-Military insider who has apparently fulfilled his Constitutional oath by providing so much 'inside' information on aerial and subsurface 'alien' activity — information which in fact coincides with other accounts given by numerous other researchers — made the following comments (Note: The 'Commander' admits to being a member of a high-level Intelligence network — intent on exposing the Illuminati 'cancer' in the Intelligence Community — called 'THE COMMITTEE OF 12 TO SAVE THE EARTH'. It is not certain however whether or not this has any connection to the notorious 'COM-12'):

"...Robert Dickhoff, in his book 'AGHARTA', mentions that the secret chambers of the Pyramid of Giza were connected by tunnels to the Subterranean World. An Egyptian informant says that at the base of this pyramid are three tunnels that radiate in different directions. Two lead to dead ends, but the third seems to go on and on and may have once connected Atlantis with it's colony in Egypt by passing under the Mediterranean and Atlantic. (There are those who have suggested that some of the ancient structures near Cairo, Egypt are in fact of antediluvian origin - Branton)

"...Two Swedes tried to traverse this long tunnel till it's end and never returned. While believed to have died, rescue parties could not find them. This caused the government to FORBID anyone from entering this third long tunnel, though they were permitted to enter the other two. There are strange reports of ANCIENT EGYPTIANS (or rather, people appearing or looking like ancient Egyptians - Branton) having been seen inside the long tunnel, coming from the Subterranean World. Many believe that the Swedes who disappeared joined these people. A popular book was selling in Egypt some time ago entitled 'THE MYSTERIOUS PATH TO THE UNKNOWN WORLD', dealing with the apparently endless third tunnel below the pyramid of Giza and the world to which it leads...

"A report has been circulating that some scientists entered a tunnel in West Africa that ran under the ocean bed in the direction of the vanished Atlantis, which was finally reached and many mechanical contrivances were seen (through some type of 'window' looking out into the depths? - Branton) on the ocean bed, including motor vehicles. How true this reporter is, the writer cannot say."

The following information was sent to researcher B. Alan Walton from Juliette Sweet, a personal friend of Sharula Dux (also known as Bonnie Condey), the self-professed resident of Telos, the city below Mt. Shasta, and was dated 2/7/93:

"...last month I had your disk transcribed and read your materials in their entirety. Very interesting, and full of well cited facts. I appreciate your sense of groundedness when presenting your ideas... I am not familiar with the saurian race, nor have I heard mention of them from Sharula or Adama (an alleged spiritual leader in Telos - Branton)... The Greys do come up from time to time, and what has been communicated by the Hierarchy is that they are indeed being asked, forcibly if necessary, to leave. The ousting process has been active for the last year or so, and Adama has indicated that Los Alamos will be one of the last areas to clear out... there has been some 'star wars' type of conflict of late, but (they) tell us not to worry about it [and] that they have things well in hand... Sharula's age is actually 267 years. Although for surface ID purposes, she says she was born in 1951. It helps where social security and passport purposes are concerned. You might want to update your materials to reflect her actual age..." (Note: of course the "ousting process" would necessitate a cessation of ILLUMINATI interaction with the Grays, as the 'Baverians' have in the past allowed the Grays access to this planet and even harbored them and protected them and their bases from public or foreign intrusion - Branton)

One report that came out of the Nevada Military Complex has not been confirmed and it's exact source is uncertain.

The report was based on information provided by a man who was involved in high-security work in the underground bases below the Nevada Military Complex. This man stated that while working at the facilities there he learned of a race of 'aliens' which were also resident in parts of the underground bases, a group known as the 'Orange'. The 'Orange' are apparently a hybrid-type of alien of humanoid form and possess some 'reptilian' genetic characteristics yet with human-like reproductive organs and capable of breeding with human beings. It is also interesting that other sources apply to them a partial cybernetic quality, suggesting that they are in fact a branch of humans who have been genetic- ally infused with reptilian DNA and also electronically or bionically altered with cybernetics. Whether or not some or all of the "ORANGE" possess a human "soul-matrix" is something which has not yet been established, at least by 'the Group'.

Since, as we've indicated earlier, evidence suggests that no TRUE 'hybrid' can exist between the sauroid and human races, because humans have an energy-soul matrix whereas true serpent race or reptilian entities do not (among many other dissimilar characteristics), we must assume that the entities encountered by the Nevada base worker were what one 'might' refer to as "Drac-Orange" (no soul-energy matrix) or "Eva-Orange" (soul-energy matrix). Please bear with us in our attempts to 'create' titles wherein non is perceived by us to exist, to describe the various new concepts which often turn up in this type of "fringe" research. Here we are simply applying the traditional names of the first recorded reptilian male (Draco) which 'tradition- ally' was the father of the serpent races; and the first recorded human female (Eva) who was 'traditionally' the mother of all the human races, as recorded in Genesis chapter 3, which also records the hatred and enmity that would exist between the two 'races' down through the ages. As for the "Orange", just which of the two categories these entities fall under (Dracorange or Evaorange or both), as we have indicated previously, remains uncertain at the time of this writing.

Another account, also unconfirmed, refers to an individual (possibly involved with military intelligence) who was reportedly invited to work with a group of 'Aryans' who were resident at a secret base in or near the Nevada Military complex, along with Secret Government Military personnel. This individual claimed that this group had access to UFO type craft and utilized the symbol of the Swastika, and were presently in conflict with the Greys, which they might have at one time in the past had associations with. As in the case of nearly every human organization that has established interactions with the sauroid Grey aliens, perhaps these particular 'Aryans' also learned of the true nature of the reptilian races after being 'betrayed' by them. There are some "Aryans" that may have broken-off from the Antarctican Empire, which we must assume (until evidence to the contrary presents itself) is still in collaboration with the Reptilian and Gray Empires, and still holds to Hitler's Nazi-nightmare of a fascist electronic NEW WORLD ORDER, complete — according to some — with human 'slaves' bearing mind-control implants inserted during abductions by joint Nazi-Reticulan saucer crews such at the one encountered by Betty and Barney Hill. It is interesting however that both the CIA as well as the 'Aryans' are said to be operating in and below the Nevada Test site, which might support allegations by some that the CIA struck a deal with the Nazi's sometime before or after World War II, and that both groups have had past and present ties with the International Bavarian (German) Illuminati.

If such an offshoot group of "Aryans" or ex-Nazis does exist it might be wise for them, considering the Nazi atrocities of the past, to RENOUNCE the swastika and all that it stands for if they intend to receive any help or support whatsoever from true Americans in their conflict with the grays. We must be careful not to equate "Germans" with "Nazis" and thus fall into the same racist trap into which the Nazis themselves fell. Nazism is a PHILOSOPHICAL problem, not a RACIAL one, and in fact there have been many Germans who have contributed to the overall benefit of humanity, including Luther and Gutenberg and others who challenged the despots of Rome (that is, until later generations of Germans sold themselves out once again to the so- called 'holy' Roman EMPIRE via the Jesuits who absolutely infested Hitler's S.S. according to Edmund Paris. This infiltration of Hitler's ranks by the Roman "militia" was accomplished in order to carry out the NEW INQUISITION against the Jews, the latest in a long history of ROMAN persecutions against the Israelite race).

Even if present Aryan 'generations' were not PERSONALLY responsible for the war crimes of their fathers during WWII, they would still have to agree to conform to Constitutional principles of HUMAN EQUALITY regardless of race, religion or culture if they are to have any future peaceful coexistence with the most powerful nation on the 'face' of the earth, the United States of America. Otherwise they might find themselves in the very uncomfortable position of being wedged between two enemy fronts: the saurian greys on one side AND indignant anti-Nazi American patriots, many of whom lost family members to the Nazi's during the Second World War, on the other. If an 'inner-planetary' or inter- planetary war does erupt between human and saurian species, as some have suggest might overtly take place in the future, then the neo-Nazi saucer groups (supposing they exist) MUST decide to join up with the human race and cast off their former FASCIST ideologies OR ELSE try and appease the alien Grays — most likely to their own ultimate destruction — or become caught up in the 'cross-fire' between the human and serpent races in whatever future conflicts might be waged between the two.

There are possible indications that 'at least' THREE groups of entirely human 'aliens' have some connection with the Nevada Military Complex, possibly involving humanoid aliens retrieved alive from crashed saucer-disks, or human-aliens who are willingly assisting certain governmental compartments in the technology department. For instance the above account suggests that some so-called ARYANS with past or present affiliation with the Antarctican Empire have some possible connection there; as well as the Pleiadean NORDICS as suggested by Robert Lazar's claim that a Pleiadean 'beamship' was seen by him on certain occasions in the hangers; and then there are the tall Telosian BLONDS who have also been known to have some connection with the underground networks of Nevada and the South-West. In fact, there may be several different 'scenarios' taking place at once within the Test Site, as if no individual 'compartment' has full control of what is taking place there (this has been suggested by different sources).

In one sense the 'Test Site' is the center of a WORLD WAR III type of scenario, the only difference is that it is a covert or 'underground' war since neither the Reptilians nor the Illuminati want this conflict to be made public, although some of the 'Constitutionals' have apparently 'leaked' information through the COM-12 and similar intelligence organizations. The allegations, as given by intelligence sources like 'Yellow Fruit', indicate that some of the 'benevolents' are operating in and below Nevada — 'aliens' who honor a Constitutional form of Government in the U.S. This would also indicate that there is more than one group of humanlike 'aliens' active there, and that there are in fact THREE general groups fighting for control, the Nordic-human FEDERATION, the 'Joint' Illuminati/Gray COMBINE, and the Reptilian EMPIRE itself. Some however would suggest that the 'Joint' activity groups are not a third power group at all but rather a 'midpoint' organization of power-hungry humans and grays that are working together on a competitive basis in an interactive and sometimes all-too-real and deadly bid for world domination. Both the Illuminati and the Grays want the planet to come under central control and both sides need each others assistance to bring it to pass, but they disagree just who will be the ultimate masters, the Humans or the Grays. Basically it is a rather sickening love- hate relationship, or a guarded "marriage of convenience".

Ancient Hebrew history speaks of a race of human beings known as the 'Anakim' in whose sight the ancient Israelites saw themselves as 'grasshoppers'. These giants were apparently very human yet of enormous stature. According to some accounts they were anywhere from 9 to 12 feet tall, and remained until the Israelites eventually drove them out of Palestine. As to their final destination or what became of them, the Hebrew records are strangely silent.

There are some who believe that men of such stature may have existed previous to the deluge and the cataclysms which accompanied it, however the Hebrew records make it clear that a human race of such great stature existed in post-deluvian times as well.

Researcher Warren Smith paraphrased, in 1976, two accounts related by Leland Lovelace describing incredible finds. The following discoveries are very similar to an account which appeared in an early issue of TAL LeVesque and Mary Martin's 'HOLLOW HASSLE' newsletter, one which described a similar cave found in the Silver Peak range of southwestern Nevada, not far from the Mojave Desert (and in which the bones of human giants, along with gigantic stone furniture and golden artifacts, etc., was reportedly discovered). The woman who submitted the account claimed to have personally known an explorer who had been in the tunnels. The cave was supposedly discovered with the help of a 'MUrian' treasure map which was said to have originated from an Native American tribe in the area. Warren Smith describes two similar incidents, one of which 'may' be a confirmation of the cavern discovered in the Silver Peak Range, in the following words:

"...Author Leland Lovelace told about such a discovery in 'LOST MINES AND BURIED TREASURES' (Naylor Co., 1965; also Ace Books, New York). Lovelace said two prospectors were searching for a gold strike in the desolate mountains of south- western Nevada. The two men were digging in the arid soil when a cave-in led them into a vast underground tunnel. Following the passageway, they went deep into the mountain and entered a large subterranean room.

"The two astonished prospectors held their torches high and saw that the cave was furnished with chairs and tables. The furniture was very large, as if manufactured for a race of giants. Dishes cast from gold and silver were also found on the tables. Other artifacts made from precious metals were discovered in the cavern.

"Lovelace did not inform his readers as to what the prospectors did with their discovery. We can assume they carried as much of the precious metal as possible from the scene, then melted down the objects for their gold and silver. This often occurs when a gold-seeker finds a rare archeological discovery. Rather than risk the treasure being taken over by the state or federal government, these men play a game of 'finder's keepers.'

"In 1904, a prospector named J.C. Brown claimed to have made an intriguing discovery in the Cascade mountain range of California. Brown had been hired by the Lord Cowdray Mining Company of England to prospect for gold in these isolated areas. During his second trip into the Cascades, Brown found a man-made tunnel carved into a solid rock wall. According to old reports, a landslide had destroyed a rock wall that hid the tunnel entrance.

"Brown followed the enormous tunnel through the mountain and came to a large, man-made cavern. The room was lined with sheets of tempered copper. Strange circular shields hammered from gold were hung on the walls. Unusual artifacts and statues were located in niches in the cavern walls. Unusual drawings, strange art, indecipherable hieroglyphics AND THE SKELETONS OF WHAT WAS APPARENTLY A GIANT RACE WERE FOUND IN ROOMS LEADING OFF FROM THE LARGE CAVERN.

"Unwilling to share his discovery with his English employers, Brown did not report the treasure cavern. Instead, he continued to work for various mining companies for the next thirty years until his retirement. Then, in 1934, he popped up in Stockton, California, with a map and an intriguing tale. Within a few days, eighty people were willing to assist the now-aging prospector in getting the precious artifacts out of the cave.

"On June 19, 1934, Brown and his followers traveled into the Cascade mountains. They camped by a small stream, waiting until morning when Brown was to show the group an entrance into the cavern. However, during the night, the old prospector vanished. He has not been seen since that night.

"Fearing that Brown had somehow duped the eighty people, detectives on the Stockton police department investigated. 'Brown didn't take a cent from anyone,' the detectives said after the check-out.

"The police chief asked, 'What was his game?'

"The detectives shrugged.

"'Was he murdered out there?' asked the chief.

"'He was probably an old liar who knew his time was up,' replied one of the detectives.

"'Brown was a kindly old gentleman of advanced years when he arrived in Stockton,' a doctor wrote several years ago. 'I was a curious young man at the time, always interested in occult lore. Anything that smelled of adventure grabbed my interest. Brown's stories were fascinating. They may have been tall stories about mythical things by an old man looking for companionship. Somehow, over the years, I've gained new respect for the old man. I believe he was telling the truth. I don't know his reasons, but I think he changed his mind at the last minute and decided not to reveal the location of the lost treasure vault of the 'Lemurian' giants.'"

In his book, 'THERE ARE GIANTS IN THE EARTH' (Doubleday & Co., Inc., Garden City, N.Y. 1974. pp. 135-136), Michael Grumley relates an ancient Hebrew tradition which suggests that remnants of a race of 'giants', possibly 'hairy' giants, survived the ancient deluge along with Noah and a menagerie of other animals:

"...in the Genesis story, there is an incident absent in the King James version but present in various scattered references in the Hebrew Midrash which concerns a giant named 'Og' who is said to have ridden on the ark during the forty days and forty nights of the downpour that caused Noah's flood. In order to be included in the ships company, so the story goes, it was agreed that he would, once the ark reached dry land and the waters receded, became a servant of Noah and ALL OF his descendants. He (and presumably a female of his kind were) the only one[s] of what was a widespread race of giants who perished, along with all men (except) Noah and his three sons Shem, Ham and Japeth (this also, Hebrew tradition holds, included the four women who were the wives of Noah and his three sons, making eight in all. Or, if the "OG" account is accurate, was it TEN "people" — eight humans and two half-humans? - Branton)."

As for the Sasquatch itself (or Yeti, Bigfoot or Abominable Snowman, etc.), in most cases they are described as being peaceable except when provoked, although such cases of retributional violence against humans are rare.

It is usually said that the Sasquatch resemble not so much a "missing link" between humans and apes, but more of a "hybrid" between the two, such as "a human head on an apes body" in the words of one witness. This might suggest that humans and apes are two distinct species, and that in some ancient time the genetic similarity might have resulted in hybrid offspring between the two groups, consigning the Sasquatch offspring themselves to a horrible and lonely existence, being outcast by men and beasts alike, being that they were neither fully human nor fully animal. If such was the case in the past, the genetic divergence's between the two groups may have long ago strayed to the point that such a 'natural hybrid' would be impossible today, except in the case of the DESCENDANTS of the Sasquatch race itself.

In the book "CHARLES BERLIT'Z WORLD OF THE ODD & AWESOME", we read of a strange being that was discovered in the Congo several years ago. "He" was given the nickname Oliver, however it was uncertain whether or not he was a mutant, a hybrid, or part of a new species of chimp. He looked like a bald chimpanzee, but his nose protruded much like that of a humans and UNLIKE APES, who prefer to walk on their knuckles, Oliver seemed to naturally walk upright. Was "Oliver" a Sasquatch, or of a race akin to the legendary hairy humanoid?

Studied by Ralph Helfer of Burbank, California, it was discovered that Oliver had FORTY-SEVEN CHROMOSOMES, FALLING BETWEEN AN APES FORTY-EIGHT AND A HUMANS FORTY-SIX, suggesting a CROSSBREED. Oliver was extremely intelligent for an "ape", and enjoyed watching television Westerns and action programs for hours, unlike chimps, which became bored after a few minutes.

Aside from the hairy humanoids, there have also allegedly been sightings of Satyrus-like creatures in connection with the underground or aerial phenomena, although these sightings are relatively rare. They are described as being small, goat-footed humanoids with horns. Because of the paraphysical phenomena surrounding such sightings however, some have suggested that they might be part of a quasi-physical pre-Adamic race which were part of the original 'fall' described in Judeo-Christian theology, a race that possessed humanoid, bestial AND angelic features and therefore immortal. Whether their humanoid/animalistic attributes allowed them to procreate is uncertain, however there are a few bizarre accounts which surface from time to time of female witches or Satan-worshippers having been impregnated by satyrus-like incubi, following which they give birth to a horrifying hybrid — a frightening and often vicious humanoid child with horns and tail, who traditionally live only a few days or weeks before dying. This may be just a myth that has been created by occultists over the years, as no actual cadavers of these supposed hybrids has ever turned up in public.

Several years ago Brad Steiger reported an incredible incident involving a demolition crew in San Francisco, who were in the process of tearing down some old buildings when they broke into an underground cavity adjacent to the basement level of one of the old structures. They gather together some equipment and entered the opening, and were surprised to find themselves in a tunnel which branched out in different directions underground. The construction workers commenced to explore the passages for some distance before they encountered something which left them shocked and trembling. Right in front of them stood a group of the strangest creatures they had ever seen. They were neither 'entirely' human nor entirely like any animal they had seen before. They were humanoid, covered from head to foot with hair, were around 5 feet tall, with eyes which reflected reddish in the light of their flashbeams.

The demolitionists decided that they weren't going to stay there much longer, and beat a hasty retreat back to the surface. The opening might have been subsequently covered-up by debris and further demolition work, although this is uncertain. Whatever may have become of the tunnel entrance is anyone's guess.

Charles Berlitz, in his 'ATLANTIS - THE EIGHTH CONTINENT' (G. P. Putnams Sons., New York., 1984., pp. 196-198), makes the following comments concerning the ancient fallen society which was apparently one of the first 'civilizations' following the deluge to release the scourge of high-tech thermonuclear warfare on the earth. He states:

"...These periodic destruction's have occurred because Earth's inhabitants failed to carry out the plan of the Creator... According to the retelling of the Hopi legends by Frank Waters, in collaboration with White Bear (BOOK OF THE HOPI: 1968), when (the ancient peoples) had acquired what they wanted 'they wanted more still and wars began again.' The peoples of the Earth created 'big cities, nations, civilizations,' and invented aircraft — PATUWVOTAS — which they used to attack and destroy one another's cities. The warfare in this previous world ceased only when continents sank and the land and sea changed places, leaving the 'third world' (the one before the present) lying on the sea bottom, 'with all the proud cities, the flying PATUWVOTAS, and the worldly treasures corrupted with evil.' (Although the 'sinking of continents' seems to be a phenomena intimately connected with the deluge, this does not mean that other island continents might not have sunk within the centuries or millennia FOLLOWING deluge as well - Branton).

"...It is in the books of ancient India, however, that we find allusions to prehistoric warfare that eerily parallel those of today as well as those of the foreseeable future (vide C. Berlitz: MYSTERIES FROM FORGOTTEN WORLDS). There are two possible explanations for them: either some scientifically minded Indians of six [or so] thousand years ago let their fancies roam at will and imagined bombs of sufficient force to destroy most of the world, or perhaps the whole concept was inherited from...a stage of development propitious to experimenting with or using the destructive power of the atom.

"In any case, passages from traditional Indian literature, such as the VEDAS, the PURANAS, the RAMAYANA, the MAHAVIRA, and especially the MAHABHARATA, contain repeated references expressed in the poetic language of their era to aircraft — VIMANAS — rockets, and space travel, but also specific allusions to what is easily recognizable as combat aircraft, air bombing, radar and other forms of aircraft detection, artillery, rocket launching, explosive bullets, detonation of mines, and bombs of cosmic destruction comparable in effect to the atom bomb of the present world. In other sections of Indian scientific and philosophical literature there are mentions attesting to the awareness of molecules and atoms of different elements, a concept that might eventually lead to the use of the power of the atom in warfare, just as it has in our day within a relatively short period of time. From the time that the atomic theory was generally accepted by modern scientists to the construction of the atom bomb WAS ONLY 130 TO 135 YEARS, while a previous world civilization, whose time span is unknown, would presumably have had as much or more time for such development.

"...When the MAHABHARATA was to be translated in the last half of the 19th century into modern languages (into English by Protap Chandra Roy and into German by Max Muller), the fanciful descriptions of ancient warfare were generally ignored, except in the case of artillery - familiar to everyone - and aircraft, then considered to be lighter than air. V. R. Ramachandra Dikshitar in his book on early Indian warfare (WAR IN ANCIENT INDIA: 1944), comments on the DECLINE of artillery in medieval times, inferring that it was more destructive in the distant past. He also defends the detailed references to heavier-than-air aircraft in ancient land and naval warfare, referring to 'the vast literature of the PURANAS showing how well and wonderfully the ancient Indians conquered the air.' Since Dikshitar was writing during the period of World War I he, like a number of Indian officers and British officers in the Indian service, was aware than many of the 'imaginary' weapons of Indian antiquity had made an appearance (or reappearance) in both world wars. Dikshitar wrote, during World War I, that the MOHANASTRA or 'arrow of unconsciousness' was generally considered 'a creature of legend until we heard the other day of the bombs discharging poisonous gases.'"

In reference to an ancient weapon known as 'the iron thunderbolt', Berlitz states: "According to the description in the MAHABHARATA its burst was as bright as the flare of ten thousand suns. The cloud of smoke rising after its first explosion formed into expanding round circles like the opening of giant parasols.

"...A strangely modern injunction in the ATHARUA VEDA cautioned opposing forces that the use of such a weapon was permissible only when the enemy 'used it first,'... There is even a mention in the MAUSALA PARVA implying that on one occasion this weapon 'capable of reducing the Earth to ashes' had been destroyed and the resultant powder had been 'cast into the sea,' another timely suggestion from the distant past of Earth.

"Whether this legendary weapon was ever used, or was destroyed, or forgotten except in Indian literature, there exists certain burned sections of our planet that may be the result of meteor strikes or even the scars of thermonuclear warfare, one of these was found in Iraq in 1947 in the course of an archaeological probe dug vertically while penetrating a number of cultural levels containing recognizable artifacts of BABYLON and SUMERIA and eventually passed through a fourteen-foot level of clay, indicating deposits following a severe and prolonged flood. Past the flood level a stratum was eventually reached that proved to be fused glass — almost exactly similar to the desert floor at Alamogordo, New

Mexico, scarred and fused after the 'first' A-bomb test." (Gen. 4:22 states that only 7 generations after Adam, 'Tubal-cain' introduced complex metalwork, and no doubt weaponry, to the antediluvians)

Some researchers and 'contactees' have referred to a 'human' group of 'aliens' from a nearby star system who are known as the 'Coldasians'. These may very well be the same group who others refer to as the 'Koldasians'. UFO PHOTO ARCHIVES (P. O. Box 17206., Tucson, AZ 85710) has released a volume detailing an alleged contact with a person from the planet 'Koldas'. It is uncertain as of this writing whether or not the 'Koldasians' (or Coldasians) are part of the alleged, although loosely-tied, Vega-Ummo-Pleiades-Andromeda-Cetus-Eridanus-Centaurus 'federation', all allegedly inhabited by 'human' spare-faring cultures. The Koldasians do however claim to have ties with the Solar "Confederation" reportedly based on the moons of Saturn.

The volume, titled "UFO: CONTACT FROM THE PLANET KOLDAS — A COSMIC DIALOGUE", is described as follows in an advertisement released by UFO PHOTO ARCHIVES:

"...This 300-page report unfolds the story behind a powerful and special friendship still continuing between two men — one from beyond Earth.

"Valdar is the extraterrestrial human being who came to Earth in preparation for his commissioning as the commander of an interplanetary spacecraft. He lived near an electronics plant and worked closely with a South African national for two years, before departing for his home planet Koldas in another solar system.

"Valdar's two years of integrated living on a more primitively inhabited planet was one last prerequisite to his new role as spaceship commander — and he chose Earth, the unique planet a friend and mentor had also visited during his own final indoctrination.

"Before his final selection of our planet, Valdar had been told by his friend of Earth's rare beauty, its great variety of living species, vast oceans, high plains, abundant vegetation — and the unusual savageness of its society.

"After some familiarization here, Valdar met and befriended F. Edwin W., a South African working in Durban. The Report tells the story of this friendship, a close relationship that has continued, up to and beyond Valdar's departure for Koldas right before the eyes of his Earth-based friend. The relationship continues today.

"More than 1,000 communications have been received (via electromagnetic energy beams) from the extraterrestrial since Valdar's departure from Earth.

"Many other witnesses and extensive documentation adequately support this case. Important material collected by lunchtime UFO researcher Carl van Vlierden includes color photographs and [an] ACTUAL PHONOGRAPH RECORD-

ING of the Koldasian commander delivering a heartfelt message to the people of Earth.

"This comprehensive report is published through the generosity and special interest of the Weaver family."

The UNICUS Group [Dept. 210., 1142 Manhattan Ave. #43., Manhattan, CA 90266], an organization allegedly devoted to 'Earthbound Extraterrestrials', related much information in 1993 concerning the research and work of a Mr. Robert M. Stanley.

Stanley has reportedly discovered a 'lost city' which he says was once inhabited by ancients, whom he postulates may have been tied-in with ancient 'Lemurians' (or rather the MU-rians of ancient California, a civilization which is not to be confused with the 'theoretical' lost empire of 'Lemuria' in the Indian Ocean - Branton). Some of the inhabitants of this ancient city were 8 ft. tall and had access to interplanetary travel, utilizing an ancient UFO 'base'.

Although Stanley has been to dozens of countries doing archaeological research, he states that the lost city — which he says largely resides in a massive underground maze of tunnels and caves below a 'Mystic Mountain' in southern California (Mojave region?) — is the most incredible site by far that he had ever encountered, and contains walls, statues and many other ancient relics from the ancient culture which built the 'city'. He has allegedly taken many scientists, engineers, archaeologists and anthropologists to the ancient site and through the underground complex and states that they agree with him on the incredible importance of the site, but wonder why it never came to light before this time.

Although Stanley is reticent of revealing the exact site of the 'Mystic Mountain' (on which he also claims, along with others, to have had experiences with UFOs beaming 'lights' down upon the group), he states that it is in SOUTHERN CALIFORNIA and one might assume from previous informations revealed that wherever this 'lost city' is located, it may very well have been connected in some fashion to the lost city of the Panamint Mountains.

Mr. Stanley can be reached through 'MYSTIC MOUNTAIN ADVENTURES'., Dept. 200., 1142 Manhattan Ave #43., M.B., CA 90266. However be warned that Stanley is adamant in his conviction that he does not wish the site to be turned into a 'tourist attraction' or amusement park with hot dog stands and all the rest, but desires to keep the site in pristine condition for the sake of future generations of researchers. However, if he sees that one has true unselfish academic motivations rather than a 'treasure hunter' mindset, one might be able to arrange a 'tour' of the site with him as have others in the past.

William Halliday, in his book 'ADVENTURE IS UNDER- GROUND', records an affidavit submitted by a Mr. Earl P. Dorr, describing vast caverns he and an associate allegedly discovered and explored in Southern California. Portions of the sworn testimonial are quoted below:

"...These caverns are about 250 miles from Los Angeles, California. Traveling over state highways by automobile, the caverns can be reached in a few hours.

"Accompanied by a mining engineer, I visited the caverns in the month of May, 1927. We entered them and spent 4 days exploring them for a distance of between 8 and 9 miles. We carried with us altimeters and pedometers, to measure the distance we traveled, and had an instrument to take measurements of distance by triangulation, together with such instruments convenient and necessary to make observations and estimations.

"Our examinations revealed the following facts, viz:

"1. From the mouth of the cavern we descended about 2000 feet. There, we found a canyon which, on our altimeter, measured about 3000 to 3500 feet deep. We found the caverns to be divided into many chambers, filled and embellished with the usual stalactites and stalagmites, besides many grotesque and fantastic wonders that make the caverns one of the marvels of the world.

"2. On the floor of the canyon there is a flowing river which by careful examination and measurement (by triangulation) we estimated to be about 300 feet wide, and with considerable depth. The river rises and falls with the tides of the sea — at high tide, being approximately 300 feet wide, and at low tide, approximately 10 feet wide and 4 feet deep. (Obviously this can only mean that, if this account is true, the "source" of the river is an underground reservoir large enough to be moved by the tides, "overflowing" into the river during the high tides and "receding" at low tide - Branton)

"3. When the tide is out there is exposed on both sides of the river from 100 to 150 feet of black beach sand which is very rich in gold values. The sands are from 4 to 11 feet deep. This means there are about 300 to 350 feet of rich bearing placer sand which averages 8 feet in depth. We explored the canyon sands a distance of 8 miles, finding little variation in the depth and width of the sands.

"4. I am a practical miner of many years' experience and I own valuable mining properties nearby which I am willing to pledge and put up as security to guarantee that the statements herein are true.

"5. My purpose of exploring the caverns was to study the mineralogy in order to ascertain the mineral possibilities and actualities of the caves, making such examination in person with my engineer necessary to determine by expert examination the character and quantity of mineral values of the caverns, rocks and sands.

"6. I carried out about 10 lbs. of the black sand and 'panned' it, receiving more than $7 in gold. I sold it to a gold buyer who offered me at the rate of $18 per ounce. 2 1/2 lbs. of this black sand I sent to John Herman, assayer, whose assay certificate shows a value of $2145.47 per [cubic] yard, with gold at $20.67 per ounce.

"7. From engineering measurements and observations we made, I estimated that it would require a tunnel about 350 feet long to penetrate to the caverns, one thousand feet or more below the present entrance, which are some 3 miles distant from my property.

"8. I make no estimate of even the approximate tonnage of the black sand, but some estimate of the cubical contents may be made for more than 8 miles and the minimum depth is never less than 3 feet. They are of varying depth — what their maximum depth may be we do not know. — Sworn by E. P. Dorr., 309 Adena St., Pasadena, Calif., November 16, 1934."

It is interesting that the "source" of this river would be some- where within or beneath the great western desert of Utah-Nevada- California where little surface water escapes by way of streams and rivers. Halliday in his book also refers to a water-filled cave annexed to Death Valley, known as "Devil's Hole", which according to some sources rises and falls slightly with the tides! This may indicate that certain underground watercourses below the Mojave Desert might ultimately connect with extensive underground lakes or small underground freshwater seas. Whether this theory proves accurate or not remains to be seen... after future adventurous 'Speleonauts' make their way once again into Dorr's secret caverns and toward the SOURCE of the 'alleged' underground river.

"Devil's Hole" itself contains a rare species of cave-fish found nowhere else in the world (at least nowhere that marine biologists are aware of). It is reported that at least two divers disappeared in this apparently 'bottomless' aqua-cave some years ago, leading officials to put the cave under government protection by making it an extension of Death Valley National Monument — much of which lies well BELOW sea level. The existence of, or the possibility of the existence of, such underground 'seas' beneath the California- Nevada regions seems to be supported by other accounts. During the 'Shaver Mystery' years Ray Palmer received a letter from a reader describing Earl Dorr's cave. This letter stated that three Paiute Indian boys had, with the help of a 'treasure map', extracted $50,000 worth of gold from these caverns, which they kept in the bank at Needle's, California. Their project was halted when one of the boys slipped from one of the lowest 'rock tiers' and died.

We will now quote from William R. Halliday's professional observations of the claims made in Dorr's affidavit, as they appear in his book 'ADVENTURE IS UNDERGROUND':

"...What is the gimmick?

"This was probably the question in the mind of every reader of the CALIFORNIA MINING JOURNAL when this affidavit appeared in it's November, 1940, issue. The question still arises whenever a caver first hears the remarkable story of this still more remarkable cave. Furthermore, the answers to the other obvious questions are not those which might be anticipated.

"'Is this just an imaginary cave?' No, the cave certainly exists. I have been in it.

"'Did Dorr keep it's location secret?' No. Dozens, perhaps hundreds, of people know it's exact location, high on the side of Kokoweef Peak in the Mojave Desert.

"'Has anyone tried to find this river of gold?' Yes, indeed. The prosperous Crystal Cave Mining Corporation owns the property. "'Then what is the gimmick?' That's quite a tale.

"The beginnings of the story of the cave of gold are shrouded in the mists of the minds of old-timers. For a long time, prowling prospectors have known of the existence of the wide mouth of a deep cavern on the limestone flank of a peak which forms part of the east face of IVANPAH VALLEY — Kokoweef Peak. Even though only four miles by dirt road from the highway between LOS ANGELES and LAS VEGAS, the area was so desolate that, in the 1920's, weeks might elapse without the passing of more than an occasional prospector and his burro. The opening of the cavern was several feet in diameter and the cave was obviously much larger farther down. There were local stories that it was bottomless, although it took 'only a few seconds' for a rock to strike 'bottom'.

"Then someone found a narrow crack leading to ANOTHER cave, high on the east face of the peak. Maybe it was Dorr. The stories vary. One version repeats the common story of two Indians with a treasure map, which in this case was supposed to have showed the entrance to the cave. Dorr was well known in the area, having a claim across the valley, several miles southwest of Kokoweef Peak. Like any experienced prospector, he certainly prowled every ledge of the area. In any event, the new cave seemed even deeper than Kokoweef Cave. Like at least seven other caves in California, it eventually became known as Crystal Cave.

"Later, in 1934, another old prospector, Pete Ressler, was resting near the bottom of the southwest slope of the barren peak. He idly tossed a rock into a crack. To his surprise it rattled back and forth for a long time until the sound died away into the depths. He strapped his load on his burro and headed for Mountain Pass Station for dynamite.

"'What do you think it is, Pete?' the men at the station asked him.

"'Quien sabe?' he shrugged.

"Pete's Spanish, however, was horrible. It sounded like 'Kin Savvy' or 'Kin Sabe,' and this name stuck to the cave he dynamited open. It wasn't much of a cave. It slanted downward, but was filled with rubble (rubble from the dynamite blasts? - Branton) to a level not far below the entrance. Old Pete dropped out of the story. Dorr is the main character.

"Dorr must have been a strange person. No one else was particularly interested in the caves, but soon he was telling of an enormous cavern into which he was gradually making his way, trip after trip. The main part of the cave was a series of vertical drops from one small chamber to another. In several areas there were small, dry pools which contained sharp little crystals. From one of the small rooms a tight tunnel led a relatively short distance to a huge cavern containing a chasm 3,000 feet deep. He told of a stalactite 1,500 feet long (Note: Both Kokoweef and Door peaks are near the SW flank of the Ivanpah Mts., just south of Highway 91. Dorr alleged that he and his engineer, following the upper rock 'tiers', discovered a huge cataract or waterfall cascading down the side of the 'canyon' below what they judged to be Dorr Peak. They allegedly followed the upper 'shelves' for 8 miles. According to a map of the caves drawn by Herman Wallace Jr., under the personal instruction and supervision of Earl Dorr, the length of the 'stalactite' was given at only 500 feet long — although this would still make it the largest "known" stalactite in the world at this writing — and was located adjacent to the underground waterfall which flowed into the underground river at the bottom of the canyon as one of its many tributaries. - Branton).

"The cavern went on for miles. He had walked to the brink of the chasm, but had not found a way to it's bottom. There were places where air came into the cavern, so other caves on the peak must open into it. And there ought to be an entrance somewhere on his claim, too. That was the direction the cave headed.

"Before long Dorr was claiming to have found a way down the wall of the subterranean canyon. Down below the wonders were even greater. He had found great deposits of placer gold. By this time he had the other old-timers half convinced. Still, THEY weren't going into that awful-looking hole for all the gold in the U.S. Mint.

"One day in 1928 Dorr again told his friends that he was going into the cave for another trip. Two days passed, three, four. His friends became worried. Gold would not tempt them to go into the cave, but they were his friends and the code of the desert is stern. Dorr might be trapped there, hurt, dying. A rescue party climbed to the mouth of the cave, where Dorr's ropes were still fixed.

"Hardly had they all entered the cave when they met a raging Dorr they hardly know. Although disheveled and wild-eyed, he was obviously in no need of rescuing. Nervously they shrank away from his needless fury. Had he gone mad from his long stay underground? (More likely it was the dreaded 'gold fever' which has affected the minds of men throughout the centuries and has often motivated them to acts of irrational cruelty - Branton) They were trying to help him, yet he was accusing them of trying to steal his gold.

"Before they quite understood, they felt the dull impact of a HEAVY charge of dynamite. Then Dorr calmed down. 'You'll never get it now,' he smirked.

"'That blast finished the tunnel to the river of gold.' (Interesting Note: Halliday himself claims to have seen within this cave, along with several National Speleological Society or NSS members, the name of DORR written in black miner's lamp soot near what appeared to be a black line left by a dynamite fuse, below which was a plugged area of shattered rock - Branton)

"We do not know whether Dorr was ever convinced that his friends were only trying to rescue him. For several years he was a familiar figure in the Mojave Desert. Continually he attempted to persuade people to run a tunnel into the cave of gold from the lower slopes of Kokoweef Peak. He would go shares with them. If they were willing to pay for the tunnel, they could have part of the profits.

"On this basis few investors were willing to consider the project. Finally, however, a small group headed by a Los Angeles capitalist was willing to speculate on Dorr's proposition. First, they tried the easy expedients. Kin Sabe Cave was the most accessible. Dorr thought it connected with the great chasm.

"They installed an inclined railway track and began to remove the rubble which filled it. Before long they had quite a respectable cave, 125 feet deep, but the air in it was completely stagnant. Over Dorr's protests, they abandoned the attempt. If there was an entrance to the great cavern from Kin Sabe, it was too deep to bother with, at least until all easier possibilities had been investigated.

"Next they turned their attention to Kokoweef Cave, the first cavern discovered on the peak. A road was built to a nearby ledge and a short tunnel was drilled, connecting the bottom of the cavern to the surface of the peak. Again, much rubble was removed without encountering the true bottom. Operations were in full swing when someone discovered a mineral vein in the wall of the peak a few dozen yards from the tunnel. It was zinc, and high- grade ore. Because of the war zinc was at a premium. The Crystal Cave Mining Company promptly went into the zinc business. Dorr was disgusted. He abandoned the project. Occasionally someone would hear of him, still telling his story of prowling the hills near his old claim, still seeking another entrance to the cave of gold..."

According to 'Sasquatch Researcher' Virginia Louis Swanson, 'Devil's Hole,' in Death Valley National Monument, NE of Death Valley Junction, CA., has been the scene of at least one disappearance. According to Swanson, two boys entered the cave several years ago and were never seen again. Navy scuba diver's were lowered on cables and reported seeing a large river which roared up from below, flowing across a wide expanse. They could not estimate it's depth because of a myriad of colonnades of black rock through which the river flowed before plunging once again down an abyss. The cave is somewhere NEAR 'Devil's Hole' (which is still open to public view, although 'fenced in'), and was allegedly sealed shortly after the disappearance.

It is interesting that Vincent Bugliosi, in his book HELTER SKELTER (pp. 232-

233, 246) refers to Charles Manson, who believed that his 'mission' was to start a race war called 'Helter Skelter', then hide with his so-called 'family' in an underground area near the Mojave Desert called the 'Bottomless Pit', and then emerge after the 'war' was over and rule the world. One version states that the Manson "family" had met with "strange people" out in the Mojave desert. Was he "programmed"? Manson was also convinced that he was Adolph Hitler's illegitimate son.

One interesting bit of information was related by Robert K. Newkirk, in a letter in AMAZING STORIES Magazine, April, 1949 issue, p. 140, stating that northern California's "...Clear Lake has many underground caverns that we know have no endings and others that run to S.F. bay."

Another anomalous account was related by Jack Peterson in a letter in SHAVERTRON, issue No. 14, describing the writer's own experience near June Lake, CA, where he allegedly observed a small humanoid being (a gray?) coming out of a strange cone- shaped machine which emerged from the depths of the earth. The alien then reentered the craft, following which its machine disappeared back the way it had come.

Turning for a moment from the subject of subterranean activity, we once again turn our sights toward the stars. Those who have been involved with research into UFOs, Underground Bases, and Secret Governments for any length of time will realize just how interconnected Aerial, Subsurface and Social phenomena actually is behind the scenes. For instance Forest Crawford's account of the recovery of a craft from Tau Ceti also involved underground bases and transportation systems, as well as top secret government activity.

In addition to Crawford's account, we have a corroborating report which appeared in 'THE UFO ENCYCLOPEDIA', by John Spencer (Avon Books., 1993). Under the heading 'DR. OTTO STROVE', we read how this astrophysicist assisted Frank Drake in establishing Project OZMA, and it's very mysterious conclusion:

"...the project began its search by focusing on the star TAU CETI. According to claims made at the time, AS SOON AS the project got underway STRONG INTELLIGENT SIGNALS were picked up, leaving all the scientists stunned.

"Abruptly, Dr. Strove then declared Project OZMA had been shut down, and commented that there was no sensible purpose for listening to messages from another world."

(Note: Or, was this merely an 'excuse' used by the secret government to keep the Project and it's findings SECRET? It would seem that Frank Drake — and Dr. Strove for that matter — has or had some connection with the Illuminati, as the Illuminati usually does not allow someone of Drake's influence for instance to operate with impunity. Usually people of such influence in economics, media, science, education, religion and politics are either 'bought off' or blacklisted. Frank

Drake, with his influence within the underground bases and disk recovery operations, is very obviously not on the Illuminati's "black list" - Branton)

Back to the underground bases, UFOs, etc., — Jimmy Ward, in a letter submitted to GRAY BARKER'S NEWSLETTER (Aug. 1982, No. 16 issue), referred to an announcement made by the Canadian Research Council in 1942 of plans for constructing a vast underground complex to be built by AVRO Corp., which was to cover an area of about 75 square miles in the region between British Columbia and Alberta, bordering on the State of Washington on the south, and the Peace River district on the north. No further word of the project has been released.

Leslie Watkins, in his book 'ALTERNATIVE 003' (First published in London, reprinted by Avon Books, N.Y., 1978. 239 pp.) quotes from an 'interview' with a government official who told of the Government's knowledge of entire ancient cities, linked by an elaborate complex of tunnels, far below the surface of the earth, which were lighted by a strange greenish luminescence, and the remains of which have been found under many parts of the world.

There have been SEVERAL documented cases of mysterious disappearances of persons in connection with subsurface and/or aerial phenomena. One such account involves the ancient Greek "Temple of Apollo", in Hierapolis (now Pamukkale), Turkey. This city was once part of the ancient Grecian empire, which covered an extensive area in and around the Mediterranean sea. One article which appeared in the January, 1989 issue of OMNI Magazine, referred to strange disappearances which had taken place in a cavern adjacent these ancient temple ruins. The article quoted from the writings of the ancient Greek philosopher 'Strabe' (who lived between 63 B.C. and 24 A.D.), to the effect that animals would often enter the cave and never return.

Also MANY PEOPLE throughout history who went past the mouth of the cave never returned. The article also quoted one Sheldon Aaronson, a professor of microbiology at Queens College, N.Y., who told OMNI that several Australian students had entered the cave and disappeared just a few days before his visit in 1987. Sheldon stated: "The Turkish government put iron bars over the opening to prevent other people from ever going in. As far as we knew, the Australians were never seen again." According to the article, the Greeks believed that the cavern was an opening into the "land of the dead ruled by the gods of the underworld."

As for the possibility of an underground subterranean 'world', scientists tell us that the lowest depths of the earth (upper and lower mantles) contain temperature and pressure extremes so great that physical life could not possibly exist there. Some however believe that there is evidence for the existence of a vast global network of CRUSTAL geothermal and hydrothermal cavities, some of these having been connected to the ancient deluge wherein the "...fountains of the great deep were broken up". This allegedly occurred as magma-heated stratas of subterranean water-filled caverns (brought to enormous pressures by an expanding and overheated mantle) suddenly burst through the crust (Gen. 7:11), like a pressure boiler of enormous proportions suddenly splitting it seams.

Looking at a map of the ocean floors, one can see what seems to be a "seam", similar to the seams of a baseball, which in ancient times apparently split or ripped its way around the entire planet. These "seams" are known as "rifts" in the ocean floor. Some have claim that the underlying basaltic rock layers within these ancient and gigantic global aqua-systems were dissolved into these global subterranean reservoirs as their temperatures and pressures increased. Eventually the pressure became so great that at the weakest point this global layer of mineralized water broke through, and the tear made its way around the world at an incredible rate. It is not difficult to imagine that such a cataclysm may have caused the sinking of ancient land masses as the underlying mega-aquifers emptied out and the overlying layers lost their support. Vast amounts of this overheated water — which had previously been dissolving the basaltic rock layers surrounding it — exploded to the surface, thus explaining why the oceans now contain a large percentage of 'salt' content. These underlying chambers, many of which collapsed yet many of which apparently remained intact, are believed to exist throughout the moho and crustal regions of the planet, just above the upper mantle. This 'Mohorovicic Discontinuity', or boundary point between the upper crust and lower mantle, is 'on the average' a dozen or so miles below the surface — or from a few miles below the ocean trenches to a few dozen miles below large mountain ranges. So it is possible that caverns of immense extent, containing life-supporting conditions, may conceivably exist to depths of 40-50 miles, especially under the larger mountain ranges. Below that (beyond the Moho) the pressure and temperature extremes would make physical life unbearable, if not impossible.

Other higher-level cavities created through geoseismic activity may also exist, cavities which may dwarf the Flint Ridge- Mammoth Caves of Kentucky or New Mexico's Carlsbad-Lechuguilla cavern systems. It is suggested that THESE may contain conditions sufficient to support physical life (i.e. air, water, subterranean flora and fauna, and perhaps even electromagnetically-induced illumination diffused throughout the underground "atmosphere" through a phenomena somewhat similar to the effect produced by the Aurora Borealis or "Northern Lights". In this case it has been suggested that powerful electromagnetic currents moving through the earth and interacting with the underground atmosphere may account for the diffused twilight illumination permeating the underground atmosphere, as has been described in various accounts of those who claim to have managed to find their way into the more extensive and deeper cavern systems).

There have been several accounts concerning individuals who have encountered human beings — some who spoke the native language and others who spoke a language entirely foreign — within deep underground tunnels and caverns. There are many such cases, but we will concern ourselves with only one of these at this point (and will reserve the others for later in the text)... an incident which may be one the most well-known and most well- documented accounts of this type:

Sometime during the 12 century, a monastic chronicler in England by the name of "Gervase of Tilbury" recorded a strange account of two "children" who suddenly appeared near a small town near Bury St. Edmunds, England. The account was also recorded in the writings of several other chroniclers who lived at the time or sometime afterwards. These include: William of Newbury — HISTORIA RERUM ANGLICARUM, written in Yorkshire, England (1136-1198?); Abbot Ralph of Coggeshall — CHRONICON ANGLICARUM; and also the chroniclers Giraldus Cambrensis and Walsingham. The account was more recently related in FLYING SAUCERS UNCENSORED, by Harold A. Wilkins (Citadel Press., New York, N.Y. 1955., pp. 97-98). From their combined accounts we can piece together the following bizarre story which the chroniclers swore to be true:

One warm, sunny day in the 12th century some farmers and other residents of the small town of Wolfpittes, England (some seven miles distant from the larger village of Burry St. Edmunds) were startled to see two young children wandering around, as if disoriented, in some ancient 'pits' or 'trenches' known to the locals as the 'Wolf-Pitts' — after which the small village had taken it's name. These excavations were ancient, but no one seemed to know when or by whom they were dug, but the consensus was that they were at least partly artificial, and very ancient. The most shocking thing about the children, which the residents of Wolfpittes encountered, was that they had skin which was olive-green in color, yet the rest of their features were as human as the average Englishman.

The villagers attempted to communicate with the children but were unsuccessful, as they soon discovered that the young boy and girl spoke a language which was completely unfamiliar to the villagers. The townspeople had compassion on the children and took them to the village and offered them various different kinds of food, all of which they seemed unfamiliar with and which they refused. However, when they were shown some beanstalks, they took them greedily, but instead of opening the bean-pods, the children attempted to open the stalks themselves, as if they had been accustomed to opening stalks in this way (apparently a practice they had learned in the land from which they emerged). Upon finding nothing in the stalks, the children began to weep. Unfortunately, the shock of entering our world was too much for the young boy, and even though he became partly acclimated to other forms of food, he nevertheless became weaker and weaker and finally died as few years afterwards. The young girl, however, adjusted quite well to her new surroundings. In fact she eventually grew into a mature, beautiful woman, and later married a gentleman from the nearby town of Kings Lynn. As time passed, her husband patiently instructed her in the complexities of the English language, and soon she was able to communicate fairly well, and the story she told of where she had come from and how she had arrived in our 'world' with her brother was even more incredible.

She told her husband that her people all had skin similar to hers, or rather similar to what her skin had once been like, as over a period of years and exposure to the outer elements the greenish tinge had left her. She described her world as a cavernous, subterranean country of enormous size, a country which went by the name of "St. Martin's Land." The land in which she lived was described as 'twilight' in nature, yet there was a large underground river, on the other side of which there was another land more brightly lit. One day, she and her brother were herding some type of underground animal when they heard something like the sound of 'bells' emerging from one of the cave passages or tunnels which lined the perimeter of this underground land. Out of extreme curiosity, they entered this tunnel and followed the passage upwards for what could have been a few days, although in their underground land it is probable that they did not have any concept of what 'day' or 'night' was. After their long and weary journey up the steep incline they suddenly emerged into the brilliant sunlight of the British countryside. The change from their twilight world was dramatic, and the children walked around in the pits or trenches starved, half-blinded and disoriented. They shortly afterwards attempted to relocate the small opening through which they had emerged, but were unable to do so, because of the blinding light. At about this point the farmers found the children and took them to the village.

A somewhat similar incident 'may' have been repeated in the small hamlet of Banjos (or Banos) Spain in August of 1887, several hundred years after the incident at Wolfpittes and several hundred miles distant. We state that it MAY have been repeated to some degree simply because there appears to be some confusion surrounding the Banjos account, apparently due to the possibility that some well-meaning researcher may have confused the two incidents, in essence attributing some of the events that in fact took place near Wolfpittes with the Banjos account. Basically, the Banjos incident reportedly involved two children with greenish skin who emerged from a CAVERN near the town (not 'pits' or 'excavations'), spoke an unknown language, and so on, although the details are sketchy. Some of the accounts of the Banjos incident repeat the Wolfpittes story almost verbatim, as if, as we said, someone somewhere mistakenly confused the two events, perhaps due to a lack of detail in the Banjos, Spain account.

Whatever the case, it seems that SOMETHING of this general nature also occurred in this Spanish hamlet, even though the exact sources of that particular story are more difficult to trace than are the sources for the Wolfpittes account. Paris Flammonde refers to this account in his book: THE AGE OF FLYING SAUCERS (Hawthorn Books, N.Y., p. 197), having learned it from an article in the September, 1967 issue of ORBIT Magazine, which in turn gave credit to an article in the Vol. XII, August 1967 issue of Dan Fry's UNDERSTANDING Magazine. Fry claimed that he got the story from an article by John Macklin which appeared in the December, 1966 issue of GRIT Magazine. The account also appears in John Macklin's book STRANGE DESTINIES (Ace Books., N.Y.); Jacques Bergier's LES EXTRA-TERRESTRES; and the July 22, 1970 issue of the British periodical 'WEEK-END'.

There are those who believe that similar cavern systems exist below the Southwest United States, and that the Dulce base in New Mexico was originally an entrance to one of these ancient underground kingdoms. Sources say that the humans, possibly the ancestors of the Pueblos, once ruled this under- ground kingdom. One abductee reported an "abduction" wherein he saw himself traveling in a craft through an immense cavern below the Grand Canyon. In one end of the cavern were the "ruins" of an ancient city, and in one of the walls he could see what appeared to be an elevator type of device that ascended the wall and disappeared through the roof.

In 1994 a file appeared over the Internet which originated from a person who claimed to be involved in a secret group of Hopi Indian youth, boys and girls, who were being trained by Hopi elders and a race of humanlike aliens code-named the "BLUES". The Blues were "star warriors" who were in conflict with the Grays, which they referred to as the "Children of the Serpent", a race of psychic vampires which feed off the passions, and in some cases the blood, of human beings. The Blues (the "Children of the Feather") were one of several humanlike races that had warned our government from having anything to do with the Grays in the first place. The reptilians have established themselves in the underground systems below the 4-corners area, in the VERY SYSTEMS from which the Hopis themselves were driven by the reptilian sorcerers in ancient times. The Hopis emerged through a cave in the Grand Canyon and, according to Hank Krastman who claims to have visited the underground city of Palatkwapi below Arizona, the Hopis today (both surface and subsurface dwelling) still consider the Grays of the 4-corners systems and elsewhere to be their enemies. Krastman says that the residents of Palatkwapi maintain some interaction with the neo-Mayan races of Mt. Shasta who maintain a large underground city near Prescott/Groom Creek, Arizona. They have also interbred with members of the Nordic or 'Pleiadean' Federation.

In relation to Dulce, researcher Paris Flammonde once gave what appears to be a description of the joint Illuminati-Gray 'Dulce' underground base-network below the 4-corners area, as described by researcher James Moseley:

"...The intimations of strange pressure groups, purportedly intent upon obscuring the true meaning of Flying Saucers, began arising in the early 1950's, the most famous of these being the 'three men in black' and the 'silence conspiracy,' which Major Keyhoe and others regard as an ominous element functioning within the Air Force. During the summer of 1956, SAUCER NEWS editor James Moseley postulated an addition to this enigmatic company in the June, 1956, issue of his magazine. Theorizing that Flying Saucers were originally being researched by the United States in 1946, were capable of speeds exceeding four thousand miles an hour, and were operating from a super- secret subterranean base below a southwestern state, he continued:

"'The whole project is so highly classified that ordinary military pilots and even the Air Force's saucer investigators on Project Blue Book could not possibly know about it. In fact, this type of saucer IS NOT built by the American Government AS WE ORDINARILY UNDERSTAND THE WORD 'GOVERNMENT.' As fantastic as this might sound... these saucers are actually built, operated, and maintained by an organization which is ENTIRELY SEPARATE from the military and political branches of the Government that we know about. Although a handful of people at the very top of the Government know about the existence of this project, they have no direct contact with it... I shall call this secret project, 'The Organization.'"

James Moseley, according to Flammonde, "considerably elaborated on the activities of this shadowy cabal with some very extravagant revelations."

In his book "ON THE SHORES OF ENDLESS WORLDS", Andrew Tomas relates the following account:

"The Jesuit Agnelio Oliva (1572-1542) recorded the words of an old Inca quipu reader to the effect that the real Tiahuanaco was a subterranean city exceeding the one above ground in vastness. It was believed that the entrance to the underground apartments could be gained through four tunnels. Last century one passage was evidently found as treasure hunters managed to get in, to look for gold, but only one came out. He brought out with him two gold bars but left behind his sanity. After this incident the Peruvian government decided to wall up the cave entrance..." This tunnel, according to other sources, was actually hidden among the ruins of Fort Sacsahuaman outside of and above the city of Cuzco, Peru. The explorers allegedly found their way into ancient treasure caves beneath the Temple of the Sun in Cuzco, and most of them subsequently became lost in the dark labyrinthine maze, except for the man who returned with two gold bars. There are however 'rumors' that the tunnels beneath Cuzco eventually connect with others below Lima, Peru — as well as different parts of the Peruvian Andes including the Lake Titicaca region.

Dr. Clifford Wilson, in his 'UFOS AND THEIR MISSION IMPOSSIBLE' (1974., Signet Books, N.Y.) relates the following account, submitted by Police Officer and 'abductee' Harold Schirmer (spelled 'Shermer' by others), who was the subject of experimentation by the alien group known as the 'greys':

"He...claimed that he was told where UFO bases were. Although he could not understand it, he stated there were UFO bases both underground and underwater. He wondered if perhaps these beings were careful to guard their own interests, for they gave no information that would actually endanger themselves. However, they did say that one base was out in the ocean away from Florida, out toward Bermuda. This is in the area of the infamous 'Bermuda Triangle' where so many ships and even aircraft have mysteriously disappeared during this century.

"Schirmer was further told that this particular vehicle was an observation craft, and that the occupants had been sent to collect samples of animals and vegetation. He remembered also that he was told that SOME HUMANS HAD BEEN USED in breeding experiments. He was convinced that something was done to the BRAIN PATTERNS of those who were captured, and was definite that he himself had been changed — as was evidenced by his earlier withholding of details of the sighting. By his obedience he had become almost robotlike, ready to do whatever they told him to do."

On July 14th, 1974 an article by Stoney Brakefield appeared in the Pennsylvania newspaper, NEWS EXTRA, reporting an incident which allegedly took place in 1944 near this small coal mining town, yet because of it's nature it had been covered-up for nearly 40 years until the son of the mining inspector who investigated the incident revealed it as his father (then deceased) had related it to him.

This mining inspector and a fellow investigator had been called-in to look into a "cave-in" in one of the Dixonville mines. About 15 men had either been killed or turned up missing altogether in the strange disaster. Once inside the mine the inspectors eventually came across the first victim. Although lying under a broken timber surrounded by some fallen rocks and rubble, they concluded that the cave-in certainly could not have been large enough to kill the man. The inspectors were shocked to find that the body of the miner was lacerated with claw-like markings from some unknown creature. They continued and found a few other bodies, all dead and some of which had similar claw-like marks covering them. Several other miners had vanished, and were nowhere to be seen in spite of subsequent diggings. This tragedy apparently took place after the miners had broken into an ancient tunnel of unknown origin deep in the mine. This tunnel (at the time the inspectors didn't fully recognize it as the recently discovered passage or drift) was then followed by the inspectors at approximately a 45 degree angle downwards for about half a mile until they arrived at a 'room' which 'seemed' to be the end of the passage. At this point the passage behind them just 'happened' to collapse (many accounts indicate that these underground creatures can manipulate the earth and rock and create "cave-ins" at will, as was the case in the Maltese incident mentioned earlier in the text).

A follow-up team was sent in to intersect the inspectors while this was taking place. This other crew followed the tracks of the inspectors into the mysterious tunnel and eventually found the "cave-in" and began digging through in hopes of finding the now missing investigators. In the meanwhile one inspector (the father of the man who released the story to the press) suddenly felt something like "hot breath" on the back of his neck. He closed his eyes, too terrified to see what the 'thing' was. As the other workers were breaking through, the 'creature' left by some unseen route, perhaps frightened away. The other inspector who was with him however observed the whole thing and in wild-eyed horror he exclaimed, "That thing was not of this world!"

One account concerning 'the underground' appeared in an early issue of CAVEAT EMPTOR magazine (P.O. Box 4553., Metuchen, NJ 08820-4533), and spoke of a physical encounter with a subterranean race HUMANS. The account was related by an individual whose girlfriend, 'Laressa', had phoned him one night. She was quite shaken up and in tears, and told him that a friend of hers at school had invited her to go for a ride with her out into the countryside. This girl friend was somewhat strange, and a loner and would often disappear and be away from school for days or even weeks at a time. As they were driving through the countryside, according to 'Laressa', this girl drove her car right towards a hill and before she knew what was happening the hill opened up into an underground 'road' and they eventually found themselves right in the middle of an underground city. She went on to say that the city was inhabited by the 'D-Forces', a human group who used the symbol of a 'wolf' (on jewelry, etc.), and who were in conflict with another human group called the 'A-Forces'. Both, she learned, possessed 'UFO' type craft, and the A-Forces were less powerful but were growing stronger day by day.

Could this somehow tie-in with Richard Shaver's scenario of an underground battle with 'Deros' and 'Teros'? The only difference would be that Shaver's 'Teros' were basically friendly people and his 'Deros' seemed to be a conglomeration of degenerate human techno-sorcerers whose minds and bodies have been affected by long-tern exposure to radiation, who seemed to be in league with a 'race' power-hungry Atlantean androids that had gone out-of-control thousands of years ago AND what Shaver refers to as the "vermin from space", a race of reptilian hominoids that are returning to planet earth to reclaim what they allege to be their native planet.

Theodore Illion, in his book 'DARKNESS OVER TIBET', told of the inhabitants of an underground city beneath Tibet, a city which the author himself claimed to have stumbled on during his extensive travels through the Far East. This underground community was allegedly ruled over by a powerful sorcerer who was part of an international secret society. This overlord kept the inhabitants of the underground city, many of whom were people who had 'disappeared' from the world above, under complete mind control to the point that they lacked any personality — their eyes were reported by Illion as being vacant and empty, and their lives emotionless and drone-like, much like an ant colony. Or in other words, they acted much like certain of the 'MIB'-like beings who have been encountered by UFO witnesses. This sorcerer was allegedly in contact with an infernal (reptilian?) race via a 'bottomless shaft' which descended through the city itself. When Ted Illion asked the sorcerer-overlord where the shaft led, he was told that if he found out he would die: "...there are such secrets." Illion claimed that he barely escaped the hypnotic hold of the sorcerer and fled the city, and after surviving a series of terrifying poltergeist and psychic attacks directed at him by the sorcerer, he finally found his way back to civilization and safe?

At this point we will quote from one of the many sources describing encounters with what may very well be a remnant of an antediluvian 'tunnel' network that the Atlanteans or their contemporaries had constructed before the deluge. The following account was given in a letter which was submitted to AMAZING STORIES (which described itself as a science fiction/science fact magazine), Dec. 1946 issue, p. 162. The letter was from a George A. Lehew of (at the time) 1918 W. Newport Ave., Chicago, ILL. Lehew wrote:

"Sirs... I have been a reader of AMAZING STORIES for a very long time... I too, know of one of these entrances into the world below. It is about fifty miles south of Pittsburgh, Pa., in the first range of the Allegheny Mountains. My experiment with the caves have been only partial explorations, consisting of traveling about a mile and a quarter down into the cave itself, and returning. The cave IS VENTILATED from below, and stays at a constant 50 degrees no matter what the outside temperature may be. It is a series of rooms or galleries with narrow passages from one to another. In about the sixth room down, there is a large tree trunk which could not have come from the surface as the stratosphere (sic: 'strata-sphere'? - Branton) is almost completely free from local fault; and it could never have come DOWN through the openings in the cave itself as they were small at the top, and kept getting progressively larger as they got deeper.

"I traveled down as long as I could find comparatively easy travel — about 45 degree descent all the way — and finally came to what I thought must be the end of the cave, for I could see no more openings into rooms, but on closer examination found instead a bore, about six feet across, straight down into solid rock. I turned my flash downward and could see that it must have gone straight down for at least a hundred feet, the sides were perfectly smooth, and the shaft, or bore, in a perfect round — no apparent irregularities anywhere — I had no way of descending any further, so I retraced my steps back up through the different rooms to the top of the mountain where the cave opens into this world. I made discreet inquiries of several old timers in that region, and found that in 1915, or about that year, six surveyors took gear and equipment, and spent a month in exploration of the cave, going 18 miles from the entrance, and down almost five miles below sea level. I have never gone back, but I hope to some day in the future, with escort, equipment, and supplies. I'd certainly love to see the machine that made that bore!

If you have any information on other caves in that area, let me know — they too may tie in with this one, though if they do, their connections are very deep. Also, if you can, please describe the equipment that made that vertical shaft. Oh, yes, one more interesting item — the surveyors in their exploration of the cave, distinctly heard the rumble of MACHINERY — but their calculations proved they were nowhere near a large city (surface), and they were too deep for surface noises otherwise. What is the answer?"

Another account also dealing with subsurface phenomena and 'creatures' appeared in the June, 1945 issue of AMAZING STORIES, in a letter submitted to that magazine by Jerry LaPriore (at the time) of 2024 Pleasant St., Fall River, Mass. The letter stated:

"You asked for stories that might relate to... the caves. My mother was told this story by an old man who said it was true as truth itself: This man and a friend were hunting, agreeing this time to go to a portion of the wood's to which they did not normally go. They saw a deer and gave chase. It jumped through a clump of bushes and they followed — to find themselves unaccountably in the strangest surroundings. They were in a huge cavern that had numerous passageways leading from it. Before them was a monster-like man they thought was the Devil himself. The monster stared, and the two men stared back. One of them fainted from fear, and the man who told my mother the story dragged the other away in panic, and as he did so, found himself just as mysteriously in the forest again. The old man's friend died a week later as a result of the shock he had suffered. The old man tried later to find the cave again, but failed. I know this story is true because my mother does not tell fairy tales and because she believes it."

In April, 1972 a reader submitted a letter to FATE magazine describing what, if true, may be one of the more remarkable 'encounters' with a subterranean civilization. The letter, which appeared below the heading 'SPIRITS OR SUBTERRANEAN BEINGS', stated:

"Two years ago my small son Danny and I were playing in his bedroom when we heard a sharp metallic sound as if a large steel hammer had struck the concrete BASEMENT floor three times. It took us so by surprise that Danny began to cry. I was merely curious because I had heard a noise like that several months earlier in or beneath the living room.

"I decided to lie down on the bedroom floor with my ear to it. I clearly heard the roar of MACHINERY or I should say a 'hum.' As I listened I heard something or somebody moving around and fidgeting with what sounded like machinery.

"I quickly got up and fetched a small hammer from my husband's took chest and began to tap the floor, 1-2-3, 1-2-3, etc. I had continued for about five minutes when to my surprise the 'being' beneath the floor began to tap back, 1-2-3, 1-2-3. As I listened I heard a series of noises and knocks and then a MAN'S voice began to speak, not to me but to someone else. His words were too muffled to understand.

"I called the local police and asked if there were any underground installations in our town and they said there were not.

"Frequently after that I would place my ear to the floor and always I could hear the hum of machinery but never again the man's voice.

"It is my opinion that races of people live far beneath the earth in vast networks of caverns and they have access to miracle machinery that can project sound and even images to the earth's surface. I wonder if we are confusing these subterranean beings with spirits? — WANDA LOCKWOOD, BAKERSFIELD, CALIF."

One researcher by the name of Frank D. Adams has written about the results of his own personal scientific experiments which may prove that giant cavities exist in granite at depths of more than 11 miles, conclusions which have also been supported by Louis V. King, a mathematician who calculated that, at normal temperatures, a cavity would exist at a depth of between 17.2 and 20.9 miles. The authors' findings are also supported by the recently discovered "16 Rouse Belts" which give planes of fracture penetrating the globe.

Dr. Ron Anjard, in an article in the Summer, 1978 issue of PURSUIT Magazine, claimed personal knowledge of 44 underground cities beneath the surface of North America, six of which are alleged to be on the West Coast. His information comes from anonymous American Indian sources. When we relate this to the large number of migration legends (to and from cavern realms) which exist among the native Amerindians, then we may conclude that certain tribes still retain intimate knowledge of underground civilizations who are related to them via distant ancestral links. In the case of the Hopi Indians, according to Dr. Hank Krastman, certain Hopi elders maintain contact with their subterranean cousin-tribes to this day. There are also indications that some entire tribes literally moved underground as a result of the encroaching Anglosaxon invasion of the America's. Similar allegations are made in relation to the Mayas, the Incas, and several other Central and South American tribes as well.

Karl Brugger, in his book 'THE CHRONICLE OF AKAKOR' (Boohi Tree Books., Delacorte Press., N.Y., 230 pp), gives the history — as given to the author by one of their chiefs — of the Ugha Mongulala tribesman, whose ancestors were allegedly part of a vast empire which covered South America in ancient times. Some of these ancient people, the chief claimed, left the planet in aerial vessels to explore other parts of the solar system and beyond, leaving behind vast subterranean cities beneath the Andes mountains and western Brazil. In 1971, due to the constant encroachment of white settlers or invaders into their territory, 30,000 survivors of the Ugha Mongulala allegedly escaped to this ancient system of underground cities, consisting of 13 separate subterranean complexes all connected by tunnels, one of which is said to extend to Lima, and others of which are located throughout the Andes Mountain range of Peru.

Michael Burke, in his article 'GREEN THING SPARKS RUMORS' (THE VALLEY NEWS DISPATCH, New Kensington, Tarentum and Vandergrift, PA., Mar. 5, 1981 issue) described a short 'lizard' like creature which has been seen walking on two legs like a man, was reportedly about 3-ft tall, and "half humanoid and half dinosaur". The creature was seen emerging from a sewer tunnel near New Kensington. A group of children chased the infant or young dinosauroid, one of the more courageous of them momentarily grabbing it from behind, at which point it let out a squealing or screeching sound, and then slipped from his hands and escaped back into the sewer tunnel. In later encounters children attempted to pour gasoline on the creature and light it on fire, although most of the fuel fell on the ground, and the reptoid escaped unscathed.

Dr. Earlyne Chaney, in an article titled 'ODYSSEY INTO EGYPT' (which appeared in her occult-oriented magazine VOICE OF ASTARA — May, 1982), tells of a discovery she and researcher Bill Cox were shown during their tour of Egypt. Their tour guides confided to the two mystics their knowledge of two tunnels, neither of which had been fully explored. One was in the temple of Edfu between Luxor and Cairo in the ruins of El Tuna Gabel; and the other near Zozer's Step Pyramid at Cairo near Memphis-Saqqarah, within the tomb of the Bull, called 'Serapium'. The Egyptian government reportedly sealed both tunnels because of fears of certain archaeologists that the tunnels "lead too deeply down into the depths of the earth," and because they found the earth to be "honeycombed with passages leading off into other depths," and the possibility of explorers becoming lost. If such labyrinths do exist, then it may explain one story concerning strange men dressed like "ancient Egyptians" who have been seen, according to witnesses, deep within unexplored tunnels below the region of Cairo and the Great Pyramids.

This may also be a possible confirmation of an account which appeared in NEVADA AERIAL RESEARCH'S "LEADING EDGE" Publication, to the effect that the U.S.(?) Government secretly maintains a HUGE base within a cavern of tremendous size (several miles in diameter) beneath the desert sands of Egypt. Could this tie-in with the vague references to the subterranean culture or cultures known as the 'Phoenix Empire' (according to "Commander X", who alleged that representatives of this empire have been seen in the deeper levels of the "Dulce" base); and the 'Giza' or 'Giza' People (a subterranean cult of Illuminati-like Imperialists who, so the "Pleiadeans" claim, are working with other power-groups in a covert attempt to take over the governments of planet earth)?

Vaughn M. Greene, in a letter which appeared in issue No. 14 of Richard Toronto's SHAVERTRON letter-zine, spoke of a possible 'entrance' to cavern systems near the bottom of the elevator landing within the Hoover dam facility near Las Vegas (not far from the Mojave Desert), which holds back Lake Mead. Several people have reported unusual "alien" encounters near this reservoir. Early construction workers allegedly broke into (and probably resealed) large caverns while blasting out the cliffs near the base of the dam. In the lower elevator landing, according to Mr. Greene, there was a "wild tile inlay on the floor, with signs of the zodiac and all sorts of stuff suggesting an entrance." He suggests a possible connection between this and the caverns which the workers reportedly broke into. Could this tie-in with similar accounts given by others that an underground base exists beneath Page, Arizona?

This underground facility is believed by several sources to connect the S-4 underground base in Nevada to the Dulce underground base in New Mexico via tube-line? The Glen Canyon — Lake Powell Hydroelectric dam in Page 'might' provide a power source for such an underground installation, and is the most likely area in or around Page for an 'entrance' (a deep gorge several hundred feet deep leading into the Grand Canyon, a large government facility, a hydroelectric power source, etc.). This is however only supposition. It is said that Navaho dam, by the way, is a major power-source that supplies a considerable percentage of electricity for the upper human-occupied levels of the Dulce Base. This may suggest that other similar bases are at least partially powered by hydroelectric dams.

Paxson C. Hayes, in writings of his which appeared in early issues of BSRF's (Borderland Sciences Research Foundation's) publication 'ROUND ROBIN,' referred to the discovery (one which he claimed to have made himself) of the mummified remains of a race of 7-ft. tall humans who lived in huge caverns 9,000 feet below the surface of North America.

Dana Howard, in her book, 'VESTA, THE EARTHBORN VENUSIAN' (Essene Press., Corpus Christi, TX. 1950), includes a chapter in her book which tells of a remnant of an ancient race or human civilization still in existence underground. These hidden people are said to reside within one of the mountain ranges adjacent to the Imperial Valley area on the outskirts of the Mojave Desert of California.

John A. Keel, on p. 145 of his book 'THE MOTHMAN PROPHECIES' (Signet Books., N.Y., 1975.), states: "An engineer, Rex Ball, swears he came upon a mysterious underground installation in Georgia in 1940, manned by small Oriental-looking men in coveralls and a few American military officers. When he was caught in the tunnels, one of the officers issued the curt command, 'Make him look like a nut!' He woke up in a field, uncertain whether his experience had been real or a dream. That seems to be the battle cry of the phenomena. 'Make him look like a nut!'" And on p. 192 of the same book:

"...A man on Long Island (informed Keel that he) was frantically making preparations for the big evacuation. He even traveled to a secret underground flying saucer base, in a black Cadillac with a dashboard festooned with flashing colored lights, where he participated in a 'dry run.' Other normal human beings were present, he said, and manned various kinds of equipment to communicate with the rescue spaceships somewhere overhead. 'Funny thing, John,' he mused, 'all the equipment was manufactured by Western Electric, Hallicrafters, and other U.S. companies.'"

Tal LeVesque, in an article titled 'UNDERGROUND UFO BASE SUSPECTED BY OFFICIALS IN WASHINGTON', which appeared in the Vol. 2., No. 2., issue of THE HOLLOW HASSLE, described a suspected UFO Base which is believed by some to lie under the Yakima Indian Reservation southeast of Tacoma, Washington.

The book 'THE LIFE OF THE CAVE', by Mohr and Paulson (1966), gives evidence of extended animal migration underground beneath the central-eastern U.S., indicated by troglodytes (cave-dwelling animals) found in widely separated caves which are identical with each other, indicating past interconnections which have become blocked. These caverns are found from time to time during deep drilling operations.

A researcher by the name of Jon Singer, stated the following in an article of his which appeared in 'THE MISSING LINK' newsletter: "Our nation's capital has it's share of Fortean mysteries. There is supposed to be a tunnel complex under the Octagon House at 1741 New York Avenue, NW. Dr. John Thornton, the architect who designed the Capitol Building, built some (but not all) of the tunnels. The course of at least two of the tunnels is known. One is supposed to go to the White House and the other supposedly leads to the Potomac. The tunnels are supposedly blocked up. Jim Brandon, on p. 58 of (his book) 'WEIRD AMERICA' (1978. E.P. Dutton & Co., N.Y.), added that the tunnels built by Dr. Thornton were only part of a much older and larger tunnel network constructed by colonists from Atlantis. Unfortunately his sources were two unidentified psychics, so this must be a fascinating rumor." (Note: This would depend upon whether these "revelations" were received by these psychics via entirely metaphysical or "occultic" means, in which case they should be viewed with great suspicion, or whether they based their claims on actual physical accounts).

However, Richard Toronto, editor of SHAVERTRON, claimed that some years ago as a result of a printed request for information on subterranean anomalies, a scientist contacted him offering a 10-page report on a system of tunnels he had personally investigated beneath Washington D.C. He stated that the tunnels were built by a very ancient race, and that the walls consisted of a diamond-hard, glassy or glaze-like substance (similar to other deep tunnels that have been described as existing beneath the surface of northern Arkansas and elsewhere). As far as we know, Mr. Toronto never did actually get his hands on the report.

THE MOJAVE DESERT'S GREATEST SECRETS

Brad Steiger, in his book 'STRANGE DISAPPEARANCES' (Lancer Books., N.Y. 1972) related the following (MIB-related?) incident:

"...at sundown on February 12, 1953, witnesses told police that they had watched an automobile enter the throat of a storm drain near Willowbrook and Greenleaf Avenues in Los Angeles. Officers arrived on the scene within ten minutes, and according to the Los Angeles HERALD AND EXPRESS, they followed the fresh tire-tread marks into the tunnel for seven miles. Other policemen and flood control district workers continued the search for the automobile by dropping through manhole covers.

"The trackdown continued until midnight when, seven miles up the storm drain, THE TRACKS VANISHED. 'HERALD AND EXPRESS' newsmen who had accompanied the police on the incredible search up the tube were witnesses to the fact that: 'In the muddy silt covering the floor of the drain, the tire-tread marks were sharp and fresh. Then no more tracks.'"

Steven Brodie was a man of many talents and hobbies, among them painting and rock collecting. Several years back he decided to investigate a certain area in Arizona where, he had heard, quartz crystals could be found in abundance. Brodie convinced a friend of his, also an avid rock collector, to join him on a rock-hunting expedition to the site. After purchasing a ticket on a passenger train, they traveled to a certain small community in Arizona, which was near the area that they desired to explore.

According to researcher John J. Robinson, who related the account as he heard it from Steve Brodie, the name of the Arizona town was not given. John J. Robinson, by the way, was a well-known UFOlogist in the 1950's, and the account as it was related to him was discussed by Robinson during an interview which was heard by tens of thousands of listeners to the 'Long John Nebel' radio talk-show on station W.O.R. of New York, in March of 1957.

The two rock hounds had their eyes on one particular bluff, which they could see in the distance from the town they were in. Other town residents heard about their plans and warned them against going to that bluff, stating that SEVERAL people had in the past disappeared without a trace in that area. Brodie and his friend blew-off their warnings, considering them mere superstitions which they should not take seriously, and set out towards the forbidden bluff. They had no sooner approached the base of the bluff than out of the shadows emerged two beings who were each cowled in a dark cloak and hood, making it very difficult to discern their features or whether they were even human or not. After being confronted, Brodie's friend panicked and attempted to make a run for it. Steve swore that at this point one of the black cloaked figures raised some kind of weapon and a brilliant pencil beam of light shot from it and hit his friend, who cried out in agony and immediately fell down motionless. From what Brodie could gather his friend had been killed, although he never did see his body after that.

Following this, one of the 'beings' came up to Brodie, who did not resist but stood where he was. While still in a state of shock, one of the creatures placed some type of device over his head, like a metal headset with two metallic 'discs' which fitted over his temples. At this point he started to lose consciousness.

The next thing Steve remembered after gaining consciousness again was of being in some type of dungeon or cavern-like enclosure, within a prison-like cell. Other humans were there as well. Most of the people there seemed to be under some type of trance or mind control, and as far as he knew, he was one of them. He dimly recalls 'waking up' a few times, but usually when this happened one of the dark-robed creatures would come over to the cage or enclosure where he was and point a rod-shaped device at him, at which point he would black out again. During one of his brief conscious episodes, he had a chance to talk to another prisoner, a girl, who told him that their dark-robed captors were known as the 'dero'.

That, basically, was all that he remembered. The incredible part of the story, however, was the fact that several months afterwards he suddenly 'came to' and found himself conscious once again. He suddenly realized that he was walking down the streets of New York City! He had no idea how he got there, or where he had been the past six months. It was like 'waking up' out of a bad dream or nightmare, the majority of which he could not remember. In addition to this, he found that someone had given him a haircut (he didn't know whom).

Whether or not this account has any connection to the many 'rumors' of strange and ancient caverns and tunnels below New York City is uncertain. Some cautiously speak of such tunnels as being used by a MIB-like secret society, some of these tunnels connecting with the lowest subbasements of the Empire State building and other Manhattan structures. Some allege that such tunnels are the possible destination of many of those who mysteriously end up 'missing' in New York City every year. Whether these are mere unfounded 'rumors' is anyone's guess, at least until solid evidence 'surfaces' to prove such accounts.

John J. Robinson made several visits to Mr. Brodie, and from his perceptions of the men he felt that Brodie was sincere in what he was saying, but Steve was constantly paranoid and in fear that he was 'being followed' or that someone or something was constantly watching or stalking him. Also, Steve Brodie would often paint bizarre other-worldly landscapes, even though he wasn't used to painting in that style until after his 'experience', which Robinson thought peculiar. Then one day Robinson stopped by Brodie's apartment to pay him a visit and he was no where to be found. No one seemed to know what happened to him, and that was the last time Mr. Robinson ever saw Steve again.

The 'Steve Brodie' account, incidentally, was also related in an article in the

Vol. 1, No. 3, 1971 issue of 'STRANGE' magazine, and also in early issues of 'SAUCER NEWS', of which John J. Robinson — who lived in Jersey City, New Jersey at the time — was assistant editor.

In his book 'ON THE SHORES OF ENDLESS WORLDS' (Souvenir Press), Andrew Tomas, in his chapter "Labyrinths and Serpents", states: "...According to legend, King Minos of Crete ordered his architect Daedalus to construct the labyrinth, a maze of passages so ingeniously devised that even the builder himself could not find his way without a plan. In the centre lived the Minotaur, half bull, half human, to whom the Greeks sent seven youths and seven maidens as a tribute every nine years. The Minotaur was slain by Theseus who was able to find his way out of the labyrinth thanks to a ball of thread given to him by Ariadne. This myth has been interpreted as an historical record of the construction of the palace of Minos in Knossos which contains innumerable galleries and rooms. On the other hand, this myth may have an entirely different interpretation, similar to a cryptogram, which conceals the existence of a secret repository of underground chambers and passages..."

Although this might seem to be just a 'legend', there are actual accounts of alleged encounters with paraphysical (part supernatural, part physical) 'demoniacal' creatures such as the satyrs, centaurs, and Minotaurs, etc., which have been described in Greek mythology. Such encounters often involve paraphysical "poltergeist-like" phenomena and manipulation of mind and matter. According to some sources, a race of beings possessing a combination of humanoid, angelic and animallike characteristics predated Adamic civilization and were involved in the original rebellion and conspiracy against the Creator (other 'mythical' beings such as mer-people, unicorns, fairies and such were also traditionally involved in the fall. Like the angels them- selves, some of them were deceived by the followers of Lucifer whereas others escaped the fall and remained true to the Creator). The creatures mentioned in the 9th chapter of the book of Revelation 'may' be this type of demonic or fallen entity. These creatures were apparently distinct from the purely spiritual angelic and fallen-angelic beings. Whether the following account describes an encounter with such a fallen race(s) remains to be seen. The letter we quote here appeared in the Winter, 1962 issue of THE HIDDEN WORLD, one of several publications which grew out of the "Shaver Mystery" controversy of the late 1940's:

"Mr. Richard Shaver: Hoping this letter finds you in the best of health. My name is Frank J. Mezta. I live in the County of Imperial Valley, City of Calexico, California.

"Through accident I happened to stumble into your book HIDDEN WORLD issue No. A-1 and just recently A-2. I sometimes wonder if it was luck or deliberate action on the part of a tero. All my life, I have been looking and asking for certain, unsolved and unanswered questions regarding civilization, our ancestors and the beginning of time. I believe your book gave me the best answers. Let me tell you a few of my expeditions.

"Two years ago, we went treasure hunting in the interior of Mexico, which turned out to be a flop. But in that excursion some strange things happened to us, which at the time we wrote off as superstition. We went to this place where we were supposed to enter; but suddenly a fright with chills came over me, something I had never felt before. Something like a sixth sense, like if I knew something was going to happen to me. I didn't go in and neither did anybody else. Next day we approached the cave again, only this time I wasn't afraid and I let the group inside. This cave was tremendous in size, and leading passages everywhere. Some of these passages or chambers, sometimes being 30 ft. high and 100 ft. long (contained) connecting tunnels. We finally gave up, but in retrieving we found two leading passages instead of the one we had entered. This startled us, and we set to investigate the second tunnel. It just kept winding and going down so we finally gave up and got out of there.

"When we got back to the village we struck a conversation with two Mexican Indians, and they told us that whatever we did, not to go into the enchanted caves. We got curious and asked them where these so called enchanted caves were. They gave us directions and that was exactly where we had entered a few days ago. We asked them what happened in these caves. They told us that people that went in there, never came out, that while in there, the entrances and tunnels would change, which happened to us, and we didn't know about this till after we had been in there. Then they told us the strangest thing, which at the time we said these people are superstitious. They said that they went with an expedition with 20 or 30 men hired by an American man to look into this cave. This happened about 10 or 15 years ago they said. Four or five of the men had revolvers, they were well equipped with lights and tools. While they were working there all of a sudden in the far end there appeared a half man and bull head like a bull upright. This description fits the one you have on your front cover on issue A-1. And next to him was a naked midget or little boy. They pulled out their revolvers but they wouldn't fire, and their lights went out. There was confusion, and several men were killed in the scramble and nobody returned after that — Frank J. Mezta, 939 Genge, Calexico, Calif."

David Perkins, in a letter of his which appeared in the Vol. 1, No. 1 issue of 'THE HOLLOW HASSLE', told of a strange "breathing well" that drillers had broken into 17 miles east of Walsenberg, CO. Other strange occurrences had been found on the ranch or farm where the well was located, including unexplained cattle mutilations. Representatives from the Colorado School of Mines came out to investigate the well, which seemed to 'breath' in and out with the rising and falling of the tides, and they excitedly suggested that a tunnel lay below which may have connected with a similar tunnel which the Colorado School of Mines had tracked from the Gulf of Mexico and as far as Oklahoma. A 'possible' connection to this: one source alleged that an 'alternative 002' type of underground 'city' maintained by a secret society, can be entered via a 'lodge' in the Uncompagre Mts., also in southwest Colorado. Also, a large "Masonic Park" exists in this same area (any connection?).

Morris K. Jessup's "THE CASE FOR THE UFO — ANNOTATED EDITION" (a classic collectors item republished by Gray Barker in a limited edition) was FIRST 'reprinted' by the VARO Corp. of Texas. This was an electronics firm which was commissioned to print the book specifically for the Navy. The original 'CASE FOR THE UFO', written by UFOlogist Morris K. Jessup, was not too revealing in itself but was merely a collection of theories and documented sightings of UFOs just like other books which were making the rounds. The interesting thing however is that Jessup was approached by Naval Officials and shown an ANNOTATED copy of his own book which had been sent to them by persons unknown. Later a 'Carlos Allende', apparently one of three mysterious informants, contacted Jessup, insinuating that he and the three other annotators were representatives of an ancient hi-tech earth-based society of possible "gypsy" heritage. The notations and comments were apparently based on the secret knowledge of their race.

They spoke of force fields, aerial ships, forces working in the Bermuda Triangle, ancient nuclear war on earth, diamond crystals, and many other subjects of a highly technical nature. What caught the Navy's interest however were references to the so-called 'Philadelphia Experiment', a Navy project which has been confirmed by others that involved an attempt to make a destroyer, the 'U.S.S. ELDRIDGE', invisible optically as well as to radar. An intense electromagnetic field was allegedly generated and the ship did go invisible to the point that it's waterline could be seen in the water — minus the ship itself.

But then something happened, a brilliant blue flash was observed and the men on the ship were thrown into chaos. Apparently the experiment in it's attempt to make a ship invisible had broken through the electromagnetic barrier between two worlds and loosed a whole Pandora's box of unknown forces. What happened from that point on has been debated. Some of these reported side effects included:

* The appearance of Greenish fogs similar to those observed in the Bermuda Triangle; nicknamed the 'molasses' or the 'push'.

* In some cases the death of servicemen who became caught up in possible underlying electrical currents which set their bodies on fire in a type of spontaneous human combustion.

* The permanent disappearance of servicemen during and after the experiments into a parallel time-space reality.

* The induced invisibility, time freezing, or teleporting of Navy workers and at least one ship at the Philadelphia Shipyard.

* Workers in the 'Experiment' state that a horrifying side effect involved the tendency of workers to phaseout into another parallel time-space existence wherein they might be able to observe our 'world' yet would be invisible and intangible, "phantoms" who are neither alive or dead as we know it. Some reports included a jet pilot involved in the original experiment who just 'disappeared' from the cockpit his aircraft, causing the death of a passenger; A man who 'walked through a wall' in the sight of his family and was never seen again; A group of men involved in the experiment who 'disappeared' into and out of a greenish fog during a bar room brawl to the consternation of their opponents; And at least one man (who was presumed to have died or disappeared in one of the experiments) who would 'appear out of nowhere' at his mother's home, crying and asking for food, etc.

* In at least one case there was the 'recovery' of crewmen who were caught in a TIME FREEZE for several decades, only to be pulled from an alternate 'timeflow' by none other than Dr. John Von Neumann and his associates. Actual non-paradoxical "time travel" (the only kind that reportedly exists or can exist) may have been involved in this recovery.

The Experiments were reportedly assisted by Nikola Tesla, Dr. Von Neumann, A. Townsend Brown, Edward Cameron, John Hutchinson, Dr. Emil Kurtenauer and other top scientists, utilizing Einsteinian theory. However Tesla reportedly sabotaged one of the first experiments after being convinced it would be harmful to the humans involved. Rumor had it that Tesla was in contact with extraterrestrials (Pleiadeans operating from the Red Planet, Mars), and that UFO's were involved with the experiment in some way, attempting to guide the experiments in an advisory capacity via their contacts with Nikola Tesla. Tesla allegedly quit the project over the fact that too many servicemen were being 'sacrificed' by well-meaning Nazi-phobes who were insistent on developing the technology to aid the War Effort before the Germans could gain the upper hand in the War. The UFO occupants in contact with Tesla allegedly warned of the dangers, however many these warnings went unheeded by Navy Intelligence...

(Note: 40 years later the project was reportedly taken over and continued by a cabal of CIA agents in league with the Bavarian Illuminati of Germany, and it's fellow occult lodge, the Bavarian Thule Society which had created the Nazi Empire. These experiments were carried out in an underground base below Montauk Point, Long Island, and involved time-space window experiments and mass microwave mind-control. However, by that time the Pleiadeans were out of the picture all-together, since these fascists who had wrested control of the 'Philadelphia' technology from Navy Intelligence were at that time in full cooperation with the alien Grays in a joint effort to establish a one- world National Socialist Empire. This war between Navy and Nazi intelligence went "underground" after the Allied Invasion of Germany. There are allegations that Navy Admiral Richard E. Byrd and 4,000 elite Navy forces even made a secret attempt to destroy a supersecret underground Nazi stronghold in Antarctica code-named "New Berlin". This massive base was reportedly inhabited by over 2,000 Nazi-S.S. scientists, and nearly 1,000,000 lay Nazis [and slave-workers from the concentration camps], all of whom had mysteriously disappeared from Germany throughout the course of the war. This secret war is said to continue today within the Nevada Military complex between Navy Intelligence's "COM-12" who maintain contact with the Pleiadeans, and the CIA-Thule Society's "AQUARIUS" cult which has maintained ties with the reptilian Grays that may date back before the beginning of World War II - Branton)

As for M.K. Jessup, who was the recipient of several of the "Allende" revelations, the Philadelphia Experiment was described in even more detail within the letters that he received from the mysterious Carl Allen, or "Carlos Allende" (could Allende's contemporaries have been tied-in with the UFO's that allegedly guided the experiments?). Jessup continued in his investigation of the Philadelphia Experiment or 'Project Rainbow'. At one point he informed a research associate that he had some startling revelations, and that he would bring the information over to him personally. Jessup left to deliver the revelations, but he never arrived at his friends house. It is almost as if some dark organization was intent on preventing these revelations, whatever they were, from reaching the public.

Jessup was found suffocated to death in his car, near a park, the result of carbon monoxide poisoning via a hose which was attached to his tailpipe and run into the car. It was said that when he was found, Jessup was still barely alive. However there were no reports of any attempts to save his life. In fact, the research documents containing the "revelations" never turned up, and Jessup took his secret with him to the grave. The "authorities" who "responded" to his death seem to be at least partially implicated. There is also the strong possibility that Jessup's death was "fixed" to look like a suicide. The mystery has not yet been solved.

John Keel, in his book 'OUR HAUNTED PLANET' (1968., Fawcett., Greenwich, Conn.) pp. 113-114, relates the following:

"...Another group of CIA-baiting researchers is now over- lapping into ufology. They are the comparatively small teams of amateur sleuths dedicated to investigating the assassination of President Kennedy. Here the black Cadillacs and the slight, dark men in black suits are viewed as Cubans and CIA agents. Paranoia runs high because now over fifty witnesses — as of 1968 —, reporters, and assassination investigators have met with sudden death, under the most suspicious circumstances. The full story of Kennedy's murder in Dallas in 1963 is filled with incredible details, many of them similar to things found in the most mysterious of the UFO incidents. Photos and physical evidence have vanished or been tampered with just as in so many UFO cases. A wide assortment of mystery men have been involved, including DOPPELGANGERS of the late Lee Harvey Oswald — see Richard Popkin's 'THE SECOND OSWALD'. This other Oswald even turned up at a public rifle range before the assassination, making a nuisance of himself (so the witnesses would be sure to remember him?), he FIRED AN UNUSUAL GUN WHICH SPAT OUT BALLS OF FIRE AT THE TARGET. He also visited an automobile showroom and went for a demonstration ride in a new car. The real Oswald could not drive. His whereabouts at the time of these incidents are known... and he was nowhere near the rifle range and auto agency. The huge WARREN REPORT contains numerous pieces of sworn testimony describing MIB-type men in the vicinity of Dealey Plaza and the School Book Depository building immediately before and after the assassination. Long-haired men were seen. This may not sound extraordinary, but remember that long hair was most unusual in 1963. The Beatles did not begin to make an impression until 1964, and the long-hair fad did not get underway until 1965-66..."

Researcher Val Valarian in the early 1990's investigated the experiences of a woman who claimed abductions on numerous occasions near Mt. Lassen, California (see: LEADING EDGE Magazine, June 1992 issue). Her 'abductors', she claimed, were humans of a generally unsympathetic and manipulating nature who were working with the reptilian 'grays'. During her encounter she saw the typical grays, a larger 'gray' with orange-red eyes and vertical-slit pupils, and of course the humans themselves. At one point a 'woman' took off a helmet in front of her, which seemed to be used to cover her features. Immediately someone from another room began cursing and told her to put the helmet back on.

This abductee also referred to a 'head-doctor' who implemented a type of 'induced psychosis' (split personality?) on her through some type of techno-hypnotic manipulation.

Mt. Lassen has been described by others as being a 'doorway to another world', and according to early contributors to Ray Palmer's AMAZING STORIES magazine during the 'Shaverian' era, strange voices have been heard there, and even rocks from the size of pebbles to basketball-size have mysteriously showered down on people who have approached certain areas of the mountain, and this without any outward sign of volcanic activity from the mountain itself.

Some years ago a man by the name of Ralph B. Fields submitted an account to AMAZING STORIES Magazine (Dec. 1946 issue, pp. 155-157), with the assurance that it was true and actually happened. He and a friend of his who lived at the base of Mt. Lassen in California stated that they had read an article in a magazine telling of the unusual quality of bat guano as a fertilizer, and that it was a very valuable resource. Hoping to make a quick buck, they decided to climb the mountain in search of caverns which might contain the valuable fertilizer.

On about the third day of their journey they discovered behind an outcropping of rock a small entrance to a cave, at about the 7000 ft. level. They immediately chose to explore, and soon found that the passage widened considerably. They noticed that the walls seemed to be smooth and glazed, as if the rock had been fused by intense heat in some ancient time.

They continued deeper until to their horror they saw a light up ahead of them. Shortly after this they were confronted with five 'normal' looking men wearing the usual surface attire that was common at the time, flannel shirts, etc. These strangers asked the two young men what they were doing, and when they explained about the 'guano' they had the impression that the 'men' did not believe them. One of them, appearing to be in his mid- 50's, said 'I think you had better come with us.' They were then taken to a large machine or contrivance nearby which appeared to be sled-like, with a copper-colored metal-like sheet covering its underside. It also seemed to hover perpetually a few inches above the ground. At that point they were taken onto the 'sled' (which they later learned was constructed, along with the tunnel itself, by an ancient and possibly antediluvian race, and was based on a 'carbon' and possibly electromagnetic propulsion system.) The 'sled' could reach great speeds and seemed to follow a metal 'strip' that ran along the center of the underground 'road'.

As if this were not enough, they were surprised once again when another 'light' quickly approached from the distance, a similar vehicle. Eventually the other 'sled' as well as the one they were on slowed and came to a stop only a few yards from each other. Their captors fled in terror while the two explorers remained on the sled, confused at this strange drama being played out before them. They noticed a brilliant pencil-beam of light which shot forth from the 'other' sled and caught the fleeing men in their path.

These new arrivals soon made it known to Ralph Fields and his friend that the men who had taken them captive were the 'horlocks'. They made it known that it was fortunate that 'they' had come this way, otherwise "you would have become horlocks yourselves, and we would have had to kill you also."

Just what a 'horlock' was they did not specify, but in connection with other accounts, they may have been mind-altered human pawns of a malevolent race, possibly even the serpent race (or Grays) if we consider later reports of collaboration between humans and reptilians near Mt. Lassen.

These 'men' did not explain much, other than the fact that there were many evil persons in the underground 'world' who have caused 'them' as well as those on the surface considerable harm. One of the men stated that such men were 'safe' because the outside world generally did not believe that they or their world existed. The dilemma of these new arrivals however, was that they felt compelled to keep the knowledge of certain of the 'ancient' technologies that had been discovered in the caverns (and much of the operation of which still remained unexplained even to these cavern dwellers) away from those on the surface, otherwise we might be inclined to destroy ourselves with these technological forces that we know very little about, based on our past experience of twisting scientific discoveries into weapons of destruction.

Fields and his friend were allowed to return to the surface, but were warned never again to enter the caves.

The above account seems to tie-in with yet another report which involved a group of speleonauts who entered one of several caverns west or northwest of Cushman, Arkansas.

These explorers claimed to have descended 5 to 6 miles (over a period of several consecutive explorations) into deep and extensive cavern systems. At one point they claimed to have broken into a glazed 'tunnel' of apparent human construction which was lined with metal-hard yet transparent tunnel walls. Through these transparent tunnel walls they were able to occasionally observe a whole "hadean" like world of bizarre subterranean creatures, including hairy humanoids who appeared to be in conflict with a race of oversized serpents or snakes, and even giant insects, cavern moths, and so on.

The most interesting part of their expedition, which was recorded in THE HOLLOW HASSLE Newsletter — formerly edited by TAL LeVesque and Mary Davis, was their alleged encounter with a race of humans approximately 8 ft. tall with pale blue skin. These people were similar in description to a certain group of 'aliens' referred to by John Lear and others which were reportedly encountered by certain astronauts on the moon — a 'top secret' which the government may never admit to. The cavers described them as about 7-8 ft. tall and possessing large 'wraparound' eyes, but nevertheless 'human' in every other respect.

The explorers insisted that they were 'led' to an underground city via a type of hidden elevator, and were even shown deeper caverns of immense size in which could be seen ancient repositories left there by a highly-advanced (scientifically) antediluvian race, some of the contents of which, they were told, remained sealed to that day! This may have been the same ancient culture which LEFT the machines that were described in the Ralph Fields account.

The explorers were told, via a type of translating device, that the inhabitants of this particular cavern city were descended from a family that in our own traditions would correspond to the Biblical description of the family of 'Noah'; that they had a 'Book of Laws' somewhat similar to our Bible; and that they had come to the Western Hemisphere thousands of years previous and discovered this already-existing subterranean 'world'. They also stated that some of their ancestors had left the earth to explore the other planets and stars long ago.

Whether the following item has any connection with the people allegedly encountered by these speleologists is uncertain. The following was related by John Keel in his book 'THE MOTHMAN PROPHECIES':

"...The Cherokees have a tradition, according to Benjamin Smith Barton's 'NEW VIEWS OF THE ORIGINS OF THE TRIBES AND NATIONS OF AMERICA' (1798), that when they migrated to Tennessee they found the region inhabited by a weird race of white people who lived in houses and were apparently quite civilized. They had one problem: their eyes were very large and sensitive to light. They could only see at night..."

Is it possible that these people may have later taken up a cave-dwelling lifestyle, if they had not done so previously, to allow themselves more comfortable living conditions?

The many caverns west of Cushman, Arkansas have given rise to many strange legends and stories. There are accounts of vast underground mazes, underground lakes, caves which lead to extremely deep pockets of stagnant air or poison gas, areas where electrical lights will not work, stories of people entering caves and never being seen again, and even accounts of hairy humanoids throwing boulders at intruders, intentionally missing them so as to scare them away. In essence it is a place which, if Jules Verne had known about it when writing his famous 'A JOURNEY TO THE CENTER OF THE EARTH', might have been the inspiration behind his novel of a daring descent into the underground world.

Lt. Col. Wendelle C. Stevens, in his book, "UFO - CONTACT FROM THE PLEIADES, A PRELIMINARY REPORT" (UFO Photo Archives., Tucson, AZ 1982., p. 79) reports on the alleged sixth face-to-face contact between Eduard 'Billy' Meier and the 'Pleiadean' Semjase. He was told of strange people, unknown to us, who live in the interior of mountains and cave's beneath the earth's surface. They are of various types, some with bluish skin, and others who often come to the surface and blend with surface inhabitants, unknown as to their true origin.

Ferdinand Ossendowski describes what may be one of the most widely accepted 'legends' in Asia, one which is in fact accepted by millions of people. This legend is described in his book 'BEASTS, MEN AND GODS' (1922. E.P. Dutton & Co., N.Y.). Quoting from the chapter 'THE SUBTERRANEAN KINGDOM' (pp. 300-311) we read:

"...On my journey into Central Asia I came to know for the first time about the 'Mystery of Mysteries,' which I can call by no other name. At the outset I did not pay much attention to it and did not attach to it such importance as I afterwards realized belonged to it, when I had analyzed and connected many sporadic, hazy and often controversial bits of evidence.

"The old people on the shore of the river Amyl related to me an ancient legend to the effect that a certain Mongolian tribe, in their escape from the demands of Genghis Khan, hid themselves in a subterranean country. Afterwards a Soyot from near the Lake of Nogan Kul showed me the smoking gate that serves as the entrance to the 'Kingdom of Agharti.' Through this gate a hunter formerly entered into the Kingdom and, after his return, began to relate what he had seen there. The Lamas cut out his tongue in order to prevent him from telling about the Mystery of Mysteries. When he arrived at old age, he came back to the entrance of this cave and disappeared into the subterranean kingdom, the memory of which had ornamented and lightened his nomad heart.

"...The favorite Gelong Lama of Prince Chultun Beyli and the Prince himself gave me an account of the subterranean kingdom.

"'Everything in the world,' said the Gelong, 'is constantly in a state of change and transition — peoples, science, religions, laws and customs. How many great empires and brilliant cultures have perished! And that alone which remains unchanged is Evil, the tool of Bad Spirits. More than 60,000 years ago a holyman disappeared with a whole tribe of people under the ground and never appeared again on the surface of the earth. Many people, however, have since visited this kingdom, Sakkia Mouni, Undur Gheghen, Paspa, Khan Baber and others. No one knows where this place is. One says Afghanistan, others India. All the people there are protected against Evil and crimes do not exist within its bourns. Science has there developed calmly and nothing is threatened with destruction. The subterranean people have reached the highest knowledge..." (Note: The 60,000 year period is probably greatly exaggerated. There have apparently been several migrations of surface tribes over the millennia and centuries into what might be referred to as this subterranean 'continent' of AGHARTA. According to an American 'monk' by the name of Ernest Dickhoff, as described in his book AGHARTA [Health Research, CA], some of the human inhabitants of this realm had established themselves as residents only within the last few centuries. This took place when an Asian Prince entered with an army of 400 followers and fought with and drove out a race of 'Reptilians' or serpent-men who had taken possession of these caverns. This invasion was initiated after it was found that these serpent beings were using black witchcraft to manipulate the minds and spirits of humans on the surface in a very negative way. According to one source, over 20,000,000 persons of various different tribes and cultures now reside in Agharti, and many more millions on the surface in Asia accept the existence of such a mysterious realm, according to writers such as Ferdinand Ossendowski, Nicholas Roerich, and others. It is said that ancient 'library' temples exists between the surface of Asia AND Agharti, in underground vaults to which certain Asian 'initiates' have access. Below or beyond these vaults, through hidden passages, the kingdom itself is believed to exist. - Branton)

"Prince Chultun Beyli added: 'This kingdom is Agharti. It extends throughout all the subterranean passages of the whole world. I heard a learned Lama of China relating to Bogdo Khan that all the subterranean caves of America are inhabited by the ancient people who have disappeared underground. Traces of them are still found on the surface of the land. These subterranean peoples and spaces are governed by rulers owing allegiance to the King of the World...'"

(Note: If the subterranea of America was once MOSTLY inhabited by humans who migrated there from the surface or other parts of the inner world, then the fact of the MODERN DAY infiltration of the saurian or serpent races [of which the Grays apparently make up the majority] into the underground of America must suggest that the major infestation occurred sometime within the last few centuries. The so-named 'King of the World' is apparently a reference to the present of a long succession of leaders over the council of Agharti, which would probably make whoever held such a position one of the most influential men in the world, for good or evil. And in fact, according to former Dulce Base security worker Thomas Castello, certain of the U.S. Presidents in the past have not only held conferences with the ruling council in 'Telos', but also with these kings of 'Agharti'. Telos, the colony below Mt. Shasta, is reportedly a western branch of the Agharti Federation. A succession of many such 'kings' have allegedly reigned over this underground realm, most of them probably receiving more adoration than they deserve, having apparently been regarded as 'gods' by some of the residents of the subterranean world, if the "King of the World" appellation is any indication. This would not necessarily be the fault of these 'kings' or leaders, many of whom according to sources HAVE acknowledged a higher potentate than themselves and prayed to Almighty 'God' on behalf of humanity. Just like the Popes of Rome or Rulers, Secretary Generals, Prime Ministers and Presidents of the surface nations, these Agharian 'kings' possessed their own personalities, some being perhaps more suited to reign than others. Nevertheless they should be respected as the elected or chosen representatives or spokes- persons for perhaps tens of millions of persons who dwell within the inner world. The name of one such king, according to one source, was 'Rigdon Jyepo'. At this writing the names of other Agharian rulers are unknown except, perhaps, to the inhabitants of Agharti or Agharta itself. - Branton)

Prince Chultun, speaking to the author, continued:

"'...In underground caves there exists a peculiar light which affords growth to the grains and vegetables and long life without disease to the people. There are many different peoples and many different tribes. An old Buddhist Brahman in Nepal was carrying out the will of the 'gods' in making a visit to the ancient kingdom of Genghis, — Siam, — where he met a fisherman who ordered him to take a place in his boat and sail with him upon the sea. On the third day they reached an island where he met a people having two tongues which could speak separately in different languages. They showed to him peculiar, unfamiliar animals, tortoises with sixteen feet and one eye, huge snakes with a very tasty flesh and birds with teeth which caught fish for their masters in the sea. These people told him that they had come up out of the subterranean kingdom and described to him certain parts of the underground country.'

"The Lama Turgut traveling with me from Urga to Peking gave me further details.

"'The capital of Agharti is surrounded with towns of high priests and scientists. It reminds one of Lhasa where the palace of the Dalai Lama, the Potala, is the top of a mountain covered with monasteries and temples.

"'...In cars strange and unknown to us they rush through the narrow cleavages inside our planet. Some Indian Brahmans and Tibetan Dalai Lamas during their laborious struggles to the peaks of mountains which no other human feet had trod have found there inscriptions on the rocks, footprints in the snow and tracks of wheels. The blissful Sakkia Mouni found on one mountain top tablets of stone carrying words which he only understood in his old age and afterwards penetrated into the Kingdom of Agharti, from which he brought back crumbs of the sacred learning preserved in his memory.'"

Ferdinand Ossendowski remembered a particular conversation with one Lama:

"'How many persons have ever been to Agharti?' I questioned him.

"'Very many,' answered the Lama, 'but all these people have kept secret that which they saw there.'"

In his book 'SHAMBHALA' (1930. Frederick A. Stokes Co., N.Y.), writer and traveler Nicholas Roerich adds some additional insights into human habitation of underground regions of central Asia. In his chapter 'SUBTERRANEAN DWELLERS' we read the following words:

"...In the Altai Mountains, in the beautiful upland valley of Uimon, a hoary Old Believer (Starover) said to me: 'I shall prove to you that the tale about the Chud, the subterranean people, is not a fantasy! I shall lead you to the entrance of the subterranean kingdom.'

"On the way through the valley surrounded by snowy mountains, my host told us many tales about the Chud. It is remarkable that 'Chud' in Russian has the same origin as the word WONDER. So, perhaps, we may consider the Chud a wonderful tribe. My bearded guide told how 'once upon a time, in this fertile valley lived and flourished the powerful tribe of Chud. They knew how to prospect for minerals and how to reap the best harvest. Most peaceful and most industrious, was this tribe. But then came a White Tzar with innumerable hordes of cruel warriors. The peaceful, industrious Chud could not resist the assaults of the conquerors, and not wishing to lose their liberty, they remained as serfs to the White Tzar. Then, for the first time, a white birch began to grow in this region. And, according to old prophecies, the Chud knew that it was the time for their departure. And the Chud, unwilling to remain subject to the White Tzar, departed under the earth. Only sometimes can you hear the holy people singing; now their bells ring out in the subterranean temples. But there shall come the glorious time of human purification, and in those days, the great Chud shall again appear in full glory.'

"Thus the Old Believer concluded. We approached some low stony hill. Proudly he showed me, 'Here we are. Here is the entrance to the great subterranean kingdom! When the Chud entered the subterranean passage they closed the entrance with stones. Now we stand just beside this holy entrance.'

"We stood before a huge tomb encircled by great stones, so typical of the period of the great migrations. Such tombs, with the beautiful remains of Gothic relics, we saw in South Russian steppes, (and) in foothills of the Northern Caucasus. Studying this hill, I remembered how during our crossing of the Karakorum pass, my sais, the Ladaki, asked me, 'Do you know that in the subterranean caves here many treasures are hidden and that in them lives a wonderful tribe which abhors the sins of earth?'

"And again when we approached Khotan the hoofs of our horses sounded hollow as though we rode above caves or hollows. Our caravan people called attention to this, saying, 'Do you hear what hollow subterranean passages we are crossing? Through these passages, people who are familiar with them can reach far- off countries.' When we saw entrances to caves, our caravaneers told us, 'Long ago people lived there; now they have gone inside; they have found a subterranean passage to the subterranean kingdom. Only rarely do some of them appear again on the earth. At our bazaar such people come with strange, very ancient money, but nobody could ever remember a time when such money was in usage here.' I asked them, if we could also see such people. And they answered, 'Yes, if your thoughts are similarly high and in contact with these holy people, because only sinners are upon the earth and the pure and courageous people pass on to something more beautiful.' (This is not to say that there are NOT subterranean areas where evil abounds, but that there are apparently protected areas where animosity between fellow human beings is greatly discouraged - Branton)

"Great is the belief in the Kingdom of the subterranean people. Through all of Asia, through the spaces of all deserts, from the Pacific to the Urals, you can hear the same wondrous tale of the vanished holy people...

(One such persistent tale is that of the "Lost Ten Tribes" of Israel. Residents of modern Israel claim descent from the tribes of Judah and Benjamin, and half of the tribe of Levi who remained behind following the great separation of Israel in the time of Solomon. The only "known" people who claim descent from other Israelite tribes are the so-called "Black Jews" of Ethiopia who insist that they are descended from the tribe of Dan. This leaves 8 1/2 tribes unaccounted for — or rather as some believe 9 1/2 tribes, because in the Book of Revelation the two Josephite lines of Ephraim and Mannassah are considered as distinct tribes. INTERESTINGLY, the tribe of DAN does not appear in the book of REVELATION among the 144,000 priests, 12,000 from each of the 12 restored tribes [this restoration has yet to take place], possibly because DAN was the tribe most responsible for leading Israel into Old Testament apostasy and idolatry. The only record of the missing 9 1/2 tribes appears in the 13th chapter of the book of II ESDRAS, one of the "apocryphal" books containing Jewish legend and tradition which were written in the 400-year non-prophetical period between the end of the Torahic or Old Testament and the beginning of the New Testement periods. This contains only a cryptic remark that the lost tribes entered an unknown land to the extreme north or northeast called ARZARETH, from where they will one day return in power - Branton)

"Even far beyond the Ural Mountains, the echo of the same tale will reach you. Often you hear about subterranean tribes. Sometimes an invisible holy people is said to be living behind a mountain. Sometimes either poisonous or vitalizing gases are spread over the earth, to protect some one. Sometimes you hear how the sands of the great desert shift, and for a moment disclose treasures of the entrances of subterranean kingdoms. But none would dare to touch those treasures. You will hear how, in the rocks, in the most deserted mountain ranges, you can see openings which connect with these subterranean passes, and how beautiful princesses once upon a time occupied these natural castles.

"From distances one might take these openings for aeries, because all which belongs to the subterranean people is concealed. Sometimes the Holy City is submerged, as in the folklore of Netherlands and Switzerland. And there is folklore that coincides with actual discoveries in the lakes and along the sea coasts. In Siberia, in Russia, Lithuania and Poland, you find many legends and fairy tales about giants who lived at times in these countries but afterwards, disliking the new customs, disappeared. In these legends, one may recognize the specific foundations of the ancient clans. The giants are brothers. Very often the sisters of the giants live on the other shores of the lakes or the other side of the mountains. Very often they do not like to move from the site but some special event drives them from their patrimonial dwelling. Birds and animals are always near these giants; as witnesses they follow them and announce their departure.

"...The endless Kurgans of the southern steppes retain around them numerous stories about the appearance of the unknown warrior, nobody knows from whence. The Carpathian Mountains in Hungary have many similar stories of unknown tribes, giant- warriors and mysterious cities. If, without prejudice, you patiently point out on your map all the legends and stories of this nature you will be astonished at the result. When you collect all the fairy-tales of lost and subterranean tribes, will you not have before you a full map of the migrations?"

According to the self-professed 'Telosian', Sharula Dux, Agharta is the largest human subterran culture in the world. Also, according to American Buddhist Robert E. Dickhoff, in his book 'AGHARTA' (referred to above), some of the Aghartan cavern networks were formerly controlled by the "serpent" people. These may have been antediluvian systems that were later taken over by the Reptilian hominoids who left the surface of the earth to preserve their race from human animosity, an animosity that was fully justified. These caverns were located beneath the region of Tibet, which would place them between the Aghartan networks to the northeast that were occupied by humans, and the Patalan networks to the southwest that were traditionally occupied by the Reptilians. This is where a major "altercation" between surface humans and subterran reptilians took place in recent centuries, according to Robert Dickhoff.

Some of the Reptilians escaped, according to other sources, back to the deeper cavern systems below the Himalayas and Hindustan, underneath which (according to Hindu legend) lies the dark and forbidden seven-leveled cavern world of the 'Nagas' or the serpent beings. Hindu legends say that the underworld 'capitol' of the Naga's empire (an empire which has been referred to in different writings as 'Nagaloka', 'Snakeworld', or 'Patala') is a major center of Reptilian activity known as 'Bhoga-vita'. The NAGAS, a race of 7-8 ft. tall green-skinned hominoid lizards, are reportedly very cunning and intelligent and have bases all over the planet. A major base which 'they' still maintain below Tibet is reportedly located in the mountains surrounding Lake Manosarowar (see: ON THE SHORES OF ENDLESS WORLDS, by Andrew Tomas., Souvenir Press. Ltd., London, England., 1974).

The Serpent Beings or the Nagas are said to possess many different kinds of machines including aerial craft. According to 'Sharula' (or Bonnie), the Aghartian Federation of humans utilizes their own space fleet (known as the 'Silver Fleet'); they assisted in the construction of Telos itself — or rather the extension of the underground metropolis from the already existing natural caverns below Mt. Shasta; and are allegedly allied to at least 100 human- occupied underground cities throughout the world, many of them in conflict with the reptilian 'Draco' species and their 'Gray' collaborators.

Sherman A. Minton Jr., a respected Reptilian and Amphibian biologist, in his book 'VENOMOUS REPTILES' (Charles Ceaibrer Sons, N.Y. 1969) quotes from some ancient Hindu legends describing the Nagas or the serpent race. These legends state that this demon-race has the ability to inflict almost instantaneous death upon a person through utilizing a cosmic 'fire' force (possibly electromagnetic energy). Minton also states the fact that the ancestors of modern-day 'snakes' once possessed limbs which became atrophied through non-use over the ages; that there are lizards with elongated snakelike bodies, a type of 'missing-link' between the saurians-lizards-and-snakes; and that nearly all reptiles with "well developed" limbs live underground! He also refers to legends which state that some Nagas were present at the birth of Guatama Siddharta (Buddha), and others which allege that a major book on YOGA was channeled at a 'well' which is believed to be an entrance to the underworld of the Naga's, located in Benares, India.

NOT ALL subterran societies are of the insidious, reptilian or reptilian-controlled variety, as further evidence of this we add the following revelations from 'Commander X', the mysterious anonymous U.S. Intelligence official who has revealed much about 'inside' government knowledge of alien civilization both beyond and beneath the earth. He is the author of the book 'UNDERGROUND ALIEN BASES', published by Tim Beckley's UFO REVIEW/Abelard Press, N.Y. Mr. 'X' was apparently very familiar with the Subterranean-world controversies that surrounded early issues of AMAZING STORIES magazine (circa 1940-1945) and 'related' publications in the early years when the science of Ufology was first beginning to emerge. This may explain his present position in U.S. Intelligence, and the sensitive knowledge that he has access to. He reveals the following paraspeleological events which reportedly took place in South America:

"..Of all the countries on the face of the Earth, none is more mysterious, or less explored, than is Brazil. Miles upon miles of this country have never been set foot upon by white man. In these areas live whole tribes of savage Indians whose civilizations are said to be akin to those existing at the time of the Stone Age. Many of those who have dared venturing into these pockets of unexplored jungle have never come out. Perhaps the case of Colonel Fawcett will be familiar to readers as an example of what I mean. He supposedly was captured by a tribe of wild Indians while in search of a 'hidden city' said to be located in the confines of the dense jungle...

"Before his death, Dr. (Raymond) Bernard had sent this writer many personal letters regarding his findings related to...underground civilization(s). We quote from these communications in the following:

"'I arrived in Brazil in 1956 and have been carrying on my research since I met a Theosophical leader who told me about the subterranean cities...that exist in Brazil. He referred to Professor Henrique de Souza, president of the Brazilian Theosophical Society, at Sao Lourenco in the state of Minas Gerais, who erected a temple dedicated to Agharta, which is the Buddhist name of the subterranean World. Here in Brazil live Theosophists from all parts of the world, all of whom believe in the existence of the subterranean cities.

"'Professor de Souza told me that the great English explorer Colonel Fawcett is still alive, living in a subterranean city in the Roncador Mountains of Matto Grosso, where he found the subterranean city of Atlanteans for which he searched, but is held prisoner lest he reveal the secret of his whereabouts (Note: Bernard refers to the inhabitants of this city as 'Atlanteans', when in fact other accounts suggest that — like the underground cities below the east coast of North America — many of these cavern cities were originally CONSTRUCTED by an ancient antediluvian race. This race might have been very similar or even akin to the lost race spoken of in the 'Atlantis' legendary, whose abandoned caverns were later re-inhabited after the flood. In 'this' sense the inhabitants might be referred to as 'Atlanteans', although the present dwellers of such underground communities probably do not have any direct 'genetic' ties to the antediluvian 'Atlanteans'. - Branton).

"'He (Col. Fawcett) was not killed by Indians as is commonly believed. Professor de Souza claimed he has visited subterranean cities, including Shamballah, the world capital of the subterranean empire of Agharta. I then went to Matto Grosso to find the subterranean city where Fawcett is claimed to be living with his son Jack, but failed to do so. I then returned to Joinville in the state of Santa Catarina, and there continued my research.

"'Just recently two explorers returned from entering a tunnel near Ponte Grosse in the state of Parana. One of them had recently entered alone and spent five days in the underworld city there. It had about 50 inhabitants plus children. The fruit orchards were recently planted, and the inhabitants received fruit from another subterranean city. During the last visit, the two explorers were met at the entrance of the tunnel by a guardian and the chief of the city, who told them that they should return in two years when the fruit trees will start to bear, but cannot enter now.

"'The same two explorers entered a tunnel in Rincon, state of Parana, and finally came to a chimney-like structure with four chains hanging down. They descended on the chains but when they came near the bottom a gas with a chemical odor started to come up and forced them to ascend. Obviously the subterranean dwellers tried to keep them from reaching the city (This seems often to be the case - Commander X).

"'Our explorer J.D. (name on file - Commander X), who is a mountain guide of the Mystery Mountain near Joinville (where there is supposed to be an entrance), said that several times he saw a luminous flying saucer ascend from the tunnel opening that leads to a subterranean city inside the mountain, in which he heard the beautiful choral singing of men and women, and also heard the 'canto galo' (rooster crowing), a universal symbol indicating the existence of subterranean cities in Brazil. He said that the saucer was so luminous that it lit up the night sky and converted it into daylight. On one occasion he met a group of subterranean men outside the tunnel. They were short, stocky, with reddish beards and long hair, and very muscular. When he tried to approach them, they vanished. Often he saw strange illuminations in this area at night which were probably produced by flying saucers (We use the name 'Mystery Mountain,' rather than reveal the true name of the mountain, so that unwanted outsiders will not come here to locate it). Throughout my many years of research I have accumulated a vast amount of data which would indicate that these entrances to subterranean cities abound throughout the region.

"'An elderly man living in Joinville once told me that he had visited a tunnel near Concepiao in the state of Sao Paulo, and saw in the distance a marvelous subterranean city with vehicles darting back and forth, evidently traveling through tunnels from one subterranean city to another.

"'Although the following report requires confirmation, it was told to me by an explorer named N.C. who said that he had visited a tunnel near Rio Casdor and had met a beautiful young woman appearing to be about 20 years of age. She spoke to him in Portuguese and SAID that she was 2,500 years old. He also met a bearded subterranean man.

(Note: Often humans encountered in aerial disks or subterranean caverns declare that they possess remarkable longevity when compared with the longevity of surface humans. On the outset this might sound next to impossible, unless a revolutionary scientific breakthrough on the part of these human 'aliens' has allowed them to retard the aging process to an extreme degree. Or, could the possibly that they are separated from the degenerating radioactive contamination and solar rays prevalent on the surface explain their greater alleged longevity? Another possibility would be that through bionics or biological transplants and prosthetics, etc., the lifespan of human beings [possessing advanced biological and technological sciences] might theoretically be dramatically increased. Incidentally, the writer and traveler Robert Stacy-Judd described in some of his books an exploration he and others had made of the peripheral areas of the Loltun cave system of Yucatan. Legend says that at least one group of people, fleeing persecution, entered en masse into the massive Loltun caves and were never seen again. Stacy- Judd tells of his own encounter with a 'cave hermit' deep in the cavern chambers who claimed to be well over 1000 years old. This unusual man said that he was a guardian of the cave and of the ancient treasures — and city? — which lay deep below in the unknown depths, 'unknown' that is, except to the strange 'hermit'. This unusual man had emerged from the inner DEPTHS of the cave when they first encountered him. Aside from photographs of this 'hermit' which appeared in some of his works, the author also revealed photographs of 'underground gardens' consisting of areas of the cave which contain small patches of 'jungle', small cave oasis' watered and lit through parts of the cavern ceilings which had collapsed in ages past, exposing them to the elements of the outer world above. Whether such claims of longevity are real or whether the "subterranean" people were just playing with the minds of such explorers who encountered them, is uncertain - Branton).

"'Still another explorer named D.O. visited this SAME tunnel near Gaspar, Santa Catarina, and behind a wonderful fruit orchard saw a subterranean woman with a child in her arms reading to it aloud from a huge book written in an unknown language... After she read each sentence the child repeated the same and in this way was taught how to read. All of these subterranean cities are illuminated by strange light...'"

Raymond Bernard (whose actual name was 'Walter Seigmeister'), writing in the Oct. 1959 issue of SEARCH Magazine, p. 48, described yet another alleged encounter with a subterranean race. What are we to make of all these stories? Are we to assume that some of the individuals who told Bernard such accounts actually made them up, as some suggest, in order to receive the financial bonus or reward that Bernard was sometimes known to offer on documentable accounts of ancient tunnels? Or, are we to accept these accounts for just what their sources claimed them to be, reports of actual encounters with a subterranean world? Bernard stated the following:

"...Last week my investigators returned and said they visited their city (i.e. the 'city' of a race of dwarf-humans whom Bernard referred to as the 'Niebelungs', who live in a subterranean region with it's own system of illumination - Branton) and are able to bring any of my American friends to visit it, but I require one condition: absolute secrecy, as I don't want governments to send armies into the tunnel to disturb these peaceful people.

"To reach them requires a 3-day journey of about 40 miles through a tunnel. This entire distance is through a tunnel carefully lined with cut stone blocks below, above and on the sides. That was quite an engineering feat. I think the tunnel was made long to keep out curiosity seekers, and only the most determined will travel that distance.

"Here is the report of my investigations: (They are two ranchers, father and son, who discovered the tunnel accidentally):

"'We left our house 5 A.M. for the tunnel on top of a mountain and reached it 3 P.M. We were tired and camped near the entrance of the tunnel. For three days we proceeded through the tunnel. We told time by our watches, as we could not tell when it was day or night. We went to sleep at 10 P.M. and awoke at 3 A.M. and continued walking. By the third day the tunnel started to go downward by steps (Note: If the entrance was on 'top' of a mountain, we must assume that it sloped downward until it became too steep to continue without a stairway - Branton). It was built of stone blocks on all sides. By the night of the third day the tunnel suddenly opened into a great space covered with what appeared as a sky with a yellow light that made everything luminous, like daylight. We saw a city with many houses and saw many people in the distance. They were dwarfs with long white beards and long hair and we saw women and children, and heard them crying. The third member of our party got frightened so we had to return.'

"These men found three such tunnels. They entered another for three days, but after hearing voices further in, got scared and returned. Now they are entering the third..."

Previously, we have referred to the alleged inhabitants of a subterranean colony below Mt. Shasta in northern California, which is believed to be one of the largest, if not THE largest, subterranean community in North America, and which allegedly has ties with the Asian empire of 'Agharti' and several South American subterranean colonies, and possibly also the 'Havmu- suvs' of the Mojave and Death Valley region. The following are some excepts from an article written by William F. Hamilton (whose other publications can at this writing be obtained via 7327 Bothwell Rd., Reseda, CA 91335), who we have referred to in earlier writings. Bill Hamilton has been in Data Processing for 22 years and is now a Sr. Programmer-Analyst. He is a writer, investigator and researcher. He has been involved in UFO research and investigations since 1953. Bill is a past member of The Foundation for Research in Parapsychology, The Spacecraft Research Foundation, The World Federation of Science and Engineering, and MENSA, the high IQ society. He has been a member of Daniel Fry's Understanding, Inc., and served on it's Board. He founded NEXUS and NEXUS NEWS, an info center for alternative energy and alternative life-styles. He also founded UFORUM, a monthly forum on the UFO phenomena. He is a UFO investigator with MUFON, an Associate Director of UFOCCI, and founder of UFORCES. Bill is the author of the following books: SPACE, TIME AND GRAVITY; CENTER OF THE VORTEX; TELOS, THE COSMIC COMPUTER; GEOMETRY OF THE GRID; CLOSE ENCOUNTER REPORT; ALIEN MAGIC; and COSMIC TOP SECRET. He has written numerous articles for publications such as 'Search,' 'Energy Unlimited,' 'New Age Science,' 'The New Atlantean Journal,' 'California UFO,' and 'UFO Universe'. The following article originally appeared in the 'New Atlantean Journal':

"...I run across some fascinating people in the course of my investigations who tell me many unusual stories. While on the trail of reports of UFO base locations, I met a young, very pretty blonde girl with almond-shaped eyes and small perfect teeth, whose name is Bonnie. Bonnie has told me an incredible story and has related a volume of interesting information... Bonnie is sincere, cheerful, and rational and says she (was born) in 1951 in a city called TELOS that was built inside an artificial dome-shaped cavern in the Earth a mile or so beneath Mt. Shasta, California.

"Bonnie, her mother (Rana Mu), her father Ra (Mu), her sister Judy, her cousins Lorae and Matox, live and move in our society, returning frequently to TELOS for rest and recuperation. Bonnie relates that her people use boring machines to bore tunnels in the Earth. These boring machines heat the rock to incandescence, then vitrify it, thus eliminating the need for beams and supports. A tube transit tunnel is used to connect the (underground) cities that exist in various subterranean regions in our hemisphere. The tube trains are propelled by electromagnetic impulses up to speeds of 2500 mph. One tube connects with one of their cities in the Matto Grosso jungle of Brazil. (They) have developed space travel and some flying saucers come from their subterranean bases...

"They grow food hydroponically under full-spectrum lights with their gardens attended by automatons. The food and resources of Telos are distributed in plenty to the million-and-a-half population that thrives on a no-money economy. Bonnie talks about history, of the Uighers, Naga-Mayas, and Quetzals, of which she is a descendant (Note: Many people have mistakenly identified the inhabitants of 'Telos' as being directly descended from the 'Lemurians', however Bonnie here seems to refute this by indicating that her ancestrage was other than this, possibly Meso-American and/or East-Indian? As in the case of the ancient 'antediluvian' cities of the eastern seaboard which were reestablished after being abandoned by the lost 'Atlanteans'; the 'Lemurians', if they existed thousands of years ago, also seem to have been devastated in a worldwide cataclysm — and their cities re- established by the Uighers, Naga-Mayas, and Quetzals as well as scattered members of other societies. The antediluvian Atlanteans apparently built underground systems below the eastern seaboard of North and South America, whereas the MU- rians apparently had control of the underground systems beneath the western seaboard. Although some island-continents may have sunk following the deluge, most accounts describe the 'Atlanteans', etc., as being antediluvians. Being that the name 'Telos' is a Grecian word meaning 'uttermost, purpose', there is a suggestion of a 'possible' connection with the Grecian-like Hav-musuvs of the Panamint mountains of California - Branton).

"I met Bonnie's cousin, Matox, who, like her, is a strict vegetarian and holds the same attitudes concerning the motives of government. They constantly guard against discovery or intrusion. Their advanced awareness and technology helps them remain vigilant...

"Science Fiction? Bonnie is a real person. Many have met her. Is she perpetrating a hoax? For what motive? She does not seek publicity and I have a devil of a time getting her to meetings to talk with others, but she has done so. There has been little variation in her story and her answers in the past three years. She has given me excellent technical insight on the construction of a crystal- powered generator that extracts ambient energy... Bonnie's father, the Ra-Mu, is 300 years old and a member of the ruling council of Telos.

"Many tunnels are unsafe and closed off. All tube transit tunnels are protected and are designed to eject uninvited guests. Does Bonnie have the answers that we are looking for? I don't know... Bonnie says she would like to satisfy our need for proof and will work with me on a satisfactory answer to that problem, but she is unconcerned with whether people accept her or not. Bonnie is humorous and easygoing and well-poised, yet sometimes she becomes brooding and mysterious. She says her people are busy planning survival centers for refugees. One of these is to be near Prescott, Arizona..." (or, more exactly, below the Groom Creek area just south of Prescott, to be exact. Another 'survival center' for refugees of the worldwide cataclysms which the Telosians are convinced will devastate the surface of the earth in future years, is said to be below the general area of Jenny Lake, Wyoming, near the Tetons. The Tetons themselves have been the alleged home of a mysterious race, according to different sources, and extremely ancient stone 'buildings' or constructions have reportedly been seen high atop the treacherous spurs of the Teton mountain range - Branton).

When Bill Hamilton asked 'Bonnie' to elaborate about the power-sources which her people utilize to propel the so-called "flying saucer" craft, she replied:

"...A lot of it is crystals (i.e. crystal-induced electromagnetism? - Branton), particularly the atmospheric vehicles. The planet-to- planet vehicles are driven by an Ion-Mercury engine. Spaceships can reach speeds way beyond light. They can enter hyperspace — you generate into the fourth dimension — this is controlled by an on-board computer that takes you into and out of hyperspace. I know this is a simplification. When your on a ship going into hyperspace, you will hear this vibration, and a loud screaming sound when you enter, then you will hear nothing..."

Bill concludes: "I have had many correlation's on this data and am researching it further toward a comprehensive theory of space travel..."

Researcher Val Valerian refers to an incident which took place in 1988. This incident indicated that at that time Project Bluebook was still as active as ever. Valerian refers to a Sgt. Robert Williams (pseudonym for his protection) who was stationed in Honolulu from 1971-1973. 'Williams' was a photographer who worked for the Aerospace Audio Visual Service (AAVS) which is headquartered at Norton AFB, CA.

In 1971 Williams was approached by PROJECT BLUEBOOK to work as a photographer, which he did until 1973. On July 10, 1973 Williams was given TDY orders and a Top Secret clearance, and was sent to Norton AFB and was briefed into a secret project involving the photographing of alien beings and craft. He was to work with a Ron Smith (also pseudonym). They were blindfolded and put into a limousine with blacked-out windows and were driven to their destination. Both felt the car descend and found themselves in an underground base. Williams noted the time on his watch, and that 45 minutes had passed since the beginning of their journey.

Both were briefed and led to a laboratory, where they found two 'aliens' in the process of being autopsied. Another alien was still alive, held elsewhere. The creatures were wearing blue uniforms, and they noticed six scientists and two MARINE guards. It was later determined that they had been taken to the 29 Palms Marine Base in S. California.

They commenced to photograph the aliens. The bodies were black with green fluid/blood. During the time when Williams was photographing the live alien it terminated and at its death he felt 'something passing through him'. The scientists there, he noticed, had bland expressions on their faces 'like they weren't all there.' He was allowed to enter the disk which appeared outwardly to be a 35' diameter disk, although inside it was almost as large as a football field, indicating some type of space-warping technology. After this, they were driven back to Norton AFB and then returned to Honolulu. The men noticed that no one would speak to them, even their wives. 'Smith' later disappeared and was never heard from again by Williams, who (as of the early 1990's) now works in Nevada.

Valerian stated that records show a disk did crash in NW Arizona and was recovered on July 10, 1973, the same day that Williams' and Smiths' Top Secret orders came through.

Aside from this, 'Williams' stated that since the age of 3 he had experienced 'abductions' by humanlike beings, during which he was often taken to a place with large white building that were LARGER WITHIN THAN THEY WERE ON THE OUTSIDE, each containing 600 family units. During these episodes he was befriended by a human girl close to his age named Karin, and this friendship lasted to later years. Through hypnotic regression, Williams recalled that during the drive to 29 Palms they (car and all?) were transported onto a starship, where he met the ships captain — none other than Karin herself. They were later dropped off just outside of 29 Palms and the memory of the episode was removed.

Actually, several contactees say that it is not so much a removal of "memory" as it is a transition into an altered state of consciousness and an alternate personality which has been conditioned to relate to the aliens, whether humans or grays. Since an alternate personality [psychosis] is involved and not the 'conscious' mind, the conscious mind itself has no memory of the events. Williams also stated that Karin's people have developed time travel (Note: There are various accounts suggesting that it is possible to travel through time without violating the laws of paradox. In short, one cannot change the past, simply because the past has already been changed — or rather SET through the intervention of past, present and future influences. It is suggested that the earth is in a universal causality loop and that there was a point where "time" began on earth or in the universe and there is a point when time will end, is ending or has ended — depending on ones perspective. This is not to say that everything is SET, because it is not. We have the power to ESTABLISH our collective reality by choices we make in the NOW, whether that NOW exists in the past, the present or the future. In a way that is difficult for finite minds to understand, events of the past help to set the present and future, events of the present help to set the past and future, and events of the future help to set the past and the present. So in reality, one cannot 'change' the past, present or future, but they can take part in establishing it. According to individuals involved with the Philadelphia and Montauk projects, a human soul is attached to the universal causality sphere or the "time" sequence at the point of conception — not birth. They are attached to the time sequence by what Nikola Tesla called a "zero-time reference" that is integrated into the human soul itself. Upon the point of physical death, the soul leaves the timeline and enters what we faintly perceive as "eternity").

In relation to Williams' experiences, and his descriptions of advanced civilizations, UFO's and 29 Palms, Valerian states:

"...Investigations of the 29 Palms underground base during April 1989 tracked down some data about the geology of the spot. During the time when the area was under the sea, an earthquake caused a large hole in the ground, causing a lot of water to create a funnel-like structure in the ground. Evidently, disks go in and out of there all the time, and the Army has tried to send cameras down there, only to have the cables cut. One group that attempted to go down on ropes were exposed to a blue gas and had to be pulled out again..."

We quote now from parts of an interview between John Lear and the National Fringe Sciences (Computer) Bulletin Board:

"Question: You just mentioned that there were... other 'species' in contact with this world... are they aware of the EBE's?

"Lear: Yes they are. The types I will mention are listed in a USAF Academy Physics book called 'INTRODUCTORY SPACE SCIENCE VOLUME 2,B.' I refer to chapter 13... which lists the ones that are most seen. They are the EBE's, the 'Blondes'... They look just like us but are invariably blond haired and blue eyed. Don't know where they come from but they do not interact with us except for a few abductions now and then. We also have a species that is similar to us in appearance but they are about seven feet tall and the main difference is that their eyes wrap around their head a little more than ours. Another type listed is a small species about four feet tall, very hairy and extremely strong for their size. We don't know where these guys come from either. All this was in the aforementioned text which was WITHDRAWN by the Air Force in the early '70's from the book. But there are several people who have the original book...

"Question: I'm curious also as to the government's plans, if any, to deal with an uprising of EBE's should that eventually occur... or would the technological gap make an attempt untenable?

"Lear: It is my understanding that we have already lost the battle. This is the reason why MJ-12 is in such a panic. They had a lot of well laid plans to INFORM us, and when the deception was confirmed about 1984 it was all out the window...

"Question: Recently in the INF treaty negotiations, Gorbachev indicated that despite prior claims, they too were working on an SDI program... Is there any connection between our program and theirs and if the battle is lost, why are those attempts being made?

"Lear: I wish I knew the answer to that. Several rumors have come out of the test site recently and one of them was that every test shot this year (1989? - Branton) has been to make a giant (underground - Branton) room. The shots are very clean and as soon as everything subsides they move in equipment to make walls, ceiling, floors and various levels."

If in fact the SDI program(s) are being used to defend the earth from foreign or alien forces, then someone 'somewhere' might not appreciate such projects. Whether it is the serpent cults or the serpent race, someone or 'something' seems to have been behind the mysterious deaths of several SDI scientists.

British UFOlogist Timothy Good, in his book 'UFO REPORT' (Avon Books., N.Y., 1989), describes the unfortunate fate of several experts who assisted in the development of the STAR WARS defense system. Apparently, they were either eliminated by those they worked for so that they would not reveal what they knew, or someone or something 'else' that was displeased with the ultimate product of their efforts was responsible for their tragic deaths. Certainly, all of these scientists dying at once cannot be explained in coincidental terms, whatever the case:

"...Reports of suspicious deaths, darkly and deeply linked to UFO's, persist, however, and continue to cause speculation. Word comes from Gordon Creighton, editor of the informative FLYING SAUCER REVIEW, who notes a possible deathly tie-in with the U.S. 'Star Wars' program. He wrote to me in Nov. 1988 as follows:

"'...here in Britain 22 scientists have reportedly either taken their own lives or died in very strange or mysterious circumstances. And it seems that most... were engaged in British work on behalf of, or related to the U.S. 'Star Wars' program. The British government, it seems, was trying to hush it up. But press statements here say that the U.S. government had put our government on the spot and demanded a full inquiry. So, quite clearly, it is either the Russians or THEM...'

"As many researchers have surmised, 'Star Wars', ostensibly conceived as a defensive system against Russian missile attack, may have had from it's beginning a 'defensive' UFO connection. Whatever the case, a 'mock test' in September, 1988, of an earth- shattering warhead — much like 'Star Wars' in reverse — was conducted at the Tonopah Test Range in Nevada. Announced as a proposed superweapon designed to destroy Russian underground command centers dug in solid rock down to 1,000 (feet), some UFO analysts believe that the real target is not Russian but another adversary deep down in cavernous installations IN NEVADA AND NEW MEXICO.

"According to the Pentagon, the proposed earth-penetrating warhead is 'urgently needed'. According to rumor-mills, an alien race — the 'grays' — in their fortified underground laboratories, are genetically experimenting with the human race. Even more ominous, rumors say that their intransigence today may lead to new perils tomorrow."

The following confirming article appeared in Washington State's 'SEATTLE' newspaper, p. 1, Oct. 8, 1988 issue. The article, which originated from the 'Hearst News Service', was written by reporter Bernard D. Kaplan, and titled: 'BAFFLING CASE OF 10 DEAD SCIENTISTS - SOMETHING SINISTER?' Below the article is quoted in its entirety:

"PARIS — They're calling it the 'Star Wars Mystery' — the enigmatic deaths of 10 British scientists and technicians, all of whom worked on projects linked to President Reagan's space-based antimissile program, the Strategic Defense Initiative.

"All of the deaths have occurred within the past 24 months, since Britain began to contribute to 'Star Wars' research.

"All took place in mysterious or violent circumstances.

"Four of the deaths were recorded as suicides and two as a result of accidents. In four other cases, coroner's juries handed down an 'open' verdict, meaning they could not determine how the victims died.

"The latest case came two weeks ago. Andrew Hall, a 33- year-old engineer with the British Aerospace company, was found suffocated in his car, a hosepipe connected to the exhaust. Verdict: suicide.

"Only a month earlier, Alistair Beckham, a senior space engineer with another major defense contractor, PLESSEY, was discovered in his garden shed, bound up in electric wires running to his house. He had been electrocuted.

"Although Beckham's death was ruled a suicide, his widow was convinced he was murdered.

"'Alistair had no personal or professional problems,' Mary Beckham said. 'He wasn't subject to depression. Murder is the sole explanation that is reasonable.'

"Member of Parliament Douglas Hoyle, who issued a call for an official investigation into the strange string of deaths even before the Beckham case, agrees that 'something sinister' appears to be going on.

"'The number of these deaths is now becoming too odd to be a coincidence any more,' he insists.

"The government has so far turned down Hoyle's demand, but last week ordered the police forces who investigated the nine deaths to 'exchange information.'

"Sources said NATO intelligence authorities in Brussels recently asked their British counterparts for a report on the affair.

"'Five of the men who died worked in sensitive posts for the same defense contractor, BRITISH MARCONI,' a NATO source said. 'Two were senior scientists at the Royal Military College of Science. We'd be remiss in our duty if we didn't take a very close look into this matter.'

"Chief Superintendent Arthur Ford, the policeman put in charge of coordinating the investigations, insists nothing has been found to link the deaths.

"Hoyle says that's 'nonsense.' He pointed out that two others, LIKE Hall, died from fumes in locked cars whose engines were running.

"Police officials continue to theorize that the deaths were attributed to personal stress to which defense industry scientists are often subjected. Marconi personnel manager John Shipley dismisses that notion.

"'We investigated each (of the five Marconi employee deaths),' he says. 'We didn't find a single instance of work stress or even suspicion of it,' he said.

"Besides Hall and Beckham, these people died:

"—Marconi scientist Ashad Sharif was found in his car with a rope tied from his neck to a nearby tree on October 1986. The car had lurched forward, choking Sharif to death. Open verdict.

"—Ministry of Defense computer specialist Richard Pugh was found with a plastic bag over his head in January 1987. Ruled an accident.

"—Royal Military College scientist John Brittan, found suffocated in his car in the same month. 'Accidental death.'

"—Marconi design engineer Victor Moore, found in February 1987 dead of an apparent drug overdose. Verdict: suicide.

"—Royal Military College scientist Peter Peapell found run over by a car the same month. Open verdict.

"—Marconi satellite project manager David Sands drove his car loaded with gasoline cans into a wall in April 1987. Open verdict.

"—Marconi weapons engineer Trevor Knight, found in a car with a hose connected to the exhaust this March. Apparent suicide.

"—Marconi scientist John Ferry, found electrocuted, in July 1988. Open verdict...."

Many UFO encounters, especially with humanlike personages, have been relatively friendly and benevolent in nature. Yet there is, nevertheless, a far more malevolent group which has reportedly caused physical harm or even death to unfortunate witnesses who became a target in a cosmic war being waged against mankind by beings which apparently have little or no regard for human life. In his article, 'INCREDIBLE UFO INCINERATION'S: CLOSE ENCOUNTERS OF THE COMBUSTIBLE KIND', researcher Larry E. Arnold describes the following terrifying encounter, only one of several cases of UFO-related 'human combustion' mentioned in his article:

"...Of the many episodes involving UFOs and the spontaneous combustion of humans, quite probably the most disastrous event — if true — in MODERN times occurred to the African village of Kirimukuya on Mt. Kenya.

"For several nights in June 1954, young Laili Thindu and his shepherd companions listened to the pounding of their neighbors' drums announcing a wedding about to take place on the mountainside. They also watched STRANGE LIGHTS soar around this 'sacred' peak in central Kenya. They naturally were startled when bright beams flashed from these soaring lights, then concerned that the drums were now silent.

"The next morning Laili learned that 'all the dancers, all the children, all the livestock, — the entire population of the village — had been seared to death by terrible streams of light from glowing objects,' report Brad Steiger and Joan Whritenour in their book , FLYING SAUCERS ARE HOSTILE. 'It was not until Laili Thindu ventured into Nairobi that he was able to tell his story to someone who recognized the tale for what it really was: the annihilation of an African village by a UFO..."

The Kenyans are not the only ones to have suffered from "alien" attacks upon its inhabitants. The U.S. Military is well aware of this threat of unknown invaders of U.S. Airspace, as is evident in the following quote:

"We have stacks ¬of report about flying saucers. WE TAKE THEM SERIOUSLY when you consider WE HAVE LOST MANY MEN AND PLANES TRYING TO INTERCEPT THEM."

— February, 1953. Statement by U.S. General CHIDLAW in charge of the United States Continental Air Defense.

There are many indications suggesting that certain humans have, in one way or another, been brought under the mental, technical or occult control of the 'reptilians' over the years — whether they are fully aware of this manipulation or not. Could the 'being' referred to in the following account, which appeared on pp. 1136-1137 of Raymond A. Palmer's 'HIDDEN WORLD' publication for Summer, 1962, be the type of subterranean- dwelling creature which at least one account has referred to as a 'dragon-worm'? Could this creature (supposing it does in fact exist and is not the result of one man's deluded and misguided fantasy experience) be one of the MANY and VARIED branches or mutations of the 'serpent' races, which many accounts tend to confirm as existing within subterranean areas? It would seem that accounts such as this one might raise more questions than answers. Remember that this letter appeared years before the advent of the famous 'Star Wars' trilogy which depicted a creature very similar to that described in the following letter. Again, one may wonder if George Lucas himself might not have been inspired subconsciously by certain evident realities, and portrayed some of these — although in a rather sensationalized manner — in his movies. The following account was submitted by a reader who chose to remain anonymous. He states:

"Dear Ray: ...This happened about 12 or 13 years ago. I was in my late teens, I think, but perhaps the time is not as important as the incident.

"In the late night hours I awoke, got out of bed, walked out of the house and was met by a group of men (?) who drove me out into the country to an old farmhouse. I don't know the location any more than the people involved; maybe I was drugged, I don't know. At the farmhouse we went immediately to the potato cellar and through a trapdoor in the floor down a long inclining tunnel. We arrived into a room, fantastically decorated, bizarre, like Hades — how can I describe it? It was of good size; and others were present. Some one asked: 'Is he ready?' and the answer: 'Yes, he is.' Two 'others' — one on each side of me escorted me into a room? Tunnel? (again beyond my description) the worm, or whoever or whatever he or it was, was huge, long, round, knobby. An immense head and mouth (which swayed back and forth) spoke to me. I don't remember what it said or my answer, but one of them put a syringe into it, and then into me! I swear the language spoken by them AND MYSELF was not English, but somehow I seemed to know, yet but not know. After some kind of warning and benediction from this being I was escorted out. Once again the car, the return trip, and home in bed. Since that time I have once in awhile visited the caves quite unhindered... in dreams and the like (since 'suppressed' memories of experiences with UFO's, etc. often surface in 'dreams' or impressions, could these be actual memories of other visits to the nether regions which were suppressed from his memory? There is also the small chance that ray-induced visions or even 'astral' interaction might be involved as well, that is, the "abduction" of the spirit body from the soul and physical bodies. The physical-soul body presumably remains attached to the disembodied spirit-essence via a silvery cord or beam of energy which maintains a kind of hyperspace link between them - Branton).

"I can only comment that the knowledge of, and use of the mechs, the architecture, the philosophies in the pictures (or whatever they are), would enable man to live like gods in comparison to how they now live. However the areas of horror beyond comprehension would have to be removed before this can be done (Note: The writer may be referring to the so-called super- human abilities brought about through the use or manipulation of powerful electromagnetic occult technologies. We must remind the reader that 'power' has NOTHING to do with benevolence or righteousness, or as the old saying goes: 'Might does not make right!' Such abilities to manipulate the forces of nature via occult technologies — such as those which were developed and utilized by the antediluvians, which by the way may have played a role in their destruction, and which is now being used by many of the inhabitants of the nether 'cavern' regions — could be extremely destructive if placed in the wrong hands - Branton).

"An interesting sequel to this (dream or reality?) is that I have prayed, hard, that this wouldn't affect my life. I believe in some ways it hasn't, but my wife feels that something, as I also have felt, is not allowing me to live as I want to. Of course I want to know, was it dream or reality? (Name deleted by request)."

The following letter appeared in the July, 1964 issue of 'SEARCH' Magazine, and was written by a Mr. Ervin M. Scott of (at that time) 536 12th St., Denver, Colorado. Mr. Scott's references to the origin of "dreams" is interesting. There are theories that the brain acts like a biological electrochemical "radio" transceiver at some levels. It is a proven fact that the brain sends very subtle neuro-electrical transmissions into the atmosphere, and that these "brain waves" can be recorded by electroencephelograph machines. An even more daring theory is that neurons can interact and affect other particles-waves in the Unified Field and that the brain has the ability to "focus" these waves as a transmitter or a receiver. Of course the success of long-range communication between minds is minimal when compared with radio waves, because of the thick morass of 'psychic static' that must be penetrated and the minimal energy output. Others claim that certain "alien" cultures have machines that are capable of electronically magnifying and focusing thought waves for transmitting or receiving. As for "dreams", some believe that they take place when the mind tunes-in to a "deeper" mental states wherein the mind is able to tap into the thought- forms of a "collective unconscious", explaining the "universal dream symbolism" which has been reported by psychologists. One symbolic explanation that has been used to explain this process is that of islands that appear to be separate and distinct when seen above water — symbolic of individual conscious minds, yet the "deeper" one goes below the "surface" the more they connect with other islands at the underlying levels — symbolic of the increasing levels of the collective unconscious mind(s). Mr. Scott describes his unusual experiences as follows:

"Dear Ray: ...Congratulations on another excellent issue of 'SEARCH' Magazine.

"I was especially interested in your article, 'Faces in Your Dreams.'

"Having had many strange, puzzling dreams over the last few years, I have become quite interested in any clues that might point towards origin and cause of dreams. I recognize a good many as probably having the subconscious as the source. However, there is an occasional dream, that is so vivid and unusual that it causes one to wonder.

"I have no connection one way or the other, on the Shaver Mystery, but, I will briefly describe... dreams that are interesting in relation to that subject.

"On Nov. 30, 1963 while in a light sleep I heard a woman's voice coming as if from a distance and she spoke urgently as follows: 'This is from a stolen farm beneath the Salt Lake flats in Utah. (I was living in Wichita, Kansas at the time.) There was a woman abducted almost three weeks ago in Boston, Mass. and taken underground. Reports indicate that an abbey in North section of the city is being used and that cellars underneath the abbey connect with tunnels leading up from caverns below. This is a continuation of the Evil one's War against Mankind.'

"Another voice broke in, 'Don't believe her. Don't you see this is a lie - a trick? (Then, warningly) Keep quiet about this.'

"I have never been in Utah nor have had no thoughts about or desire to visit, so if this was caused by subconscious, it is certainly puzzling, as is the reference to 'a stolen farm'..."

This letter suggests that a conflict of sorts has been and is taking place in cavernous levels below Utah, as in other states.

Earlier in this file we revealed an incident which was originally described by 'Commander X', from a source in Dulce, N.M., stating that a certain chemical was secretly (via certain 'doctors' tied in with the aliens) being injected into individuals via sulfa drugs which in turn lodged in the bone-structure of the victim. This chemical allegedly makes their bodies extremely sensitive to ELF (Extremely Low Frequency) radio waves, which can be 'tuned in' to the deep encephalographic wave bands of the human brain, and these transmissions could apparently be used to subliminally control or at least influence human minds from a distance.

Perhaps some individuals, such as the writer of the letter just quoted, are naturally sensitive to these extremely low frequency waves, in that their brains to some extent act as an electrochemical biological ELF radio receiver. Certain accounts suggest that various subterranean groups utilize ELF radio transceivers capable of penetrating many miles of solid rock.

The letter just quoted might "suggest" that another group, more malevolent, utilize a similar form (of ELF radio wave transceivers?) such as the one through which the woman apparently sent out the 'distress' or warning call.

Could this 'other' voice be tied-in with a subterranean group similar to the 'Horlocks' mentioned earlier in this File? Or could it have originated from the Reptilians? The 'Horlocks' are, as we've suggested earlier, a group of human 'mind-slaves' who are possibly manipulated and kept under reptilian mind-control via implantation, technosis, and so on.

Various sources have described many strange subsurface phenomena associated with the Salt Lake or Great Basin subnet. Some of these include:

1) A reference to a system of tunnels and catacombs allegedly existing below the Salt Lake Valley, which were said to exist long before the first settlers moved in. Unusual stories have made the rounds to the effect that early construction workers in downtown SLC broke through into these underground tunnels. Some of these passages were later expanded by early polygamists who entered them to take refuge from government prosecutors. Others who entered certain of these tunnels never returned. Additional "rumors" say that "Lizard People" have been encountered in some of the deeper tunnels, as well as unusual footprints of creatures with three toes. There are also reports of seemingly "bottomless shafts". Also huge passages "large enough to drive a truck through" are said to lead southwest from downtown Salt Lake City to other chambers below the western Rockies, especially below the Cottonwood Canyons.

It is interesting that the Mayan- Telosians claim to have a large base under Big Cottonwood Canyon, The Mormon Church has a huge underground storage shelter below Little Cottonwood Canyon, and the tunnels in down- town SLC are also said to connect with the basement of the Masonic Temple there. ALL THREE groups possess an initiatory order of "Melchizedek" within their structures... interesting! Also, there have been reports of encounters with NORDICS as well as abductions by REPTILIANS near these canyons. One witness swore that at night she was taken out of her house in Salt Lake City by a blond man in a black "astronaut" uniform, who showed her a "Star Wars" scenario taking place above the Cottonwood Canyons. She saw [cloaked?] disks emerging from Twin Peaks only to fire beams of energy at incoming UFOs. The beams hit what appeared to be the force shields of the incoming craft and in "Star Trek" like fashion the energy crackled around the UFOs, many of which seemed to lose motive power and drift away. Could this area be one of the "Stand-off" zones between the Benevolent Ones and the Reptilian Grays that John Lear, Agent YF and other sources have referred to?

Aside from these mountain bases, other underground systems are said to run southwest under Trolley Square [where workers also reportedly "broke in" to underground catacombs in years past] and also the old Sugerhouse Mall district. At least two individuals have reported "abductions" from this area. One man stated that he was taken underground just north of Sugerhouse, and was "operated on", his right leg removed and reattached. Although the experience seemed "dreamlike", when he found himself at home once again he stood up and his right leg gave out under him. Another person, a woman, reported being abducted and taken into huge underground chambers by way of a maze, just west of Sugarhouse Mall. She was placed in an altered state — it also seemed to be "dreamlike", but she did experience "missing time". She reportedly encountered a tall, dark haired man who was in the company of a "Gray" alien, and he gave her and several other people in the chambers different instructions — which she cannot consciously remember. One other incident was reported by a woman who was part of a night cleaning crew in the multi-levelled Crossroads Mall. She claimed that one night a creature came around a corner, wobbled up to her, and snarled viciously as it went past. She could only describe it as a "demon", however the apparent physical tangibility of the creature may suggest that it was one of the so-called "lizard people" or reptilians that are rumored to stalk the lower tunnels below the Mall. One worker who had gone into the tunnels reportedly placed his hand against one tunnel wall at which point his arm went THROUGH the wall — an extremely unnerving experience. The next time he was there he attempted the same thing, but the wall was "solid". Could the "aliens" temporarily "phase shift" the molecules within an underground passage in order to pass through to hidden chambers beyond? Others have reported passing rooms from which an unusual greenish luminescence emanated. Others speak of tunnels that have been sealed or locked by wooden doors that seemed to be ancient, or by metal doors or gates. There are also reports of people entering the sewer or drainage tunnels under downtown SLC, peeking into huge chambers, and seeing "men in suits" carrying Uzi machine guns. Could these be Mormon Church security officers protecting the basement levels of "Temple Square" from unwanted alien intruders from BELOW?

2) Certain geologists state that the Great Salt Lake has an underground counterpart deep below it, and that a certain type of earthquake could 'conceivably' empty the entire contents of the lake into it's subterranean counterpart. There are vague rumors of underground streams or rivers which allegedly flow from HUGE caverns in the heart of the Wasatch Mts./Western Rockies (caverns which can supposedly be entered by following the right path through the underground maze), and westward below the valley floor, possibly to the underground 'counterpart' of the Great Salt Lake.

3) A former worker in Utah's 'Dugway Proving Ground' (where former Dulce Base worker Thomas Castello alleges there is an 'entrance' to the underground systems) reported that he witnessed 'people' working at the base-facility who were NOT human. He could not explain, but he did state that he learned of top secret robotics and even 'Philadelphia-Experiment' like teleportation research that was being conducted at the base. Also, there have been reports (similar to those at Dulce, NM; the Nevada] Test Site; the Madigan Medical facility in Washington State, and at Deep Springs, CA), particularly from a former hairdresser at the Dugway base whose name was Barbara, that there were several reptilian beings working at the base who were masquerading as humans. She stated that even one of the base commanders was NOT human — she saw him momentarily transform before her eyes!

4) There are many accounts of various alien 'bases' throughout Utah occupied by the Nordics, the Grays, secret societies, the large 'EL' humans, possibly

the 'Orange', and of course the 'hubrids' — and possibly even natural-born humans who are being held prisoner in 'reptilian' strongholds.

This latter possibility was confirmed by Val Valerian in 'THE LEADING EDGE' Newsletter, in which he stated his belief that, based on the numerous accounts that he had gathered:

"...Scores of underground installations hold citizens of virtually every country on the planet in captivity."

Valerian is of course referring to the Dulce facility, as well as other such facilities throughout the world where permanent abductees' reportedly end up. This may also include other people who have disappeared in other ways.

One possible subterranean 'abduction' was described by researcher John Grant. In his book 'GREAT MYSTERIES' (Chartwell Books., Secaucus, NJ., 1988), Grant records the following frightening incident: "...In 1975 Mr. and Mrs. Jackson Wright were driving to New York through blinding snow; in the Lincoln Tunnel they agreed to pause and wipe snow from the front and rear windows. Jackson Wright never saw his wife, Martha, again."

People just don't 'disappear' without a trace, never to be heard from again, especially in a place like this unless SOMETHING intentionally causes such a disappearance to take place. There have, incidentally, been reports of 'UFO' like objects and/or alien creatures being seen in connection with 'abductions' which took place in underground tunnels, some 'deserted' by our standards and others not. One case involved some teenaged boys in Europe who swore that their abductors (grays) took them to a base underground via a long-abandoned World War II railway tunnel.

It is uncertain just how many human casualties the human race may have suffered as a result of the Da'ath or Dah'ath wars over the centuries (Da'ath is the Hebrew name of the 'tree' where, tradition holds, the human and serpent races first came into conflict), yet based on the various accounts which we have covered in this Fil, we can assume that the victims have been in the tens of thousands AT THE VERY LEAST.

In the meantime, the abductions of humans, an integral part of the 'evil ones' warfare against God and men's souls, are still taking place. Whether the victims are taken to underground or off-planet areas is difficult to tell in any given case, although there is reason to believe that both possibilities are a reality.

There have, believe it or not, been abductions which have occurred in connection with 'UFO' activity that have involved not a few, not dozens, nor hundreds but THOUSANDS of people who have disappeared without a trace, or been abducted, en masse. Such is the case with the following well-known and documented incident that has baffled the many researchers who have mentioned it in their writings:

"In the Winter of 1930 a profoundly disturbing incident took place in Canada. Trapper Arnaud Lauret and his son observed a strange light crossing the northern sky. It appeared to be headed for the Lake Anjikuni area. The two trappers described it as being alternatingly bullet-shaped and cylinder-shaped...

"Another trapper named Joe LaBelle had snowshoed into the village of the Lake Anjikuni people, and been chilled to discover that the normally bustling community was silent, and not a soul was moving in the streets. Even the sled dogs, which would normally have bayed welcome, were silent. The shanties were choked with snow, and not a chimney showed smoke.

"The trapper found the village kayaks tied up on the shore of the lake. Inside the shanties the trapper found a further surprise: there were meals left hanging over fires, long grown old and moldy, apparently abandoned as they were being cooked. The men's rifles were still standing by the doors. This really frightened the trapper, because he knew that these people would NEVER leave their precious weapons behind.

"He reported his discovery to the Royal Canadian Mounted Police, who investigated further. They discovered that the town's dogs died of hunger, chained beneath a tree and covered by a snowdrift. More disturbingly, the town graveyard had been emptied. The graves were now yawning pits. Despite the frozen ground, the graves had been opened and the dead removed..."

Whitley Strieber, who claimed to have had several abduction- type experiences since a young age involving different types of beings — both apparently physical and paraphysial — does not hold to the idea that these creatures are originally from deep space. He believes that some of them MAY come from the nether regions of the earth, and may have been here for millennia, being part of an ancient conspiracy to occultically control or manipulate the human race. He is not certain exactly what the creatures behind his abductions were, but he did suggest that the ancient (fallen?) 'elementals' might be involved. Strieber had some comments of his own concerning the strange mass abduction near the Lake Anjikuni area. In his book 'MAJESTIC', he stated:

"The RCMP continues the case opened to this day. A check with the records department indicated that the matter remains unsolved, and despite a search of the whole of Canada and inquiries throughout the world, not a single trace of the MISSING TWELVE HUNDRED MEN, WOMEN AND CHILDREN were ever found." Strieber related still another incident in this same book, of a mysterious abduction (apparently) to underground regions:

"...The first seemingly related case of disappearance in the U.S. history (that is, 'related' to cases given by Strieber earlier in his book, concerning people who were allegedly pursued by unknown objects and experienced NEAR abductions yet managed to escape — and others who were captured in the full sight of witnesses and never seen again - Branton)... took place on 23 September 1880 near the town of Gallatin, Tennessee. At approximately three-thirty on that sunny afternoon, Mr. David Lang, a farmer, dematerialized in front of five witnesses, including his wife, his two children, his father-in-law and a local judge.

"The father-in-law and the judge had just pulled up in a carriage. Mr. Lang moved toward them across a field followed by his family. Without warning, he simply ceased to exist. There was no cry, no sign of distress. Mrs. Lang, distraught, rushed up and pounded the ground where he had been walking. All that afternoon, and into the night the field was searched. Subsequently the county surveyor determined that there were no hidden caves or sinkholes in the area of the disappearance.

"The subsequent April, seven months later," Streiber writes, "the children heard their father crying distantly UNDERNEATH the field. He seemed desperate and tortured, and was begging for help. His voice gradually died away and was not heard again. Where he was last seen, there was a circle of WITHERED yellow grass twenty feet in diameter.

"The family moved away from the farm.

"It can be surmised that Mr. Lang was not removed above ground, but rather was taken INTO THE EARTH and kept alive there for some months," Strieber continues, "judging from the cries that were heard the next April. What the poor man suffered during that time, and what finally put him out of his misery, can scarcely be imagined...

"He was apparently left to languish in some subterranean prison, presumably dying when his food and water ran out."

Evidence is beginning to mount that many of the human and animal organs from mutilation victims are being used by an entirely different 'alien' group than the reptilians-saurians, although the sauroids are apparently working in full cooperation with this "other" group by assisting in the construction of physical-biological 'forms' which can be 'possessed' and animated by an insidious group of SUPERNATURAL nonphysical entities, the 'infernals' or 'poltergiests'. Whitley Streiber stated that he encountered some of these entities during an abduction, and noticed an area on their craft where these malevolent, fearful creatures stored these 'bodies' when they were not in use. These energy beings, he came to realize, used such physical shells to operate in the physical dimension, much like a human being enters a diving suit in order to operate under water.

The LEADING EDGE Magazine for March, 1990, quoted one 'inside' source as saying that: "These beings... have a PHYSICAL presence generate biological structures that function as CONTAINERS for them... the aliens manufacture containers for themselves... fabricate their own bodies — using biologicals gained from humans and cattle..."

THE MOJAVE DESERT'S GREATEST SECRETS

A publication titled 'AMERICA'S MISSING & EXPLOITED CHILDREN' (published by the U.S. Department of Justice, Office of Juvenile Justice and Delinquency Prevention, Washington D.C.) made the following statement: "Even the most conservative estimates suggest that SEVERAL HUNDRED THOUSAND children are missing within the course of the year." (in the United States alone). Also: "...In 1983, the U.S. Dept of Health and Human Services put the number at 1.5 million a year — a figure that has been widely circulated by private organizations. But experts say roughly 95 percent of these are runaways — many of whom return home within days and are counted repeatedly if they run away more than once a year." This would apparently put the number of those who are 'abducted' in one way or another to AT LEAST 75,000 per year... STILL A CONSIDERABLY LARGE NUMBER.

'Commander X', from his apparent though guarded vantage- point within the Intelligence Community, claims to be privy to much 'deep-level' inside information, as we have seen in earlier writings. One of the reports that crossed his desk involved the experience of a woman who was 'abducted' and taken over 1000 miles to the underground facility below Dulce, New Mexico:

"...One woman I have spoken with was abducted from the roof of a New York City apartment building and apparently held underground at the Dulce facility. She was taken to a cabin in the desert which was being used as a camouflaged entrance to the 'alien' base. She was eventually escorted to the laboratories to be used as a test subject, but at the last minute managed to escape thanks to the aid of one of the Nordic-type, tall aliens, who befriended her and showed her a secret way out, down an unguarded shaft.

"Back in the desert, she was rescued by members of the Blue Berets, and eventually flown back to Manhattan. During a de- briefing session with the military, she was warned to remain silent about her experiences. Anyone hearing such a bizarre tale would certainly think she had gone insane. It was inferred she could be committed to a mental institution at any time should she refuse to go along with the cover-up conspiracy, which she was told was being conducted 'for the sake of the country, and the sake of the world!'" (if you believe that excuse, then I have some beachfront property on Mercury that you might be interested in! - Branton)

William Cooper stated at the MUFON symposium in Las Vegas in 1989 that over 3,000 children disappear yearly in one section of Manhattan alone. Could there be some connection!?

The accounts of disappearances around underground tunnels and caverns are seemingly endless, as we see in the following incident recorded in Harold T. Wilkins' book 'FLYING SAUCERS UNCENSORED', p. 47:

"June 7, 1954: Three German tourists who entered the vast Lamprecht Cave, near Lofer, in the Salzburg mountain region of Austria have never been found.

Their automobile was left locked outside the cave.

"...The above may very well be merely a case of amateur speleologists getting lost in labyrinthine caves, although it is unusual for THREE men to vanish in this fashion. But I must risk the charge of being accused of fancy and moonshine, when I say that both in England and the United States, there are regions of limestone caverns and mountains from which...queer phenomena associated with white lights descending to ground level from great altitudes have been reported!"

Similar disappearances were recorded by John Keel in his book 'OUR HAUNTED PLANET', pp. 202-208:

"...There are periodic waves of disappearances which create brief sensations in the newspapers and are quickly forgotten. No one ever manages to find out where these people have gone. In 1912 five men, all unrelated, disappeared unaccountably in a single week in Buffalo, New York. Montreal, Canada, had a wave of missing persons in July, 1883, and again in July, 1892.

"Children vanish MORE FREQUENTLY than any other group. We're not talking about ordinary runaways. In August, 1869, thirteen children vanished in Cork, Ireland. No sign of kidnapping or foul play. The same month there was a wave of disappearing children in Brussels, Belgium. Another group of youngsters melted away in Belfast in August, 1895. And again in August, 1920, eight girls (all under twelve years of age) disappeared forever in Belfast...

"Actually, children have been disappearing in large numbers for centuries all over the world, and most of these cases have remained unsolved. In the Middle Ages it was popularly believed that fairies and leprechauns frequently stole children away. The Indians of North and South America also have many myths and stories about children being kidnapped by little people. The notion that parahumans kidnap children is deeply entrenched in every culture...

"The celebrated Pied Piper of Hameln, Germany, is more than just a charming children's story. A stranger actually did appear in Hameln in the Middle Ages, and he lured away 150 children never to be seen again. The event is still commemorated with an annual festival in Hameln (one of the old versions of the story says that the children were taken to a subterranean cavern - Branton).

"In A.D. 1212 a teenaged boy in France, Stephen of Cloyes, BEGAN TO HEAR VOICES which inspired him to collect together fifty thousand children for the pathetic Children's Crusade. They marched off to do battle with the infidels and disappeared EN MASSE. The popular explanation is that they were all seized by slavers.

"...Ufologist Jerome Clark uncovered an extraordinary item from an old 1939 newspaper. 'On a day in the late summer, 1939, a military transport left the Marine Naval Air Station in San Diego, California, for a routine flight to Honolulu,' Clark wrote in FLYING SAUCER REVIEW. 'About three hours afterwards several urgent distress signals sounded from the plane and then silence. Later the craft came limping back to execute an emergency landing. When Air Station personnel entered the plane, they found every man of the crew, including the copilot who had lived long enough to pilot the craft back to its base, dead of unknown causes.

"Each of the bodies carried large, gaping wounds, and the outside of the ship was similarly marked. Air Station men who touched parts of the craft came down with a mysterious skin infection.

"One of the most puzzling aspects of the whole affair was that the .45 automatics carried by the pilot and copilot as service pieces HAD BEEN EMPTIED, AND THE SHELLS LAY ON THE FLOOR. A smell of rotten eggs pervaded the atmosphere inside the plane... Mysterious skin infections and rotten egg odors (hydrogen sulfide) are phenomena familiar to all UFO researchers. It would seem that the transport was attacked — apparently without provocation — by some sort of strange aerial intruder."

The following account, taken from the May, 1946 issue of AMAZING STORIES magazine (pp. 171-173) seems to contain information which would explain many of the 'missing pieces' of the overall 'Men In Black' phenomena. At least some of the 'MIB' have been variously described as oriental or 'androidal' like beings, although as John Keel has stated, others seem to portray reptilian characteristics. Abductee Christa Tilton allegedly encountered some 'MIBs' in a black automobile within Boynton Canyon, near Sedona, Arizona (a reported base site). She described them as follows: "The men did not look right. Their faces had no expression on them whatsoever. They looked like they were wearing chalky tan makeup. Their movements were robot-like and unearthly." The AMAZING STORIES letter, which was quite lengthy and excerpts of which we quote below, was submitted by a Mr. Edward John of (at the time) 475 Fell St., San Francisco, CA.:

"Sirs... I have enjoyed your stories for many years as I have read AMAZING since the first issue back in 1928 if I remember right.

"...I think I can show you an entrance to this subterranean city that he (Shaver) has written about several issues back. Here is what happened to me and you may judge for yourself. In 1931 my mother and I took up a section of land as a cattle raising home- stead from the U.S. Government and naturally it was not a choice piece... a person who turned out to be our nearest neighbor gave us some hints and as the place was only six miles from his we stayed at his ranch until we built our house. Then we moved into our own and all in all we stayed there about two years before we quite; and now I will relate the things that caused us to quit, which at the time I did not know much about, but since Mr. Shaver wrote, now I know and marvel that we managed to stand two years without getting killed by these things from below.

"As a note of interest I have had to use 30,000 rounds of ammunition in the period and perhaps that is why we are still here. At night I would sit up fully dressed all night with a rifle in my hands, ready, and an extra one by my side. In about five hours after dark I would hear things moving outside the house and after a while something would try to open the door quietly and I would wait until I saw the knob turn, then let go a clip right through the door and then pull it open and look around outside and there was nothing to be seen. After a couple of nights like that, that performance would stop and something new would be tried.

"There are too many incidents to be told in one letter, the best one was the two disappearing automobiles, which happened at about ten at night over at the neighbor's place. It was as follows: the neighbor and we were sitting on the porch after supper when he saw headlights come over the hill to the fence then along the fence for about half a mile, then go out and that was all that night. So next morning we went to the trail along the fence and there were tire tracks of seven inch width tires and they went along the fence into the box canyon and right up against a smooth boulder about 20 feet in diameter and ended there. Now the car could not turn around anywhere in that place because the road is a trail five feet wide and one side is against our neighbor's fence, which was not damaged and the other was a steep hill that no car could even make in compound low. You know, we have a few mountains here, and as far as backing out I tried that myself in the daytime with help and I could not steer a straight enough path without crossing my other marks so they did not back out or we would have trailed them as my neighbor has lived around there since 1848 and he sure knew his tracking. We never did get an answer to the question of where did the cars go.

"The cars were very large and black and very heavy and now that I compare them they were about twenty years ahead of anything I have ever seen anywhere and I had worked in the auto business for about five years before we took up the land. They were silent, smooth, no wavering of the lights and the trail is extremely rough; in places it has hollows a yard deep, but these cars went through at about 25 mph, and it would even wreck a jeep to do that, so you figure it out and let me know the answer if you can. By wavering of lights, I mean that the beams were steady and not flashing up and down as an ordinary car would do when a rough road is traveled.

"I have been away from there since 1933, but just about three months ago, I drove through with a friend for safety and my place is razed to the ground and everything that was made by human hands has been carried off — even the old tin cans, and the place would not be noticed unless you knew where is was. The Coast and Geodetic survey had a marker near my house in the front yard and even that is gone; who would want to take a concrete marker and carry it away?

"...after two weeks, you can hear insects running on the ground, (also) forest fires will not burn there. They burnt 250,000 acres, then burnt all around this area; and that stopped the forest rangers. They never could understand because most of it is on the slope of a mountain and it should have gone, but they saw that the wind came down and blew from the top down and blew North, South, East and West at once and that was the only time that the wind ever blew there.

"Also you can detect an ATMOSPHERE of FEAR within 30 miles of the area and you will not get a statement from anyone who lives around there and the people in the valleys are afraid of the people in the hills. One farmer erected 20 foot barbed wire fences and a heavy gate across the road that leads to my old place. The gate would take a tank to knock down, so maybe there is something there, after all. (Note: Richard Toronto reprinted a news article in his SHAVERTRON newsletter concerning a Krishna Sect temple that had been built on a mountain BETWEEN Hopland and Lakeport, California — the same area that Edward John refers to. This sect had come under Federal scrutiny when it was discovered that they had been stockpiling weapons for some unknown purpose. Interesting... - Branton)

"It is located 110 miles north of San Francisco in Mendocino county and is directly on the old Pieta toll road that ran between Hopland and Lakeport in Lake county of which Clear Lake is quite a summer resort. If you care to look it up on a map get a good auto road map and look due south off the road midway between towns and you will note an area with no roads bounded by Sonoma Lake and lower Mendocino counties and there is it. If you wish to go there, be sure that enough people know where you went. Maybe they will be able to find you. There have been several disappearances along that stretch of road, even trucks have vanished. All the U.S. Government's.

"The U.S. Government has noted the area as rough, unsurveyable and UNEXPLORED...

"Personally I do not care to go near the place, but if there is some way of driving the things out I would help if I can so that someone else could live there safely.

"...Also I forgot to mention there is a cave on the property that has steps leading down and there is no sound when a rock is thrown in. I have never seen it, but I understand that it is there... Also, several people (in the area) have died of heart failure and some have gone insane, I found out later.

"I think the thing that saved us was the fact that I am not surprised at anything and that I am quick to shoot and I can shoot without sighting and by ear and not having the THOUGHT of shooting fixed SO THAT the things would be warned. After that place, I was able to outshoot U.S. Marine sharpshooters. I tried competing in a match and I just never missed any target at any range. If I could see it, I could hit it, 5 out of 5. I have tried practice machine guns at plane models and I hit 3 out of 5 at speeds up to 700 mph scale without using the sights. So the old ranch gave me something worthwhile after all.

"Due to my physical condition, I cannot get into any armed forces, so that talent is wasted, for you see I have a bad leg and cannot walk more than a mile at a time. Since I left the ranch I have been in the radio business and have not owned a gun since '34, because as long as I stay away from there I don't need one..."

An interesting postscript to this story. Several years following this incident, some people who had befriended Edward John stated that he claimed to know of an man who was not from this planet. He was a radio expert in the Navy and, according to Mr. John, he was born on a world with no temperate zone but where the tropics and the arctic regions were almost adjacent to each other. Still later, others made references to Mr. John as having actually met up with the 'space brothers', essentially becoming another 'contactee' like those who frequented California during the late 1950's and early 1960's.

Aside from the area referred to by Edward John, there are apparently other "danger zones" in different parts of the world that have been associated with underground phenomena. The 'I.N.F.O. JOURNAL' (box 367., Arlington, VA, 22210), a publication devoted to 'Fortean' research, in it's Vol. IV, No. 2 issue related one of the most frightening and disturbing accounts of subterranean abduction that we have come across yet. The article, titled 'MOUNTAIN OF DEATH', was written by David D. Browne, and originally appeared in the June 1972 issue of WALKABOUT, published in Sydney, Australia:

"Black Mountain comes almost as a shock when you see it first.

"Traveling by bus just south of Cooktown, North Queensland (Australia), a bend in the road suddenly discloses it and the visual impact can bring an involuntary exclamation, as you see it — black, bare and sinister, a 1,000 ft. high pile of enormous boulders two miles long, rearing out of the rain-forest.

"This is 'the Mountain of Death.' Aborigines will not go near it. An ancient legend warns them of danger. White men fear it too, because of the numbers of men who have gone there and disappeared without a trace, as if the earth — or the mountain — had swallowed them. Birds and animals shun the area.

"The rocks give off a curious metallic ring when struck, and the only sound is the croaking of countless frogs sheltered in the depths where the great granite boulders lie against each other.

"In Brisbane's Public Library, a yellowing newspaper cutting tells some of the story:

"'Grim tragedy has been associated with the mountain ever since it has been known to white man.

"'Three men with horses completely disappeared at the mountain. They vanished as if the earth had opened and swallowed them up, for absolutely no trace of them has ever been discovered, although police and backtrackers and hundreds of local residents scoured the mountain and surrounding country.'

"Then following (were) the names and occupations of several others who disappeared, and the dates of their disappearance.

The cutting continues:

"'This constitutes one of the most amazing stories in the police history of the far north, for not one of the mysteries has been solved and probably never will be.'

"Another newspaper cutting, signed Nancy Francis, reads:

"'The formation of these mountains is unique; their appearance grotesque. They are mountains of huge boulders full of chasms that go down to unsounded depths. Only a few rock wallabies and a few turkeys live near these grim, forbidding hills. The Aborigines regard the Black Mountains with dread.'

"In the files of the Cooktown police, dating back 25 years, there is a report made by a Sergeant of Police who discussed the mountain with a man whom he refers to as Mac. Mac began:

"'Know anything about Black Mountain, or so-called 'Mountain of Death'? Its aboriginal name is Kalcajagga.'

"'What does it look like at close quarters?' I asked.

"'Just a mass of tumbled granite blocks; hardly any vegetation. The only living things there are black rock wallabies and enormous pythons 16 feet or more long and able to swallow a wallaby whole. The ridge is honeycombed with caves, nearly all unexplored. They dip down below ground level but nobody knows their extent or what they contain.'

"The latest fatalities, he reported, had occurred only a few years earlier when two young men set out to solve the riddle of earlier disappearances in the caves. They were never heard of again. Two black trackers who tried to trace them disappeared too.

"Then Mac went back to the beginning of the mountain's grim story.

"The first-known fatality was that of a carrier named Grayner, in 1977. He had been searching on horseback for strayed bullocks when he, with his horse and bullocks, vanished without a trace. Thirteen years later, Constable Ryan, stationed at Cooktown, tracked a 'wanted' man to the scrub at the foot of the mountain. Other trackers followed his trail to the entrance of one of the caves, but he was never seen again. Nor was the 'wanted' man.

"More recently a gold prospector named Renn was added to the list of mysterious disappearances.

"Well-organized police teams with trackers combed the whole area for weeks without finding him.

"Then there was the case of Harry Owens, a station owner from Oakley

Creek. One Sunday morning he rode over towards Black Mountain looking for strayed cattle. When he didn't return on time his partner, George Hawkins, alerted the police then went out to look for him himself. But by the time the police joined in the search, Hawkins had also disappeared. Two of the native police trackers entered one of the caves. ONLY ONE OF THEM CAME OUT. He was so unnerved by what seemed to have been an experience of terror that he could give no clear account of what happened to them both.

"Mac even knew a white men who had penetrated the caves and lived to tell the tale, and produced a newspaper cutting of his story. It read:

"'Armed with a revolver and a strong electric torch I stepped into the opening. Like other Black Mountain caverns it dipped steeply downwards, narrowing as it went.

"'Suddenly I found myself facing a solid wall of rock, but to the right there was a passageway just large enough for me to enter in a stooping position. I moved along it carefully for several yards. The floor was fairly level, the walls of very smooth granite. The passage twisted this way and that, always sloping deeper into the earth.

"'Presently I began to feel uneasy. A huge bat beat its wings against me as it passed, but I forced myself to push on. Soon my nostrils were filled WITH A SICKLY, MUSTY STENCH. THEN MY TORCH WENT OUT.

"'I was in total darkness. It was inky black. From somewhere that seemed like the bowels of the earth I could hear faint moaning of bats.

"'I began to get panicky and I groped and floundered back the way I thought I had come. My arms and legs bleeding from bumps with unseen rocks. My outstretched hands clawed at space where I expected solid wall and floor. At one stage where I wandered into a side passage I came to what was undoubtedly the brink of a precipice, judging by the echoes.

"'The air was FOUL and I felt increasing DIZZINESS.

"'Terrifying thoughts were racing through my mind about giant rock pythons I have often seen around Black Mountain.

"'As I crawled along, getting weaker and losing all hope of ever getting out alive, I saw a tiny streak of light. It gave me super strength to worm my way towards a small cave mouth half a mile from the one I had entered.

"'Reaching the open air, I gulped in lungfuls of it and fell down exhausted.

"'I found I had been underground for five hours, most of the time on my hands and knees. A king's ransom would not induce me to enter those caves again...'

"Such are some of the weird stories told of the mountain.

"These and the extraordinary structure of the mountain itself give rise to many questions, scientific and otherwise.

"On the scientific aspect, the following comments come from a member of the staff of the James Cook University of North Queensland, Dept. of Geology, Associate Professor P.J. Stephenson.

"He says, 'I have visited and climbed the mountain concerned. It is composed of huge granite boulders covered with black lichen. The complete black surface coating may be uncommon but the boulder pile is less so. Near Chillagoe and at several other localities in north Queensland similar phenomena exist.

"'The occurrences are somewhat puzzling because of their relative rarity. However, they must have been produced by rapid erosion of the 'skeletal' soil profile. Many soil profiles contain fresh rock 'kernels' in them and removal of the soil component would produce a boulder pile. But such removal takes place so slowly the 'kernels' also weather completely...'

"There are still some practical questions to ask, however.

"What really did happen to those people who at various times in the last hundred years, have been said to disappear, vanish without a trace?

"...Any party that decides to unravel the mystery of the mountain will need to be very carefully organized and equipped to meet any hazard, likely or unlikely — not forgetting the possibility of meeting a very real python. CR: Simpson."

At this point we will diverge from the subject of underground disappearances and reenter the realm of conspiracy... In apparent relation to William Copper's allegations concerning the connections between the Kennedy assassination, MJ-12, UFO's and so on, we have the following very interesting yet very disturbing 'connection' which was related by John Keel in his book 'OUR HAUNTED PLANET' (1968., Fawcett Crest., Greenwich, Conn.):

"In his detailed report on the Maury Island UFO (incident) of 1947, Kenneth Arnold also describes meeting a small, dark foreign looking man who was tinkering with the motor on a beat-up boat in TACOMA HARBOR. Ray Palmer, editor of 'AMAZING STORIES' in Chicago, had commissioned Arnold to investigate the puzzling Maury Island affair, which began when a 'donut-shaped object' (according to other sources, one of six such craft seen at the time - Branton) had rained 'slag' onto a boat near Maury Island. Pieces of that slag had killed a dog aboard the boat and slightly injured a boy, the son of Harold Dahl, who was piloting it. Early the next morning, according to Dahl's story, a 1947 Buick drove up to his home and a black-suited man of medium height visited him. This man, Dahl said, recited in detail everything that had happened the day before AS IF HE HAD BEEN THERE. Then he warned Dahl not to discuss his sighting to anyone, hinting that if he did there might be unpleasant repercussions which would affect him and his family. Since Dahl and the others had not yet told anyone of their sighting, and since UFOs were still publicly unknown (Arnold's sighting over Mount Rainier and the attendant publicity did not occur until three days later), Dahl was naturally nonplused by his strange visitor. This was the first modern MIB report (although Edward John might disagree... - Branton).

"Dahl's boss, FRED L. CRISMAN (he also owned the boat), became a central figure in the mystery. DAHL HIMSELF VANISHED SOON AFTER HIS INTERVIEW WITH ARNOLD, and the efforts by later investigators (such as Harold T. Wilkins, a British author) have failed to locate him. Crisman had been A FLIER IN WORLD WAR II, and he was suddenly RECALLED into the service in 1947, FLOWN TO ALASKA, and later stationed in Greenland. In recent years amateur sleuths engaged in investigating the alleged conspiracy to assassinate President John F. Kennedy have tried to implicate CRISMAN. District Attorney JAMES GARRISON of New Orleans subpoenaed one FRED LEE CRISMAN of TACOMA, WASHINGTON, to testify before the Grand Jury listening to Garrison's evidence against Clay Shaw (Jim Garrison was portrayed by Kevin Costner in the popular motion picture "JFK" - Branton), according to wire service stories in November, 1968. Crisman was identified as a radio announcer, but Garrison's investigations implied that HE WAS EITHER A MEMBER OF THE CIA OR HAD BEEN 'ENGAGED IN UNDERCOVER ACTIVITY FOR A PART OF THE INDUSTRIAL WARFARE COMPLEX.' He allegedly operated under a cover as a preacher and was 'engaged in work to help Gypsies.' These stories caused a chain reaction in UFO circles, since UFO believers have long accused the CIA of being somehow connected with the flying saucer mystery. Of course, the CIA was in its infancy in 1947 at the time of the Maury Island case and was then largely staffed by NAVAL personnel from World War II intelligence units.

"Clay Shaw was tried early in 1969, accused by Garrison of having conspired to murder President Kennedy. He was found innocent and freed. The exact nature of Crisman's testimony before the Grand Jury IS NOT KNOWN. He did not testify at the actual trial...

"The Maury Island case fell apart in Arnold's hands. The slag samples given to him by Dahl and Crisman WERE SWITCHED BY SOMEONE; two investigating Air Force officers, Brown and Davidson, WERE KILLED WHEN THEIR PLANE CRASHED shortly after leaving Tacoma; DAHL VANISHED; Crisman was literally exiled to Greenland for two years; Tacoma newsman Paul Lance, who helped Arnold in his investigation, DIED SUDDENLY A SHORT TIME LATER. Palmer claims that a cigar box filled with original slag samples WAS STOLEN from his Chicago office soon afterwards.

"At one point Ted Morello of the United Press took Arnold aside and told him:

"'You're involved in something that is beyond our power here to find out anything about... We tried to find out information at McChord Field (the Tacoma

Air Force base) and drew a blank, and we have informants there who practically smell the runaways for news... We've exhausted every avenue attempting to piece what has happened together so it makes some sense... I'm just going to give you some sound advice. Get out of this town until whatever it is blows over.'

"Arnold got into his private plane and headed for home. He stopped in Pendleton, Oregon, to refuel, and shortly after he took off again, HIS ENGINE STOPPED COLD. Only quick thinking and expert flying saved him from a serious crash..."

Yet another apparent 'casualty' of what appears to be a cosmic warfare between Mankind and certain 'Draconian' forces of darkness, was described in a letter addressed to SEARCH Magazine, which appeared in it's September, 1960 issue:

"Dear Rap (i.e. Raymond A. Palmer):

"I have been following your pursuits of UFO(s)... through your magazines for some time with consuming interest, especially the Shaver Mystery. There's an item or two concerning this that I have been intending to write you about for some time. Some- times during the year about 1946 to 1947 I heard that Dr. William Beebee wrote an article published in the 'Atlantic Monthly' in which he made a remark about 'the coming invasion of the earth by the underground race.' When I remarked on this to a fellow worker of mine he said 'Isn't he the scientist-oceanographer who disappeared?' I was startled by his sudden question and said that I didn't know, and asked if he knew anything of the circumstances surrounding his disappearance. He said he understood or heard that on one of Dr. Beebee's descents to the ocean floor OFF THE COAST OF FLORIDA, he was missing from the inside of the diving bell when it was brought up! Do you have anything on this? I had been wanting to look for some corroboration of this to see if it could be true or if the present whereabouts of William Beebee is known. Then I am reminded of the disappearance of another prominent person, the world traveler and explorer Richard Halliburton. I am sure I read only a few years ago that he was presumed to be lost at Sea in a storm...."

The number of 'casualties' keep pouring in...

In his book 'THE UNDERPEOPLE' (1969. Award Books., N.Y.), author Eric Norman relates an interesting account of a 'disappearance' of another sort, involving the possible fate of the Inca Indians of South America. In chapter 2 — 'Strange Caverns and Terrifying Tunnels', he relates:

"Conquest in South America (involved) natives hacked to death by Spanish swords, arrogant priests absolving Conquistadors for their murderous atrocities, sharp Toledo steel lances running through children and, pervading it all, a dark lust for native gold.

"In the autumn of 1582, Francisco Pizarro hid his 168 Spanish horse soldiers behind the doorways and walls of the Incan town of Cajamarca. Atahualpa, the absolute emperor of the sun- worshipping Inca's empire, had agreed to meet Pizarro in the village plaza. Atahualpa's procession entered the village with a flair of pageantry. Incan warriors and the emperor's litter bearers were dressed in the finest cloth. The Royal Guard were armed with spiked helmets, feathered war clubs, poison-tipped lances and dazzling gold-inlaid swords. Thick gold bracelets encircled their bronze wrists and rich silver discs dangled from their pierced ear lobes.

"Pizarro and his Conquistadors remained hidden behind their guns and cannons as Atahualpa and his entourage entered the main plaza. 'It is like leading hogs to the killing pen,' Pizarro sneered. The bandy-legged Spaniard knew hogs; prior to his service for Spain's king, Pizarro had been a swineherd in the province of Estremadura. He lived by a harsh personal code that equated kindness with weakness; deceit was the trick of a clever man and lying, duplicity and thievery were proper.

"Atahualpa's group stirred nervously when they found no sign of the visitors to their land. Spanish fingers twitched on gun triggers and a hawk-faced soldier stood ready to torch the cannon. Suddenly, a solitary figure left a building and walked into the plaza. He was dressed in the faded robe of a Dominican (Roman Catholic) friar. His bald head glistened contemptuously toward the Incan emperor.

"Friar Vincente Valverde announced that all of South America now belonged to the king of Spain. He stared coldly at the emperor and snapped, 'The Papal Bull of 1493 provides this right...'

"Proud and regal, Atahualpa glared at the haughty friar before him. 'Your POPE must be CRAZY to give away land that does not belong to him,' he said...

"The friar was stunned momentarily, then he turned and ran toward the safety of a building, shouting: 'Pizarro, attack, attack! Kill all of them! I will absolve you!'

"With hoarse cries of 'Santiago!', the Spaniards slaughtered the unsuspecting Inca warriors. In a few minutes the battle was over; the emperor's royal guard was dead, or dying, in the bloodstained dust of the plaza and Atahualpa was a prisoner of Pizarro. Greedy Spanish hands ripped the emerald necklace from his body. A wild gleam entered Pizarro's eyes when the emperor handed over his exquisitely carved bracelets of thick gold.

"'I want my freedom,' Atahualpa informed Pizarro. 'I will fill this room with gold for ransom.' The room was 17 feet wide and 22 feet long! The emperor's subjects delivered $8,443,456 in gold to Pizarro and, afterward, Pizarro and Friar Vincente Valverde condemned Atahualpa to be burned alive at the stake.

"While the Spaniards were burning the emperor, a pack train of 11,000 llamas was headed toward the Spanish encampment. Each beast was burdened by a heavy load of gold. Native messengers brought news of the Inca king's death — and the fantastic caravan disappeared! During the past centuries, thousands of gold-greedy adventurers have searched for the 'loot of the 11,000 llamas.' None has discovered a single clue to the treasure's site.

"Believers in the Under-People theory are firm in their contention that the Incan llamas disappeared into a gigantic tunnel that led to the inner earth kingdoms. 'Even the population figures show that these conquered people outwitted their bestial conquerors,' according to one South American researcher. 'Incan census figures reveal that there was 10,000,000 subjects when the Spaniards arrived. Forty years later, in 1571, the Spaniards took a census. There was approximately 1,000,000 Indians. I admit that the Spanish method of slave labor took a tremendous toll. But could 9,000,000 Incas have died in Spanish mines?'"

Eric Norman relates the words of one correspondent who described the ancient subterranean tunnels, predating the Incan Empire itself, that were believed by many to exist beneath the Andes:

"'...at first I scoffed at such stories about mysterious tunnels and an alien civilization beneath the surface... I joined an inner earth group for the simple enjoyment of discussing outlandish ideas in a humorless, serious manner. Gradually, I became interested by the considerable volume of circumstantial evidence. I now believe the earth is absolutely honeycombed by a web of tunnels that run beneath the continents, under the oceans, and these passageways link the subterranean cities of the inner world.

"'...There are many reports concerning a vast tunnel called the 'Roadway of the Incas' which has an entrance somewhere in Peru. It runs south more than a thousand miles. There is another entrance to this fabulous tunnel in the Desert of Atacamba in Chile. The 'Highway of the Incas' passes under Cuzco, the legendary city of Peru. There is another, smaller, but very well hidden entrance to the tunnel in the mountains near Machu Picchu, which is the capital city of the first and last Inca emperor. It is called 'The Lost City of the Incas' and was not discovered until 1911 by an American, Hiram Bringham. It is considered the 'Eighth Wonder of the World... everything at Machu Picchu is in excellent preservation.'

"His mention of the 'Highway of the Incas'," Eric Norman continues, "strikes a familiar note... A physician in Argentina has devoted his spare time to an investigation of this legendary inter- continental tunnel of the Under-People. He commented:

"'...I have always been intrigued by the unknown and please convey my thanks to Dr. H—— for providing the opportunity to publish my views... I started to investigate the 'Highway of the Incas' when I was a young, curious youth and I have hundreds of witnessed, notarized statements. These documents and tape recordings fill one room of my home. The Incas knew of the tunnel and, although gold was of little value to them, they hid their treasures in these caverns to keep it from the greedy Spanish conquerors. No one had provided a satisfactory explanation for their mysterious disappearance. There was an empire of several million people that vanished from the surface of the earth. They entered the tunnel and left the Quechua Indians behind. As few Incas have been seen since then, they possibly took up residence in a cavern city or followed the tunnel to the interior of the earth.

"'...The 'Highway' is the largest of the tunnels and it connects all continents. In addition to the openings in South America, there are entrances in Canada, in British Columbia; in America, you should investigate Mt. Shasta in California and Mt. St. Helena in Oregon. The tunnel is connected with Tibet and another opening in Central Asia. I believe the African entrance is in the Atlas mountains in the north of that continent.

"'...I also suggest that you explore the 'highways' which have been found in the oceans. These ancient underworld civilizations may be mining our seas!'"

Alexander Von Humboldt, in his volume 'VIEWS OF NATURE' (London, Henry G. Bohn, 1850) relates on pp. 412-413 the following account which he collected while in Cuzco, Peru:

"...The son of the Cacique Astorpilca, an interesting and amiable youth of seventeen, conducted us over the ruins of the ancient palace. Though living in utmost poverty, his imagination was filled with images of the subterranean splendor and the golden treasures which, he assured us, lay hidden beneath the heaps of rubbish over which we were treading. He told us that one of his ancestors once blindfolded the eyes of his wife, and then, through many intricate passages cut in the rock, led her down into the subterranean gardens of the Inca. There the lady beheld, skillfully imitated in the purest gold, trees laden with leaves and fruit, with birds perched on their branches. Among other things, she saw Atahuallpa's gold sedan-chair (UND DE LAS ANDAS) which is alleged to have sunk in the basin of the Baths of Pultamarca. The husband commanded his wife not to touch any of these enchanted treasures, REMINDING HER THAT THE PERIOD FIXED FOR THE RESTORATION OF THE INCA EMPIRE HAD NOT YET ARRIVED, and that whosoever should touch any of the treasures would perish that same night.

(Note: This may or may not be the same as the legendary underground 'garden cavern' below the 'fort' of Sacsahuaman near Cusco, referred to by other sources. Through that cavern is said to flow a large under- ground spring, a vast chamber which can only be entered by navigating a confusing labyrinth of underground tunnels. This account would also seem to tie-in with various rumors that not only the Inca treasures, but many of the Incas themselves escaped the Conquistadors through ancient tunnels which led to vast cavern cities built in antediluvian times by the lost 'Atlantean' race. There are actually people who claim to have met these subterranean 'Incas'. One person who claimed to have been descended from the Incas themselves, told the former editor of AMAZING STORIES magazine Raymond A. Palmer, that he had encountered one of these ancient 'cousins' of his who acted as a sentry or guard of an entrance to one of the underground abodes. This entrance was in the form of a shaft which was situated on the top of a mountain peak hidden somewhere in the Matto Grosso region of Brazil. The sentry, who spoke to the man through a transparent partition near an elevator shaft that descended into the depths, stated that he and his family could enter their abode if they so wished, but that they would have to undergo a decontamination process to remove the radioactive pollutants, contaminants and infections that their bodies had acquired from a lifetime of living in the outer world - Branton)

"These golden dreams and fancies of the youth," Humboldt continues, "were founded on recollections and traditions transmitted from remote times. Golden gardens, such as those alluded to (JARDINES O HUERTAS DE ORO), have been described by various writers who allege that they actually saw them; viz., by Cieza de Leon, Parmento, Garcilaso, and other early historians of the Conquista. They are said to have existed beneath the Temple of the Sun at Cuzco, at Caxamarca, and in the lovely valley of Yucay, which was a favorite seat of the sovereign family...

"The son of Astorpilca assured me that underground, a little to the right of the spot on which I then stood, there was a large Datura tree, or Guanto, in full flower, exquisitely made of gold wire and plates of gold, and that its branches overspread the Inca's chair. The morbid faith with which the youth asserted his belief in this fabulous story, made a profound and melancholy impression on me."

The following account appeared on page 52 of the Nov. 1954 issue of FATE magazine. The article was titled 'GATE TO THE UNKNOWN':

"In March, 1954, a French Jesuit priest in Sorata, Bolivia, told a strange story of an exploring trip he had made in the cavern of San Pedro on 20,000 foot Mount Illampu of the Andes chain.

"The cavern must be entered on all fours through a narrow passage which widens after a few yards and leads into an immense cavern filled with stalagmites and stalactites. At one end of the cavern is a subterranean lake.

"The French priest claimed to be the first person to cross to the far end of the lake. After several HOURS of rowing a small boat by artificial light, he related, the cave narrowed and gave way to a trail barred by an enormous gate of wrought iron. The grille, he said, bore all the characteristics of 17th century Spanish ironwork.

"The priest tried unsuccessfully to break through the barrier. He was eager to see what lay beyond but he had to return to Sorata without solving the mystery."

The question one might ask in this case is: Did the early Spanish explorers of this cavern go through all the trouble to forge the gate in order to keep someone out, or did they do it to keep some 'thing' in...?

SERIA DOCUMENTAL DEL PERU, a Peruvian newspaper describes an expedition which explorers from Lima University, accompanied by experienced speleologists, undertook in 1923. After entering a tunnel in or near Cuzco, Peru, the explorers lost communication with the point of entry. After 12 days only one member of the expedition, almost starved, returned to the surface. But his report of a confusing labyrinth was so incredible his colleagues declared him mad. Police prohibited entry into the mysterious passage and dynamited the entrance to prevent further loss of life.

In his book 'THE GOLD OF THE GODS', Erich von Danniken relates some interesting thoughts concerning an ancient tunnel system that had been discovered below the mountains and jungles of Ecuador, which reportedly consist of straight 'glazed' tunnels with intermittent 'air shafts' that stretch for hundreds of miles. Although he has come under criticism from many researchers for his tendency to embellish certain accounts, and twist certain archeological and historical facts in an attempt to support his own theories, some of his research is nevertheless interesting and reliable enough to include here. On pp. 59-60 of this particular work, he stated:

"...I can refute the objection that the tunnel-builders must have 'betrayed' themselves by the enormous quantities of debris excavated while making the tunnels. As I credit them with an advanced technology, they were presumably equipped with a THERMAL DRILL of the kind described in DER SPIEGAL for 3 April, 1972, which reported it as the latest discovery. The scientists of the U.S. Laboratory for Atomic Research at Los Alamos spent a year and a half developing the thermal drill. It has nothing in common with ordinary drills. The tip of the drill is made of wolfram and heated by a graphite heating element. There is no longer any waste material from the hole being drilled. The thermal drill melts the rock through which it bores and presses it against the walls, where it cools down. As DER SPIEGAL related, the first test-model bored almost soundlessly through blocks of stone 12 ft. thick. At Los Alamos they are now planning the construction of a thermal drill that is powered by a mini atomic reactor and eats into the earth like a mole, in the form of an armored vehicle. This drill is intended to pierce the earth's crust, which is about 25 miles thick (on the average - Branton), and take samples of the molten magma that lies underneath it..."

A Navaho Indian legend speaks of ancient migrations involving a cavernous realm below the four corners areas. The Hopi's speak of a similar legend involving an alleged opening, sometimes described as a hill and sometimes as a 'pond', covering the path to the cavern world. The Hopi 'emergence' point is called the 'Sipapu' or 'Sipapuni' and is said to be near the confluence of the Colorado and Little Colorado rivers. According to the Hopi tradition not all of the people who dwelt in the cavern world came up with them. Others chose to remain below. As for the Navajos, they state that:

"At one time all the nations, Navajos, Pueblos, Coyoteros, and white people, lived together, underground in the heart of a mountain near the river San Juan. Their only food was meat, which they had in abundance, for all kinds of game were closed up with them in their cave; but their light was dim and only endured for a few hours each day...

"Then the men and the animals began to come up from their cave, and their coming up required several days. First came the Navajos, and no sooner had they reached the surface they commenced gaming at patole, their favorite game. Then came the Pueblos and other Indians, who crop their hair and build houses. Lastly came the white people, who started off at once for the rising sun and were lost (from) sight...for many winters.

"While these nations lived underground they all spoke one tongue; but (with) the light of day and the level of the earth came many languages..."

If there is even a grain of truth to this ancient legend, then it would seem that the caverns in which the southwestern Indians formerly and allegedly lived were void of the nefarious influence of the reptilian hominoids. Although the reptilians may have moved in later, some Hopi sources state that their people were actually forced to the surface by the sudden invasion of the serpent people or reptilians from caverns beyond. We will make one comment, and that is the amazing coincidence between this legend and the more modern accounts of cavernous labyrinths below this very same region of the Four Corners. As they say 'Where there's smoke there's probably fire.' Most of the accounts that refer to subterranean conflicts between human and reptilian forces within the compartmentalized world of the cavern systems state that the warfare within that realm is overt and deadly real. Reports of whole human tribes or communities within the caverns being wiped-out by sudden and unexpected attacks from reptilian forces are not uncommon in "Inner Earth" literature. Out in the "open" surface world, however, these draconian forces must work in secrecy and engage in covert attacks and psychological warfare since the outer world has not yet been subjected to the point where there will be minimal resistance to an overt invasion. However, the reptilians have had much success in programming, implanting and buying-off human political, intellectual and spiritual leaders who are all too willing to do the will of their alien "bene- factors" in exchange for the "Trojan Horse" promises given by the serpent race. These human collaborators are members of all those secret societies that are tied-in with the conspiratorial hub of the BAVARIAN EMPIRE or ILLUMINATI [aka the BILDEBERGERS] — the Thule Society, Vril Society,

Nazi Party, Knights of Malta, Knights Templar, Jesuit Order, Black Nobility, Council on Foreign Relations, Trilateral Commission, Scottish Rite, Skull & Bones, Ordo Templi Orientis, etc.

Migration legends concerning vast caverns are not restricted to the southwest however. Many of the Indians of the southern states and New England in fact repeat this same theme almost verbatim. Nor should we limit such accounts to North America, since they are found profusely throughout the world.

If the Navaho's did in fact migrate through the cavern world from some distant land, then could they have 'emerged' from the caves with their neighboring Hopi Tribesmen?

Harold Courlander, in his book 'THE FOURTH WORLD OF THE HOPIS' described an ancient Hopi legend about an underworld. Whether or not the account is accurate, it nevertheless shows that the POSSIBILITY for the existence of such a 'world' was and is foremost in the minds and legends of many native American tribes.

Courlander describes the Hopi legend which states that the Hopi ancestors, before their 'emergence' to the surface world, migrated through different cavern regions until they came to the 'third' cavern world — or the realm below the general 'Four Corners' area of the Southwest, a series of caverns that were very extensive and in which crops were able to grow to some extent. Life there eventually became very oppressive for the majority of the Hopis when a few of their numbers turned to practicing sorcery, making it very difficult for the rest. The 'peaceful' Hopi's later left this cavern world (in an attempt to escape the influence of the sorcerers who were collaborating with the advancing reptilian forces?) on a journey which took several days, leaving the sorcerers below. If true, this does not necessarily mean that all Hopi ancestors who remained below are presently collaborating with the reptilians. Dr. Hank Krastman, who claims to have been allowed into an underground "Hopi" city below the Grand Canyon beginning in 1960 and beyond, states that those humans he encountered there were presently at war with the Grays. The surface Hopis themselves have legends of those who have revisited the ancient traditional site of 'emergence'. Some suggest that the 'Sipapu' is covered by a mound, while others hold that a small pond seals the entryway to the cavern world. Whatever the case, most Hopis agree that the ancient site is somewhere near the convergence of the Colorado and Little Colorado rivers. As Courlander reveals on pp. 213-214 of his book:

"...The story of the journey to Grand (Salt) Canyon to transfer the salt deposits to that place conforms to an account given in the 1930s by Don Talayesva or Oraibi, as recorded in Mischa Titiev's article, 'A Hopi Salt Expedition' (AMERICAN ANTHROPOLOGIST, vol. 39, 1937). That account contains detailed reference to all the shrines and sacred spots along the salt trail, and the ritual observations at those places. The legend primarily belongs to the Third Mesa villages — Oraibi, Hotevilla and Bakavi (Bocobi) — and to Moencopi, an offspring of Oraibi. In former times these villages sent expeditions to Grand Canyon to gather their salt. According to the belief of some Third Mesa clans, Grand Canyon contains not only the sacred salt beds and shrines, but the sipapuni through which mankind emerged from the Third (Lower) World. As Titiev paraphrases the description given by Don Talayesva:

"'It was not long before the expedition found itself approaching THE Kiva, the original SIPAPU through which mankind emerged from the underworld. Its outlines are indicated by soft, damp earth and an outer circle of bushes called pilakho... Pushing their way through the fringe of vegetation, the party stepped into the inner ring within which the Kiva is located. The sipapu is full to the brim with yellowish water, of about the same coloring as the surrounding earth, which serves as a 'lid' so that ordinary humans may not see the wonderful things going on beneath the surface.'

"The Walpis and other First Mesa people do not agree that the sipapuni is at that place, asserting that its location is no longer known. The salt myth given here is not part of First Mesa belief. Walpi customarily sent its salt expeditions to Zuni in the south- west. In recent years, of course, virtually all Hopi salt expeditions have been to the nearest trading posts..."

It may be a coincidence, then again maybe not — but an early issue of the 'HOLLOW HASSLE' newsletter reported one woman's belief (she did not state where she got her information) that within caverns a mile-and-a-half beneath the surface of northern Arizona and New Mexico lies the remains of one of the most ancient human civilizations on (or rather, within) the earth.

In a letter dated January 28, 1991, Norio F. Hayakawa added the following comments concerning the 'Dulce' facility and it's possible connection with the 'Mystery of Iniquity' of Bible prophecy:

"...I've been to Dulce with the (Japanese) Nippon Television Network crew and interviewed many, many people over there and came back with the firm conviction that something was happening around 10 to 15 years ago over there, including nightly sightings of strange lights and appearances of military jeeps and trucks. And I am convinced that the four corners area is a highly occultic area. The only stretch of highway, namely Highway 666, runs through the four corners area from southeast Arizona to North- western New Mexico and up. I have also heard that this Highway 666 came into existence around 1947 or 1948, fairly close to the time of 1947, the modern-day beginning of OVERT UFO APPEARANCE, i.e. the Kenneth Arnold incident, and coincident- ally or not, the establishment of Israel in 1948."

Paul Bennewitz sent out a letter on June 6, 1988 describing 'PROJECT BETA', which referred to the alien base in New Mexico (near Dulce - pronounced 'Dul-see'), the lower extremities of which are reportedly inhabited by the Grays, the Reptons and the Draco. NASA CIR film was allegedly useful in locating this base and revealing U.S. (or rather 'secret government') Military involvement with the 'Greys'. Another group called the 'Orange' is said to be based below the west slope of Mt. Archuleta near 'the Diamond'. Some suggest that the 'Orange' are a so-called 'hybrid' race with PARTIAL reptilian-like features yet possessing human-like reproductive organs and even certain artificial or cybernetic features. It is possible that the 'Orange' consist of hu-brids and re-brids in that some or most of them may possess a human soul- matrix and therefore may be 'human', although information on the 'Orange' is presently sketchy. They have also been described as being involved in the scenarios taking place in the tunnels below the Nevada Military Complex as well.

William Cooper briefly mentioned the 'Orange' based on memories of top secret documents he had read while in Navy Intelligence:

"...there were four types of aliens mentioned in the papers. A LARGE NOSED GREY (Reptoids? - Branton), a blond human like type described as the NORDIC, a red haired humanlike type called the ORANGE. The homes of the aliens were described as being a star in the Constellation Orion, Bernard's star, and Zeta Reticuli 1 & 2. I cannot remember even under hypnosis which alien belongs to which star." (Note: Zeta Reticuli is most often associated with the Grays. The 'Orange' — which sources seem to indicate 'may' actually be a double term used to describe two different types of entities, a reptilian hominoid group with scaly orange skin and a more humanlike group with 'red' hair — may have established themselves in Orion or Bernard's Star. Contactee Hal Wilcox allegedly has experienced interaction with HUMANS based near Bernard's Star, although he did not describe them as particularly "Nordic" appearing. Orion has long been associated with imperialistic human and predatory hybrid reptilian- insectoid cultures, excluding the Orion "Nebula" itself which lies hundreds of light years BEYOND the Orion open cluster and has been identified as a "gateway" to an infinite realm beyond the physical universe, or the abode of the angelic forces and the Supreme Being).

"...There were over 650 attendees to the 1959 Rand Symposium." 'Commander X' related in one of his reports. "Most were representatives of the Corporate-Industrial State, like: The General Electric Company; AT&T; Hughes Aircraft; Northrop Corporation; Sandia Corporation; Colorado School of Mines, etc.

"Bechtel (pronounced BECK-tul, a San Francisco - base organization - Branton) is a supersecret international corporate octopus, founded in 1898. Some say the firm is really a 'Shadow Government' — a working arm of the CIA. It is the largest Construction and Engineering outfit in the U.S.A. and the World (and some say, beyond).

"The most important posts in the U.S.A. Government are held by former Bechtel Officers. They are part of 'The Web' (an inter- connected control system) which links the Tri-lateralist plans, the C.F.R., the Order of 'Illuminism' (Cult of the All-seeing Eye) and other interlocking groups..."

"MIND MANIPULATING EXPERIMENTS... The Dulce Base has studied mind control implants; Bio-Psi Units; ELF Devices capable of Mood, Sleep and Heart-beat control, etc.

"D.A.R.P.A. (Defense Advanced Research Projects Agency) is using these technologies to manipulate people. They established 'The Projects,' set priorities, coordinate efforts and guide the many participants in these undertakings. Related Projects are studied at Sandia Base by 'The Jason Group' (of 55 Scientists). They have secretly harnessed the Dark Side of Technology and hidden the beneficial technology from the public.

"Other Projects take place at 'Area 51' in Nevada... 'Dreamland' (Data Repository Establishment and Maintenance Land); Elmint (Electromagnetic Intelligence); Cold Empire; Code EVA; Program HIS (Hybrid Intelligence System): BW/CW; IRIS (Infrared Intruder Systems); BI-PASS; REPTILES, etc.

"The studies on Level Four at Dulce include Human Aura research, as well as all aspects of Dream, Hypnosis, Telepathy, etc. (research). They know how to manipulate the Bioplasmic Body (of Man). They can lower your heartbeat with Deep Sleeve 'Delta Waves,' induce a static shock, then reprogram, Via a Brain-Computer link. They can introduce data and programmed reactions into your Mind (Information impregnation — the 'Dream Library').

"We are entering an era of Technologicalization of Psychic Powers... The development of techniques to enhance man/ machine communications; Nano-tech; Bio-tech micro-machines; PSI-War; E.D.O.M. (Electronic Dissolution of Memory); R.H.I.C. (Radio-Hypnotic Intra-Cerebral Control); and various forms of behavior control (via chemical agents, ultrasonics, optical and other EM radiations). The Physics of 'Consciousness.'...

"SURVIVING THE FUTURE... The Dulce Facility consists of a central 'Hub.' the Security Section (also some photo labs). The deeper you go, the stronger the Security. This is a multi-leveled complex. There are over 3000 cameras at various high-security locations (exits and labs).

"There are over 100 Secret Exits near and around Dulce, many around Archuleta Mesa, others to the source around Dulce Lake and even as far east as Lindrich.

"Deep sections of the Complex CONNECT INTO (EXTENSIVE) NATURAL CAVERN SYSTEMS.

"...INSIDE THE DULCE BASE... Security officers wear jumpsuits, with the

Dulce symbol on the front, upper left side (the Dulce symbol consists of an upside-down triangle with an inverted "T" superimposed over it - Branton)... The ID card (used in card slots, for the doors and elevators) has the Dulce symbol above the ID photo. 'Government honchos' use cards with the Great Seal of the U.S. on it. 'The Cult of the All-Seeing Eye' (The NEW WORLD ORDER) 13. '666', The Phoenix Empire... '9', 'Illuminism'... 'One out of many.' (and so on)."

The Feb.-Mar. 1991 issue of 'UFO UNIVERSE' carried an article titled 'THE DEEP DARK SECRET AT DULCE', written by Bill Hamilton and 'TAL' LeVesque. We are sure the reader will agree that the following article serves to tie-together much of what has been revealed earlier in this file. If planet earth is the main 'battleground' for the final cosmic conflict, and the U.S. is one of the major areas on earth where the 'final outcome' may be decided, and since the Dulce or New Mexico subnet is considered to be the MAJOR site where reptile-saurian activity is taking place (an alien 'empire' in conflict with various 'human groups' based in California and elsewhere, with the Nevada subnet itself being a major 'battlezone') then we should focus our attention not only on what has been going on within the Nevada Military Complex and its subbranches in Utah and Idaho, but also on what has been taking place in the subterranean complexes deep below the small southwestern town of Dulce itself.

More than any other area in the U.S., if not the world, this small town has been the epicenter of nearly every form of para- normal and top-secret activity one can imagine, including: UFO sightings, UFO landings, top secret CIA and Air Force activity, experimental Aircraft, secret Special Force operations, High-Tech Research, Abduction scenarios, implantation's, Human & Animal mutilations, PSI warfare studies, Secret Government-Alien interaction, armed conflict between human and alien forces, sightings of Grays, Reptilians and 'Mothmen', Underground bases and construction activity, conspiracy scenarios, alien infiltration of human society, deep-cavern phenomena, unusual Native American legends, MIB or Men In Black encounters and other activity related to the above. In fact a higher CONCENTRATION of such activities has been evident in the vicinity of Dulce than most other areas in the world, even to the point that the inhabitants of this town have, for the most part, resigned themselves into accepting the reality of such activity — whether they like it or not.

Bill Hamilton and 'TAL' LeVesque take us deep 'inside' the Hadean-like labyrinthine depths of this underground megacomplex through the eyes of those who have been there:

"...Dulce is a sleepy little town in northern New Mexico. It's population is about 900 and it is located above 7,000 feet on the Jicarilla Apache Indian Reservation. There is one major motel and just a few stores. It is not a resort town and it is not bustling with activity. Yet, according to a few outsiders, Dulce harbors a deep, dark secret. That secret is said to be harbored deep below the tangled brush of Archuleta Mesa. That secret involves a joint government-alien biogenetic laboratory designed to carry out bizarre experiments on humans and animals.

"New Mexico State Police Officer Gabe Valdez was drawn into the mysteries of Dulce when called out to investigate a mutilated cow on the Manuel Gomez ranch in a pasture 13 miles east of Dulce. Gomez had lost four cattle to mutilations between 1976 and June 1978 when a team of investigators which included Tom Adams arrived from Paris, Texas to examine the site of the carcass.

"Curious as to how cattle were being selected by the mysterious mutilators, an interesting experiment was conducted on July 5, 1978 by Valdez, Gomez, and retired scientist Howard Burgess. The three penned up about 120 of the Gomez beef cattle and moved them through a squeeze chute under an ultra- violet light. They found a 'glittery substance on the right side of the neck, the right ear, and the right leg.' Samples of the affected hides were removed as well as control samples from the same animals. Some investigators attribute the mutilations to aliens from UFOs. Sightings of strange lights and other aerial phenomena have been reported in many areas where the cows have been found at the time of the reported mutilation. UFOs have been seen frequently around Dulce.

"I arrived in Dulce on April 19, 1988, to visit with Gabe Valdez and to inquire about the sightings, the mutes, and the rumors of an underground alien base in the area. There was still snow on the ground by the Best Western motel when I checked in and called Valdez. He made an appointment to see me at 9:30 PM. I found Gabe to be a very congenial host as he offered to show us around the roads of Dulce that night and point out the various locations where he had found mutilated cows or had seen strange aerial lights. He made the astounding statement that he was still seeing unidentified aircraft at the rate of one every two nights. We took a look at the Gomez Ranch, the road by the Navajo River, and the imposing Archuleta Mesa. Gabe had found landing tracks and crawler marks near the site of the mutes. Gabe was convinced that scientist Paul Bennewitz of Thunder Scientific Labs in Albuquerque was definitely on the right track in his attempts to locate an underground alien facility in the vicinity of Dulce.

"I had first heard of Paul Bennewitz in 1980 when my friend Walter called me from Albuquerque and told me he had been working with Paul on electronic instruments. Walter said Paul had not only photographed UFOs, but had established a communication link with their underground base at Dulce. Bennewitz had first come to prominence during the August 1980 sightings of UFOs over the Manzano Weapons Storage Area and Kirtland AFB. A Kirtland AFB incident report dated October 28, 1980 mentions that Bennewitz had taken film of UFOs over Kirtland. Paul was president of Thunder Scientific Labs adjacent to Kirtland.

Bennewitz gave a briefing in Albuquerque detailing how he had seen the aliens on a video screen. The aliens were transmitting signals... from a base underneath Archuleta Mesa.

"Researcher William Moore claims that government agents became interested in Bennewitz' activities and were trying to defuse him by pumping as much disinformation through him as he could absorb. Whether Paul's communication (or rather his "interrogation" of their mainframe computer core via a computer-video-radio link - Branton) with supposed aliens at the Dulce Base was part of this disinformation campaign is unclear. If one were to believe that Paul is the single source of reports on the Dulce Facility, then it could also be a tactical maneuver to discount and discredit Paul's allegation of an underground base if such reports were meant to remain secret. Then the actual disinformation maneuver would be to disinform the public and not a single individual.

"In a report entitled 'PROJECT BETA' Paul states that he had spent two years tracking alien craft; that he had constant reception of video from an alien ship and underground base viewscreen; that he had established constant direct communications with the aliens using a computer and a form of Hexadecimal code with graphics and printout; and claims to have used aerial and ground photography to locate the alien ship's launch ports and charged beam weapons. Paul claimed that the aliens were devious, employed deception, and did not adhere to agreements. Paul and Walter were working on a weapon that would counter the aliens.

"Some will think at this point that we have crossed-over from the land of clear thinking concerning anomalous phenomena to the land of science-fiction. But let us remember that bizarre phenomena such as the UFOs represent may have its roots in a bizarre reality. It is expected to be bizarre at first, but as we continue our studies we will evolve to understand it.

"Paul Bennewitz had investigated the case of abductee Myrna Hansen of New Mexico who reported having been taken to an underground facility in May 1980. Christa Tilton of Oklahoma has reported that she had an experience of missing time in July 1987 where she had been abducted by two small grey aliens and trans- ported in their craft to a hillside location where she encountered a man dressed in a red military-like jump suit. She was taken into a tunnel through computerized checkpoints displaying security cameras. She reported having been taken on a transit vehicle to another area where she stepped on a scalelike device facing a computer screen. After the computer issued her an identification card, she was told by her guide that they had just entered Level One of a seven-level underground facility. Christa goes on relating how she was eventually taken down to Level Five. She reports having seen alien craft and little grey alien entities in some of the areas that she passed through.

"Christa reports going into one large room where she saw large tanks with computerized gauges hooked to the tanks and large arms that extended from some tubing down into the tanks. She noticed a humming sound, smelled formaldehyde, and was under the impression that some liquid was being stirred in the tanks. Christa has made drawings of much of what she had witnessed during her abduction.

"These tanks Christa talks about were depicted in a set of controversial papers called the Dulce Papers. These papers were allegedly stolen from the Dulce underground facility along with 30 black and white photos and a video tape by a mysterious security officer who claims to have worked at Dulce up until 1979 when he decided that the time had come to part company with his employers. The rest of the story is about this security officer who has met with one of us in an attempt to tell us the truth about the aliens, the U.S. Government (Note: although some sources claim that another 'government' completely separate from our Constitutional elected government is involved with this base, a 'secret' government that is - Branton), and the Dulce base. He is announcing his intention to come out of hiding and present soft and hard evidence of his claims. It will be up to you to decide whether this evidence constitutes an addition to the growing proof that a government cover-up exists.

(Note: At the time this article appeared, 'Thomas C.' was still an anonymous individual. More recently the authors have given permission to state his full name as being Thomas Edwin Castello. The reason for this is due to 'rumors' that he had passed away in 1994 while hiding out in Costa Rica. It is interesting that at this time Costa Rica was experiencing one of the largest UFO flaps of that year in the entire world, one that was OFFICIALLY RECOGNIZED by the Costa Rican government. Some suggest that the UFO's chose Costa Rica because its Air Defenses were minimal and therefore they were less likely to fire upon their craft. - Branton)...

"In late 1979, Thomas C. could no longer cope with the awesome reality he had to confront. As a high level security officer at the joint alien-U.S. Government underground base near Dulce he had learned of and had seen disturbing things. After much inner conflict, he decided to desert the facility and take various items with him.

"Using a small camera, he took over 30 photos of areas within the multilevel complex. He removed a security video tape from the Control Center which showed various security camera views of hallways, labs, aliens, and (secret government) personnel. He also collected documents to take with him. Then, by shutting off the alarm and camera system in one of the over 100 exits to the surface, he left the facility with the photos, video, and documents. These 'originals' were hidden after five sets of copies were made.

"Thomas was ready to go into hiding. But, when he went to pick up his wife and young son, he found a van and 'government' agents waiting. He had been betrayed by K. Lomas (a fellow worker) who was instrumental in the kidnapping of his wife and child. The agents wanted what Thomas had taken from the facility for which he would get his wife and son back. It became apparent to him that his wife and son would be used in biological experiments and were not going to be returned unharmed. That was a little over ten years ago.

"How did Thomas get involved in all this covert intrigue?

"Thomas is now about 50 years old (i.e. at the time the article was written - 1991 - Branton). When he was in his mid-twenties, he received top secret training in photography at an underground facility in West Virginia. For seven years, he worked for the Rand Corp. in Santa Monica, California when in 1977 he was transferred to the Dulce facility. He bought a home in Santa Fe, New Mexico and worked Monday through Friday with weekends off. All Dulce Base personnel commute via a deep underground tube-shuttle system.

"At the time, one of us (TAL) was working security in Santa Fe, M.M. and was privately investigating UFO sightings, animal mutilations, (and) Masonic and Wicca groups in the area. Thomas had a mutual friend who came to Santa Fe in 1979 to visit both of us. This individual would later view the photos, video tape and documents taken from the Dulce Base. Drawings were made from what was seen and circulated later in the UFO research community as the 'Dulce Papers.'

"Thomas alleges that there were over 18,000 of the short 'greys' at the Dulce Facility. He has also seen (tall) reptilian humanoids. One of us (TAL) had come face-to-face with a 6-foot tall Reptoid which had materialized in the house. The Reptoid showed interest in research maps of New Mexico and Colorado which were on (TAL's) wall. The maps were full of colored push-pins and markers to indicate sites of animal mutilations, caverns, the locations of high UFO activity, repeated flight paths, abduction sites, ancient ruins, and suspected alien underground bases.

"...The security level goes up as one descends to the lower levels. Thomas had an ULTRA-7 clearance. He knew of seven sublevels, but there MAY have been more. Most of the aliens are on levels 5, 6, and 7. Alien housing is on level 5. The only sign in English was one over a tube shuttle station hallway which read 'to Los Alamos.' Connections go from Dulce to (the) Page, Arizona facility, then to an underground base below Area 51 in Nevada. Tube shuttles go to and from Dulce to facilities below Taos, N.M.; Datil, N.M.; Colorado Springs, Colorado; Creed, Colorado (where gravity anomaly maps have shown a large adjacent area of negative density suggesting massive subterranean cavities below - Branton); Sandia; then on to Carlsbad, New Mexico. There is a vast network of tube shuttle connections under the U.S. which extends into a global system of tunnels and sub-cities.

"At the Dulce Base, most signs on doors and hallways are in the alien symbol language and a universal symbol system under- stood by humans and aliens.

Thomas stated that after the second level, everyone is weighed, in the nude, then given a uniform. Visitors are given off-white uniforms. The weight of the person is put on a computer I.D. card each day. Any change in weight is noted. Any change in over three pounds requires a physical exam and X-ray. The uniforms are jump suits with a zipper.

"In front of all sensitive areas are scales built into the floor by doorways and the door control panels. An individual places his computer I.D. card into the door slot, then presses a numerical code and buttons. The person's card must match with the weight and code or the door will not open. Any discrepancy in weight will summon security. No one is allowed to carry anything into sensitive areas. All supplies are put on a conveyor belt and X-rayed. The same method is used in leaving sensitive areas.

"All elevators are controlled magnetically, but there are no elevator cables. The magnetic system is inside the walls of the elevator shaft. There are no normal electrical controls. Everything is controlled by advanced magnetics, including lighting. There are no regular light bulbs. The tunnels are illuminated by Phosphorous units with broad, structureless emission bands. Some DEEP TUNNELS use a form of phosphorous pentoxide to temporarily illuminate certain areas. The aliens won't go near these zones for reasons unknown (Note: This suggests that these deeper tunnels may have originally been built by ancient beings other than the reptilians - Branton).

"The studies on Level 4 include human-aura research, as well as all aspects of telepathy, hypnosis, and dreams. Thomas says that they know how to separate the bioplasmic body from the physical body and place an 'alien entity' force-matrix within a human body after removing the 'soul' life-force-matrix of the human (or, in more simple terms — 'kill' the human being and turn it into a vessel to be used by one of the 'infernals', 'paraphysicals' or 'poltergeists' in order to allow it/them to work and operate in the physical realm? This appears to be a complex version of the ancient 'zombie' traditions, if in fact such horrific things are taking place in this installation. Many have stated that the Antichrist Force, symbolized by the number '666', is fully at work within the Dulce Base Network, suggesting that what is in fact involved there may be a sophisticated form of high-tech Satanism. Incidentally — according to one source — the inter-networking underground systems converging below Dulce is only PARTIALLY described in accounts such as this. In fact, this source alleges, the vast extent of the underground mega-complex can actually be compared to the size of the island of Manhattan! - Branton).

"Level 6 is privately called 'Nightmare Hall'. It holds the genetic labs. Here are experiments done on fish, seals, birds, and mice that are vastly altered from their original forms. There are multiarmed and multi-legged humans and several cages (and vats) of humanoid bat-like creatures up to 7-feet tall. The aliens have taught the humans a lot about genetics, things both useful and dangerous.

"The Greys, the Reptoids, the winged Draco species are highly analytical and technologically oriented. THEY HAVE HAD ANCIENT CONFLICTS WITH THE EL-HUMANS (or 'Anakim'? — human 'giants' who reportedly maintain underground and off-planet colonies - Branton) and may be STAGING here for a FUTURE CONFLICT...

"Principal government organizations involved with mapping the human genetics, the so-called genome projects are within the Department of Energy (which has a heavy presence on the Nevada Test Site); the National Institute of Health; the National Science Foundation; the Howard Hughes Medical Institute; and, of course, the Dulce Underground Labs 'run' by the DOE.

"Is the alien and human BIO-TECH being used to nurture and serve us or is it being used to CONTROL AND DOMINATE US? Why have UFO abductees been used in genetic experiments?

"IT WAS WHEN THOMAS ENCOUNTERED HUMANS IN CAGES ON LEVEL 7 OF THE DULCE FACILITY THAT THINGS FINALLY REACHED A CLIMAX FOR HIM. He says, 'I frequently encountered humans in cages, usually dazed or drugged, but sometimes THEY CRIED AND BEGGED FOR HELP. We were told they were hopelessly insane, and involved in high-risk drug tests to cure insanity. We were told NEVER TO SPEAK TO THEM AT ALL. At the beginning we believed the story. Finally in 1978 a small group of workers discovered the truth. THAT BEGAN THE DULCE WARS.'

"We may find it hard and unpalatable to digest or even believe Thomas' story and why should we even give it a hearing at all? Probably for no other reason than the fact that MANY OTHERS are coming out and telling bizarre stories and the fact that there may be a terrible truth hidden behind the continuing phenomena of UFO sightings, abductions, and animal mutilations. Our government intelligence agencies have had an ongoing watchful eye on all UFO activities for many decades now. This bizarre phenomena must have a bizarre explanation. We may be only one outpost in (a) vast interstellar drama.

"Recently, researcher John Anderson went to Dulce, N.M. to see if he could see if there is anything to the reported UFO activity. He says that he arrived in town coincidentally to see a caravan of cars and a McDonnell Douglas mini-lab in a van going up a rural road near the town. He followed them to a fenced-in compound where he waited to see further developments. Suddenly, six UFOs descended rapidly over the compound, hovered long enough for him to snap one picture, then shot up and out of sight. When later stopping in a store to tell the owner of the UFO photo he had taken, the store owner listened and revealed how he had been a victim cattle rancher of cattle mutes. Their conversation was interrupted by a phone call after which the store owner told John to leave at once, then closed the store after John went to his car. John then saw a mysterious van drive up to the store and a man got out and went in. John decided to leave Dulce at that moment but WAS FOLLOWED BY TWO MEN IN A CAR as he left town.

"Even more recently a research team has gone up to Archuleta Mesa to take soundings under the ground and preliminary and tentative computer analysis of these soundings seem to indicate DEEP CAVITIES UNDER THE MESA (one source said that according to the data these cavities extended to a depth of over 4,000 FEET! - Branton).

"Perhaps, someday, we will discover the deep dark secret of Dulce... Whatever the future brings it won't be dull."

Gabe Valdez, former State Police officer in Dulce, New Mexico, was contacted by a certain researcher in 1990, in an attempt to confirm some of the information which had appeared previously concerning his involvement in the UFO-mutilation investigations. The following was learned:

"—He and others HAD seen strange flying objects in the area, however he himself was unsure whether these were 'UFO's' of alien origin, or some type of top secret aircraft being tested by some secret faction of the government.

"—Something DID crash near Mt. Archuleta several years ago, but again, he did not find any evidence conclusively proving whether it was an object of human OR alien origin.

"—There is another road leading to the Mt. Archuleta area (and mesa) aside from the one which goes through the Ute Indian reservation. As for the restricted road that runs south from the Ute Reservation, much of it is in good condition (paved?). Only the area around the Archuleta region itself requires four-wheel drive vehicles.

"—He did investigate cattle mutilations, and at least in SOME cases a known nerve agent was discovered in the carcasses, and other indications suggesting that the cattle were being used for research in 'D.N.A.' experiments."

The following document (among others) originated from a U.S. Intelligence worker who has been missing for quite some time. A nephew of the OSI-CIA intelligence worker discovered the following (as well as other documents, many of which applied to the Dulce and Dreamland base systems) in a locker in which the missing Intelligence agent, a Mr. 'Tucker', apparently kept some of his papers. The document(s) may have had something to do with his disappearance, although exactly what connection this might be is uncertain.

Copies of this and other documents eventually ended up in the hands of several researchers as a result of one investigator who was approached by the family of the missing agent and given the documents. This source indicated that this family was extremely disturbed not only about the disappearance, but about the nature of the documents themselves, and the role they may have played in connection with the disappearance.

In the copy of the document which is quoted here, some annotations were made. These seem to have been 'corrections' on the ms. made by Paul Bennewitz. These will be indicated by an (*):

"SUMMARY OF NOTES TAKEN BY JIM MCCAMPBELL CONCERNING... TELEPHONE INTERVIEWS WITH DR. PAUL F. BENNEWITZ:

"This is Jim McCampbell making a recording of a remarkable episode on July 13, 1984. It has to do with a UFO base, cattle mutilations, advanced weaponry, contact with aliens, etc.

"The episode began about a week ago when I received a little semiannual periodical titled STIGMATA. It is number 21, the First Half of 1984. This little bulletin is prepared by Thomas Adams at P.O. Box 1994, Paris, TX 75460...

"He has a rather lengthy article. One finds point of interest on page 9 and I suppose the only way to pursue this is to read what he has here as it is fundamental to the entire story.

"Quoting: 'In May of 1980 a most interesting event occurred in northern New Mexico. An event similar in many respects to the Doraty Case. A mother and her young son were driving on a rural highway near Cimarron, New Mexico. They observed two or more craft and as Judy Doraty did, they observed a calf being abducted. Both observers were themselves abducted and taken on separate craft to what was apparently an underground installation, where the woman witnessed the mutilation of the calf. (* Woman witnessed mutilation in the field — dead animal taken with them.) It has been alleged that she also observed a vat containing unidentified (* cattle) body parts floating in a liquid, AND ANOTHER VAT CONTAINING THE BODY OF A MALE HUMAN. The woman was subjected to an examination and it has been further alleged that small metallic objects were implanted into her body as well as into her son's body. More than one source has informed us that CAT-scans have confirmed the presence of these implants.

"'Paul Bennewitz, President of his own scientific company in Albuquerque and an investigator with the Aerial Phenomena Research Organization, has been the principal investigator of the case. Interviewed in his office in April 1983, Bennewitz reports that through regressive hypnosis of the mother and child and his own follow-up investigation (including communications received via his computer terminal which ostensibly is from a UFO-related source), he was able to determine the location of the underground facility, a kilometer underground beneath the Jicarilla Apache Indian Reservation near Dulce, New Mexico. (Since 1976, one of the areas hardest-hit by mutilations coincidentally or whatever).

"'...The mother and son, by the way, were returned back to their car that night. Since the incident, they have suffered repeated trauma and difficulties as they attempt to recover from the episode. We pass this along because the account is, of course, most crucial if true; but we are not in a position to confirm the alleged findings. Hopefully, more information regarding this incident will be aired in the near future. We can only consider such reports while continuing to seek the evidence to refute or confirm.'

"That's the end of this remarkable quotation from STIGMATA.

"...I got in touch with Dr. Bennewitz by telephone and indicated that I had seen this reference to him and his work and I wanted to find out whether he was being misrepresented or whatever... It is rather mind boggling and here is the substance of that telephone conversation.

"He is a physicist and he started four years ago to determine in his own mind whether UFOs exist or do not and he has gotten much more deeply involved than he ever intended. IT HAS CAUSED HIM A GREAT DEAL OF TROUBLE FROM THE GOVERNMENT INTELLIGENCE GROUPS. He has pictures from the location. He went with a Highway Patrol Officer and they saw a UFO take off from the mesa at the location. He obtained photographs and what he calls launch ships were 330 ft. long and 130 ft. across. The cattle rancher named Gomez and he went back to this location which is a mesa and saw a surveillance vehicle which was about 5 ft. by 10 ft., like a satellite, he said. He had been using a Polaroid camera and then got a Hausel-Bladd to produce much better pictures. He set up a monitoring station and observed that UFOs are all over the area... He has been dealing heavily with a Major Edwards (somebody) (* Security Commander) who was with Manzano Security and two (* My wife & I) of them saw four objects outside of a warhead storage area at a range of about 2500 feet and obtained movies of them. He now has about 6000 feet of movie footage, of which 5000 ft. is in Super Eight. THE OBJECTS HAVE THE ABILITY TO 'CLOAK,' that's the word, spells CLOAK like cloak and dagger, like cover up and he says that they can cause themselves to GO INVISIBLE by a field that caused the light waves to bend around the object and that one sees the sky behind them.

"He confirmed the fact that the woman was picked up when she accidentally observed the calf being abducted. He has paid for a pathology work and medical doctor work. The pathologist is a former head of the microbiology department of New Mexico University. They have done CATscans to show that the woman and her son did in fact have implants in their bodies. (* We confirmed the woman — not her son) She has a vaginal disease like streptococci-bulbie(?) and tried many antibodies to destroy the bacteria. That it has survived off the antibodies themselves. THE ALIENS KEEP HASSLING HER. (* Still true to date).

"Paul kept the woman and her mother at his house and the UFOs were flying overhead constantly. THERE IS NO ESP INVOLVED, BUT IT IS JUST PLAIN PHYSICS.

"They beam down (* They send a beam down — not 'beam down'). They can communicate THROUGH THIS BEAM. She picked up their transmissions. He devised a means of communication based upon her alfbic (?) code; one is equal to 'no' and two being 'yes.' Through this code he has been able to 'talk' to the aliens. He then computerized the system that would reject extraneous inputs. HE SAID THAT THEY CAN BE VERY THREATENING AND MALEVOLENT...

"He then told the O.S.I. OF THE AIR FORCE and he has been requested to give (* Did give) several presentations to high level Air Force people in briefings on the subject, wing level Command and many others including this fellow Edwards. And he took a helicopter to the site (* No — Twice to site — 1st by OSI agent, 2nd by a Col. Carpenter). It turned out that the WING COMMANDER, after a presentation that this fellow made, then took a helicopter to the site and MADE PHOTOGRAPHS.

"He says that you can see saucers on the ground. He says there is a kind of cone — a large cone and the larger vehicles come and land on top of the cone with the top of the cone fitting into a hole in the bottom. There is an elevator inside of the cone and that goes down into the mountain or ground about one kilometer. You can see the aliens running around the base getting into the vehicles and stuff. They use small vehicles to get around that have no wheels. They are rectangular in shape and they levitate. They do not show up in color BECAUSE THEY ARE HIGHLY REFLECTIVE, but in B & W they are visible. He says that there are beam weapons that are floating in strategic locations and there is a road into the base. He obtained infrared photos of the area from an altitude of 14,000 Ft. There is a level HIGHWAY going into the area that is 36 ft. wide. IT IS A GOVERNMENT ROAD (i.e. apparently, part of the off-limits road that originates within the Ute Reservation on the Colorado-New Mexico border, and leads southward through the Jicarilla-Apache reservation toward the Archuleta plateau - Branton). One can see telemetry trailers and buildings that are five sided buildings with a dome. It is standard military procedure. There are many guard points and 'stakes' and there are launch domes that one can see. Next to the launch dome HE SAW A BLACK LIMOUSINE AND ANOTHER AT SOME DISTANCE OFF (* Apparently). The careful measurements showed that the limousine was the same length of his Lincoln Town car. IT IS A C.I.A. VEHICLE. ALSO THERE WAS A BLUE VAN. He has been cautioned about these limousines as they will run you off the road if you try to get into the area and in fact some- body has been killed in that manner. To the north is a launch site. THERE ARE TWO WRECKED SHIPS THERE: they are 36 feet with wings, and one can see oxygen and hydrogen tanks. There are four cylindrical objects Socorro type — two carrying something while flying. The whole operation is based upon a government agreement and a technology trade. We get out of it atomic ships that are operated by plutonium. The Cash-Landrum case was one of them. The doors jammed open and neutron radiation came out. They are based at Kirtland AFB and Holloman AFB (* No — only know of one based at HAFB) and some place in Texas (possibly Ft. Hood, Texas — a guess only). He said the government is paying the hospital bills for the Cash-Landrum victims (* OSI Input — found out later unless someone covering — not true). Refueling of the plutonium is accomplished at Los Alamos. He had...pictures of this base back to 1948 and it has been there starting in 1948. Pictures in 1962, you can see many saucers and the base and truck... The road was 'passed off' to the local inhabitants as a lumber contract. He has photographs (I believe) of the firing of a beam weapon that (?) in two directions. (That would be necessary on a flying saucer. The reaction forces would impede the vehicle.) He has computed the speeds of (the) flying saucers at 15,000 mph and indicates that THE PILOTS (* of ours) ARE FROM N.S.A., THE NATIONAL SECURITY AGENCY. The aliens (i.e. one particular group? - Branton) have had atomic propulsion system for 48 years and the saucers themselves operate on an electric charge basis having to do with crystal semiconductor and (* Maybe) a super lattice. I think he said 'as you increase the voltage, the current goes down.'... At present there are six to eight vehicles, maybe up to ten over the area and sometimes up to 100. THEY CAN BE SEEN IN THE CLOUDS. They go into cumulus clouds and produce nitrogen nitride. (* I assume or speculate it is this) YOU WILL SEE BLACK SPOTS IN THE CLOUD. They eat holes in the cloud. If you can see black spots in a cloud, then you can tell that a vehicle is in there.

"He says that they come from six different cultures and in his communications (he learned that) some come from a binary system, possibly Zeta Reticuli and from distances up to and larger than 32 light years away. They also (* appear to) have one to three ships in (geosynchronous? - Branton) earth orbit at 50,000 KM altitude (* Based upon data). He had to form the words to try to communicate and he produced a vocabulary of 627 words in a matrix form and used a computer. The Flying Saucers (* we see) are limited to operation in the atmosphere.

"Now with regard to the cattle problem, the ALIENS are using the DNA FROM CATTLE AND ARE MAKING HUMANOIDS. He got pictures of their video screen. SOME OF THE CREATURES ARE ANIMAL LIKE, some are near human and some are human and short with large heads (the so-called hybrids? One abductee reported viewing an 'apparent' genetic experiment involving possible human-cattle hybridization. She viewed another woman abductee who was put asleep on a table, something — possibly ova — being removed from her abdomen by a Gray, at which point the Gray went over and worked on a cow that was laying unconscious on another table. Could SOME of the 'hybrids' be the result of genetic crossbreeding between humans and cattle rather than humans and reptilians? - Branton). They grow the embryos. After (that) the embryos become active by a year of training presumably that is required for them to become operational. When they die, they go back into the tank. Their parts are recovered.

"In 1979 something happened and the base was closed. There was an argument over weapons (Robert Lazar states that the Nevada DREAMLAND conflict between human and alien security was sparked by an argument over weapons. Since the DREAM- LAND and DULCE base are reportedly connected via tube shuttles then this "argument" may have spread to the Dulce Base, although Thomas Castello states that one of the major reasons for the DULCE WARS was the discovery of humans who had been permanently abducted or mutilated in a blatant violation of the joint- interaction treaties - Branton) and our people were chased out, more than 100 people involved. (Someplace later he indicates further details on this point.)

"The base is 4000 ft. long and our helicopters are going in there all the time. When it became known that he was familiar with all this, the mutilations stopped. (* True) They are taking humanoid embryos out of this base to somewhere else. I asked if it was Albuquerque or Los Alamos, but he said he didn't know. (Note: 1/8/86 — looks like it is Albuquerque) [subterranean bases below Albuquerque? - Branton] He said there are still quite a few helicopters in operation. They fly at night. (* all unmarked) HE WENT UP THERE HIMSELF IN A HELICOPTER AND THE O.S.I. BRIEFED THE COPTER PILOT AND HE THOUGHT PERHAPS THE COPTER PILOT HIMSELF WAS AN UNDERCOVER MAN. They saw helicopter pads up there — Viet Nam type, with bearing markers and trees pushed off away from the location. It is such a wild area he said. He agreed to send me the coordinates of this base.

"Regarding abductions of people, they pick out medium to low IQ personnel. They are able to scope out each one (so we can do the same thing with electromagnetic spectrum analyzers). (* I don't know this part — word mixup — drop). They pick up these people and then put implants into them and then take tissue samples, including ovum from the women, sperm from the men and DNA.

"THEY CAN PROGRAM THESE PEOPLE AS SLAVES TO DO WHATEVER THEY WISH AND THEY WILL HAVE NO MEMORY OF IT. THEY (The Hard Core type) STAUNCHLY REFUSE TO BE X-RAYED OR HYPNOTICALLY REGRESSED. YOU CAN RECOGNIZE THEM BECAUSE OF THEIR EYES. HE SAYS 'PECULIAR LOOK IN THE EYES AND A FUNNY SMILE.' (* An expression) Hynek knows about all of this and has been in contact with Coral (Lorenzen). He regards Hynek as a threat. (* Not really — I just think he is still a Gov. cover) At his house, he showed Hynek films and out in the back yard a flying saucer. He asked Hynek about his view with regard to abductions as to how many people might have been abducted. Hynek, unhesitatingly said ABOUT ONE OUT OF FORTY.

"He said that many people come to his door to see him, just 'out of the blue' and HE SEES SCARS ON THE BACK OF THEIR NECKS (Note: Refer to the remake of the movie INVADERS FROM MARS and also the movie THE PUPPETMASTERS based on Robert A. Heinleins book. The former depicted a mind-control implant inserted into the lower brain through the BACK OF THE NECK — leaving scars, whereas the latter depicted an alien parasite that attached itself in a controlling capacity to a human brain through the BACK OF THE NECK. - Branton). That previous old scars are easy to detect and that new ones are hard to detect. HE FEELS THAT THIS IS A SICKENING SITUATION.

"THE ALIENS HAVE GONE WILD AND USE HYPODERMICS (and notes a 'parallel four times.') (McCampbell: I don't know what that means) (* I don't know either). He has been paralyzed four times and has been hit 250 times by hypodermics. He says they knock you cold and they do whatever they want to do and the above points have been verified medically.

"A man came to see him with a top secret document that was dated in the 50's, indicating if anybody found out about all of this they would kill them. He was asked 'doesn't that bother you?' He said 'no it didn't.'

"He said he had sent in some film to Kodak and there were seven rolls. They were Ectrochrome G which could not be processed locally, so they had to go to Kodak. He does all of the film work commercially so that nobody could claim that he had 'monkeyed' with the film. His films came back, but one of them — one was plain Ectrochrome, but (* Was missing for 2 months — when received) nine feet was missing and this was close-ups of UFOs that he had taken. THE MISSING PICTURES OF THE NINE FEET SHOWED UP (* The 9 ft. didn't — others known only to me did) IN A TOP SECRET DOCUMENT THAT HE STUDIED AND THE CODE NAME IS AQUARIUS AND IT IS A PROJECT OF THE NATIONAL SECURITY AGENCY (* I was told NASA). They are the ones that kept his film and copied it with deletions on Ectrochrome and sent it back (* I suspect).

"THERE HAVE BEEN INDIRECT THREATS BY THE AIR FORCE INTELLIGENCE AGAINST HIM.

"THE LOCATION OF THE BASE IS 2 1/2 MILES NORTH- WEST OF DULCE AND ALMOST OVERLOOKS THE TOWN. IT IS UP ON THE MESA. We discussed the similarity between everything we have been talking about here and the movie 'CLOSE ENCOUNTERS OF THE THIRD KIND'. He said he speculated THAT seemed to be a plan of disclosure, that is the movie. The coordinates of the location are not far off and the mountain where the actual base is looks much like the mountain in the movie.

"The next thing was — Discussing the trade off — alright. Here is what we got in the trade off. We got atomic technology, the atomic flying ships. Several of them, the first one wrecked on the ground and it can be seen and photographed from the air. A second one wrecked. A third one was wrecked. Apparently this last one was repaired and was the one that was in Houston — near Houston in the Cash-Landrum case. The second item was that we get out of it, are the beam weapons, the beam technology and third (* I speculate) is the thought beam. That is the means by which communication is accomplished. It is electrostatic in character with a magnetic component (* artifact) and it is the only way of communicating with people. They have to have the implants in order to use it. The crash that occurred at the base WHEN THERE WAS A DISTURBANCE OF SOME SORT, THE ALIENS KILLED 66 OF OUR PEOPLE AND 44 GOT AWAY. (* Alien computer input — True? I do not know.) (Note: Did the grays destroy that craft? Even if Bennewitz was able to LINK INTO and INTERROGATE the alien computer mainframe and discover certain secrets, there is the possibility that the aliens 'may' have used this in reverse and fed him with false information, as is their nature. As for the 'altercation' at the base, other human sources such as Thomas Castello have CONFIRMED this - Branton). Over an argument — they turned on us.

THE MOJAVE DESERT'S GREATEST SECRETS

The Dulce Wars: Underground Alien Bases and the Battle for Planet Earth: This is Not Science Fiction. . .A True-To-Life "War Of The Worlds"

Authored by B. Branton, Introduction by Commander X

ISBN-10: 1892062127 $21.95

IN THE CORNER OF A SMALL TOWN IN AMERICA'S SOUTHWEST SOMETHING VERY STRANGE IS GOING ON! IS AN ALIEN "FIFTH COLUMN" ALREADY ACTIVE ON EARTH PREPARING TOTAL CONQUEST VIA IMPLANTATION'S AND MIND CONTROL?

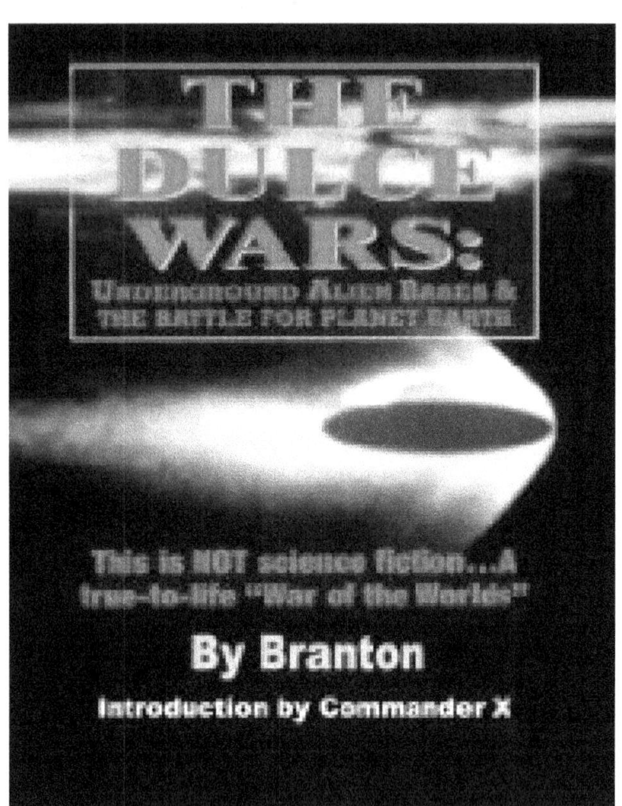

According to the author — who only used his first name for privacy reasons (and because he is deathly afraid!) — "The repercussions of what is taking place here will soon be felt throughout the whole country, when the beast has reached out with its deadly tentacles to invade our seemingly impregnable fortress, causing it to crumble and fall."

Did U.S. Military Forces perish recently in hand-to-hand combat with a group of hostile Greys who subsequently seized control of one of our Top-Secret underground bases? And has the New World order established an unholy alliance with this group of ETs?

In Dulce, New Mexico, seemingly everything has gone haywire, becoming the epicenter of: Cattle mutilation phenomena. . .Energy Grids. . .Secret Societies. . .Underground Anomalies. . .Conspiracies Between Townsfolk and "Outsiders". . . Unexplained Legends and Mythology Concerning Various "Lost Civilizations". . . Geomagnetic Enigmas. . .Abductions and Missing Time. . .Hostile Alien Beings. . .Peculiar Sounds and "Movements" Coming From Beneath The Earth.

THE MOJAVE DESERT'S GREATEST SECRETS

The Omega Files; Secret Nazi UFO Bases Revealed: Special Limited Edition

Authored by Branton, Notes by Timothy Green Beckley

$24.00 — ISBN-10: 1892062097

If, as the late J. Allen Hynek claimed, over 1 in 40 people have been abducted and 'processed' by the 'alien/secret government' agenda — or 1 in 10 according to more recent sources — then you are bound to know SOMEONE who is an abductee and KNOWS it. This information is for THEM.

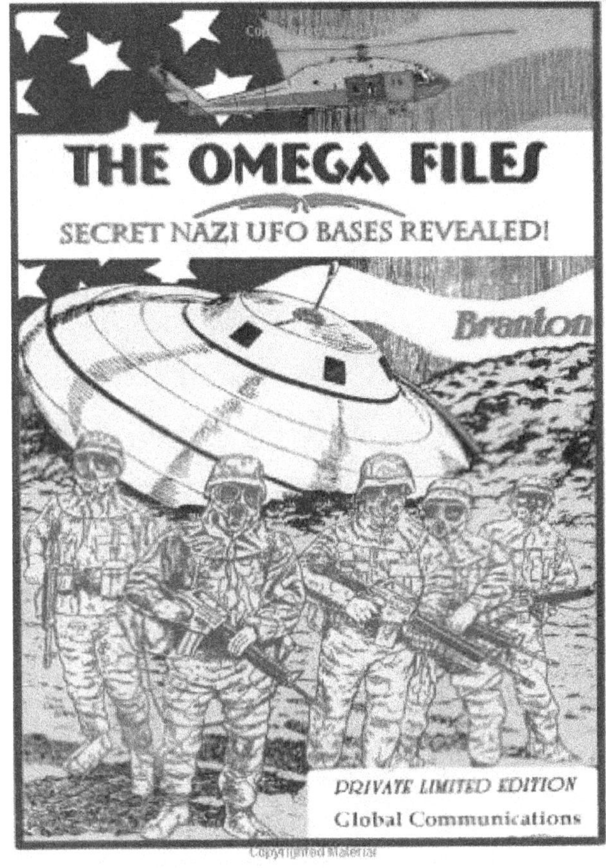

For those who are not "UFO Abductees", the information in this file is nevertheless vital and applicable, and may one day save your life!!! If you believe that information about "Aliens" is only for those who have lost all touch with reality, then PLEASE accept that information in this document that you CAN accept, and pass over the rest, at least for now. Your future may depend on it. As I have said, this information may save your life.

This file contains the most intricate and intimate details of a global conspiracy which seems to be rooted in an alien - military - industrial collaboration which is intent on bringing all freedom-loving peoples of this world under its control, through the implementation of a global government which has commonly been referred to as the 'New World Order'.

We have pulled no punches and are laying everything out on the table in regards to the New World Order agenda as I and those who have contributed to this document perceive it. If you are one who is easily offended, then be warned. Most of you who read this will realize that you may have personally supported in one form or another — albeit unknowingly — certain religious, economic, or political organizations which are on various levels being controlled by those forces that are working towards the implementation of the New World Order.

Those who have contributed to this file have not compromised nor held

back on what they perceive to be the truth in regards to this conspiracy. We make no apologies, since we feel that this agenda has already been responsible for damaging this American Republic in ways that most cannot even begin to comprehend, and will continue to be a threat to its very existence and prosperity until this 'enemy' is forever purged from our nation and those traitors responsible for violating our national security and 'selling out' this Constitutional Republic of the United States of America are brought to justice.

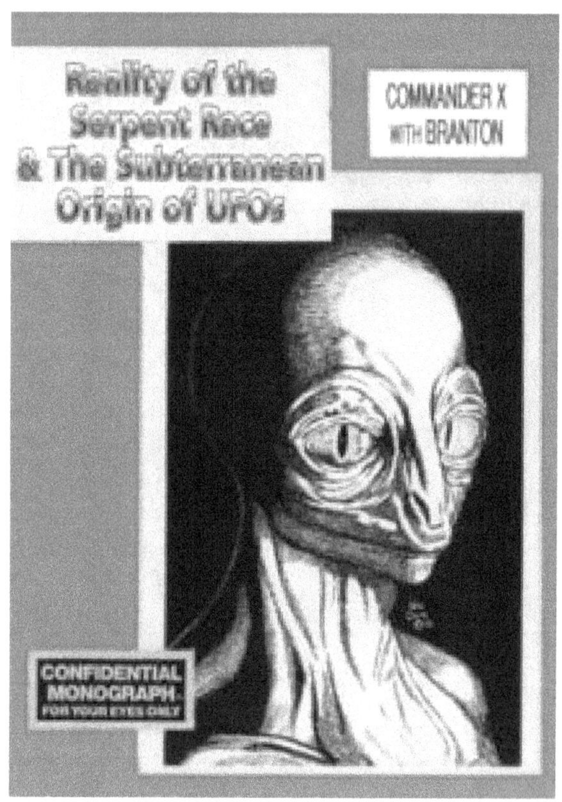

Reality of the Serpent Race and the Subterranean Origin of UFOs
Authored by Commander X.,
Authored by Branton
$25.00 — ISBN-10: 1892062542

WARNING: TO BE USED BY MEMBERS OF THE 'HUMAN RESISTANCE' AS A GUIDE TO ALIEN STRATEGY!

This manuscript contains expositions of an extremely revealing and concentrated nature. There are powers of spiritual origin that will attempt to interfere with the dissemination of this information. In the event that the reader begins to sense such an oppressive influence while reading this book, the author strongly recommends that they stop and read the 23rd Psalms aloud and then continue. This will break the power of the spiritual attacks.

SUBJECTS COVERED IN THIS AMAZING WORK. . .

* The great cosmic conflict between humans and the REPTILIANS.
* The Serpent Race and its influence throughout history.
* The Missing Link between Lizards an Snakes.
* Horrible battle between humans and aliens.
* AGHATRA - Contact with the subsurface world beneath our feet.
* What this group of ETs WANT!
* The great Biblical Deluge.
* Tribal memories of Flying Saucers.

THE MOJAVE DESERT'S GREATEST SECRETS

* TELOS — city beneath Mt Shasta.
* Chinese on the moon 4300 years ago.
* Underwater Bases.
* The Seven Sisters Constellation.
* Tunnel Beneath Salt Lake City.
* Secret Microwave Stations identified.
* Mysterious Disappearances in the Black Mountains.
* The Illuminati Connection.

Learn about the underground base beneath Dulce, NM. Cross breeding with aliens. The Skull and Bones Society and its connection with the Reptilians.

www.ingramcontent.com/pod-product-compliance
Lightning Source LLC
Chambersburg PA
CBHW081144270326
41930CB00014B/3026